The Magellan Fallacy

The Magellan Fallacy

Globalization and the Emergence of
Asian and African Literature in Spanish

Adam Lifshey

The University of Michigan Press

Ann Arbor

Published in the United States of America by
The University of Michigan Press
Manufactured in the United States of America
⊗ Printed on acid-free paper

2015 2014 2013 2012   4 3 2 1

A CIP catalog record for this book is available from the British Library.

Library of Congress Cataloging-in-Publication Data

Lifshey, Adam.
    The Magellan fallacy : globalization and the emergence of Asian and
African literature in Spanish / Adam Lifshey.
        p. cm.
    Includes bibliographical references and index.
    ISBN 978-0-472-11847-2 (cloth : acid-free paper) — ISBN 978-0-472-02866-5
(e-book)
    1. Spanish literature—Asian authors—History and criticism.   2. Spanish
literature—African authors—History and criticism.   3. Southeast Asian
literature (Spanish)—History and criticism.   4. African literature
(Spanish)—History and criticism. 5. Literature and globalization.   I. Title.
PQ6042.A75L54   2012
860.9'95—dc23   2012019743

For Jen and Landon

Contents

Acknowledgments

In the course of researching and writing this book, I was fortunate to have the support of people who believed that this sort of thing was worth doing. The world can feel large and small at once, and I appreciate the solidarity of family, friends, and colleagues who accompanied me through it this time. The sunrises and sunsets are more memorable as a result.

In Berkeley and Manila and many places elsewhere, diverse individuals went out of their way to assist my efforts and listen to my enthusiasms. I thank them all, deeply.

I am grateful in particular to Ben Goldberg, who long ago cheerfully encouraged me to read up on Equatorial Guinea; to Jane McAuliffe, who offered a generous grant that enabled me to return to the Philippines for a second summer when others sources had fallen through; to David William Foster and Eugenio Matibag, who gave repeated support for the publication of my work; and to Tom Dwyer, who backed my manuscript at the University of Michigan Press.

The most rewarding part of creating this book was the opportunity to develop friendships with kind people in the Philippines. I could not possibly have researched or written much herein without the original support of Nerissa Balce, who encouraged me wholeheartedly to research Filipino literature in Spanish. She put me in touch with wonderful colleagues and friends in Manila, such as Shirley Lua and Ricky Torre, whose generosity of time and knowledge was critical to my endeavors and enriched greatly my stays. In the Philippines, I also received unique assistances from Fe Susan Go, Oscar Campomanes, Resil Mojares, F. Sionil José, and many others. The lasting friendships that I made in Manila with Melanie Preza and Imee Teves are an enduring testimony to the value to me of my time in the Philippines.

Here in the United States, the University of California, Berkeley, the University at Albany (SUNY), Georgetown University, and the Northeast Modern Language Association provided me with grant support at different stages of this project.

Various journals and conference panel organizers gave space for me to present earlier thoughts on Asian and African literature in Spanish. Preceding versions of my work that appear in revised forms in this book include three essays. The first, which is reprinted by permission of the copyright owner, the Modern Language Association of America, is "The Literary Alterities of Philippine Nationalism in José Rizal's *El filibusterismo*," *PMLA* 123:5 (October 2008): 1434–47. The second is "And So the Worm Turns: The Impossibility of Imperial Imitation in *Una lanza por el Boabí* by Daniel Jones Mathama," *Chasqui* 36:1 (May 2007): 108–20. The third, whose copyright owner is *Hispanic Journal*, is "Ideations of Collective Memory in Hispanophone Africa: The Case of María Nsue Angüe's *Ekomo*," *Hispanic Journal* 24:1–2 (Spring and Fall 2003): 173–85.

One of the challenges in researching Asian and African literature in Spanish is the considerable difficulty of locating source materials. I have been lucky to work with a series of talented research assistants who tracked down one rare text after another: Christina Marzello, Scott Noble, Susanne Stover, Nina Gleiberman, Anne Micheau Calderón, Jason Robinson, Ha Na Park, Cecily Raynor, and Yovanna Cifuentes. Many other individuals, including librarians, administrative staff, other colleagues, and my own students also assisted this project one way or another. I thank them all.

As always, I am fortunate most of all for the love and support of my family. As the new generation of Katarina, Joshua, Elliot, Megan, and Connor comes along, I feel again the luckiest of people. Jen, I am thankful for having in you a loving partner and an astute editor. Landon, your mom and I love you with all our heart. When someday you become old enough to read this, know that you were born in the last days of the voyage that is this manuscript. And as you travel round your own worlds, may all your paths be of peace.

Introduction

Magellan sailed the ocean blue but never made it home. A Portuguese captain who commanded under the Spanish flag, he arrived in 1521 at what later would be called the Philippines. The archipelago was unknown to Europe and so Magellan claimed it for Spain. He died a month after contact. The reason he died is that Lapu Lapu, an indigenous king on a small island, resisted evangelization and Magellan decided to press the point through war. The foreign captain launched an amphibious attack on the local sovereign and, in short, lost. The narrator who would carry news of the defeat back to Europe was Antonio Pigafetta, an Italian tourist who survived the inaugural circumnavigation thanks to, among other things, the luckiest poisoned arrow in the forehead in history.

The dynamics of Magellan and Lapu Lapu are symbolically compelling, with the world-historical European, whom many people mistakenly think to have been the first to travel around the world, felled by an individual of profound insularity. This originary victory of the local over the global, however, is complicated by the fact that Magellan's ship did complete the circumnavigation without him and that Spanish claims to the archipelago held until 1898. Moreover, it is the voice of Pigafetta that tells us of Lapu Lapu, not vice versa. The death of Magellan marks the birth of modernity, for it is his voyage, half-completed by him, subverted dramatically by Lapu Lapu, and finished for the moment by Pigafetta, that intertwines provincial and planetary powers into an irreducibility that is the definitive hallmark of the world today. The Magellan fallacy is the conviction that captains can control the consequences of globalization. They cannot. Narrations of the world are always written with one intent of domination or another, yet all elude the command of their navigators, they who are authors and readers alike. We are all heirs of Magellan and Lapu Lapu and Pigafetta, we all

bear their mark every day. And we all commit the Magellan fallacy whenever we will the world in our image, which is to say, whenever we set our
sails, whatever their silhouettes, to the winds.

Lapu Lapu defeated Europe in the form of Magellan in what was, from
a Western perspective, an utterly peripheral space, a minor and previously
unknown island whose antipodality seemed both literal and figurative.
When three and a half centuries later a generation of young Filipino intellectuals began arriving in Spain, they followed, metaphorically, the path of
Pigafetta. These men, though from the most distant of colonies, possessed
substantial European educations. Unlike Lapu Lapu, they negotiated the
transnational forces affecting the identities of their homelands not on
archipelagic beaches but in the heart of Madrid and Barcelona, and not
with lances but with prose. They perceived the Philippines to be part of
Spain and therefore part of Europe, notwithstanding the evident reality
that Spain did not treat its colonial subjects as it would Europeans. Men
such as Pedro Paterno and José Rizal consequently took up their pens in the
1880s to illustrate that Europe was a transgeographical concept that could
be realized fully back in the Philippines. In so doing, Paterno broke new
ground by publishing the first Filipino book of poetry in Spanish, the first
Filipino novel in Spanish, the first Filipino opera in Spanish, and so on. By
definition this makes him radical, yet history primarily remembers him as
a fatuous bon vivant. Meanwhile, Rizal, despite never embracing independence for the archipelago, was executed by colonial authorities in 1896 for
the alleged subversiveness of his two novels.

When the United States defeated Spain in a war in 1898 and became the
new foreign power in the Philippines, Spanish became a language whose
literature was apparently destined for near extinction in Asia. Nonetheless,
the tradition continued to develop vibrantly for many decades more. New
literature in it still emerges today in a different sense, for many twentieth-
century Filipino texts in Spanish come to light whenever anyone decides to
look for them. For instance, Félix Gerardo, an astonishing short story writer
likely from the central island of Cebu, may be the greatest pre–World War
II fictionalist of globalization whom no one has ever read. His narratives
were discovered only in 2007. Gerardo was one of the last Filipinos to produce a major creative work in Spanish before armageddon arrived. Japan
bombarded and then occupied the archipelago from 1941 to 1945 and, in
the process, obliterated the primary Spanish-speaking community in Asia.
The audience for local literature in Spanish never recovered and a critical

mass of new authors did not come to be. By the end of the 1960s, the readers and writers of Filipino literature in Spanish who had survived the war were, for the most part, dead.

After the war, on the other side of the world, the first African novel in Spanish appeared amid a blend of village color and fascist colonialism. Although Pigafetta paid almost no attention to West Africa as he returned home northward along its coasts, the first circumnavigation signals here too a transhistoric sequence in which literature in Spanish, the inaugural language of globalization, would be produced one day by locals and distributed in imperial metropoles. A novel by Leoncio Evita, a young man from the colony of Spanish Guinea, was published in Madrid in 1953; his text was edited and prologued by a lackey of the autocratic rule of Francisco Franco. Nine years later, another author born in the colony, Daniel Jones Mathama, released a much lengthier novel in his longtime home city of Barcelona. Subsequently, however, Spanish Guinean literature fell silent. The colony gained independence in 1968, becoming the nation of Equatorial Guinea, but was promptly tyrannized by a horrific dictatorship that permitted no freedom of expression. It was not until 1985 that the next Guinean novels were published, a reemergence that this time would prove continuous. These fictions by María Nsue Angüe and Juan Balboa Boneke also appeared in Spain, far from the geographies they depicted. As with the earlier Filipino authors, narrations of a homeland circulated largely in exile.

These Asian and African texts are not antiquated or parochial curiosities but the most modern and global of phenomena. And the world of today, wrestling with migrations and displacements and hybridizations of all sorts, is not newborn, for the unsettled negotiations between localisms and world-scale transformations have defined humanity ever since Magellan. His inaugural voyage of globalization, unfinished by him and quasi-completed by others, including by Asian and African authors hundreds of years later, initiates modernity. Globalization is often perceived as the tensions that result when Western forces of vast reach penetrate asymmetrically into non-Western local spaces, but this is always parried by the asymmetrical insertion of the local into global spaces. The narratives that result from these dynamics are never as clear as their narrators might claim, whatever the provenances of people and texts at stake. The transmutations of local resistances from a purported periphery upon a supposed center blur the difference between metropole and colony, axis and orbit, for when bodies circle or pass through each other nothing is left discrete. Power relations and their consequent disciplinings are not challenged and upturned so much as enmeshed. Put another way, people carry mainlands with them whenever they arrive on islands, but also islands with them whenever they appear anew on the main. Modernity is distinguished by the arrival of the global in lands that hitherto had been culturally and politically isolated, followed immediately by diverse forms of local resistance and, ultimately, by the itinerant and unstable narrations of a planet whose poles and provincialities prove increasingly inextricable.

The Magellan Fallacy interrogates how the local, versed in the global, reimagines the seeming centers and presumed peripheries of the modern world. This book is not primarily a recovery of unknown literary artifacts, not an archaeological expedition, not an encyclopedic accounting, not a taxonomic tourniquet, and not, entirely not, an illumination of anything dark. Ahead are passages with many paths, none of which is finished, not by Pigafetta or any of his progeny. This is to say that there are many questions but no quests, at least not consolidated ones. What permutations of globalization arise when marginalized literatures develop in metropolitan centers? What are the paradoxes of colonized elites who propel non-Western national literatures in Western languages and forms? How do creative works of the ostensible periphery escape the limitations of localism and redefine the ostensible center in the process? Can the most passed over artistic phenomena pass as the most pivotal? Such queries put many fields into play and many bogus boundaries into bold relief. The aim of *The Magellan Fallacy* is not to reveal that certain traditions and texts exist. It is to argue that such literature is imperative to altering our basic understandings of how marginalized arts refract modern power and recast it altogether.

When the Filipino intellectuals who reached Spain in the late nineteenth century began producing literature, they carried with them the dynamics of Magellan and Lapu Lapu. Theirs was no simple relationship, however, between thesis and antithesis, between the global and the local. As they became the founding fathers of the Philippines through their varied authorships, they formed a community of writers who were literally insular insofar as they came from an archipelago but who were in no metaphorical sense insular as they tried to bridge the cultural currents that separated them from a European continent about as distant from their homeland as geographically possible. Like the Africans who later also published in Madrid and Barcelona, the early Asian writers who launched literary traditions in Spanish are not minor writers of peripheral importance, however critics see them and however they saw themselves, but actors in complex geopolitical dramas of worldwide scale. The Filipinos and Guineans are characterized in every way by displacements, ruptures, hybridizations, transculturations, and transnational forces. In sum, they are profoundly modern and global figures. Their significance is thus inverse to their reception. They are, almost across the board, unknown or obscure even to scholars who specialize in the Spanish-speaking world.

Though antipodal to each other geographically, the countries overlap on some points. For instance, both the Philippines and Equatorial Guinea are acutely artificial productions of colonialism. Prior to their respective political aggregations by the Spanish empire, these were lands whose diverse societies were unbound, even at an elite level, by a common language or culture. Moreover, before being yoked into existence as colonies, the Philippines and Equatorial Guinea each enjoyed plentiful, complex, and rich oral literatures but no lengthy written texts. It was an imperial tongue, Spanish, not a vernacular language, that ended up yielding the first novels in both places. These fictions suffered from the same fate of being alienated from a home audience, who could not be counted on to know Spanish, or for that matter to be literate in any language, and who certainly were not in Madrid, which is where the two inaugural novels were published. The prospective readership for Paterno and Evita was in the common metropolis, not the respective colonies, which raises the question of what it means for Asian and African literature in Spanish to begin with narratives that are, for various reasons, illegible or inaccessible to the very Asians and Africans who are its subjects.

This sort of tension is not as manifest in Spain and Latin America, where the originators of novelistic traditions could count on the existence of fellow readers of Spanish who formed a potential audience and market, even if only among the elite. Yet Filipino literature in Spanish before 1898 and Guinean literature after 1968 was produced largely in exile and with little presumption of widespread textual circulation back home. Other shared elements are rooted in the joint cultural legacy of Spanish colonialism, such as the presence of Catholicism in general and the macrohistorical decline of Iberian power. As a theoretical matter, however, a more striking commonality is the apparent paradox of forming national literatures almost entirely outside the nations in question.

Asian and African literature in Spanish emerges in moments of late colonialism that do not fit into the accepted frames of when, where, how, and why literatures in Spanish outside Spain came into existence. The tradition—and this book argues for the advantages of taking these disparate phenomena as a tradition—is invisible to nearly all those who study or teach in Spanish programs worldwide. Asian and African arts in Spanish, as a result, unveil multiple contours of the Spanish-speaking world while imaging them anew. How might the indigenous literatures of Peru or Guatemala, for example, compare to those of Filipinos and Guineans beset by the same imperial institutions of Spain? Which native responses to Spanish colonialism might prove unique to Latin America and which might span the Atlantic and the Pacific? Without consideration of Asia and Africa, there is no way to begin to talk about the possible exceptionalisms of Latin American texts within the larger empire. A host of issues with a long legacy in Spanish-language literatures resurfaces in Filipino and Guinean texts in alternative ways. These include the roles of local elites in colonial superstructures, the tensions of linguistic imperialism, the import of persisting precolonial cultural practices, and so forth.

The aim of *The Magellan Fallacy* is not to rescue two national traditions from oblivion and award them a modicum of scholarly respectability. The intent instead is to question the many ways in which the captains of globalization are betrayed by their own vehicles, by the characters they enlist to serve in them, by the blood and ink they spill in the name of creating a world in their image. The fall of Magellan is in one sense a very old story, that of one more demihero whose hubris results in his clinging to a shoreline, unrepentant, as his life seeps away. But it is also the most modern of stories, for ever since Magellan the flow of capital and narrative around the world has been unstoppable. As a result, fresh cadavers still float to the foam all the time. Yet there is no easy division between the local and the global, between resistance and conquest, between those who are narrated and those who narrate. We are all world travelers now, like it or not, whether we leave home or not, because from Magellan onward those of us who least move geographically from our birthplace are assaulted nevertheless by the world that keeps arriving ineluctably at our front door, by the currencies of all kinds that keep coming at us in even the calmest of harbors, by the captains who keep forcing entrance and evangelization upon us of one sort or another. We cannot escape the most brutal consequences of those currencies, for we travel with them every time we employ them in our own service or simply struggle against them. We cannot escape the most egregious of those evangelizations, for we participate in them every time we wade in the waters to do them battle. We are condemned to this postmagellanic planet and there is no going back.

There are good fights to fight and better peaces to plan, but however we resist globalization we are not reducible to Lapu Lapu, and however we pick our purveyors we are not reducible to Pigafetta. All authors, too, try to captain the vessels they lead forth, those ships of narrative that set sail not only from imperial countries but from colonies as well. And all ultimately fail to command those vessels, their directions always skewing in winds unplanned, their docks always those that they did not attempt to reach. Paterno, Rizal, Gerardo, Evita, Jones Mathama, Nsue Angüe, and Balboa Boneke are all betrayed by their own attempts to will forth a world in their books. So is the author of this book. The most obvious conquistadors are Magellan and his kind, but the act of writing is itself, even in an anticonquering cause, an attempt to circle the world too. And the consequences of globalization cannot be controlled. There are always unexpected and effective subversions by local forces and their world-traveling retellings by others. To believe otherwise is to commit the same mistake as Magellan. And to mimic his miscalculation is to fall face forward on one more shore, unremorseful, as what is left of humanity wavers in the waves.

THE CONTEXTS

This book operates in an scholarly space that is replete with obscurities and invisibilities. For starters, the field of Asian and African literature in Spanish does not exist as such. *The Magellan Fallacy* proposes its existence. Rizal is the lone Filipino author whose texts in Spanish are occasionally read. And Equatorial Guinea is a nation so little known that most specialists in Latin America or Spain probably could not find it on a map, much less speak to its history or literature. For the moment, therefore, Asian and African literature in Spanish remains isolated in practice from many disciplines and many potential publics. There is no reason to assume that a person leafing through this book, however knowledgeable in general, will have any substantive familiarity with the traditions at hand, or for that matter the countries. Yet *The Magellan Fallacy* aims for a broad readership of varied backgrounds and interests, popular as well as academic, without succumbing to the strong tendency in what scholarship does exist on Filipino and Guinean literature in Spanish to provide brief overviews of authors and texts. The hope here is instead to weave the micro and the macro together in a way that delves deeply and analytically into the details of unknown literary texts while retaining potential readers, whatever their starting point, rooted enough to follow the arguments and engage with them, even refute them, on the evidence presented. The ultimate hope, of course, is that *The Magellan Fallacy* inspires such readers to forge further arguments about Asian and African literature in Spanish, to develop them passionately, and to render this book obsolete as soon as possible.

Why the lack of attention to Asian and African literature in Spanish? One reason is the long-running division of professors in university departments of Spanish into peninsularists (that is, people who focus on Iberia) and Latin Americanists. Such institutional binarism does not leave space to acknowledge, much less analyze, the literary results of Spanish colonialism in Asia and Africa. Though the fact is often ignored, the Spanish empire was transpacific as well as transatlantic. And usually forgotten is that its transatlantic dimension extended southward to sub-Saharan Africa as well as westward to Latin America. The colonial and postcolonial literatures that emerged from the full reach of imperial Spain are therefore inherently global in nature. A consideration of fiction, journalism, poetry, theater, music, films, blogs, and streaming video in Spanish from Asia and Africa consequently would require rethinking multiple markers of any broad assessment of the entire world. After all, Spanish itself is the second or third mostly widely spoken language on the globe, following Mandarin and perhaps, depending on how a count is done, English. As of now, however, there are extremely few, if any, scholars who specialize in the full sweep of Filipino literature in Spanish; Rizal studies are a cottage industry and an exception. In the case of Equatorial Guinea, a small but growing coterie of exiled intellectuals and Western academics has been publishing increasingly in the past two decades. But until *The Magellan Fallacy,* no investigation of Guinean literature has moved beyond its specificities to include Filipino texts as well.

As of this writing, all lengthy considerations of Asian or African literature in Spanish are closer to guidebooks, some more nuanced than others, than to what is considered analytical criticism in other fields. The existing compendiums of literary names, facts, and synopses can be extremely useful points of departure for research but should not stand as a destination. The rare efforts at argument about Asian or African literature in Spanish are usually restricted to general characterizations of what are deemed to be national traditions. Compounding the dearth of comparative and theoretical approaches is the consanguineity of the tiny corpus of scholarly texts. Given so little published criticism with which to dialogue and so narrowly national a focus, essayists keep citing the same conclusions from the same few earlier essayists. This often creates a whisper-down-the-lane sequence of paraphrasing that takes scattered academic pronouncements as definitive frameworks and produces distortions in the process. The least helpful consequences of this phenomenon include the homogenization of much of the commentary and a limitation of the potential for disagreements that would dramatically diversify the field. The circular nature of these critiques also curbs the opportunities for ideas to travel to other academic disciplines and vice versa.

The Magellan Fallacy attempts to interact directly and extensively with a succession of literary texts without pausing to recycle once again the same scholarly narratives that are available elsewhere. At the same time, no reader can be expected to have familiarity with those narratives or to be able to access them, particularly if they are untranslated from Spanish (this book assumes only an anglophone reader) or are unavailable via inter-library loan or electronic databases, which is often the case with Filipino and Guinean texts. The rest of this introduction is therefore a sketch of the basic historical, literary, and scholarly contexts in which Asian and African literature in Spanish appears, plus an explanation of some of the terminological and methodological decisions made for *The Magellan Fallacy*. Most of this slips into other passages of the book later on, whenever needed to inform a specific point, but is relayed here more concisely as a general orientation and frame of reference.

When Magellan arrived across the Pacific from the South American strait that now bears his name, he visited but a fraction of the more than seven thousand islands and diverse peoples of what is now the Philippines. Subsequent naval expeditions likewise sponsored by Spain resulted in the first permanent settlement by Europeans in the archipelago in 1565 and, a few years later, the possession of Manila. Spain stayed on as the principal imperial power for over three hundred years, naming the islands after its Prince Philip, the future King Philip II. Throughout those centuries there was no large indigenous government in place nor any shared culture or language among the many different island communities subsumed into the colony. As the most distant possession of the Spanish empire, the Philippines was governed via the viceroyalty in Mexico until the independence of that country in 1821. Revolutionary movements across Latin America had commenced a decade or so earlier and by the 1820s had succeeded in producing new states throughout the Western Hemisphere. The Spanish empire, once the largest in the world, thereby had disintegrated with few exceptions. Asian and African literature in Spanish, phenomena of the late nineteenth century through today, thus emerged upon the rather earlier collapse of most of imperial Spain.

According to nearly all accounts, that empire ended definitively in 1898 when Spain lost a Carribean and Pacific war to the United States and consequently its final colonies of the Philippines, Cuba, Puerto Rico, and Guam. A cohort of Spanish writers who mourned this apparent end to Spanish power overseas was canonized eventually as the "Generation of '98" literati. This widespread historical-literary narrative of imperial finality, however, ignores the fact that Spanish Guinea, constituted by a few islands off the West African coast and a larger swath of mainland, remained a colony long thereafter. The narrative also does not acknowledge that a quite different generation of intellectuals in Spain initiated a Filipino literary tradition in Spanish in the 1880s. That tradition kept developing throughout the more than four decades of U.S. control over the archipelago. It weakened permanently only with the Japanese assault on the Philippines in December 1941 and ensuing occupation and, ultimately, the apocalyptic battle between Japanese and U.S. forces in 1945 in Intramuros, the old Spanish walled city inside greater Manila. Intramuros for centuries had been the heart of the colonial community in the Philippines and of those Filipinos who spoke Spanish. Most of its residents and buildings were destroyed in the war.

Immediately after the losses of 1898, Spain and its introspective intellectuals did not pay particular attention to the remaining imperial possessions on the western coasts of Africa. Through a combination of territorial claims and international treaties, Spain had come to hold not only Spanish Guinea but also Spanish Sahara, currently named Western Sahara. Before 1898, occasional Spanish missionaries and adventurers had set foot in both territories, the usual array of people and forces who appear once an imperial flag has been planted. In the first half of the twentieth century, more and more Spaniards arrived. Meanwhile, Spain established a protectorate over stretches of Morocco from 1912 to 1956. Such external advances took place while Spain was fracturing in its own internal struggles that culminated in the Spanish Civil War of 1936 to 1939, in which the fascist armies led by Francisco Franco emerged triumphant. The first African novel in Spanish appeared in 1953, that is, during the extensive middle of the Franco regime. This period also saw continuing growth in the foreign population of Spanish Guinea, to the point where, according to Ibrahim Sundiata, "In 1968 the European presence was one of the strongest in equatorial Africa with relation to the indigenous population" (*Equatorial Guinea*, 32).[1] General international pressures against colonization led to the independence of Spanish Guinea that same year, but freedom did not correlate to democracy or, for that matter, freedom. When Franco died in 1975, the young nation of Equatorial Guinea was suffering from the homicidal regime of Francisco Macías Nguema. Approximately a tenth of the country was murdered by the Macías government and a third of the population fled into exile. In 1979, the nephew of Macías, Teodoro Obiang Nguema Mbasogo, launched a successful coup d'ètat and installed himself as dictator. As of this writing, Obiang is still the president of Equatorial Guinea, having lasted in power longer than any other ruler in Africa. Such is the historical context for African literature in Spanish.

At first glance, therefore, the modern history of Guinea seems unrelated both directly and indirectly to that of the Philippines. The latter, unlike the former, did not emerge independent from Spanish colonialism but instead was occupied by a second foreign power and then a third. Moreover, the two autocracies that constitute the entirety of postindependence Guinean governance are incomparable to the variegated democratizations of the Philippines, however spotty and superficial they have been, and notwithstanding the long dictatorship of Ferdinand Marcos. The Philippines may lead the world today in the assassinations of journalists, but, still, it does have a press that is independent of the government. It also has bookstores, thriving universities, and relatively free institutions of civil society that have no equivalents at all in Equatorial Guinea.

Notably, the U.S. colonization of the Philippines and the consequent privileging of English in the archipelago left the Spanish-speaking community in Manila in an internal exile that was not political but linguistic. Relatively few Filipinos ever knew Spanish in any case, and as the twentieth century unfolded, Filipino authors who wrote in that language found themselves yet further isolated from a potential national readership. They also were increasingly alien to the younger intellectual elite, among whom knowledge of Spanish was no longer necessary. Filipino literature in Spanish, like its opposite number in Guinea, was thus always conditioned by one sort of expatriation or another, whether that of the pre-1898 intellectuals like Paterno and Rizal who wrote in Europe or that of the post-1898 generations who wrote inside the literal and metaphoric walls of Intramuros. The particular sequence of three different colonial powers does distinguish the Philippines from Guinea, but the African writers in Spanish also have had to compose first under colonialism and then amid two regimes marked by harsh disciplinings from above. Here too is a tripartite succession of repressive political contexts that authors have had to work within and without. In both countries, literature in Spanish has emerged and circulated in ways consistently apart from the people and lands that are its subject. In both countries, the national literature in that language has developed largely in division from the nation it notionally represents.

Asian literature in Spanish arose and flourished and trailed off just before its African counterpart began. Before Magellan, there was little tradition of written literature in the Philippines, though a limited script had developed among some peoples on the islands. After Magellan, Spanish priests eschewed the dissemination of their language among Filipinos, a policy that was forced to liberalize somewhat only after reforms in 1863. That is why virtually all Filipino literature was oral or written in vernaculars, such as Tagalog, prior to the arrival of Pedro Paterno in Madrid in the 1870s.[2] A high-society aficionado, he was in no sense representative of the rural Filipinos who constituted the bulk of the islands' population. Paterno spoke Spanish and probably French better than Tagalog. His writings, such as his 1885 novel *Nínay*, sought to convince European readers that Filipino culture, both ancient and contemporary, was European in essence and that the archipelago belonged on the roster of civilized places. Yet Paterno never could stabilize the map on which he situated the Philippines. His celebration of European globalization always proved inescapable from his resistance to the same. In his mind, the Philippines offered a unique contribution to a worldwide European culture. This posture is paradoxical at its core.

The two novels now hailed as foundational of the Philippines, José Rizal's *Noli me tangere* (*Touch Me Not*) of 1887 and *El filibusterismo* (*Subversion*) of 1891, were composed in Spanish shortly before the colonial master changed to the United States and the imperial language of the archipelago to English. A whole generation of Filipinos who learned Spanish at the tail end of the Spanish reign thus ended up producing the bulk of their literature under the occupation of a different empire altogether. Four decades of

Filipino literature therefore were produced under circumstances that were simultaneously colonial and postcolonial. The poets of the Filipino revolution, which was waged first against Spain and then against the United States, wrote in Spanish. And the decades leading up to World War II are referred to in dusty volumes as the "Golden Age" of "Fil-Hispanic" literature. With the exception of Rizal's texts, virtually none of this canon has been translated into English or Filipino languages. Since few Filipinos today know Spanish, the lack of translations means that the mere existence of an archipelagic literature in that language after Rizal is almost unknown in the country, including by scholars in the humanities. The increasing temporal distance from the tradition does not ameliorate matters any. After World War II, the remaining Filipino writers in Spanish were mostly aging men born before 1898 or the descendants of a small number of elite families who had survived, one way or another, the ravages of history in the islands. Apart from a handful of attempts in recent decades, often by Filipinos living abroad, the last significant array of creative texts by Filipinos in Spanish appeared in the early and middle 1960s.

Counterintuitively, the end of a continuous Filipino literary tradition in Spanish does not mean that its individual examples have ceased to emerge. There is a tremendous quantity and variety of texts in all genres that remains to be discovered in archives, both public and private, in the Philippines and elsewhere. An unpublished anthology of short stories by Félix Gerardo, for instance, is the subject of the third chapter of this book. These complex fictions by Gerardo, who wrote in the late 1930s and early 1940s, were found just several years ago. The stories are set in the central Philippines and feature characters who speak Cebuano as a native language, not Tagalog. Gerardo worked, therefore, with historical and cultural points of reference other than those of Manila and Intramuros. His contributions diversify in important ways the contours of Filipino literature in Spanish. And beyond the likely discoveries of more such writers in coming years, the twenty-first century may be marked by new Filipino literature not in Spanish but Chabacano. This language, developed from Spanish, Cebuano, and other tongues over the course of several hundred years, has experienced a rapid growth as of late and already has yielded short narratives and poems. The possibility of an inchoate Chabacano tradition is raised in the final chapter of this book. The emergence of Asian Hispanic literature is not confined to the chronological or linguistic boundaries that might be assumed.

As Filipino writers in Spanish struggled to resume their tradition after the devastation of Intramuros, Guinean literature in Spanish commenced with the publication of *Cuando los Combes luchaban* (*When the Combes Fought*) by Leoncio Evita in 1953. A much longer novel, *Una lanza por el Boabí* (*A Spear for the Boabí*), by Daniel Jones Mathama appeared in 1962, but the brutal Macías regime put an end to any possibility that independence in 1968 would afford a chance for a national literary tradition to flourish. The dictatorship eliminated virtually the entire intellectual class in the new country. A few young men who had gone to Spain to study in the late colonial years and thus escaped the persecution back home formed eventually, along with post-1968 refugees, the nucleus of the first generation of Equatoguinean writers. Without exception, dictatorship has conditioned the production of every text of Guinean literature from Evita onward. Spain too was a dictatorship throughout the late colonial period and so, during the overlap of the Macías and Franco regimes, Guinean writers were doubly subject to autocracy. Exile and expatriation, both personal and textual, provides a dominant background as well. Nearly all major works have been published in Spain, many of them composed there too or elsewhere abroad. The continuous written literary tradition of the country begins only with the publication of an anthology of local authors in 1984. That volume was edited by Donato Ndongo-Bidyogo, who remains the most prominent Equatoguinean intellectual. The next year, two novels appeared, *Ekomo* by María Nsue Angüe and *El reencuentro: el retorno del exiliado* (*The Reencounter: The Return of the Exile*) by Juan Balboa Boneke. A stream of texts in various genres has surged since. In contrast to Filipino literature in Spanish, Equatoguinean literature in Spanish is booming.

The chronological span of Asian and African literature in Spanish therefore parallels that of modern Latin American literature, which most scholars would identify as starting in the 1880s with José Martí of Cuba and Rubén Darío of Nicaragua, both of whom were innovative writers of poetry and prose. Filipino literature in Spanish extends mostly between 1880, when Paterno published a small book of poetry, and the aftermath of World War II. Notwithstanding the occasional fluttering of life since then, the tradition is pretty much dead. Despite the strenuous efforts of the Manila branch of the Cervantes Institute, an organization of the Spanish government designed to promote Spanish culture worldwide, the Spanish language is unlikely to reemerge in any significant way in the islands. But the 1953 novel by Evita, though forgotten for decades, is enjoying something of a recuperation as the initiator of a Guinean tradition that since the mid-1980s has broadened dramatically. The 1990s saw major growth in Moroccan and Cameroonian literature in Spanish and the early 2000s in Western Saharan literature in Spanish as well. In other words, just as Asian literature in Spanish winds down in the mid-twentieth century, African literature in Spanish winds up. This sequence suggests the possibility of imagining the global tradition of literature in Spanish as running directly from Paterno and his first volume of poetry to today. Latin Americans such as Martí and Darío are not the only writers in the 1880s who launched the modern history of literature in Spanish.

The aggregate of Filipino literature in Spanish, authored by hundreds of known individuals, remains for the moment far greater in number and range than that of Guinean literature in Spanish. Many of the extant texts have not yet been identified or located, however, and the sub-Saharan corpus continues to grow. Moreover, the African writings, though not particularly accessible, are far easier to obtain than their Asian counterparts thanks to their coincidence with contemporary technology. If an African book is published in Spain today, however limited its initial printing, it may be available via a few Internet clicks or, failing that, an email to the right person or attendance at the right academic conference. The surviving Filipino texts in Spanish, all much older, are not in print (again, the Rizalian oeuvre is the sole exception) and do not circulate nearly that readily. Most of those that are unavailable through interlibrary loan, which is to say, nearly all of them, are either collecting dust in small archives in Luzon (the large island where Manila is located) and Cebu that deliberately discourage research, or moldering in forgotten corners of random homes throughout the islands, or, quite likely, sitting in the Philippines among the private holdings of elite families and bibliophiles. The tradition is so offline that there is no way of tracking down many of the known titles and authors other than going to the archipelago and sleuthing out those inheritors and collectors who might be willing to open their doors. Furthermore, the names of most titles and authors may not be listed anywhere. Meanwhile, successive natural forces, including floods and strong heat and humidity, slowly destroy the remaining examples of many old texts on the erratic local used-book markets and in public libraries and private collections where stable temperatures are not maintained. The bulk of Filipino literature in Spanish was published in magazines and newspapers, media that do not survive well physically even when not having to make it through the multiple environmental and man-made catastrophes of the sort the Philippines endured in the twentieth century.

Nonetheless, thanks to a smattering of scholars over the last 130 years, an ample number of authors and titles have been signaled for posterity. Yet despite the eight decades or so of the mostly continuous production of Filipino literature in Spanish, and notwithstanding the paradoxical centrality of Rizal in the Filipino national imaginary, only one guide to the tradition has been published in English. That language is key because it is the lingua franca not only of the Western academic world but of the Philippines too. The book in question is *81 Years of Premio Zóbel* by Lourdes Castrillo Brillantes and appeared in 2006. Like the clutch of other retrospectives that were published in Spanish in the twentieth century, the overview by Brillantes emphasizes the who and what of the literature. There are capsule biographies of authors, lists of titles, summaries of plots, reproductions of poems, and so on. The text is therefore an extremely useful compendium of data but not a critical intervention. Now on sale throughout the Philippines, *81 Years of Premio Zóbel* was commissioned by an elite family that oversaw a prestigious literary prize. It was originally written and published in Spanish, but that version circulated only hand to hand and never was made commercially available. Furthermore, the book starts chronologically with the 1920s and therefore long after the inaugural era of Paterno and Rizal.

With respect to the entire tradition, the most comprehensive and incisive panorama is *La literatura filipina en castellano* (*Filipino Literature in Castilian*) by Luis Mariñas, a slim study that appeared in 1974 and that has never been translated or republished. The sentences that Mariñas offers on various texts are often the lone commentary in existence about them. Unpublished graduate student theses whose single copies may survive in a sole university library in the archipelago are sometimes the only other scholarship with which to engage. There are also occasional academic essays that have been published in Filipino journals at different points in the past fifty years, but since those articles are rarely indexed in major or minor databases, it may take diligent detective work and a fair amount of luck to learn of their existence. Substantive and extant scholarship on Filipino literature in Spanish may not, ever, enter into wider dialogue as a result. Meanwhile, the few relevant articles published in foreign journals tend to be of an introductory nature, along with the usual emphasis on Rizal. The consequence of such a tiny number of circulating texts is that, as in the case of Guinean literature, later scholars end up repeating the sparse comments of their few predecessors. Oddly, the impression left is that there is little space to redefine a field that barely exists in the first place.

A principal reason for this anemic academic environment is the marginality in the Americas and Europe of Filipino studies as a discipline. The Philippines remains virtually unacknowledged by Spanish departments despite over three centuries of Spanish colonialism; by English departments despite being, according to some measurements, perhaps the fourth largest anglophone country in the world; and by Asian departments, despite geography, because of all the successive Western presences in the islands. The ceaseless flux of cultures and languages and peoples that constitute the Philippines, however, is precisely what makes its literature in Spanish a leading example of the unsettled and asymmetrical forces of modernity. Rizal studies are always popular in the archipelago but he is read almost entirely in translation and in isolation from the rest of the tradition, which overwhelmingly remains untranslated and unavailable. Professors in the Philippines teach and study Filipino literature, of course, but because of the events of 1898 their common Western language is English, not Spanish. All are multilingual but those other languages are either indigenous to the islands or, in some instances, Mandarin, as Filipinos of Chinese heritage have long played important roles in various sectors of national life. In addition to the language barrier, another impediment to the local study of Filipino literature in Spanish is that the economic infrastructure of Filipino universities is impoverished compared to that in North American and European peer institutions. The basic conditions that support academic production, such as decent library budgets, journals that publish regularly, fellowships for scholars to learn Spanish abroad, and occasional freedom from teaching responsibilities, are not consistently available and therefore not propitious for the local development of studies of Filipino literature in Spanish. There are some Filipino scholars who do know Spanish and who do offer groundbreaking work, often in a philological vein, but they are few in number.

Critical studies of African literature in Spanish are less rare but still quite thin by the measure of any other field that analyzes cultural production in Western languages. As with Asian literature in Spanish, only one guidebook to the subject exists in English, *An Introduction to the Literature of Equatorial Guinea: Between Colonialism and Dictatorship* by Marvin Lewis. Published in

2007, a year after *81 Years of Premio Zóbel*, it too mostly proffers author biographies and plot summaries and thematic overviews. Once again, this is helpful information that provides starting points for future investigations, but the little that might be called analysis in the book tends to repeat the general conclusions reached by two earlier writers, Donato Ndongo-Bidyogo and Mbaré Ngom. The former is the most important Equatoguinean figure of letters; the latter is a scholar based in the United States whose 1993 journal article, "La literatura africana de expresión castellana: la creación literaria en Guinea Ecuatorial" ("African Literature in Spanish: Literary Creation in Equatorial Guinea"), and its many subsequent reincarnations seem to be the texts that made Guinean literature known to an increasingly broader slate of academics in the Americas and Europe. Yet these later investigators almost always have been trained in the literatures of Spain or Latin America, not Africa. Meanwhile, scholars of African literary traditions, including those in other Romance tongues such as French and Portuguese, confront a linguistic hurdle with Guinean texts, few of which are translated. Inside Equatorial Guinea, the dearth of basic freedoms and the meager higher education system—the lone university is controlled by the state—result in inordinately fewer opportunities for local academic investigations and publishing than in the Philippines. There are writers who do appear and choose to stay in the country but they have no institutional spaces in which to develop independent scholarship. And it is hard to pursue antidictatorial arguments in fiction or poetry or, for that matter, scholarship, when the dictator and his cohort live around the corner.

Since most major Guinean writers work in exile, however, and since their tradition, unlike its Filipino counterpart, is very much alive and vibrant, Western scholars have had easier access to authors and texts and have produced academic publications in consequence. There is a small array of professors in North America and Europe who specialize in Guinean literature, at least at times, and there are now occasional gatherings at which scholars, exiles, and, recently, even diplomats from the Obiang government meet to exchange ideas. In the late nineteenth century in Madrid and Barcelona there were frequent interchanges in person and via mail among Filipino intellectuals and their European colleagues, but there is no longer a community of Spanish-speaking Asian authors in existence. This means that the opportunities for translation inspired by direct personal interactions no longer exist either, whereas the opposite is true for contemporary African writers. Although Equatorial Guinea is far less populous than the Philippines and far more obscure, it easily outdistances the archipelago in terms of the number of people interested in its literary tradition in Spanish.

Despite the current burgeoning of Guinean literary studies, however, the basic contours of the scholarship stay essentially unchanged. The early verdicts of Ndongo-Bidyogo and Ngom on disparate texts remain virtually uncontested. Many of the academic publications continue to be of the surveying nature, intent on providing paragraph summaries of authors and texts and little else. There are very few lengthy monographs of any kind. With a handful of exceptions, there are no innovative theoretical interventions attempted in the criticism and there is scarce effort at framing Guinean literature in something other than a strictly national context. Furthermore, much of what is presented as study of African literature in Spanish is actually study of Spaniards' perceptions of Africa and of Africans in Spain. Probably, all the scholarly initiatives help create academic space for a subject otherwise ignored worldwide. But African literature in Spanish, as with Asian literature in Spanish, is far more significant than the repetition of originary judgments and taxonomies would suggest.

The Magellan Fallacy suggests new ways of navigating these global waters. In the meanwhile, this trip around the world may fail to reach its many destinations. Perhaps, arguably, it should. Yet the endeavor seems worth launching, and its stories, hopefully, worth reading. But that is for others to decide.

TERMINOLOGIES AND METHODOLOGIES

Nomenclature and working practices for research on Asian and African literature in Spanish are not well developed. Consequently, certain choices regarding vocabularies and approaches had to be made. The results in *The Magellan Fallacy* of these decisions are as follows.

Filipino literature. This phrase is not as self-evident as would seem. In the nineteenth century, "Filipino" traditionally meant a person of Spanish descent born in the Philippines, not someone whose ancestors were originally from the Philippines. To characterize the early works of Pedro Paterno as Filipino, therefore, is somewhat anachronistic, because his family tree features indigenous and Chinese forebears. Yet there does not seem to be a way around this issue better than accepting the anachronism, so "Filipino literature" throughout *The Magellan Fallacy* can be taken on its face as following the current usage of "Filipino."

Guinean. The nation of Equatorial Guinea emerged in 1968 from the colony of Spanish Guinea. All references in *The Magellan Fallacy* to the combined literary tradition of the two polities is denominated as "Guinean," with "Equatoguinean" reserved only for postindependence texts and authors.

Expatriate. Technically, authors from the colonial eras who wrote and published in Madrid and Barcelona were not, in fact, abroad, nor were they expatriates, for the pre-1898 Philippines and pre-1968 Guinea were legally part of Spain. Authors such as Paterno, Rizal, and Jones Mathama did not regard themselves as exiles per se. Nonetheless, *The Magellan Fallacy* uses "expatriate" as the most useful way of characterizing the geographical alienation of these writers from the lands of their birth. Similarly, "compatriot" will be used to describe colonial-era authors in a sense exclusive of Spaniards, though legally all shared the same patria.

Fil-Hispanic. This term is used occasionally in the surveys that appeared over the course of the twentieth century. It simply means Filipino literature in Spanish, with "Filipino" equivalent to the current use of that term.

Asian and African literature in Spanish. At first glance, this book is concerned almost entirely with literature from two countries, not two continents. The frequent substitution of "the Philippines" and "Equatorial Guinea" with "Asia" and "Africa" is not meant to indicate synonymity so much as multiple broader issues at stake. Among the implications are the wider geographies that African literature in Spanish comprises, including places such as Western Sahara, Morocco, Cameroon, and Gabon. And Asian literature in Spanish should embrace cultural phenomena beyond the Philippines, such as from Latin American immigrant communities in Japan, Australia, and elsewhere in the Pacific. The final chapter of *The Magellan Fallacy* discusses these possibilities further.

Asian Hispanic and *African Hispanic.* These phrasings offer broader possibilities at linguistic as well as geographic levels. "Asian Hispanic" is useful to encompass emergent written and audiovisual phenomena in Chabacano in addition to older Filipino texts in Spanish. It also points to the need for research into the possibility of Spanish-inflected literatures in Pacific lands such as Palau and Guam. "African Hispanic" likewise opens greater potential breadths of language. Perhaps some day, for instance, researchers will collect oral narratives from the more than fifty thousand Guineans, most of the Fang ethnicity, who live in francophone Gabon as refugees. Such narratives very well might appear in some combination of Spanish, Fang, and French. A term like "African Hispanic" is wide enough to include that.

Hispanophone. This helpful adjective means "in Spanish" yet is almost never used by scholars of Latin America or Spain. In contrast, "francophone" (in French), "anglophone" (in English), and "lusophone" (in Portuguese) are common words in academic circles and are routinely used to describe literatures in those languages that appear outside of France, Great Britain and the United States, and Portugal. The implication of these terms is generally of the colonial and postcolonial contexts of artistic production in European tongues. The reason "hispanophone" has little currency is the widespread assumption that there is no phenomenon of literature in Spanish outside the binarism of Spain and Latin America and, therefore, little need for a word to describe it.

Global literature in Spanish. This phrase points to conceivable remappings of literature in Spanish not only beyond Latin America and Spain but also beyond Asia and Africa. There is already a book in English on Canadian literature in Spanish, *Latinocanadá: A Critical Study of Ten Latin American Writers of Canada* by Hugh Hazelton, which thereby equals the number of corresponding texts on the Philippines and Guinea. Abundant scholarship on Chicano, Puerto Rican, and other U.S. literary traditions in Spanish and Spanglish exists too but tends to be claimed by academics in English and American studies programs. Newer cultural phenomena in Spanish and Spanglish of disparate immigrant communities in Europe north of the Pyrenees seem yet to be the subjects of extensive published scholarship. Despite their diversity, all these marginalized arts can be envisioned collectively as forming global flows.

Humabon and **Zzula.** These are two terms *not* in *The Magellan Fallacy* that merit registering nonetheless. Whenever the story of Magellan and Lapu Lapu is relayed via Filipino monuments and other media, the historical presences of two additional indigenous leaders is generally left out of the narrative. Pigafetta, however, extensively depicts the rajah Humabon from the island of Cebu, where Magellan made his last major port of call. Pigafetta also writes, briefly, of Zzula from Mactan, the adjacent and smaller island that was ruled over by Lapu Lapu. On the arrival of Magellan, Humabon asked the foreign captain to offer tribute to him, as was customary from visiting ships, whereupon an imperial interpreter explained that "if he [Humabon] did not wish to be his [Magellan's] friend and treat his subjects well, he would send to him again so many men against him that he would destroy him" (Pigafetta, 75). Humabon considered the situation and soon agreed to be baptized and to swear loyalty to the king of Spain. Once Magellan was dead, however, he oversaw an ambush in which two dozen of the surviving Europeans were slaughtered. As for Zzula, a figure who is sometimes not mentioned in other early accounts of the circumnavigation, he appears momentarily in Pigafetta as a less powerful leader than Lapu Lapu on Mactan. Zzula secretly sends a son to Magellan to convey that he wants to submit to the king of Spain but cannot because of the opposition of Lapu Lapu, so he pleads for a military intervention by the foreigners (87, 163). By this narrative, therefore, Magellan is cued into the fatal attack by an indigenous rival to Lapu Lapu.

In sum, both Humabon and Zzula are indigenous figures who occupy an unstable middle space between the two famous protagonists. They are temporary surrenderers of local sovereignty whose actions nonetheless result in the deaths of a number of the foreigners. *The Magellan Fallacy*, as with most Filipino representations of the foundational episode, does not engage tropologically with either Humabon or Zzula. This metaphoric absence is a strategic decision made on two grounds. First, neither figure seems to correspond particularly well to any of the Asian or African writers at hand, for all seem to have embraced both Spain and Christianity fairly willingly. Although general colonial duress may have conditioned their disparate leanings in those directions, it did not arrive at the immediate barrel of a gun, as in the case of Humabon before Magellan; as for Zzula, he is too thin a figure in Pigafetta to hazard any substantive guesses about his motivations for petitioning Magellan. Second, additional allegorical actors in an uncertain center stage are not needed because Magellan and Lapu Lapu, as this book argues, already occupy that space. Theirs is not a binarism in the first place but a dialectic in a permanent state of common collapse and endless inversion.

Sources. The principal texts studied herein by Paterno, Rizal, Gerardo, Jones Mathama, Nsue Angüe, and Balboa Boneke were chosen as illustrative of varying problematics of artistic emergence rather than as correlative to the full breadth of Asian and African literature in Spanish. As for genre, notwithstanding the prominence of poetry in both the Filipino and Guinean cases, fiction was selected as the focus of this book for the generally greater opportunities available for extended analyses of specific texts. The deliberate length of the chapters in *The Magellan Fallacy* reflects a will to show that multilayered and deep engagement with particular issues of Asian and African literature in Spanish is possible and desirable and, even so, leaves much still open for further questioning. Regarding cited scholarship, an unusually high number of unpublished theses by students at different levels are referenced in *The Magellan Fallacy,* as these often represent the only or leading commentary on certain texts.

Translations. All those in this book are by the author. Readers of Spanish will note various irregular orthographic features in some of the quotations. These are all reproduced verbatim from source texts.

Play. All the play in this book, in every sense of that word—the primal scene that grounds it in water, the alliteration for art's sake, the ludic leanings here and there—are in no way meant to obscure the horrendous realities that permeate every page: the theaters of war, the staging of coups, the bloody mise-en-scènes in the foregrounds and backgrounds, whether markedly visible or not, that are the many hundreds of thousands of dead Asians and Africans whose cadavers pile high during the Spanish empire, the U.S. empire, the Japanese empire, and assorted homegrown dictatorships. The century of literature that this book spans is a hundred years of inordinate suffering. A dirge, however, is not the only response demanded for tragedy, however acute and however profound, and the sundry modes of play in *The Magellan Fallacy* operate via other tones. All of them, no matter how light, are laced with mourning and more. But readers turn to literature for various reasons, chief among them entertainment of one kind or another; few are those who turn similarly to literary criticism. Yet why should reading fiction be so often a gesture of play while reading about fiction so often a burden? All narrative, including and especially those about the arts, is play, and this book hopes to entertain its reader even as it mourns the postmagellanic pummelings of the world over.

Qualifiers. The frequent repetition in the forthcoming chapters of "known" and "seems to" and synonymous phrases is unavoidable and is meant to caveat any number of declarations. The underlying issue is that many primary and secondary sources of African and especially Asian literature in Spanish remain off the grids of international scholarship. If or when those sources appear, some and perhaps many of the statements in this book may prove to be in need of revision. The use of "known" and "seems to" throughout *The Magellan Fallacy* attempts to acknowledge that reality. There is virtual certainty, however, that a number of individuals in the Philippines in particular, and possibly some institutions too, keep significant archives with texts beyond those consulted for this book; to varying extents, such individuals and institutions may be aware of the information they possess. But as with, say, relevant graduate student theses that are not indexed online (nor perhaps in any offline, local computer system anywhere) and so may not yet be discovered, private holdings whose existence is either deliberately hidden or otherwise inaccessible to researchers cannot be said to be "known" in any public or social sense of that concept. The judicious proliferation in *The Magellan Fallacy* of an adjective such as "known" is not typical in scholarship about such recent literature but is, in this case, necessary.

One of the challenges facing a study like this that attempts to be the first word, not the last, on many aspects of a field that does not presently exist, is the multiplicity of lines in sight and the desirability of not foreclosing any of them. The endeavor here is to develop sundry trajectories but also to try to indicate the many possible paths that could be taken by others. Most intellectual efforts are interventions in debates, but in this instance there is often no debate in which to intervene. There are relatively few coordinates by which to be guided. As a result, there are no doubt many mistakes and missteps in the movements that lie ahead. Every attempted circumnavigation misses many marks. The ones that continue anyway are carried on by others. That is the hope, in any case, and the melancholy as well.

CHAPTER ONE

Novelizations of Asia:
Pedro Paterno's Nínay *(1885)*

The first Asian novelist in Spanish completed the journey of Magellan three and a half centuries later. He did not, however, conclude it. As Pedro Paterno sailed from the Philippines to Spain in the early 1870s, he must have thought of Antonio Pigafetta, the Italian wayfarer on the circumnavigation of 1518–21 who survived the death of Magellan in the archipelago and returned to Iberia along with fewer than a tenth of the original crewmen. In the European context, it is Pigafetta whose account of the round-the-world voyage and the demise of Magellan put the Philippines, literally, on the map. It is Pigafetta whom Gabriel García Márquez cites as a starting point of Latin American fiction in the opening paragraph of his acceptance speech for the Nobel Prize for Literature. And Pedro Paterno, the first major Filipino author in Spain, composed new texts and contexts for the world as much as did Pigafetta. He too made the radical trip west that Magellan never did.

Paterno cut a singular figure in the fin de siècle world. He was an absurdly aristocratic national of a nonexistent nation who sided for and against a dying European empire, for and against a frustrated Asian revolution, and for and against a triumphant North American colonizer. By all accounts, his personality was extraordinary. He was a self-proclaimed lord of royal indigenous blood, an inveterate organizer of parties for whatever high society surrounded him, and a walking pomposity whose obsession with footnotes in his early novel is matched only by his obsession with virgins in his late stories. He wrote erudite tomes that passed fantasy off as fact. He assumed authoritative voices for readerships that barely existed. He made history, literally, time and again, and he knew it, and history unmade him just as quickly, time and again. In his person and his texts, he trans-

posed islands and continents without end, and in so doing he created cartographies capacious enough to unmoor all the maps onto which he wrote
both the Philippines and the world. If the death of Magellan marks the
birth of modernity, then the fictions of Paterno are the fulcrum on which
the powers of the planet pivoted.

During the two dozen years that Paterno spent in Madrid in the late
nineteenth century, his mind kept traveling to the Philippines in an unbounded flux of there and back again. This incessant movement, however,
never followed a strictly linear path between the peninsula and its colonized archipelago, for Paterno offered a globalized rather than binary vision of the world. In that vision, he, as the pathbreaking Filipino intellectual in Spain, could promote the Philippines in the metropole as a unique
component of Europe. He saw himself, for all intents and purposes, as the
captain of a ship arriving from the Philippines with news of distant but civilized lands and culture. Controlling the representation of those lands and
culture, however, always eluded him despite his voluminous literary and
scholarly output on the subject. That is why Paterno never concluded Magellan's journey in any definitive sense. An essentialized Philippines always
slipped beyond his reach despite his sustained efforts to the contrary. Paterno's *Nínay* of 1885, the first Filipino novel in any language and the first
Asian novel in Spanish, is a remarkable testament to the global ebbs and
flows of a man and a country that spill out over their banks even when
most apparently confined within them. His *Aurora Social* (*Social Dawn*) of
1910–11, a flurry of fictional narratives produced after a generation of absence from the genre and on the eve of his death, is equally overlapping of
its borders, albeit in a different way. As a result, Paterno subverted far more
in his writings than anyone has acknowledged, indeed, far more than he
intended.

That probably fewer than a dozen people today have read even two of
Paterno's fictions is a sign of how inordinately the Philippines has been ignored as the symbolic birthplace of globalization. Paterno, like the Philippines he tried to imagine into existence, was a derivative of everything and
nothing. His person and his oeuvre embodied both Magellan and Lapu
Lapu, that is, both the Western captain and the indigenous leader who defeated him, while being resolvable to neither the foreign aggressor nor the
local sovereign. It is this inability to pin Paterno down to any particular
character or country or continent that makes him the critical author of
globalization that he is. Only via *Nínay* and *Social Dawn* does the circum-

navigation of centuries earlier resume in the form of fiction from where it first fractured.

Magellan himself does not appear in these texts, but Paterno could not have written a new world without him. The ending point of the voyage for one man is the starting point for the other. Together, which they never were, they opened novel spaces for Asian literature in Spanish. Paterno began by publishing in Madrid the first Filipino book of poetry, *Sampaguitas,* in 1880.[1] A *sampaguita* is a white flower that would be a recurring symbol of both Filipino nationhood and virginal purity in all later archipelagic literature in Spanish. As far back as 1593, with the publication of the first book in the Philippines, entitled *Doctrina Christiana en la lengua española y tagala* (*Christian Doctrine in the Spanish Language and Tagalog*), locals had collaborated with Spanish priests in diverse ways to translate religious teachings fron Spanish (Mojares, *Origins,* 47–50). The early seventeenth-century Filipino printer Tomas Pinpin even had written some poetry in Spanish (Mojares, *Origins,* 51). The creative writings of Paterno, however, stand apart from the obscured work of such predecessors because his texts are foundational to a largely secular and institutionally autonomous Filipino literary tradition in Spanish, notwithstanding the religious references and leanings of many of its authors. Paterno was highly influenced in style and substance by his European contemporaries and, regardless of the moralizing thrusts of his fictions, wrote outside the power grid of church and pedagogy. As a result, the flowery poems of *Sampaguitas* function in effect like the travel narrative of Pigafetta, as an initial secular attempt to process a modern world in which the Philippines and the West were now forever intertwined.[2]

This endeavor evinced itself at greater length in 1885 with the publication by Paterno of *Nínay* in Madrid and in the language bequeathed to him by the flag under which Pigafetta had sailed. When Paterno returned to the Philippines for good in 1894 (his only previous return home was a trip in 1882–83), he continued navigating new waters through the end of Spanish rule in 1898 and the consolidation of the U.S. occupation thereafter. He founded numerous newspapers and wrote in 1902 the first Filipino opera in Spanish, entitled *La alianza soñada* (*The Dreamed Alliance*). As his days ended early in the 1910s, now contextualized by the heavy colonial promotion of English, Paterno produced the hispanophone narratives of *Social Dawn* to proclaim in a bygone imperial language the necessity of carving out a patriotic space amid the dominance of a new one. In between his permanent return to the Philippines and his final writings, he became an indisputable father of his country in his roles as director of the Museo-Biblioteca de Filipinas (Museum-Library of the Philippines) in 1894; as mediator between the Spanish governor-general and indigenous revolutionaries in negotiations that resulted in the Pact of Biyak-na-Bato of 1897, a milestone that marked for the moment the end of armed anticolonial hostilities; as president of the revolutionary Congress of Malolos in 1898; as legislative sponsor of the forerunner of the Philippine National Library; as assemblyman in the first Philippine congress under U.S. rule; and as a failed candidate for Speaker of that congress and for provincial governor (Mojares, *Brains*, 16–40). Despite all this, Paterno was ridiculed throughout his career and forgotten by the end of it. His posthumous life in historiography is scant, sometimes only amounting to brief characterizations as a traitor for his role in the Biyak-na-Bato accord. Significantly, Nick Joaquín, perhaps the most respected Filipino essayist of the twentieth century, leaves Paterno out of his *A Question of Heroes*, a study of the mixed legacies of ten founding fathers of the Philippines. All were contemporaries of Paterno. Despite the manifest efforts and impacts of Paterno as a national figure, Joaquín apparently deemed him so unheroic as to not make this list of even the conflicted luminaries of his era. This is in keeping with the consensus on Paterno, both in his time and since. History is embarrassed by his paternity, but such fathers are what most patrias are made of anyway.

There is no getting around the fact that the fictions by Paterno are awful by almost any measure. There is no denying that his scholarship—he produced copious histories and cultural and scientific studies of the Philippines in between *Nínay* and *Social Dawn*—was considered even by his Filipino contemporaries as apocryphal and vainglorious.[3] There is no refuting that *Nínay* was read by very few people at the time and the entire run of *Social Dawn* perhaps by no one. Moreover, Paterno the man has been regarded by historians and contemporaries in a spectrum that ranges from fatuous ass at one end to sycophantic treasonist at the other. Yet none of this is relevant to an examination of the singularly important globalized phenomena that are his fictions. They created new coordinates that many later authors would assume in turn, regardless of whether they acknowledged or knew that Paterno first mapped them out. Máyolo G. Torres, one of the few scholars to praise Paterno without caveat, has gone so far as to call Paterno "el gigante de los gigantes de su época" ["the giant of the giants of his epoch"] (13).[4] Although Paterno, it is true, did not see further than other men, that is largely because he spent his life trying to stand on his own shoulders. He was a bizarre type of giant, a sort of Atlas manqué who created the world he then tasked himself with carrying, but he was a giant nonetheless. And all giants, whatever the burdens they bear, must be reckoned with at some point.

Paterno should be read because of his stupendous failures, because he so dramatically achieved the opposite of what he sought. In this he is a man for all modernity, a writer who understood postmagellanic Europe and Asia and everything in between, whichever direction the earth might turn, despite the mammoth amount of evidence that he understood next to nothing at all. He tried to cohere antipodal cultures in his writings and his person, probably convincing himself that he succeeded in doing both while spectacularly demonstrating that he did not. The currents of his prose and poetry rush against each other in unending proof that the cultures he sought to align were no longer antipodal anyway, that since Magellan and Lapu Lapu they occupied the same unstable spaces of Pigafetta and his progeny and were condemned to a common world evermore.

John Schumacher summarizes Paterno's scholarship as "miscellanies of history, irrelevant erudition, and outright plagiarism" (*Making*, 108). But there is nothing less miscellaneous than the choosing of certain histories, nothing less irrelevant than seemingly unneeded decisions to cite certain snippets of academic knowledge, nothing more original than moves to steal someone else's lines. Benedict Anderson, who likely has done more than any other Westerner to make North American and European scholars aware of the importance of *Noli me tangere* (*Touch Me Not*), a novel published by the Filipino national hero José Rizal in 1887, dismisses Paterno's *Nínay* of two years earlier as "minor, experimental trash" (*Spectre*, 232). Without the allegedly minor, however, the supposedly major cannot be determined and defined. Without the experimental, the normative cannot possibly be codified. Moreover, the experimental is, at the very least, alluring. And there is nothing, of course, more revealing than trash. As the first Asian novelist in Spanish, Paterno should be of interest to anyone broadly engaged with international literature. As the first novelist of the Philippines, as an unknown and flexible foil to the overly known and stiffly molded Rizal, Paterno should rearrange the allegories of Filipino nationhood. But as a globalized writer who took on the world, Paterno should occupy a central place in any canon of the leading artists of modernity.

Most scholarly references to Paterno make a note of his political posts, perhaps indicate his major publications, and leave it at that. Only one sustained biography of him has been published, as the first third of Resil Mojares's exemplary *Brains of the Nation* of 2006. (In a number of fields of scholarship on the Philippines, if Mojares has not written about a subject, no one has.) There is no known extended analysis of any of Paterno's fictions save for the dissertation on *Nínay* from 1967 by Torres and an essay on the novel published in 2010 by Eugenio Matibag. Torres notes that at the moment of his own writing, more than eighty years after the publication of *Nínay*, "hasta ahora ningún filipino se ha preocupado de estudiar detalladamente esta dicha primera novela filipina publicada" ["until now no Filipino has bothered himself to study in detail this first published Filipino novel"] (2). The bulk of his thesis, however, consists not of textual analysis of *Nínay* but of biographical, historical, and Spanish literary contexts for the novel. The reasons for the academic and popular aversion to Paterno are not hard to discern, as he was laughed off various stages even in his own time. His protean political sympathies and steadfast elitism made him far less viable a character for the creation of a patriotic Filipino narrative than the generation of doomed intellectuals that succeeded him. Despite his stature as the first Filipino of the era to make a name for himself, the coterie of compatriots who arrived after Paterno in Europe proved much more serviceable in building a national identity for the Philippines. Their reformist newspaper *La solidaridad* (*Solidarity*) ran from 1889 to 1895 in Barcelona and Madrid and has been analyzed far more than Paterno's fiction. The periodical was dedicated to achieving ameliorations in the way Spain governed the Philippines, not independence.

The foremost figure among the intellectuals behind *Solidarity* was Rizal, an essayist and poet as well as novelist who was executed by Spain in 1896 for the alleged anticolonialism of his oeuvre. Rizal was invoked in his last years and against his will by Filipino revolutionaries as their symbolic leader. His martyrdom posthumously confirmed him as the easy choice for the role of principal author of the Philippine nation. Various powers, including the U.S. regime that wrested the archipelago from Spain and local revolutionaries in 1898, found it helpful to have in Rizal a man who had perished at Spanish hands. Other key contributors to *Solidarity* such as its successive editors, the florid orator Graciano López Jaena and the polemicist Marcelo H. [Hilario] del Pilar, usefully died in 1896 as well. While this cast of characters exited the proscenium, Paterno, who maintained oblique relations with them while all were in Europe, had the fortune or lack thereof to survive past the imperial shift. He died in Manila in 1911 as an anachronism, an aristocratic relic of an age and empire and cultural geography that had changed beyond anything foreseeable in his youth.

This inconsistent relationship with his era helps make Paterno the key international figure that he is. The Philippines and the world are not, in an age of globalization, in sync with themselves. There is no master narrative of what Magellan wrought that has a beginning, middle, and end. There is no heroic trajectory. There is no unifying story. The archetypal, static national narrative of Rizal as a martyr with a coherent moral and literary-political trajectory is the most unrepresentative iconography conceivable for a world of forces in perpetual flux. Time was always out of joint for Paterno and so was space. His novelizations, consistently at odds with their own premises, reflect this and therefore reflect both his world and ours. Mojares lends a relatively sympathetic ear to Paterno and his writings, attuned to the nuances of his contradictions and their reasons for existing (*Brains,* passim). The portrait is of an aristocratic buffoon who accepted European ways of seeing and defining the world as universal but who believed as well that Filipino culture and history offered a valuable contribution to the overall history of humankind. Paterno crafted scholarship that was shoddy even by the standards of the time, and sometimes he fabricated his facts outright, but all this was in the service of illustrating that the Philippines deserved a rightful place on the European map of the world. Paterno, like Lapu Lapu and Magellan and Pigafetta, inserted the Philippines into that map and so changed it forever.

For readers today of Latin American and Spanish literature who would encounter Filipino fiction in Spanish for the first time, Paterno and the Asian tradition he inaugurates might seem a cartographic outlier, an island or archipelago way off the charts of history, both literary and otherwise. In some ways this is true, for Paterno does augment and arrange anew the atlas of the arts. He was cognizant of such, but at the same time he took great pains to demonstrate that he was operating in territory that was quite familiar to readers throughout the Spanish-speaking world of his day. In the Iberian context, for example, the audience for *Nínay* would have recognized in Paterno's detailing of Filipino customs the twinned influences of Spanish realism and *costumbrismo*. The latter is a well-established genre of hispanophone literature in which fictional texts are set in peripheral places in order to reveal local color and culture to metropolitan readers; the plot is a heuristic device intended to be more sociological, anthropological, and naturalistic than anything else. Earlier nineteenth-century *costumbrista* texts of Spanish realism that Paterno probably would have read before writing *Nínay* include such canonical novels as *La gaviota* (*The Seagull*) by Fernán Caballero, published in 1849. He certainly read and was influenced by the extremely popular *Doña Perfecta,* published in 1876 by Benito Pérez Galdós, the leading Spanish writer of the time. Paterno saw his own literary contributions as participating in an existing Spanish patrimony.

As for potential Latin American frames, readers today might view Paterno as an author of what Doris Sommer has termed foundational fictions, that is, novels of the nineteenth century written in Spanish or Portuguese whose characters and plots served as allegorical imaginings of inchoate national identities throughout the Americas. Which characters developed relationships with whom often can be interpreted in these Latin American novels, as in *Nínay,* as analogues to the fusion or fission of larger social classes and cultural forces, real or proposed. Paterno's novel bears such readings well. Another way of analyzing *Nínay* within Latin American literary discussions would be by focusing on how it relates to the *indigenista* tradition, that is, fiction by and about indigenous peoples. Paterno is the first indigenous novelist of the Philippines in any language, and as such his social and class concerns, plus his mix of autochthonous and foreign vocabularies, could be contrasted to better-known counterparts in Peru, Guatemala, Bolivia, and elsewhere.

The contextual fact of the ongoing colonial status of the Philippines, meanwhile, suggests the particular possibility of situating the unknown *Nínay* within the more familiar contours of Cuban literature. The comparison of nineteenth-century Filipino and Cuban texts in Spanish makes sense because of the lingering political position of the islands that, along with Puerto Rico and Guam, remained in Spanish possession long after most of the New World gained independence. To take one Cuban predecessor of *Nínay* that Paterno may have read, *Sab* by Gertrudis Gómez de Avellaneda of 1841 is similarly a novel written and published in Spain by an expatriate from an island colony. Like Paterno in *Nínay,* the author looks back on her distant homeland through the allegorical national drama of an elite local family whose virginal daughter is beset by a young foreign suitor and his sinister father. The supporting casts in both *Sab* and *Nínay* include a character who represents the persisting indigenous inheritance of the islands, and a girl who plays an important role as a symbolic sister to the heroine.

Any move to outline Paterno with Spanish and Latin American markers so that he and his novel and his birthplace become more comprehensible is understandable, reasonable, and insufficient. Such attempts offer the advantages of inclusion but also the risks, premised as they are on the supposition that Filipino literature in Spanish cannot stand on its own terms. Furthermore, the subsumation of an author like Paterno into canons and analytical conventions established elsewhere elides the possibility that his work might force a restructuring of those canons and conventions in the first place. For while the author of *Nínay* is from an island, his views and literary production are in no way insular. They cannot be confined within familiar linguistic borders or inside recognized regional, national, or continental traditions because Paterno and his texts are indivisible from a globalized world. At no point did Paterno write as if the Philippines or he, as its self-selected cultural representative to Europe, were parochial or peripheral to the story of humanity. In fact, Paterno in *Nínay* repeatedly contests European authority in matters of knowledge production. In *Social Dawn* a generation later, he does the same vis-à-vis the United States. The Filipino characters who populate his texts do so not as objects of foreign gazes and powers but as subjects with high degrees of autonomy who reverse the presumed hierarchies of colonizer and colonized. His early novel turns Westerners into passive, ignorant, astounded receptors of Filipino traditions of knowledge. Because of his classism and reflex obeisance to Western thought, certainly, Paterno tried to compose narratives that complemented rather than upturned postmagellanic orders. Despite that effort, the inherent asymmetries and instabilities of his novelizations destabilize any notion of a world globalized simplistically along European or North American lines. The unexpected resistances in his stories function as a sort of inner Lapu Lapu. In the tosses and turns of his fictions, Paterno circumnavigates the earth, but doing so entails upending Magellan all over again.

INTRODUCTIONS AND INFRASTRUCTURES

The streaming together of the global and the local in *Nínay* is noticeable throughout the introduction of the novel and the nine chapters that correspond to the nine days of Pasiám, a Filipino mourning tradition. The introduction opens in a cemetery where a young man, serving as a first-person narrator, sees an old man making his way to a tombstone. The narrator offers him an arm for support and, upon seeing a large procession of other mourners carrying an opulent coffin, asks the old man who is inside it. Surprised, the old man asks, "Es V. forastero acaso, que no conoce á la hermosa Nínay?" ["Are you perhaps a foreigner who does not know the beautiful Nínay?"] (10). The narrator responds, "Como si lo fuera; partí de niño á la otra orilla del mar, y después de larga ausencia vuelvo á pisar esta patria querida. Mas, ¿quién es esa Nínay?" ["It is as if I were; as a child I left here for the other side of the sea and after a long absence I return now to step upon this dear fatherland. But who is that Nínay?"] (11) The old man says that he cannot remember all the details of Nínay's story and urges the narrator to attend the Pasiám about to be held in her honor. Paterno then interrupts the plot to "explicar al lector lo que es un Pasiám, antigua costumbre filipina" ["explain to the reader what a Pasiám is, an ancient Filipino custom"] (11). In this tradition, the house of the deceased is kept open for nine days and every evening friends of the family arrive and "se reunen en círculos para contar los actos laudables del difunto, la historia de nuestras islas, los cuentos y leyendas y las mil poesías que consuelan el espíritu. A media noche todo concluye con la cena acostumbrada" ["gather in circles to tell of the praiseworthy acts of the deceased, the history of our islands, the stories and legends and thousand poems that console the spirit. At midnight all concludes with the customary dinner"] (12–13). Paterno, in a seemingly needless act of repetition, then notes again that this mourning custom is called "*Pasiám*" and adds the footnote, "**Pasiám.** Costumbre antigua que también se encuentra en Europa, por ejemplo, en algunos pueblos de Santander, Bretaña, Irlanda, etc." ["**Pasiám.** Ancient custom that is also found in Europe, for example, in some towns of Santander, Brittany, Ireland, etc."] (13). After the authorial intrusion in both text and footnote, the young man presses some coins into the old man's hands and declares, "Como filipino y amante de nuestras costumbres . . . nos une amistad desde ahora" ["As a Filipino and lover of our customs . . . a friendship unites us hence"] (13). The old man takes the narrator to the house of a friend who knows where the Pasiám of Nínay is going to take place. The narrator bids the old man goodbye and the principal plot of the novel is ready to begin.

The *costumbrista* function of the introduction seems straightforward: a narrator is inspired by a chance meeting to learn of a local woman's story that will reveal to the Spanish reader of *Nínay* certain Filipino practices. Acting as cultural mediator, Paterno addresses that reader directly in the main text. At the same time, he hastens to limit the very peculiarities of Pasiám that he wants to describe by seeking to show in the footnote that the Filipino custom is really not all that different from those found in Spain, France, and Ireland.[5] The introduction therefore lends credence, apparently, to the general criticism of Paterno that his goals in *Nínay* and other writings are fundamentally assimilationist in nature, that his valorization of Filipino culture as part of the global human tapestry is really just an attempt to insert the islands into a map distinctly European in origination and orientation. Such analysis is accurate but partial, for an interpretation of the introduction along these lines fails to reveal the potency of many of its narrative gestures. For starters, the cemetery setting, the coffin of Nínay, and the geriatric mourner all suggest that a symbolic death is going to be replaced in this novel with life: the relative gaiety of the house where the Pasiám will take place, the resurrection of Nínay in the form of her life story, and the youthfulness of the narrator. The nature of the symbolic death is unclear, but the transition from silence and passivity and the past to voice and action and the future marks, too, the radical production of the novel itself. This introduction, after all, commences not only a novel but also a protonational literary tradition, synonymous with the moment when Filipinos began articulating themselves in genres hitherto claimed only by the Westerners who colonized them. With the introduction to *Nínay*, a doubly novel structuring of a particular social life has begun.

In the process, the young man sustains the old man with his arm and his money while the old man conveys news of the Pasiám. The import of the relationship is of a shared cultural heritage. The bond between the two strangers, confirmed in the key phrase, "As a Filipino and lover of our customs," is fundamentally social, national, and transgenerational in nature. The line is also quietly powerful. Under Spanish rule, indigenous Filipinos were known as *indios* (Indians), like their presumed counterparts in the Americas, whereas *filipinos* referred primarily to creoles, that is, people born in the Philippines but of Spanish ancestry. Spaniards born in Iberia who lived in the Philippines were known as *peninsulares*. Merely describing the two men as "Filipinos" therefore points to a dramatic reimagining of what it means to be from the archipelago. As Resil Mojares notes, "By the 1860s . . . the word [*filipinos*] was increasingly used by natives (*indios*), Chinese and Spanish mestizos, and creoles to identify themselves as members of an emerging, multiracial community politically set apart from Spanish peninsulares" (*Brains*, 202). Paterno concretizes this nascent identity by his use of a charged and changing term that seems, to twenty-first-century readers, a neutral and static national category. When Taríc, the *indio* narrator of most of *Nínay,* later issues the phrase "entre nosotros, los filipinos" ["among us, the Filipinos"] to indicate a collectivity of indigenous rather than Spanish origins, the implications are of a new sense of social bonding (107). This use of "filipinos" by Paterno conflicts directly with the supposition that his ideological inclinations are conformist with Spanish concepts of the colony.

The introduction of *Nínay* is also notable for its narrator, who is evidently a stand-in for Paterno. The author and his alter ego have common biographies as youths who crossed the seas and only now return to a beloved homeland, a "patria" that significantly is not Spain but the Philippines. That is, via the novel, set in Manila, Paterno, writing from Madrid, returns metaphorically to the archipelago to reengage with customs there. This is a metamagellanic journey in which Paterno allots Filipino traditions an autonomous cultural space. He raises a local standard here rather than a foreign one. The novel thereby is not only the narrative strut of a pompous pseudointellectual but, in the bond of the old and young men, also a response to the West from a collectivity of indigenous others. Pasiám, clearly, is not an act of individual mourning but that of a community formed around a historical and literary trajectory perceived as particular. The stories of the life of the deceased ("the praiseworthy acts") will flow naturally among those of her people ("the history of our islands"), whether veridical or fictional.

This communal resurrection (or, arguably, creation) of a collective legacy serves as the structure of the novel as well as its content. The chapters of *Nínay* correlate to the successive nights of Pasiám. At the outset of each chapter, the narrator listens as Taríc, "Un joven indio" ["A young Indian"], commences a new section of the life story of the dead Nínay (16). At all times, Taríc is surrounded by a group of Europeans who "habían acudido allí sólo para el estudio de las costumbres tagalas" ["had gone there just to study Tagalog customs"] (16–17). The foreigners are obvious placeholders for Paterno's anticipated readership, just as the ex/repatriated narrator of the introduction and then Taríc substitute for Paterno himself. And as the voices of Paterno mediate all authority of the narration, the listeners/readers are passively subject to that authority. This entails a series of metatextual passages, such as that on the second night of Pasiám (correspondingly, the second chapter) when the narrator asks that Taríc keep in mind that the attendant Europeans "ignoraban por completo los pormenores de nuestro suelo y de nuestras costumbres, por lo que procurase detallar lo más posible, como si relatara la historia sólo á los europeos" ["did not know at all the details of our land and our customs, which is why we encouraged him to be as specific as possible, as if he were telling the story only to Europeans"] (52–53). That, for the most part, is the intention of Paterno with the novel itself.

At the start of the fourth night, Taríc quotes Plato upon resuming the story of Nínay, but the recitations of Tagalog poetry and drama that commence each of the next four nights frustrate the Westerners because "los europeos, ignorando el idioma, deseaban más oir contar la historia de la difunta" ["the Europeans, not knowing the language, desired to hear more telling of the story of the deceased"] (197). The ignorance of the European audience reaches its peak on the ninth night when, just moments after Taríc finishes his story, they see some leaves of a local tree with bioluminescent properties: "los europeos, que ignoraban la cualidad de esta planta, no salían de su estupor contemplando el ramaje luminoso, y se aproximaron para examinarlo sin poner en él las manos temerosos de quemarse" ["the Europeans, who did not know the qualities of this plant, did not come out of their astonishment as they contemplated the luminous branches, and they neared to examine it without touching it with their hands, fearing they would be burned"] (314–15). The scene is reminiscent of the opening chapter of *Cien años de soledad* (*One Hundred Years of Solitude*) by García Márquez, when a rural family in the tropics sees ice for the first time and ascribes to it amazing properties.

Yet there is a key difference: in that famous passage of Latin American literature, the rubes are the locals. In Paterno, the rubes are the Westerners. The whole structure of the novel consequently complicates the assumed hierarchies of colonizers and colonized. Though the genre at hand, the novel, is Western, Paterno configures it with the Filipino form of Pasiám. Though the novel is a written genre, Paterno converts it into Taríc's oral narrative and thereby privileges a more traditional means of storytelling. The narrator who at first serves as Paterno's alter ego, the privileged youth who now has returned to his country after years abroad, is replaced by an *indio* who can cite Plato in one moment and Tagalog artists in another. By contrast, the Europeans who form Taríc's audience, both those inside the text in Manila and those outside it in Spain, are passive ignoramuses who are unable to access Filipino literary traditions, who make fools of themselves in front of unknown local flora, and who sit at the mercy of the *indio* oral narrator and in thrall to his narrative and authority. In a Filipino house, subject to Filipino discourse, they and not Paterno in Madrid are the strangers in a strange land.

Paterno himself is not resolvable to any side of these dynamics. He is the expatriate returned *and* the foreigner abroad *and* the indigenous narrator; he is the writer *and* orator *and*, to a great extent, his own audience. As a result, his text betrays his many attempts at consolidating the Philippines as a colonial object of *costumbrista* interest. Florentino Hornedo thus underestimates the potential of the Pasiám structure when he dismisses it as an "incredible device [that] appears to have been chosen to serve Paterno's central purpose—to give the readers in peninsular Spain a costumbrist picture of Filipino types, places, and customs" (388). Similarly, Schumacher suggests that "the entire structure of the novel is quite artificial" ("Literature," 490). No narrative structure, however, is any more "artificial" than any other. All carry within them certain ideological and cultural presumptions, including chronological. In the case of Paterno, at issue are the implications of the Pasiám structure for Filipino social spaces, temporalities, and cultural histories, given the author's ostensibly Europhile agenda.

The story that Taríc relates is melodramatic, complicated, and unintentionally hilarious. Nínay is a "joven de diez y ocho años acariciada por la belleza y la fortuna" ["young woman of eighteen years caressed by beauty and fortune"] (17). She spends a great deal of time in an Edenic garden where she delights in butterflies. Her innocence, youth, sunshine, and virginity are evident wherever she goes. Dawn accompanies her, often literally and always metaphorically. On one such occasion, a little pet bird of hers who knows how to say "Nínay, Nínay" is flying free in the garden when a hungry bird of prey appears (26–27). Nínay is desperate. A shot rings out. The evil bird falls from the sky. Nínay and her gardener rush toward the river and spot an elegant youth with a gun on a boat. He motions for them to stay silent as his servants row him quietly away into the distance. Nínay wonders who the hero might be and the gardener replies that it is Don Carlos, who has just inherited "muchísimas tierras y un capital que puede cubrir todo este pueblo" ["very many lands and enough capital to cover all this town"] (28). Thus begins the love between Nínay and Carlos that forms the dramatic axis of the book. Both are members of the Filipino upper class, both are gendered along conventional lines, both are apolitical in any meaningful way, and both, as it turns out, are doomed.

The culmination of the novel in a marriage between Nínay and Carlos would suggest a strengthening of the indigenous colonial aristocracy that they represent. Their children would be proof of the fecund potential of that class to lead the Philippines forward. That Nínay herself represents the archipelago in general is unquestionable, as the same prelapsarian qualities of vernal purity attributed to her are constantly identified with the islands as well. Her biological potential as a beautiful virgin and untapped mother is clearly meant to be analogous to the rich, unpenetrated natural resources of the archipelago. Yet Nínay and Carlos never do marry and they never even have sex, though there are moments of temptation represented by Paterno with extended ellipses so as to not articulate the unspeakable (186).[6] The failure of their union is significant. By extrapolation, it is the failure of the Filipino upper crust trying to pass for Spanish and of the Philippines trying to pass for Europe. There is no production of future generations in the novel, no bright hope for the land. Nearly everybody in the end dies.

There is no acute political protest either. Paterno was the leading elitist of his generation and, as an avid hispanophile and equally avid Christian, unlikely to lambast either the secular or religious forces running the archipelago. The various orders of Spanish priests who wielded much of the de facto power in the colony and whom Rizal later would satirize acerbically are well-nigh invisible in *Nínay*. León Ma. [María] Guerrero suggests that Paterno went out of his way not to "offend" any of the ruling class, adding "One might think, [sic] reading his novel that there was not a single friar in the Philippines" (*First,* 135).[7] According to Schumacher, "Peaceful and conciliatory by temperament, Paterno in his writings would seek to serve nationalism in this way—by making his country and the virtues and abilities of his people known to others rather than through any polemical campaign against abuses or for liberties" ("Literature," 489). If so, the tale that unfolds in *Nínay* would be puzzling. Nationalism, even of a conservative kind, would not seem particularly advanced by a foundational fiction that founds nothing.

Within the plot, the literal reasons why the two protagonists never conjoin either physically or legally begin with Carlos's evil doppelgänger, Federico, a young man of Portuguese descent who has just arrived in the Philippines. Federico desires Nínay as much as does Carlos. Meanwhile, Nínay's evil doppelgänger, Pilar, desires Carlos. In related news, Federico's evil father desires Loleng, a parallel figure to Nínay due to her own beauty and virginity. Loleng is loved by Berto, a bandit of sorts who, as a strapping youth with a heart of gold, parallels Carlos. Long story short, Berto and Loleng escape from Federico's father but Loleng dies in the process. In a cave, transfixed by the beauty of Loleng's cadaver, Berto swears revenge on Federico's father in front of Carlos, and the two young men become fast friends. Eventually, Pilar suggests to Federico that he somehow put Nínay's father in danger and then save him, which would surely cause a grateful Nínay to love him thereafter. This in turn would leave Carlos available for Pilar. Federico subsequently orchestrates the arrest of Nínay's father by colonial authorities on trumped-up charges; and then, acting on his own, arranges for soldiers to arrest Carlos as well. Fortunately, Berto, thanks to his outlaw connections, gets wind of this and alerts Carlos, who consequently flees aboard a ship named *María*. Federico then tells Nínay that he can save her father from a certain death sentence so long as she writes a letter in which she begs him to marry him before anyone realizes that she is pregnant by him, which she is not. Nínay, sobbing, consents. The vile Federico is then slain by the heroic Berto, denominated at this moment as a "joven indio" ["young Indian"] like Taríc was earlier (252). Subsequently, out at sea, a tempest shipwrecks Carlos and he spends the next three years as king of an island tribe, whose topless queen Tik yearns for him. In the meanwhile, Nínay's parents die and she, presuming her boyfriend drowned, condemns herself to a convent. Finally, Carlos gets off the island and returns to Manila. On discovering that Nínay is now a nun, he goes to see her. At the door of the convent he collapses, struck by the cholera epidemic that opened the novel. He dies. Berto buries him. Then Nínay dies, though not first without forgiving Pilar. End of story.

Along the way, there are enough serpents, caves, surveillants, totems, phallic weaponry, displacements, doubles, and necrophilia to keep a Freudian busy for months. There are also stupefyingly plentiful footnotes and appendices. *Nínay* as a result seems to most critics (a reduced number exist, to be sure) more of a contraption than a novel, a sort of Rube Goldberg machine that is preposterous in its design and content and, from a narrative point of view, outlandishly inefficient.[8] Its combination of the worst of multiple genres and literary styles (melodrama, romanticism, *costumbrismo*, encyclopedic entries, naturalist description, etc.) has led to excoriations such as the following by Schumacher, probably one of the few historians of the Philippines to have read it: "it fails quite completely as a literary work" ("Literature," 489). Later, Schumacher adds that *Nínay* "is important for what it symbolized rather than for any artistic merit. Its setting is in the Philippines, but it has little to do with real Filipino life, which Paterno has to explain to his readers in a series of lengthy and pedantic footnotes. Indeed, it is not much of a novel at all" (*Making*, 122). In a third assessment, he writes, "As a novel, it is of less than mediocre worth, being little more than a framework into which were inserted various scenes and customs of Philippine life. These are frequently explained in long footnotes, and the entire structure is contrived. The novel is without political implications" (*Propaganda*, 55).[9]

Mojares, nearly the only scholar to offer interpretive analysis of the actual details of the novel, sees *Nínay* as a luxurious product of its author's class:

> The novel is a deliquescent romance that conjures a world filled with laughter, poetry, music, good food, and contemporary fashion. Nature imagery celebrates sensual pleasures (gardens are scenes of romantic trysts rather than metaphors for the soul); scenes of the lover gazing at the beloved dramatize self-conscious, self-absorbed heterosexual love; descriptions of person, dress, and ornament convey a sense of bodies cultivated, autonomous, and even vain. A wealthy Manileño [citizen of Manila] who fancied himself a Filipino-Hispanic *hidalgo* [nobleman], Paterno was engaged in a bit of self-promotion, a celebration of social class ("Tagalog nobility") that posed native bodies equal to the Europeans. ("Catechisms," 189–90)

Whereas Schumacher considers *Nínay* as poor art for its ham-fisted attempts at *costumbrismo*, Mojares instead concedes it a coherent literariness in its evocations of the customs, real and projected, of a particular elite stratum of Manila society: "One notes the cataloguing of the symbols of this class: Ninay paints, plays the piano and speaks four languages; articles from India, China and Japan adorn the spacious habitations of the rich; the love of exotic native products and arts exists side by side with a taste for Strauss and the artistic refinements of Europe" (*Origins*, 134).[10] Paterno cultivated the metropolitan counterparts of this colonial class throughout his many years in Madrid. *Nínay*, read as such, seems not radical but reactionary. As Mojares observes, "It is obvious that Paterno depicts local customs with the end of showing them off for their charm and demonstrating that they partake of the grace of aristocratic feudal life in Europe itself . . . [he] romanticizes native mores to claim recognition and rights not so much for his people as for his own class" (*Origins*, 134).

Although Schumacher and Mojares diverge on their evaluations of *Nínay*, they do coincide in signaling its importance as an inaugural literary at-

tempt by Filipinos to represent themselves. Thus Schumacher writes, "The
novel appears to have had little or no effect on Spaniards or Filipinos in
Spain or at home. But it deserves notice as an indication of the growing
awareness among the Filipinos of what was peculiarly their own, and a belief in the value of what was properly Filipino" (*Propaganda,* 55). Mojares
adds that Paterno "tried to write a Filipino novel and although his integration of materials may leave much to be desired, the making of a conscious
attempt is in itself an achievement" (*Origins,* 135). These conclusions render
the novel as primarily an artifact of an era, an initial appropriation by Filipinos of a certain type of discourse, the novelistic, from which they had
been previously excluded. This was a step forward even if both the mes-
senger and message were deemed severely flawed in terms of artistic skill
and class bias. Mojares recognizes the worldly outlook of Paterno much
more than Schumacher but emphasizes that the contours of that world
were decidedly Europhile in nature (*Origins,* 135). The real and presumed
cosmopolitanness of Paterno, both in life and in art, was rooted in a notably Western notion of the cosmos in which he sought a rightful place for
the Philippines and Filipino culture (*Brains,* passim).

There are structural and thematic incoherences in *Nínay,* however, that
work against the conclusion that the novel is just an attempt to fit Filipino
society, or at least its elite versions, into European cartographies of culture.
These incoherences are the key to Paterno and to all the legacies of Lapu
Lapu because once coherence is granted to a system of knowledge, it is the
lack thereof rather than an equally coherent oppositionality that reflects a
resistance true in form as well as function. Looking for a programmatic
anti-Western stance in Paterno will produce no results. He was, after all,
slavish to the Spanish throughout his two decades in the metropole. It is
only in the hints of dedication pages and footnotes and appendices and
other marginalia, including apparently minor metaphors and seemingly
throwaway subplots, that the plural significances of *Nínay* can be perceived
in their acuity and magnitude. The marginalia themselves are not internally consistent either; this, indeed, accentuates their importance.

The title page of the lone edition of *Nínay* in Spanish contains no clues
as to the subversive and unstable potential of the text but rather much the
opposite: the helpful subtitle "(*Costumbres filipinas*)" [(*Filipino Customs*)],
the listing of Madrid and a local press as the source of publication, and the
year 1885.[11] The implied audience for the book is clearly the Spanish literate classes for whom the faraway colony is a matter of curiosity. Since the

title of the novel is to that readership an unrecognizable Filipino word (it will turn out to be the Tagalog nickname of the presumptive heroine), Paterno hastens in the subtitle to explain that the novel is *costumbrista* in nature. Again, this genre, in which fiction was crafted in order to reveal the local color of out-of-the-way places both inside Spain and beyond, was very familiar to nineteenth-century Spanish audiences. Any cognitive disjunction caused by the unfamiliar language of the title will be smoothed away for the reader as Paterno uses the novel as a vehicle to explain the customs of the distant archipelago to armchair colonialists in Madrid.

Paterno offered *Nínay* in a historical moment in which there was no sign of a significant revolutionary movement in the Philippines, unlike in Cuba, nor agitation for independence among the Filipino expatriates in Madrid.[12] Rizal had arrived in Spain in 1882, more than a decade after Paterno, and would not produce his novels critical of colonial rule until 1887 and 1891, while *Solidarity,* the journalistic organ of the reformers, would not issue until 1889. Neither the novels nor the newspapers would advocate independence in any case. Quite the contrary, when Paterno published *Sampaguitas* and then *Nínay,* he showed every appearance of being willing to be the object of a Spanish gaze with himself in the position of its mediator.[13] Nonetheless, the fact remains that the first word of this first Asian novel in Spanish was unintelligible to a metropolitan audience and that Paterno knew this to be the case, hence his parenthetical subtitle. There is already a subtle inversion of relations here in that it is a writer from the colony who implies that a reader from the empire is in need of translations and explanations, not vice versa. Paterno sets himself up as an authority while Spaniards are revealed as those who lack certain privileges of knowledge and power.

This understated implication of the title page is magnified by the dedication page that follows, on which two lines of what appear to be scribbles form a banner headline in an otherwise blank top two-thirds of the page.[14] The scribbles are so foreign that it is not clear whether they are meant to be read left to right or right to left or perhaps in some triangular order. Nor is it clear whether they are alphabetic, syllabic, or pictographic in nature. In the bottom third of the page, Paterno offers a translation as follows: "Traducción: A mi querido padre Pedro Alejandro Molo Paterno" ["Translation: To my dear father Pedro Alejandro Molo Paterno"]. This translation apparently corresponds to the wavy lines above and seems innocent enough. Yet quite a few forces are struggling for supremacy in the dedication. Here, more than on the title page, Paterno has framed his Spanish reader with a headline beyond the ken, for this time it is in a language that the reader cannot even identify as such. Paterno gives no explanation here as to the nature or provenance of the illegible script. This destabilizes further the metropolitan reader who opens the novel expecting to find what it promises, namely, a presentation of indigenous customs draped onto the form of a novel. The words of the dedication appear apolitical, but its reversal of knowledge and power—who is framing whom and in what system of discourse—is sharp.

Contrasting tendencies therefore arise in the opening frames of *Nínay*. One, exemplified by the subtitle, configures a colony as an object of an imperial gaze. The other, implied by the title and the dedication, configures the empire as an object of a colonial gaze. This opposition, however, is neither binary nor straightforward. Nothing in Paterno is. The script of the dedication is actually a premagellanic seventeen-letter writing system called *baybayin* that developed before Spaniards laid claim to the archipelago. The indigenous alphabet had been used in a limited way by various communities, and presumably only by certain of their members, for short correspondences, chants, brief poems, rites, and the like (Mojares, *Origins*, 21–25). As Spanish powers consolidated on the islands, Christian missionaries began impressing vernacular Filipino languages into the Latin alphabet rather than trying to utilize *baybayin* for written communications. At first glance, the dedication in *Nínay* in *baybayin* may not seem surprising, for it fits in with Paterno's later massive scholarly efforts, as analyzed by Mojares, to show Europeans that Filipino culture was distinctive and accomplished before Spanish colonization began (*Brains,* passim). By invoking *baybayin* in the dedication, Paterno signaled the existence of an indigenous literacy and orthography that was a unique contribution to the breadth of human cultures.

Invisibly complicating this gesture, however, is a matrix of factors. For instance, at no point does Paterno explain to his Spanish readership the name or source or functions of the unintelligible script. He translates it but leaves its origins and purpose a mystery. This is akin to claiming absolute power over a discourse that he knows his metropolitan readers cannot recognize. At most, they might guess that the script is that of Paterno's native language. Yet this conclusion is not true. Paterno spent so much time in hispanophone environments, both in the Philippines and in Spain, that he was not even a fluent speaker or writer of Tagalog, the language whose sounds the *baybayin* dedication represents.[15] Furthermore, he certainly could not write or read *baybayin* with any great ease. Perhaps few in his era could. After all, the script preceded the arrival of Magellan centuries earlier and was of narrow usage in the first place. To dedicate *Nínay* in *baybayin* was to frame, for unspecified reasons, a relatively young genre from Europe, the novel, with a relatively old script from Asia. This is a posturing for political purposes that upends hierarchies by casting the Spanish reader as the ignorant outsider and Paterno as the knowledgeable insider. That he was perpetrating a fraud insofar as his own knowledge of Filipino linguistics goes lends the move a still more intricate subversiveness.

The challenges of the *baybayin* dedication are underlined by its exclusion from all subsequent editions of *Nínay* in English and Tagalog. Later translators and editors attempted to smooth out the marginalia of the novel and thereby render it more digestible. This was not an apolitical approach, whatever the intentions of the revisers, for the effect of bowdlerizing not only the *baybayin* but also the diverse footnotes and appendices is to transform the novel from an unsettled world flux of cultural forces into a more linear plot of local heroes and villains. Such excisions betoken a literary artifact of national rather than global import, a text of primarily aesthetic rather than subversive character. This can be seen in the only translation of *Nínay* into English, which was published in Manila in 1907. Nearly a century later, in 2004, the National Historical Institute of the Philippines decided to reissue the translation, with its chairman, the popular public historian Ambeth Ocampo, announcing in the foreword, "We presume that having Paterno's approval this translation is authoritative" (v). One sense of authority, however, is not necessarily another, and 1907 was not 1885. A new world order was at hand. What and who was "authoritative" for Paterno and the Philippines had changed dramatically in the twenty-two years between the original publication of *Nínay* and its first translation. Thanks to the 1898 war, the United States had replaced Spain as the imperial master of the archipelago and initiated a massive pedagogical effort to make English the lingua franca of the colony. This was surely the rationale for producing an English version of *Nínay* in the first place: the assimilation of the islands to a new reality. The idea of an English translation would have made little sense prior to 1898. Paterno himself in 1907 was an aging has-been in Manila trying to stay in the good graces of U.S. elites in the Philippines, much as he had clung previously to its Spanish counterparts in Madrid in 1885. And the 1907 translation of *Nínay* bears little resemblance to its source text. Gone along with the footnotes and the appendices is the *baybayin*. In its place is an unctuous dedication to "Mrs. William H. Taft," wife of the former governor of the colony who was later to become president of the United States and chief justice of the Supreme Court.[16]

An elision also befalls the one other place in the original *Nínay* where Paterno uses *baybayin*. The wronged youth Berto uses it while inscribing an oath of vengeance into hardwood with his dagger. Paterno interrupts the typescript of the novel to insert the oath by hand as a *baybayin* graphic right in the middle of a sentence (165). This time, an accompanying footnote translates the *baybayin* oath into Spanish and refers readers interested in "los caracteres tagalos" ["the Tagalog characters"] to an article written by the Filipino scholar T. H. Pardo de Tavera (165).[17] By contrast, in the 1907 English translation still considered "authoritative" a century later by an official publishing arm of the national government, the visual representation of the *baybayin* and the actual contents of the oath, along with the footnote, are simply censored out of existence. There is no acknowledgment of their former inclusion. No English reader would be aware that anything had been excised. The scene now is rendered simply as "Berto had inscribed with the point of his dagger" (55). The nature of what he "inscribed" is not addressed at all. In the lone Tagalog version, which appeared first in 1908, the oath is translated in the body of the text and not in a footnote, but the *baybayin* is absent (125). The 2002 reprint of the 1908 translation follows suit (47). The cultural challenges of the *baybayin* to a previous imperial center redouble quietly in its censorship before a new and stronger colonizer.[18] As the scene of potential contestation has shifted from Madrid to Manila and the occupying power from Spain to the United States, the implicit confrontations of the *baybayin* have been taken out of play.

FOOTNOTES AND APPENDICES

The complete elimination of Paterno's copious footnotes in both the English and the Tagalog translations also suggests a forced nationalization of an otherwise internationalized text and a suppression of the original potential of its possible resistances from the margins. The imposition of linearity over hypertextuality is a conquest in the name of local order, for it is in the literal subtext of *Nínay* that many of Paterno's negotiations with the global take place. The footnotes are variegated in nature. Many are definitions by Paterno of Tagalog words, such as the names of artifacts and flora and fauna of the archipelago, that he has italicized in the main body of the text. Others consist of long citations of studies by Europeans, often anthropologists, of various non-European societies. Still others are seemingly random comments inspired by something that has just taken place in the novel.

There is no question that the footnotes as a whole, which Hornedo estimates as amounting to a full third of the text of *Nínay*, are cumbersome to any reader intent on following only the advancement of the plot (388). And there is no question about their ostensible purpose: first, to provide to the Spanish reader the *costumbrismo* explanations promised in the subtitle of the novel; second, to show that non-European cultures have been taken seriously as objects of study by learned men; and third, to show that Paterno has ruminated on a wide range of scholarly readings. This is why Mojares says of *Nínay* that "its author's show of erudition [is] superfluous and exhibitionary" (*Brains,* 45). In general, the footnotes confirm the conclusion that Paterno was a pretentious sycophant eager to do for Spain in person what Magellan himself did not survive to accomplish: reveal and situate the Philippines on a world map drawn up by Europeans.

The narcissism of Paterno that permeates all the footnotes scarcely can be underestimated. In this, counterintuitively, lies the legacy of Lapu Lapu. Paterno's unflagging efforts to flaunt his knowledge of the Philippines and other cultures peripheral to Europe—a knowledge born not so much of lived experience as of readings of what Europeans had written on those subjects—constitute an appropriation of power rather than a subsumation to it. By inserting his own voice to declare one thing or another, he reminds the reader ceaselessly that the author in charge of this text is from the archipelago, not the peninsula, and that the balance of erudition favors Paterno over any Spaniard due to his mastery of both Filipino and Western knowledge. When Paterno italicizes the name of an island plant or animal or cultural practice and then footnotes it with elaborate precision, he commands authority as an indigenous subject, not as a colonized object. When he cites a European text written in French and does not bother translating the passage, he demonstrates his control over metropolitan knowledge production as well. The reader is but a bystander who can only equal Paterno's command of French but not trump it. If the reader does not know French, the unexpected hierarchy of discursive power is accentuated even more.[19]

And when Paterno uses the footnotes to ramble about subjects that bear at best a tangential relation to the details of the novel, his mere ability to interrupt at will the expectations of the reader reinforces the discrepancy between who is captaining this vessel from the Philippines and who is not.

Paterno did tend to produce sophistry at least as much as sophistication. He was ridiculed by Filipino contemporaries as a pseudointellectual whose accounts of the archipelago were rife with misconceptions and outright fictions. The incessant citations and metacommentary in *Nínay* do substitute referentiality for knowledge. Nonetheless, apocryphal or not, the footnotes are not marginal to the text but fundamentally formative of it. The voice that apparently issues from below deck actually emanates from above deck. And as Paterno charts the course to and from the Philippines, proclaims the directions and identifies the topographies that arise, his Spanish reader is a passive passenger who accompanies him around the world of knowledge, island hopping, as it were, from footnote to footnote. The interference by Paterno from the apparent periphery is therefore not inconsequential at all. Dismissing his novel as retrograde bombast from a fop, which is how existing criticism mostly summarizes *Nínay,* renders invisible some of the most interesting textual maneuvers at hand.

The political possibilities inherent in the footnotes are demonstrated from the very first one onward. It accompanies the opening line of the novel, which is "En 18 . . . el cólera hacía estragos en *Manila*" ["In 18 . . . cholera ravaged *Manila*"], and reads as follows:

> **Manila.** *(La insigne y siempre leal, y la muy noble ciudad de), capital del archipiélago filipino y sus inmediaciones, tiene alrededor de 400,000 habitantes. "En esta población numerosa se presenta verdaderamente un mundo cuya vista sorprende al que llega por primera vez al país, y nunca lo considera bastante estudiado el hombre pensador. Hállase éste rodeado de chinos, tagalos, visayas, pampangos, americanos, españoles, ingleses, franceses, alemanes, etc.; pues casi no hay pueblo que no tenga algunos individuos en Manila." (Diccionario geográfico-estadístico-histórico de las islas Filipinas, por Fr. Manuel Buzeta, t. II, pág. 243.)*

> [**Manila.** (The famous and always loyal, and very noble city of), capital of the Philippine archipelago and its surroundings, has around 400,000 inhabitants. "In this numerous population a world is truly apparent whose sighting surprises he who arrives in the country for the first time, and the thoughtful man never considers it sufficiently studied. He finds himself sur-

rounded by Chinese, Tagalogs, Visayans, Pampangans, Americans, Spaniards, Englishmen, French, Germans, etc.; for there is almost no people who does not have some individuals in Manila." (Geographic-Statistical-Historical Dictionary of the Philippine Islands by friar Manuel Buzeta, vol. 2, p. 243.)]

This footnote might be seen as setting the tone for the descriptive text promised in the subtitle of the novel. Hornedo relegates it as the product of "some sort of a writer of a prototype of modern day tourist reading" (228). Yet the footnote is contestatory. It contains within it a number of subtleties that work against the "siempre leal" ["always loyal"] toadyism with which it begins. First, the decision to footnote the word "Manila" is unnecessary. It is the one Filipino noun, after all, that any Spanish reader of the novel already would recognize, the one indigenous concept presumably least in need of further explanation. Such an apparently superfluous footnote suggests that it functions not to confirm a metropolitan reader's existing frame of reference for the Philippines but instead to substitute for that frame another.

The second surprising move is the interruption of the opening line of the novel in the first place. The reader is not allowed to proceed even one sentence into *Nínay* before the foreign authority of the author is affirmed. This authority from the colony then encompasses a European authority via the citation of Buzeta. This move would be interpreted in Paterno criticism (such as exists) as that of an insecure author from the periphery seeking to justify his text by quoting a published writer from the center, or, less generously, as the product of an intellectual show-off. Equally true, however, is that the appropriation deftly subsumes an apparently greater authority into an apparently lesser one. That is, Paterno uses the priest for his own purpose, which is to emphasize that Manila is anything but a colonial backwater. On the contrary, it is a microcosm in which Tagalogs, Visayans, and Pampangans—these are all different Filipino ethnic groups of distinct languages and regions—are given equal weight as polities to Americans, Chinese, and various European nationalities, including the colonizing Spaniards.[20] There is nothing peripheral at all about Manila, suggests Paterno, because though halfway around the world, it is a center of the same. In truly *costumbrista* novels, the point is to show the local in all its parochial colors. In *Nínay*, the point is to show the local in its global resplendence.

Such slippages in *Nínay* resist the placement of the novel as the forerunner of only a particular national tradition, which is how Schumacher sees it, or primarily as a case of international mimicry—a Filipino aristocrat's literary attempt at approximating European upper-class ideals—however undeniable the analysis by Mojares. Overly delimiting as well is the comment by Manuel García Castellón: "Hay asimismo algo cervantesco en las narraciones extrapoladas, bizantinos exilios y aventuras e inclusión de piececillas líricas" ["There is also something akin to Cervantes in the extrapolated narrations, byzantine exiles and adventures, and the inclusion of little lyrical pieces"] (*Estampas,* 151). This attention to the hodgepodge of genres that constitute *Nínay* is on target, but the characterization of it as Cervantine suggests an incorporation of the novel into the mainstream of the Spanish literary world. That is what *Nínay* never could do any more than Paterno himself. Given the reality of colonialism, an elite Filipino who tried to pass for an elite Spaniard was, like a novel written for a parallel purpose, destined to the inevitable tensions of pretension. Yet these tensions flourish rather than fail; they create rather than eviscerate. In the interstices between the metropolitan and its mimicry emerge exactly those phenomena that cannot be assimilated to the dominant model. The hypertextual nature of *Nínay*—its stops and starts, its apparently haphazard movements among subplots and footnotes and appendices—makes it function avant la lettre like a web page bound to no enclosure in particular, not to national or even Western confinements. The random passages of the narration, linked by association rather than linearity, are escape routes rather than dead ends. The Philippines that appears amid this cartography of half-chance is not an inchoate national project nor an approximation of Europe but a planetary plurality whose gaps and overlaps and accidental wanderings spill out over its own boundaries into an unending and uncontrollable global arena.

The four appendices of *Nínay* amount to another place where the novel, literally, overflows its borders. Spatially less intrusive of the plot than the footnotes, the appendices have been excised nonetheless from all translations to date. Their elision alone merits their study. No doubt the exclusion results from the swirling transnationalisms that mark the appendices as seemingly tangential to the romantic story line of Carlos and Nínay. The first appendix tells the history of the icon of the virgin of Antipolo that was brought from Acapulco, Mexico, to the Philippines in 1626; many miracles were attributed to it in subsequent centuries. The second appendix, without any segue whatsoever from the first, announces its subject in its title: "Bailarinas de la India: Sus danzas, sus trajes y sus joyas.—El Mahl ó el harém de la India" ["Dancers from India: Their Dances, Their Outfits, Their Jewels.—The Mahl or Harem of India"] (332). The third appendix offers information on ancient Filipino burial and mourning customs, such as Pasíam. The fourth and most intriguing appendix seeks to debunk the "creencia común que, las islas descubiertas por Hernando de Magallanes en Marzo de 1521, se encontraban pobladas por una raza completamente salvaje. Error tan grande merece se rectifique" ["common belief that the islands discovered by Fernando Magellan in March 1521 were found peopled by a completely savage race. Such a great error deserves to be corrected"] (343). Paterno takes pains to show in this last appendix that "No fueron los españoles los primeros conquistadores de aquel archipiélago" ["The Spaniards were not the first conquerors of that archipelago"] (343). This is an unusual statement. Most authors launching a literary tradition in the language of a prevailing empire probably do not go out of their way to stress how many other cultures have previously taken over their homeland. Yet with great enthusiasm, this is what Paterno does. He notes that emigrants from India arrived long before Magellan and were followed by Arabs, whose cultural accomplishments Paterno clearly respects. He ends the appendix by adding that "los japoneses, aislados del resto del mundo, sostenían ya á la llegada de los españoles, relaciones comerciales con aquellas islas" ["the Japanese, isolated from the rest of the world, already maintained commercial relations with those islands when the Spaniards arrived"] (352).

Like the footnotes, the appendices are characterized by a lack of linearity and apparent irrelevance to the plot of the novel. They are notable too for their yoking of a disparate world into a Filipino context: Mexico, India, the Middle East, and Japan all play their roles in globalizing the archipelago along with Magellan and Spain. What is most remarkable about the appendices, however, is that Paterno may not be the principal writer of any of them. Each of the four culminates in bibliographic citations of texts composed by Europeans in Spanish or French. All the passages on Christian miracles, Indian dancers, Arab travelers, and Japanese merchants may be taken from these other publications. That Paterno did not author his own appendices in the sense of creating them singlehandedly, however, does not mean that his voice and control are absent. Quite the contrary, he assumes an omnipotent role in the way he subsumes the European discourses to his. Through his manipulation of the Western texts—selecting them in the first place, choosing where to start and end the excerpts, cutting and pasting them, using ellipses to skip past their passages that he deems least important—Paterno vaults his voice over theirs by rearranging the transnational and transoceanic movements of which they speak into his own production of the Philippines. At the end of the day, he is in charge of the European world of discourse rather than vice versa. He lifts plot lines and environments in *Nínay* proper from other texts too, but he is not so much a solitary plagiarist as a cosmopolitan collagist.

ISLAND DISPLACEMENTS

Nowhere is a globalized Philippines more evident than in the most seemingly bizarre interlude of the novel, the episode in which Carlos, having fled on the brigantine *María* (virgin vessels are one of Paterno's favorite fictional subjects, particularly later in *Social Dawn*) from Federico's diabolical plans, is shipwrecked on a ludicrous island replete with warring savages, a half-naked queen, dancing around bonfires, hidden treasure and such. The island sequence takes up most of Taríc's storytelling on the penultimate night of Pasiám, though its beginning (the boarding of the *María*) and end (a climactic escape back to Manila in hopes of boarding Nínay) are narrated in the seventh and ninth chapters. On the eighth night, Taríc relates how a tempest sinks the *María* somewhere outside Manila Bay and Carlos sinks into the waves "pronunciando el nombre querido de Nínay" ["pronouncing the beloved name of Nínay"] (261). He washes up exhausted onto unknown sands. The next day, he wakes up on the beach to a noisy battle raging in the distance. Suddenly, "Una mujer con suelta cabellera, perseguida por un grupo de feroces salvajes, huye del centro de la batalla y se dirige aterrorizada hacia donde se encontraba Carlos. Éste, movido por generoso impulso toma la defensa de la débil perseguida, y armado de dos piedras de granito, derriba al primer perseguidor con un golpe certero" ["A woman with loose hair, pursued by a group of ferocious savages, flees the center of the battle and makes her way in terror toward where Carlos was. He, moved by a generous impulse, takes up the defense of the pursued weakling and, armed with two granite stones, topples the first pursuer with a sure strike"] (261–62). The valiant Carlos then strips the saber from the downed savage and fights off all the others, who flee. The dead warrior turns out to be the king of the invading tribe. As for the woman he saved, she is "una isleña de negros ojos y ardiente mirada, labios abultados, de torso y brazos desnudos" ["an island woman with black eyes and an ardent look, thick lips, and naked torso and arms"] (263). Her name is Tik and she is a queen.

Structurally, the island subplot sets up a panoply of inversions in roles and narrative dynamics. Carlos flees dangerous chaos in Manila, whereas on the island he promptly resolves dangerous chaos. Previously at the mercy of adverse and powerful forces human (Federico and the colonial military) and natural (the storm that shipwrecks the *María*), Carlos now takes control of both (the savages and the granite stones) and reestablishes himself as a real and potential hero. At the same time, however, he has no idea where he is. He wonders whether the topless woman is an Indian queen or perhaps an Indian concubine, possibly from Malabar in southern India or some other subcontinent locale (264–66). How he was tossed by the waves from Manila Bay to India in a single night is unclear; the distance is over three thousand miles by air alone. In any case, the locals are happy that their royal leader was saved. In thanks, they give Carlos some bits of human flesh, a shield made of elephant skin, a *cris* (an Islamic dagger from the southern Philippines), and a *khouttar* (a type of Indian dagger). Tik also presents him with some ostrich feathers to wear in his hair. Dancing around a bonfire seems sure to be next, and indeed it is as the queen, watching the ceremonies, is fanned by slaves.

The next day, the king of the island is found dead in the field of battle. This puts Carlos in an unexpected position.

Proclamado jefe de tribu, á pesar suyo, teniendo que recibir los homenajes de aquella corte salvaje de ceremoniales tan varios y extraños, no sabía cómo huir, ni cómo orientarse para volver á Manila, ó al menos comunicarse con Nínay. En vano recorrió la isla de Norte á Sur, de Este á Oeste; en vano subió los más elevados picos, en vano se paseó una y mil veces por las desiertas playas para ver si descubría una vela salvadora, que llevara sus mensajes á su patria. (274)

[Proclaimed chief of the tribe to his sorrow, having to receive the homages of that savage court of so varied and strange ceremonies, he did not know how to flee nor how to orient himself to return to Manila or at least communicate with Nínay. In vain he traversed the island from North to South, from East to West; in vain he climbed the highest peaks, in vain he walked a thousand and one times along the deserted beaches to see if he might sight a sail of salvation that could carry his messages to his fatherland.]

As Carlos paces the sands, Tik falls in love with "el extranjero que le arrancó de las garras de los feroces invasores, librando á su pueblo de la esclavitud" ["the foreigner who pulled her out of the claws of the ferocious invaders, freeing her people from slavery"] (275).[21] Carlos, however, thinks only of Nínay. Desperate one night atop a mountain, he decides to jump to his death, "pero en el momento de lanzarse al abismo" ["but at the moment of hurling himself into the abyss"] he feels the hand of Tik (277). She, "mostrando su desnudo pecho, todo agitado" ["showing her naked breast, all agitated"], confesses her love (277). Just at this moment when Tik displays "la lava de pasiones que desbordaba de un pecho volcánico" ["the lava of passions that overflowed a volcanic breast"], shouts ring out (277). The clamors of her people rise from below and Tik and Carlos learn that another enemy tribe has invaded the island and is scaling the mountain. At this point, Carlos turns to Tik and announces, "Sálvate; vive para tu pueblo. Yo no tengo patria, ni hogar y debo morir" ["Save yourself; live for your people. I have no fatherland, nor home, and I ought to die"] (278). Notwithstanding this assessment, he faces the oncoming invaders and wades through them with his dagger, defending Tik. A poisoned dart penetrates her bare bosom. As the queen dies in his arms, she tells him that in a cave by the beach she has hidden her treasures. Carlos puts her cadaver in the cave, takes the booty, and sails off the island in one of the invaders' canoes (279–80). The narration then switches back to Nínay's home, where three years have passed. Carlos's story resumes on the following (and final) night of Pasiám, when Taríc notes that it is reminiscent of when Aeneas left Dido behind in Carthage. As Carlos rows toward Manila and sights the southern Philippine island of Mindanao, he feels like Columbus and then Magellan, then Ulysses, then Herodotus and, finally, Marco Polo. His arrival at Nínay's home puts an end to the island sequence.

At first glance, the whole episode seems utterly superfluous. (This is perhaps the most charitable reading of it.) In terms of narrative function, the flight and shipwreck of Carlos adds nothing to the larger plot of the novel, which is affected by his adventures only in the sense that his absence in Manila allows time for Nínay's father to die in exile and for Nínay to enter the convent. What would have been a doubled heroic opportunity in Manila does not have a chance to come to pass, for Berto slays the cretin

Federico in Carlos's stead, and no jailbreak or dramatic courtroom scene appears in which Carlos might liberate Nínay's father. A marriage that could have followed such events is therefore never possible, nor, by extrapolation, is a symbolic founding family of the Philippines in this first Filipino novel. In other words, the sole apparent literary reason for the island sequence is to whisk away Carlos so that the novel ends in death rather than new life, in tragedy rather than comedy. This again begs the question of why a novel that launches a national tradition ends in the destruction of all those characters who might metaphorically launch the nation itself.

An extraliterary rationale for moving Carlos out of the Philippines and onto Tik's island is that the twist allows Paterno a major opportunity to wax intellectual. Thus Mojares writes, "An episode in the novel where the hero is marooned in the company of a tribe on an exotic and indeterminate island occasions comparative notes on India and Africa and esoteric topics like music and costume, culled from European authors" (*Brains*, 45). Mojares adds that the "exotic island episode seems inspired by late eighteenth-century European travel writing on the Pacific . . . rather than a personal knowledge of local geography" (*Brains*, 45). This explanation, which is surely accurate, is in keeping with Mojares's overall assessment of Paterno as keen to demonstrate that his erudition was in step with that of any high-brow European intellectual. Paterno aims for his Spanish readers to recognize that he, and by extension the land he represents, does not flounder somewhere in the distant wake of Europe but arises fully in the flow of the main currents of Western thought. Paterno has perused the academic authorities of Europe who have looked out toward the rest of the world and he wants the reader to know it. Moreover, he has read many of those learned books in French and he deliberately does not translate his citations of them to show it.

Yet this analysis does not cover all the questions raised by the island episode. The key word in Mojares is "indeterminate." Where is this island, exactly? And what is its allegorical import? Fictional castaways on desert islands are inevitably symbolic of something. The number of tenure cases built by Robinson Crusoe is proof enough of that. Desert islands are never as deserted as they appear, even when described as such. What happens on Tik's island, really, and what does it signify for the Philippines? Why move a hero off one island and have him shipwreck onto another? Why take Carlos, like Paterno himself, out of the Philippines, and why bring him back? The first thing to note is that Taríc's narration on the eighth night of

Pasiám begins, as on the three previous evenings, with recitations of Taga-log literature. In this case, the oral performance is a continuation of the recital on the seventh night of *Segismundo,* "drama el más notable de la lit-eratura tagala" ["the most notable drama of Tagalog literature"] (225). The fifth night had begun with a "celébre poeta tagalo" ["celebrated Tagalog poet"] and the sixth with "un literato indio" ["a literate Indian"] reciting poetry in Taglog to other *indios* (169, 225). The orality and language of these successive openings frame the faraway, indeterminate, and unknown island within the literary forms of local and specific island traditions. As a result, the familiar genre of the castaway narrative, with its long European history, is nested within Filipino literary currents rather than vice versa.

This inversion of West-East hierarchies then is dispersed broadly as Pa-terno bounces in the main body of text and in the footnotes from one re-gion of the planet to another. After writing that Carlos grabbed a saber from one of the first invading "salvajes" ["savages"], Paterno pauses to ob-serve that the weapon is "análoga á la usada por los Bertas, pueblos nó-madas del alto Nilo" ["analogous to that used by the Bertas, nomadic peo-ples of the upper Nile" (261–62). He then expounds upon the Bertas in a footnote by paraphrasing and translating passages about them from two francophone sources, whose authors and titles he cites. In the next foot-note, inspired by Tik's bare bosom, he summarizes in Spanish yet another scholarly source written in French, this one about how "las indias" ["In-dian women"] adorn their breasts (263). Subsequent footnotes comment on diverse aspects of various Indian cultures. Back in the plot, the grateful islanders give Carlos the bits of human flesh, the elephant skin shield, the Islamo-Philippine dagger, the Indian dagger, and the ostrich feathers. Pa-terno elucidates this passage with a footnote that cites three works in French that discuss the use of human flesh in battle in Abyssinia, that is, Ethiopia (267). He promptly adds another footnote to note that there is a *khouttar* (the Indian dagger) in the Louvre.

What on earth is going on here? Just about everything on earth, actu-ally. The predominance of references to cultures in India implies that the is-land is somewhere in South Asia, but just how the *María,* a tiny ship, could have been swept in a few hours by a storm near Manila Bay to an island off-shore India beggars the imagination. Even Gilligan could not manage such a feat on his most inadvertent day. Meanwhile, the references to Africans in Ethiopia and the upper Nile, to ostriches (native to African savannahs and deserts but not India or further east in Asia; and, for obvious reasons, unlikely to make their way to an island in any case), to Muslims of the southern Philippines (the dagger) not to mention the francophone authorities and the Louvre, constantly displace Tik's island across a global map. The Philippines, via the persons of Carlos and his author—Paterno, moreover, is writing from Spain—weave through this cartographic chaos as well. The footnotes cannot be dismissed as unimportant marginalia in these pages. After all, they fill up approximately half the space on each of them. Indeed, the argument can be made that if anything is marginalia, it is the narrative involving Carlos rather than the hypertext that comments it. Later footnotes in the chapter compare the island women's hairstyles to those of "los pueblos africanos del Gabon" ["the African peoples of Gabon"], the musical instruments to those of Hindu dancers in India, and the fans that wave over Tik to Indian devices derived from Tibetan yak tails (269). When the second savage tribe invades, however, Carlos wades through them flourishing a knife, which Paterno footnotes as a "Sable recto y largo usado en Filipinas" ["straight and long saber used in the Philippines"] (279). Carlos penetrates the barbarian imperialists with his Filipino weapon and absconds from the island with one of their canoes. He heads home to his love and his land, which are metonymically just about the same thing. He leaves behind an island that is not so much "indeterminate" as overly determinate, an isolated nowhere that is a planetary somewhere: a land marked improbably by South Asian referents but, in repeated ways, by a more global South that also stretches from Gabon to the Nile to wherever ostriches roam.

This, therefore, is the function of the island chapter: to show that Carlos, and by extension the Philippines that he represents and, of course, Paterno himself, are not part of that global South. Carlos leaves his islands so that they can be distinguished from other islands that are less developed, islands over which he might rightly be made king and enjoy a volcanic naked beauty as his queen and a retinue of fan-waving slaves. It is the dream scenario of every European imperialist. For the first time in the novel, absent are the salons and gardens of aristocratic Manila, an eastern Versailles of sorts or at least a Merchant-Ivory production, replaced instead by war and slavery and even hints of cannibalism. In a structuralist sense, therefore, the island is to Manila as Federico is to Carlos and Pilar is to Nínay: the dark double that is invoked to reveal the purity of the original. That purity is sexual and religious and political all at once, which is why Carlos never acculturates to island life, never goes native, never seeks to modify the island

with his presence in any way (build a home, learn to spear local fish, eat local fruits, invent labor-saving contraptions, etc.), unlike all the fictional
castaways before him. He is given a queen but ignores her, given a kingdom
but ignores that, given slaves but ignores them. Yet even as he denies his
phallus to Tik, he does use his other Filipino weapon, his "straight and long
saber" to cut through barbarians and fight his way toward home. By this
point, the differentiation has been made: the Philippines offers civilization
and Tik's island does not. The hero can return home now, his weapon in
hand, to a land that approximates Europe rather than the islands of the
global South with which the Spanish readers of the novel might instinctively confuse it. That South is global, in fact, not because Paterno is cosmopolitan but because he is parochial. After all, he sees the world only
through the prism of the West. The point of the island chapter and of the
whole novel is to ensure that readers place the Philippines within that West
and from there look outward in pseudoanthropological fashion to the rest
of the world. Filipinos are from European islands, so much so that when
they show up on other, less civilized islands, they naturally play the role of
rightful rulers. They are, as is said, greeted as liberators.

Yet this reading also is overly simple. There are slippages and paradoxes
even in this point of view that prevent any fixed location or identity for the
Philippines from coming into being. The conversion of Carlos from island
subject of foreign invaders to island leader against foreign invaders is too
complex to allow any dualisms to survive much examination. For one, Tik
and her island are hardly dark doubles for Nínay and her islands. Although
Tik offers her body, her people, her land, and her treasure to Carlos, she is
as honorable and pure as her alter ego in Manila who withholds all such
things. With the original island king dead, Tik's desires for Carlos are unimpeachable. And she belongs to an even more elite class in her society than
does Carlos in his. Her people may be associated with the ostensible sav-
ageries of the global South but they behave respectfully at all times toward
Carlos. Their characters are never impugned by the narrator. Indeed, because of the unconsummated sympathies that Carlos has for Tik and her
subjects, he utters that astounding pronouncement at the second and climactic battle scene, "Save yourself; live for your people. I have no fatherland, nor home, and I ought to die" (278). This is an extraordinary moment. What can "I have no fatherland" possibly mean in this scene and in
this protonationalist novel? At a literal level, Carlos figures that he will
never get off the island and therefore is alienated forever from a patria con-

stituted by the Philippines and Nínay as interwoven entities. Symbolically, however, the declaration runs deeper than geography. What he really avers here is an absent national identity, without which he may as well be dead. He recognizes that Tik, by contrast, does have such a collective identity that provides a reason to live. Her island, for her, is not a nowhere but a somewhere, and for that reason she and her people deserve an autonomous existence free of foreign occupation. Her community is and ought to be, Carlos implies, an independent state. Tik's people, microcosmic of all island peoples beset by invaders, are not uncivilized savages but possessors of the basic right to rule themselves. Meanwhile, Carlos's Philippine identity is eviscerated to nothingness.

There are no political statements in *Nínay* in any formal sense. There is no criticism of Spanish secular or religious regimes, no listing of historical grievances against Spain, no mention of imperialist invasions of the Philippines. Yet there are two moments when Carlos does take a political stand: when he defends Tik from both groups of foreign invaders. And his declaration that he has no fatherland reads as a certain longing for nationhood accomplished already by the islanders who embrace him. Tik and her people are not southern barbarians akin to others studied by European anthropologists, not a savage contrast to a civilized Philippines, but rather a consolidated nation that leads where Carlos only can hope to go. In *Nínay*, the violent colonial dramas of the Philippines play out not in the archipelago but on Tik's island. This displacement unexpectedly aligns Carlos with the dreams and accomplishments of islanders rather than with those who arrive on their shore and turn them into political and discursive objects. He takes the side of the embattled and nationalized locals, not the martial intruders. Carlos is a Crusoe before whom Friday transmutes from a slave to a sovereign.

This paradoxical displacement and will to nationhood reappears via the epics associated with Carlos as he rows from the South Asian island to Manila aboard the invaders' canoe (itself an interesting example of taking an imperialist's tools and using them for nationalist endeavors). According to Paterno, Carlos is a "Nuevo Eneas sobre las olas de la esperanza huyendo de Cartago. ¿Quién no recuerda en Tik la pasión de Dido?" ["New Aeneas upon the waves of hope fleeing from Carthage. Who does not remember in Tik the passion of Dido?"] (293). The learned persona of the author is displayed anew as again he sees the global South through the prism of Western tradition. Tik and her island are now metaphoric to a classical story of

coastal Africa, the *Aeneid,* while Carlos stands for a hero bound for Europe
rather than the Philippines. The destiny that drew Aeneas across the seas
was the founding of Rome. His flight from Carthage would lead to the birth
of a new state whose civilization would be the center of a world order, not
an underdeveloped margin. That center would result in the production of
a peripheral Spain. If Carlos is Aeneas, then Manila is to become Rome and
Spain one of its distant backwaters. This inversion recalls the contestations
of the *baybayin* dedication and the devices of Taríc's oral tale that unsettle
any conclusion that the ideological underpinnings of *Nínay* result from a
simple attempt to place the Philippines on a map drawn by Europeans. The
novel implicitly, if not Paterno consciously, challenges that cartography
every time it seems to settle on one set of contour lines or another.

The protean subject position of Carlos emerges on all sides of the European map. This is particularly the case in the breathtaking paragraph that
compares him to a litany of major historical and literary figures. When he
sights at last Mindanao, Carlos "sintió al fin la alegría del ilustre Genovés al
descubrir las islas Lucayas" ["felt at the end the happiness of the illustrious
Genoese upon discovering the Bahamas"] (297). That Genoese is Columbus, whose putative role as discoverer of the New World is filled by Carlos.
But of course, the Philippines is no new world to Carlos. His is a return, not
a first-time encounter, and he is somehow indigenous and foreign at once.
He is a fused version of both the arriving mariner and the local population
who receives him. Paterno next compares Carlos to Magellan, but this too
is a contradiction. In voyaging to and from Tik's island, Carlos has sailed
around the world via the global associations of the footnotes, whereas Magellan only traveled in one direction to the Philippines. It was no round trip.
By this point, however, Carlos has long been considered dead by Nínay, so
his reappearance in the Philippines marks a certain if short-lived rebirth,
something Magellan never even enjoyed temporarily.

The third mariner in this metaphorical current is Greek rather than Genoese or Portuguese: "Como Ulises, visitando Chipre, la Fenicia, el Egipto y
la Libia, Carlos pasó en bancas, canoas ó en goletas las cien islas que forman
el Archipiélago, esas islas semejantes á las de Grecia" ["Like Ulysses visiting
Cyprus, Phoenicia, Egypt, and Libya, Carlos traveled in dugouts, canoes, or
in schooners through the hundred islands that form the Archipelago, those
islands similar to those of Greece"] (297–98). This classical reference echoes
that to Aeneas invoked earlier. Although Aeneas and Ulysses fought on opposite sides of the Trojan War, they shared a sort of seafaring peregrination

akin to that of Carlos upon his departure from Tik's island. Aeneas represents the front end of the wandering, with Tik playing Dido, while Ulysses represents the back end, with Nínay in the role—substituting sisters for suitors—of Penelope. The legendary heroes evoked by Paterno, however, are separated from Columbus and Magellan by antiquity and myth. What the four figures do share, though, is that they all experience otherworlds at sea and bear news of such (via Pigafetta, in Magellan's case) to once and/or future geopolitical centers. Their voyages upturn known cartographies so that those centers, defined now in relief by the distant lands and polities they are *not*, necessarily force into existence new collective identities. Meanwhile, although Tik is secure in who her people are, the same cannot be said for Carlos. The onomastic succession of heroic identities for him shows that the Philippines is unresolvable to any particular South and any particular North, to any particular temporality whether ancient or modern, and to any particular imaginary whether mythic or historical. The national identity of Carlos and the islands to which he returns as a metaphoric founder is scattered in diverse subjectivities across the globe. He has no patria not because he is nowhere but because he is just about everywhere.

This apatriotism of the Filipino hero in the originary Filipino novel is consolidated in the final two allusions of the paragraph: "Y cuando podía contar cosas maravillosas de tierras desconocidas, como Herodoto en la antigüedad, ó como Marco Polo en los tiempos modernos, llegó al fin al deseado puerto de Manila" ["And when he could tell marvelous things of unknown lands like Herodotus in antiquity or like Marco Polo in modern times, he arrived at last at the desired port of Manila"] (298). As voyagers abroad, as strangers in strange lands, Herodotus and Marco Polo are alter egos for Carlos alongside Aeneas, Columbus, Magellan, and Ulysses. As narrators, they are also alter egos for Paterno himself. Herodotus went to Athens as an intellectual from the margins. His writings on his wide travels throughout the Mediterranean more or less invented the field of history. After *Nínay*, Paterno the armchair traveler would do the same for the Philippines. He, like Herodotus, arrived at the metropolis, in his case Madrid, as a thinker from the periphery who would tell stories of the past. As for Marco Polo, his travels led him to inform the West of cultures of the East, the primary goal of Paterno as well. These superficial similarities, however, are less interesting than the comparative logic that produces them. Paterno again classifies the world into antiquity and modernity along decidedly Western lines—these are not heroes and storytellers indigenous to the

Philippines—but his insertion of Carlos into analogies that bridge a Greco-Roman past (Aeneas, Ulysses, Herodotus) with a European present (Columbus, Magellan, Marco Polo) means that Carlos and Paterno and the Philippines emerge as wandering simultaneously in both classical and modern times around the Mediterranean, the Atlantic, and the Pacific.

Paterno may have traveled from Manila to Madrid, east to west, but in his novel he does not linearly retrace that journey backward to its starting point. Nor does he have Carlos's odyssey repeat his own. Carlos leaves the Philippines and ends up not in Spain but on Tik's island. There he finds a microcosmic South differentiated from his presumptively European archipelago but also an admirable nationhood elusive to himself. Unlike traditional castaways in fiction, he does not arrive on the island with one identity and then forge a new one amid his isolation. On the contrary, his subjectivity has been fluid from the beginning, as he has played the roles of both indigenous Filipino and elite European. When Carlos returns to the Philippines, he is revealed explicitly to be a polytemporal, polygeographic adventurer-author whose every move is a succession of slipping signs of globalization. This is both the classical version of globalization in which European protagonists moved beyond their known world, redrawing its maps in the process; and the later version, whose protagonists forged linkages among the full breadth of hitherto unconnected regions of the planet (this is why Marco Polo marks "los tiempos modernos" ["modern times"]) (298). None of the analogies and metaphors that describe Carlos ever comes to rest on him or Paterno or the Philippines. Each one slides into the next. No organic composite ever emerges either.

This incoherence is appropriate to the subjects at hand. The stream of national signs through Carlos is not a lack of an identity but the primary features thereof for an archipelago that exists due to the transoceanic currents that flow among it. The Philippines is always *not* the Philippines, and this is precisely why Paterno cannot insert it into some unproblematized linear march of European civilization from Greco-Roman antiquity to late nineteenth-century Madrid or Manila. He cannot stylize it into any essence. Paterno wishes to show the Philippines as part of a Europe that looked outward to the global South, but contestations in the text to his conscious navigations undermine his own captaining. Such resistances are plural, appearing, for example, as the *baybayin* dedication, the introduction to the first footnote that posits Manila as a center rather than a periphery, and the inability to settle on a consistent metaphorical identity for Carlos either on or off Tik's island.

The incoherence of the inchoate nation is the coherence of incipient globalization. The significance of *Nínay* for world literature is not that of a strictly national artifact (as the first Filipino novel in any language) nor continental (as the first Asian novel in Spanish) but of a text of unending dynamics of circumnavigation and resistance thereto. If Lapu Lapu repelled the onslaught of Magellan, that inaugural captain of globalization, the text of *Nínay* so resists the will of its own author, Paterno. He was dedicated to "[p]utting the country," as Mojares writes, "in the map of European consciousness" (*Brains*, 45). Yet Paterno's powers of cartography escape and evade him in a flux of here and there that never settles into any particular latitude or longitude. This incommensurateness with itself is what makes *Nínay* so telling a text of globalization. Unfortunately, it has never been recognized as such. The novel disappeared into popular and academic oblivion almost from its date of publication.

That oblivion is due in part to the dearth of scholarship on Filipino fiction in Spanish outside the many studies on Rizal. With the exception of brief analyses by Mojares and Schumacher in several texts and by Hornedo and Matibag in single journal articles, the critical commentary mostly appears in three forms: unpublished graduate school theses, published literary histories, and language textbooks that attempt to teach Spanish to Filipinos via literature. These isolated works do not coalesce into any particular intellectual tradition. Their only shared motivation is an irregular sense of patriotism. All of them offer lists of authors and attendant biographical blurbs, truncated plot summaries, and perhaps a few words of aesthetic description. There is virtually nothing in them that would count as interpretation. A chronological survey of a number of the twentieth-century secondary texts known so far reveals the little importance given to *Nínay* in particular to date:

1935   Delfina de San Agustín's graduate thesis "La literatura castellana en Filipinas" ("Castilian Literature in the Philippines") spends seven pages on Paterno but does not mention *Nínay*.[22]

1950   Araceli Pons García's graduate thesis "Filipino Writers in Spanish and Their Works: Historico-Bibliographic Study," mentions Paterno among thirty-five "major writers" but does not elaborate on *Nínay*.

1955   Margarita Zaragoza Viuda de Preysler's graduate thesis "Temática de
        la poesía filipina en su siglo de oro—(1870–1930)" ("Thematics of Fil-
        ipino Poetry in Its Golden Age—[1870–1930]") discusses Paterno's
        poetry but does not include even a passing reference to *Nínay*.
1958   Mercedes C. de Sánchez's graduate thesis "El desarrollo de la liter-
        atura hispano-filipina" ("The Development of Hispanic-Filipino
        Literature") does not mention Paterno at all.[23]
1964   Estanislao B. Alinea's *Historia analítica de la literatura filipinohispana
        (desde 1566 hasta mediados de 1964)* (*Analytical History of Hispanic-
        Filipino Literature (from 1566 to the middle of 1964)*), which provides
        the most complete published listing of texts and authors, devotes a
        single clause to *Nínay* that dubs the novel "muy popular durante su
        tiempo" ["very popular in its time"] (61). There is no reason to be-
        lieve that this judgment is accurate.
1965   Rosa Reyes Soriano's *Cultura Hispano-Filipina: Breve historia de la lit-
        eratura hispana filipina* (*Hispanic-Filipino Culture: Brief History of His-
        panic-Filipino Literature*), second edition, a book that teaches Span-
        ish to anglophone Filipinos by offering passages of Filipino
        literature in Spanish, describes *Nínay* in just one sentence as well.
        Reyes Soriano writes of Paterno that "es famosa su novela costum-
        brina [*sic*] típicamente oriental y auténtica de colorido filipino"
        ["his *costumbrista* novel is famous. It is typically oriental and au-
        thentic in its Filipino color"] (83). Again, the novel hardly was fa-
        mous even at the time. Its orientalisms and authenticity are also
        questionable frames of analysis.
1973   Luis Mariñas's *La literatura filipina en castellano* (*Filipino Literature in
        Castilian*), which usually is the most useful guide to the subject, of-
        fers only two sentences on *Nínay*. The novel is "sentimental . . . lig-
        eramente anticlerical, nos ofrece ya las características que práctica-
        mente sin excepción . . . se darán entre los escritores fil-hispanos"
        ["sentimental . . . lightly anticlerical, it already offers us the char-
        acteristics that practically without exception . . . will mark the Fil-
        Hispanic writers"] (37).
1976   *Literatura Hispano-filipina (Selecciones)* (*Hispanic-Filipino Literature
        (Selections)*), an anthology designed to teach reading comprehen-
        sion in Spanish to Filipinos, offers two short prose texts by Paterno
        but neither is from *Nínay*.
1981   Vida Ma. [María] Madrigal y Centenera and Arlene de León y del
        Rosario's *Filipinas es mi patria: Español 4-N; Selecciones de literatura*

filipina en español (*The Philippines Is My Fatherland: Spanish 4-N; Selections of Filipino Literature in Spanish*), a Spanish language primer, offers excerpts from various contemporaries of Paterno but none from Paterno himself.

1993 Edgardo Tiamson Mendoza's graduate thesis, "A Re-appreciation of Philippine Literature in Spanish," notes in three sentences about *Nínay* that it "was more of a socio-anthropological treatise on Philippine customs than a literary work" (84–85).[24]

1999 Pedro Ortiz Armengol's *Letras en Filipinas* (*Letters in the Philippines*), a review of texts written about the Philippines by both Spaniards and Filipinos, dedicates a section to Paterno but only a paragraph of that to a plot summary of *Nínay* and a few sentences of commentary (211–12).

An interesting exception to the nearly complete inattention to *Nínay* is Victoria Sycip's graduate thesis of 1972, "The Golden Age of Philippine Literature in Spanish." Her two and a half pages of commentary on the novel—an epic length of criticism, in the scheme of things—dismiss it as a "mediocre" attempt at *costumbrismo* in which "because Paterno gets so engrossed with details, *Nínay*, on the whole, lacks continuity. Often the events follow each other without being linked in any way . . . [Paterno] does not effectively unite his thoughts" (13, 14). What Sycip criticizes as the weakness of the novel, however, is actually the key to its significance. The apparently chaotic jumping from irrelevant detail to irrelevant footnote to irrelevant subplot makes the novel, like the Philippines, uncontainable. It constantly spills out over itself. Its illogic is actually a logic of surplus from a person and place supposedly acting from a position of paucity. The unending disunity of *Nínay* is that which unifies it as a shifting matrix of the asymmetrical and obliquely opposing forces of globalization. The conclusion that *Nínay* is a cut-and-paste job by a hyperbolic and pretentious amateur is accurate. The assumption that that conclusion renders the novel immaterial is not. *Nínay* is the most modern of novels from the place where modernity began.

MOURNING AND MARGINALIA

At the end of *Nínay*, nearly everyone is dead: Carlos, Nínay and her parents, Federico and his father, Tik and her consort, plus much of Manila from cholera.[25] Again, what kind of foundational fiction ends with all the potential founders killed off? The body count is inexplicable if Paterno in Madrid, as the forerunner of a seminal generation of Filipino intellectuals, and *Nínay* in literature, as the first Filipino novel, mark a certain start to a Filipino sense of national self-consciousness. After all, the collective tragedy that is the novel suggests that rather than looking forward, Paterno is looking back. The plot is not a comedy that culminates with a wedding and the implication of children to come. On the contrary, *Nínay,* which begins and ends in a cemetery, can be seen as a kind of mourning work in which Paterno tries to come to grips with all the sterility, all the death, of the Filipino upper class whose affairs he depicts.[26] And that class is the local elite who prospered hand in hand with the foreign rulers, indeed, tried to mimic them as much as possible. It is a class, Paterno among it, that tried to pass as Spanish. Paterno hoped to succeed at that in his own life and with his novel, but the text of *Nínay* shows the precariousness of the endeavor and its inevitable collapse. There is no explicit sign in the novel that the fall of the house of Nínay symbolizes the advent of a major class revolution in the Philippines, but the death of all the representatives of the upper class in the novel does leave space open for alternative structurings of social power.

Tensions often reveal what intentions do not. In *Nínay,* there are no overtly political polemics of any kind taking place in the Philippines. There is no haranguing against either contemporary Spanish priests and governors-general or against their forebears such as Magellan. Yet not all the novel takes place in the Philippines. And it is suggestive that the one episode not set in the archipelago, that of Tik's island, is also the one part of the novel in which imperial contests do play out. In both cases of invasion, the good guys are the local islanders, the bad guys are the foreign aggressors, and Carlos defends the natives heroically and instinctively. Protonationalism proves incommensurate with imperialism. Once again, the Tik sequence emerges as a critical displacement of the plot rather than as a superfluous addition to it. Carlos in his regular life in Manila, like Paterno in Madrid, may be too bound by his class position to become aware of his deepest sympathies, but when freed of his own moorings his latent anticolonialism becomes manifest. Neither the author nor his protagonist can summon the consciousness to take up arms for his own island community against its own occupying power, but the Tik episode shows that such efforts are justified and worthwhile.

Carlos, however, does not represent ultimately the survival of local re-sistance nor of anything else. Like the rest of the doomed Filipino elite in *Nínay* who style themselves Spanish, he produces no apparent challenge to Philippine social structures and no apparent heirs. He cannot even bring himself to consummate his relationship with his beloved. In the most pas-sionate scene with Nínay, Carlos clutches her body against his with an ar-dor so lustful that Paterno retreats into a lengthy ellipsis of over fifty peri-ods, unable to verbalize the sexual heat. When the description resumes, Carlos drags Nínay toward a grotto with the apparent intent of deflowering her, but he desists upon seeing a white image of the Virgin Mary (186). Catholicism, the most persistent of the Spanish inheritances, stops him from challenging social codes and thereby producing possible offspring. This is not say that Nínay does not have sex in this scene. Although Carlos does not violate her virginity, "el fuego de la pasión penetró en el pecho de la inocente joven, sin menoscabar su pureza, como el rayo solar atraviesa la piedra preciosa sin mancharla" ["the fire of passion penetrated the breast of the innocent young girl without harming her purity like the sun ray passes through the precious stone without staining it"] (187). This is virgin inter-course. It is ardent and innocent at once.

Nevertheless, it is not quite true that all the key figures are silenced at the end of *Nínay*. Berto and Pilar survive. And herein lies the true potential of the novel as an exemplar of the Magellan fallacy, as a legacy of Lapu Lapu, suggestive of new social forms and collective identities unrecognized no doubt by Paterno. Although Carlos is the ostensible hero of the novel, he is remarkably feckless and passive by comparison to Berto. It is Berto who is introduced not while shooting a bird about to eat Nínay's pet, as is Carlos, but while singlehandedly saving a whole town from an enraged wa-ter buffalo and then singlehandedly saving a poor widow's son from a house fire (114–15). Next, it is Berto who elopes with his girlfriend Loleng, a chaste and beautiful young woman parallel in life and death to Nínay (the two are also good friends), rather than hang around sentimentally un-til larger forces overwhelm him, which is what Carlos does. It is Berto who swears revenge on Federico's father, a "capitalista portugués" ["Portuguese capitalist"] who has arrived in the Philippines intent on controlling and exploiting its economic resources as "el hacendado más influyente de An-tipolo" ["the most influential landowner of Antipolo"] (45). Berto thereby rises in opposition to a foreigner who towers over the religious site so sym-bolic for Paterno of the Philippines and over its parallel sexual resources, embodied this time in the virginal Loleng. Magellan too was a Portuguese operating under a Spanish flag whose arrival ultimately betokened a conquest that was economic, religious, and sexual. It is Berto who flees after Loleng's death to a "pueblo de la libertad" ["liberty town"] that promises to harbor him as long as he proves his mettle by leading a group of brigands to sack Nínay's house and kidnap her (192).[27] It is Berto who is the only character to use the *baybayin,* in an oath of vengeance no less (165). It is also Berto who tells Carlos to flee aboard the *María,* who slays the evil Federico, and who, in the final account, buries Carlos. All of these scenes happen on the outskirts of the text, to be sure, for the narrator of *Nínay* focuses on Carlos throughout. But there is no question which young man is stronger in thought and deed, which one represents outside challenges to the status quo rather than hopes of succeeding within it, and which one survives in the end. And whereas Carlos is a rich heir to Filipino lands, Berto is described as "pobre" ("poor") (114). Carlos may be the central figure of *Nínay,* but Berto, operating always from the margins, is the leading man.

As for Pilar, her machinations to ensnare Carlos and eliminate Nínay as a rival go horribly awry. At the end of the novel, she remonstrates herself bitterly for her actions, lamenting, "no ceso de sufrir; los remordimientos destrozan mi corazón. Cada rayo de sol que nos alumbra, es una lima ardiente que tortura mi alma . . . debo arder en el fuego de mi desesperación" ["I do not stop suffering; remorse destroys my heart. Every ray of sun that lights us up is a burning lime[28] that tortures my soul . . . I ought to burn in the fire of my desperation"] (311). This is a hell, but at least it is a living one. Pilar survives in the end, which is more than Nínay can say. In other words, the principal female character who brought disorder to the elite cast of characters is the one who manages to keep going. Unlike Berto, Pilar is well-off financially, but she is also orphaned halfway through the novel and taken in by Nínay's father as a ward.[29] This makes her symbolically Nínay's sister, a relationship confirmed when Nínay's father tells Pilar that "desde ahora será una hermana que tenga Nínay" ["from now on you will be a sister that Nínay will have"] (121). This sororal status accentuates her role as a double for Nínay and therefore a potential replacement. In short, the antiheroine, like the bandit Berto, remains viable, while the protagonizing sweethearts do not.

Of the three young men (Carlos, Berto, Federico) and three young women (Nínay, Loleng, Pilar) whose interrelations drive the novel, only

Berto and Pilar are left at the end.[30] There is no hint of romance between them, but they, though marginal, are the real protagonists of *Nínay*. They are the true foundational couple. Their potential fertility is not only biological. What they represent is the possible birth of a new social order, one that stood up against the forces of the elite of Manila and brought them crashing down. This explains why everyone else dies, why Carlos and Nínay produce no progeny, either biologically or culturally or politically. Their ultimate sterility is that of the Spanish ruling class for which they tried to pass. The Filipino sources of disorder in the novel win the day, not the Filipino sources of order. As a result, *Nínay* is a foundational fiction that implies a new day with outlaw forebears, even if such is the last thing that Paterno himself ever wanted. He was a backward-looking man, but his own novel, the first in Asia in Spanish, betrays him. He tried to captain the Philippines in Madrid and to captain Filipino literature in *Nínay*, but local forces of resistance transmuted the intended consequences of his efforts at globalization. They always do.

CHAPTER TWO

The Imperial Shift: José Rizal's El filibusterismo *(1891) and* Pedro Paterno's Aurora social *(1910–11)*

Pedro Paterno was the first novelist of the Philippines but his *Nínay* is barely known inside the country, much less read. This is not the case with the next two Filipino novels that appeared, José Rizal's *Noli me tangere* (*Touch Me Not*) of 1887 and *El filibusterismo* (*Subversion*) of 1891. Neither the author nor the texts suffer from a lack of national fame. Whereas Paterno and his literary output languish somewhere between obscurity and obsolescence, every Filipino schoolchild is legally required to study Rizal and read his novels in one form or another. Rizal even has a modicum of international renown, the only Filipino author of his era to achieve that. Like Paterno, he wrote his novels in Spanish and published them in Europe. Rizal moved around that continent more than Paterno, but the two men knew and read each other. History has consigned one of them as a dead end and the other as a death that leads to national life itself. Paterno survived the collapse of Spanish colonialism in Asia and the imperial shift that followed, which may very well be a prime reason that his homeland has ignored him. Rizal, in large part because of his execution in 1896, retained a veneer of purity that has kept his image shining for generations. The antipathies and sympathies of history, however, tend to say more about present moments than past.

Both Paterno and Rizal were authors of global visions, but neither is read as such. This raises the issue of where a nationalized author like Rizal, acknowledged as foundational to his country, fits into a larger discussion of world literature when the Philippines is commonly framed as a historical and cultural hybrid neither quite Asian nor quite Western. *El filibusterismo*, a novel sharply critical of Spanish colonialism yet reluctant to promote

Philippine independence, provides a particularly complicated space in which such tensions are engaged. The sinister, American and procolonial protagonist, Simoun, freshly arrived in Manila from years of supporting Spanish imperialism in Cuba, actually turns out to be an equally nefarious but Filipino and anticolonial revolutionary named after the South American independence hero Simón Bolívar. The incipient national project that is the Philippines is thereby imagined in a literary sense not in Asia at all but amid complex allusive dynamics that originate from the Americas. It is via the apparently American body of Simoun/Simón, for instance, that projections emanate of an unexpectedly non-Filipino Orient as he and an American proxy enrapture the Philippine colonial elite with tales of Middle Eastern pyramids and sphinxes and jewels once belonging to Cleopatra. In effect, Rizal and Simoun, like the Philippine nation they in large part authored, appear in global frameworks as both Asian and American in that currents Eastern and Western interact in a ceaseless flow that resists any easy categorization.

A search for limited nationalisms and coherent regionalisms has typified traditional divisions in the way nineteenth- and twentieth-century literature in Spain and Latin America has been studied and taught. For example, the literary repercussions of the war between Spain and the United States in 1898 have been categorized as a strictly Spanish phenomenon in which the leading writers of the day tried to process the implications of a military debacle in the Philippines and Cuba that putatively marked the end of the Spanish empire. After Columbus, Spain had developed an expansive identity brimming with powers and conquests of all natures. In geopolitical and religious spheres, Spain had led Europe and the world and accumulated unimaginable riches along the way. But the imperial heights of the so-called Golden Age, featuring in the arts such luminaries as Miguel de Cervantes, Diego Velázquez, and El Greco, had been followed by a long decline in all areas. A particular nadir was the successful independence movements in most of Latin America in the early part of the nineteenth century, but it was the loss in 1898 of the Spanish colonies of Cuba, Puerto Rico, Guam, and the Philippines that definitively (and inaccurately) ended the correlation of Spanish identity with empire.[1] Spain, so the story goes, would have to come up with a new self-definition from that point onward, one aimed inwardly at Iberia. The accomplished novelists, essayists, and poets who wrote in the wake of the perceived national disaster, authors such as Azorín, Pío Baroja, Ángel Ganivet, Antonio Machado, and Miguel de Unamuno, turned their gaze to a Spain no longer defined by the wake of 1492. Eventually labeled as the "Generation of '98," these authors were institutionalized within Spanish letters, where classifying diverse writers into generational groups remains an expected practice. Still today in the North American academy, taxonomic codifications in the form of graduate student reading lists, like that at the program at the University of Virginia, may refer to the Generation of '98. To study 1898 in literature has meant, for most of the decades since, to study reflections by Spanish writers on Spain in its provincialism.

In recent years and in some quarters, the above narrative has been amended and nuanced. These modified imaginings of 1898 often include José Martí, the Cuban poet and essayist who wrote mostly from New York as a leader of the movement against the ongoing Spanish colonialism of his island in the 1880s and 1890s. Martí, whose return to Cuba in 1895 to take up armed revolt promptly ended with his death, hitherto had been considered mostly within national frames, as the Cuban writer par excellence, and within continental frames (exclusive of North America) as an aesthetic innovator who, along with Rubén Darío of Nicaragua, was one of the two greatest Latin American writers of his era. Dubbed as exemplars of *modernismo,* a term of variable meaning, Martí and Darío are generally credited with the launching of modern literature in Spanish throughout the New World. It always has been clear that Martí cannot be cordoned off as an insular nationalist because his stature as a Latin American writer is unquestionable. Yet his international influence, all too often, has been defined within aesthetic terms that cast him predominantly as a renovator of language and form; and within continental terms as an imaginer of Latin America per se via his landmark essay "Nuestra América" ("Our America"). The consideration of Martí by various scholars of 1898 amounts to a move to understand the literature of the era as not only an introspective Iberian phenomenon—a Eurocentric delimitation of obvious narrowness to anyone studying coeval Caribbean authors—but also as a broad matrix of voices that emerged, geographically, on both sides of the Atlantic Ocean and, temporally, on both sides of the year in question. Efforts to discuss Martí, in turn, could comprise as well analyses of the anglophone writings of men like Theodore Roosevelt, who fought in Cuba in 1898 and praised himself for it thereafter in various texts. And Martí could lead the way for the inclusion in 1898 studies of his contemporary across the Pacific Ocean, another foundational writer and martyr from another island controlled by Spain, José Rizal.[2]

Although globalized studies of 1898 have yet to predominate, the advantages are multiple. Depriviledging the narrownesses of various nationalist groupings can only be a good thing. What happens if Martí and Rizal and Roosevelt and Azorín do not seduce scholars into national rhetorics but globalized ones? Why not read Unamuno next to Rizal—for that matter, why not read what Unamuno wrote *about* Rizal—and Ganivet next to Roosevelt? Why not stop sequestering Martí into the modern Latin America section of syllabi and anthologies and doctoral exams and read him in the actual worldwide spatial and temporal contexts in which he moved? At a minimum, everyone should put literature from the Philippines, starting with Rizal, into considerations of the era. This may be the biggest blind spot in the last hundred years of scholarship on modern literature in Spanish. If the Generation of '98 is conceded to exist, then at least it should go beyond the definition of parochial peninsular writers suffering from a national postpartum depression after an orgy of global conquest. The meaning of life in Spain may have seemed to them to have little sense with the colonies gone, but Iberia was hardly the only place where prominent authors writing in Spanish were trying to come to grips with altered national identities in the post-1898 world. Pedro Paterno, in the texts of *Aurora social* (*Social Dawn*) and elsewhere, was one such person.

The narrative of 1898, both before and after the titular year, looks very different when viewed from global vantages rather than peninsular. The wars among foreign troops and local revolutionaries did not lead to the end of empire but the transition, as in Cuba and Puerto Rico, to a different one. The Caribbean islanders soon gained legitimized legal statuses, however, as Cuba became independent in 1903, at least nominally (the United States wielded heavy powers there until the Cuban Revolution in 1959), while Puerto Ricans all became U.S. citizens upon the Jones Act of 1917. In contrast, Filipinos in the years after 1898 became citizens of neither their own country nor someone else's. To grapple with the changing identity of Filipinos around the turn of the century, it is requisite to return to Rizal. He, like Martí, did not live to see the eruptions of 1898 proper, but both men are indivisible from what happened following their deaths. Their names were invoked posthumously in war by revolutionary forces in the Pacific and the Caribbean because of the literature they had produced that processed and fueled the struggles at hand. Since then, Martí has been canonized every which way, including by Pete Seeger singing his verses in "Guantanamera" in the name of human solidarity across borders.[3] Rizal, in contrast, remains almost unstudied and unknown beyond his country and those scholars who specialize in it.

FRAMES AND TRANSPOSITIONS

In *Under Three Flags,* Benedict Anderson focuses on the European context of Rizal, who wrote the *Fili* (as *El filibusterismo* is tenderly called in the Philippines today) in various European cities and published it in Ghent (45).[4] Anderson situates Rizal and his second novel within trends in the political environment of his era, particularly the rise of anarchism. Noting that the Philippine colonial society depicted in the novel generally lacks correspondence with the historical reality of Manila in the 1890s but bears a striking resemblance to the Madrid of the 1880s that Rizal knew intimately, Anderson concludes that the author effects in the *Fili* "a massive, ingenious transfer of real events, experiences, and sentiments from Spain to the Philippines" (110, 121). Anderson acknowledges, however, that "Simoun is another matter altogether. He . . . enters the novel not from Spain, but from an imagined Cuba" (121). Anderson convincingly recontextualizes as European the historical space in which Rizal's Philippine setting emerges but does not develop analyses of the American spaces of that same nation-narration. This additional displacement of the Philippines in another of its foundational novels—Paterno also resituated the archipelago in *Nínay*—is critical. The paradoxes of Rizal, as of Paterno, are that he and his works are not one with themselves. The moment any posture on them is taken is the same moment in which they dissolve in their own contradictions. They are alienated from their own isolation. As a result, otherness in Rizal and Paterno, perhaps in the Philippines in general and in our globalized world by extrapolation, is always other than it is.

In the *Fili,* the mysterious protagonist Simoun enters and exits the novel associated with Cuba. His struggle is thereby linked with an independence movement long under way in a different island colony ruled by Spain. But his identity is not only Cuban, for both at the start and end of the *Fili* he is called a "yankee," a term uniquely identified with the United States (37, 345). Though these geopolitical markers are varied and unstable, their aggregate presence, as John Blanco notes, "cues the reader to examine the colonial question in the Philippines through the lens of the Americas" ("Bastards," 100). Moreover, flush in the middle of the book, Simoun appears to be doubled by an itinerant ventriloquist of sorts, Mr. Leeds, also dubbed a "yankee" and also a fluent speaker of Spanish thanks to his lengthy stay in South America (201). America in the hemispheric sense is therefore, symbolically, as much a deterritorializing presence in the *Fili* as is the historical European context signaled by Anderson. Notably, Southeast Asia is displaced in a third way as well, for although the plot of the novel transpires superficially in the Philippines, the conjoined Simoun/Leeds character produces a discourse that consistently invokes an ancient and stereotyped Middle East. In sum, the slippages that Simoun signifies equate to a transoceanic whirlpool of global discourses. His American body and its orientalizing projections are metonymic to a nascent national corpus that is, at the same time, a diverse world uncoalesced. As a result, the *Fili*, like *Nínay*, may be viewed as a foundational novel of globalization itself.

The American heritage of the Philippines was self-evident to Rizal's contemporary compatriot in Spain, Graciano López Jaena. An editor of the reformist newspaper *La solidaridad* (*Solidarity*), he announced in an homage to Columbus, "En nombre del pueblo filipino, brindo por América, enviando su más cordial saludo, su fraternal abrazo a todo el pueblo americano cuya historia hasta entrado ya el siglo presente, historia era del Archipiélago filipino" ["In the name of the Philippine people, I toast America, sending its warmest greeting, its fraternal embrace to all the American people whose history through the beginning of our own century was the history of the Philippine archipelago" ("Homenaje," 25). The legacy of Columbus in the New World, implies López Jaena, extends to the Philippines as well. Moreover, the concept of "America" here embraces not exclusively the United States but all the lands of the Western Hemisphere. After 1898, however, a more specific type of American presence began making itself felt in the Philippines with the impositions of the U.S. regime and of English as the new imperial language. The result, as Blanco suggests, was that "barely a generation after Rizal's death, Filipinos had already forgotten they were once a part of Latin America" ("Bastards,"102).[5]

The Philippines is the only Asian country to be governed first via Latin America (through the Spanish viceroyalty in colonial Mexico) and then, after 1898, via North America. Independence did not arrive until after World

War II. This is to say that the Philippine spaces in which to situate national imaginaries were never entirely located either in the islands themselves or, to be sure, simply in Europe, but also in the Americas. Through most of the nineteenth century, counterintuitively, Filipinos were not even Filipinos. Colonial society under Spanish rule was understood to have three principal sectors: *peninsulares* (people born in Spain, i.e., the Iberian peninsula), *filipinos* (people of Spanish descent born in the Philippines, i.e., those who in Latin America would be considered "creoles"), and *indios* (people of indigenous ancestry, i.e., those who occupied the position of the "Indians" of the Americas). Thus Anderson writes, "In Rizal's novels, the Spanish words *filipina* and *filipino* still mean what they had traditionally meant—i.e., creoles, people of 'pure' Spanish descent who were born in the Philippines. This stratum was, in accordance with traditional imperial practice, wedged in between *peninsulares* (Spain-born Spaniards) and mestizos, *chinos,* and *indios*" (*Spectre,* 233).[6] With Rizal, the argument therefore can be made that literally as well as symbolically, the *filipinos* of the *Fili* are not even Asian. At hand instead are colonial designations mapped after Spanish experiences in the Americas. And yet the *Fili* and the *Noli* are, as Victor Sumsky puts it, "for all practical purposes, the sacred books of Filipino nationalism" (237).

Rizal was born in 1861, a moment when broad-based independence movements had yet to exist in the Philippines. Colonial rule, overseen by governors-general sent from Spain but dominated by Spanish priests of various religious orders, seemed firmly in place. The signature event of his early life, however, was the Cavite Mutiny, a very brief and ill-fated local uprising in 1872 that jolted the colonial status quo. The excessive Spanish response climaxed with the executions of three innocent priests. This injustice, which would rally Filipino revolutionaries a generation later, affected Rizal immediately and throughout his life. His brother Paciano lived with José Burgos, the most famous of the condemned priests, and the entire family was stained by association to the point where they had to begin using their alternate surname, which was "Rizal." As Nick Joaquín writes, "The importance of '72 can be seen just in its effect on one person: Rizal, though he was only ten years old at the time. But because his brother, Paciano Mercado, was a disciple of Burgos, '72 meant for Rizal the childhood trauma of a change of name—from Mercado to Rizal—and the wound was obviously still festering when, years later, he defiantly dedicated his second novel [i.e., the *Fili*] to the martyred priests" (9).[7]

Regarding the rest of his youth, Rizal grew up as a native speaker of Tagalog, which was then just a regional language spoken in the area around Manila.[8] He mastered Spanish quickly, one of the few *indios* to gain such proficiency. In the *Fili,* notably, the Spanish priests deliberately suppress the teaching of their tongue so as to maintain a near monopoly on European knowledge. At the age of twenty, Rizal went to Europe for the most important ten years of his life. His polyglot talents and general brilliance were readily apparent and he joined forces with a group of hispanophone Philippine intellectuals of whom López Jaena, mentioned above, was one. In Spain from 1889 to 1895 this cohort produced *Solidarity,* the periodical that sought reforms in the way the metropolis governed the faraway archipelago. In 1887, Rizal published the *Noli* and, in 1891, the *Fili,* the second and third Filipino novels to come into existence. The *Fili* in particular, with its extensive space given to various voicings of all sides of the debates over colonial governance, landed him in trouble with Spanish authorities whose nerves and resources were already frayed by their increasingly unsuccessful efforts at squashing successive rebellions in Cuba.[9] Rizal returned to the Philippines in 1892 and was put under house arrest for four years, toward the end of which an armed revolution broke out led by an organization called the Katipunan. Inspired by his literature, the Katipunan named Rizal its president in absentia and used his name as its "secret password" (Rafael, 64). Rizal, however, explicitly abjured any connection with the independence movement and signed up to join, as a physician, a military expedition being outfitted to repress the Cuban revolutionary forces. This was not enough to save him. Although in July 1896 he was allowed to leave house arrest behind and make his way toward Cuba via Spain, the moment he landed in Barcelona in October he was imprisoned. The very next day he was sent back to the Philippines to await trial there. In Manila on December 30, 1896, a firing squad executed Rizal for subversion.[10]

A few significant oddnesses stand out in the background. Spanish, for starters, was never spoken in the Philippines by more than a clutch of individuals. Estimates of the 1890s colonial population tend to range between only twelve to fifteen thousand Spaniards in an archipelago with some seven million indigenous inhabitants. Very few *indios* had the opportunity to learn the language. A recent estimate is that under 1 percent of the population could read it at the time of Rizal (Rafael, 36).[11] Rizal thus produced in the *Fili* a novel so provocative on the question of anticolonialism that it would lead to his own execution, yet it was entirely inaccessible to the vast majority of his compatriots supposedly inspired by it. Moreover, he chose a Western genre, the novel, in which to convey his thoughts; and he did so at a time when an autochthonous novel tradition was entirely absent. The lone example of a previous Filipino novel is *Nínay* in 1885, but Rizal did not seem to have much respect for Paterno, and, in any case, a single predecessor text does not constitute a tradition.[12] Rizal's general adoption of foreign forms amounts to quite a different move than, say, writing on colonial issues in his native Tagalog and in literary genres indigenous to the Philippines, perhaps even attempting to do so in the premagellanic local script *baybayin*.[13] Paterno, at least, gestured in that direction on the dedication page of *Nínay* and in one of his character's oath of revenge.[14] The choice of language and script do carry implications of intended audience: there were virtually no readers for *baybayin* (the most dramatic option), some in the Philippines for Tagalog (still mostly an oral idiom at that point), but potentially all of literate, polyglot Europe for Spanish either directly or via translation into other Western tongues. The novels of Rizal are considered, unusually for any tradition, as both the start and summit of a national literature, yet the macrohistorical paucity of Spanish speakers in the Philippines means that very few in the islands have ever read them in their language of composition.

Rizal has long been converted into the leading national hero despite his lack of local readers in Spanish, despite his articulate rejection of the independence movement, and despite the fact that Simoun, his radical protagonist, dies at the end of the *Fili* in apparently just punishment for the errors of his revolutionary ways. And again, when sentenced to death by Spanish authorities, Rizal was planning to go to an ongoing revolution in Cuba not to join the forces of liberation but to lend a hand, albeit as a doctor, to those of colonialism. Yet it is this same antirevolutionary, European-educated, Spanish-writing individual who was marked as an *indio* in his own life and who identified with the American *indios* who had fought against their own conquest. As Blanco observes, "the name of Rizal's group of friends in Europe, 'los indios bravos,' ["the brave Indians"] hearkened to the Native American Lakota and Cheyenne peoples, led by Sitting Bull, who defeated General George Custer at Little Big Horn" ("Patterns," 21). In his literary and biological corpus, Rizal continually falls outside traditional binaries. His voice emerges multivalent, suppressed and suppressing at once. The *Fili*, in short, is the product of an *indio* inspired in Europe and by the Americas to focus a uniquely hybrid gaze upon his distant compatriots

and the colonial elite that ruled them. There are displacements and deter-
ritorializations here of unending complexity as the Philippines is transplanted and transformed only to return, differentially, to itself. This movement of there and back again never settles into either here and there, this
or that. The constantly deferred conclusions of scenes and subplots of the
Fili that frustrate many readers are thus amply representative of the inability of the protonation in question ever to be anchored simply in itself.

The complexity of colonized elites trying to write new states in imposed
tongues is hardly a parochial concern. Nonetheless, the canonization of
Rizal within the archipelago as national author and national martyr has
tended to reinforce a more local view of his importance. Successive Philippine governments have made this clear with such statutes as Republic Act
No. 1425, enacted in 1956 and commonly referred to as the "Rizal Law." It
opens as follows:

> WHEREAS, today, more than any other period of our history, there is a need
> for a re-dedication to the ideals of freedom and nationalism for which our
> heroes lived and died; WHEREAS, it is meet that in honoring them, partic-
> ularly the national hero and patriot, Jose Rizal, we remember with special
> fondness and devotion their lives and works that have shaped the national
> character; WHEREAS, the life, works, and writings of Jose Rizal, particularly
> his novels *Noli Me Tangere* and *El Filibusterismo,* are a constant and inspiring
> source of patriotism with which the minds of the youth, especially during
> their formative and decisive years in school, should be suffused . . . Be it en-
> acted by the Senate and House of Representatives of the Philippines in Con-
> gress assembled: Section 1. Courses on the life, works, and writings of Jose
> Rizal, particularly his novel [*sic*] *Noli Me Tangere* and *El Filibusterismo,* shall
> be included in the curricula of all schools, colleges and universities, public
> or private.[15]

The Rizal Law remains in effect today. All high school students, for instance, are supposed to be assigned versions of the *Noli* in their junior year
and the *Fili* in their senior year. Other state sanctionings of the novelist
abound. Every December is officially Rizal Month. Every December 30, the
day of his death, is the national holiday known as Rizal Day. The primary
urban park in Manila, site of the execution and symbolic center of the nation, is officially called Rizal Park and features an obelisk above his remains.

Although the *Noli* and the *Fili* are mentioned in the same breath in all formal sanctifyings of Rizal, in practice the first novel always receives more popular and scholarly attention. Its episodic plot is not directly related to most of the events in the *Fili,* its supposed sequel. Amid a broad diversity of characters and locales, the *Noli* generally privileges the story of Crisóstomo Ibarra, a young man who, in the opening pages, returns from studies in Europe to the Philippines. There he finds out that his father has died in jail because of dark forces that include local priests and politicians. These same forces now turn their enmity to Ibarra as he tries to build a school for his compatriots and as he renews his affections for his childhood sweetheart, the angelic María Clara. As the powerful conspirators keep up their overt and covert attacks, Ibarra forms an alliance with a mysterious man named Elías. By the end of the novel, the dark forces essentially have won, as Ibarra and Elías flee and one of them dies (the *Noli* is ambiguous on this point) and María Clara is condemned to a tragic life in a nunnery. This plot summary, however, is far more linear than the novel itself, an itinerant text that features a panoply of minor characters and subplots that have been endlessly extracted and transposed into stand-alone texts such as poems, songs, paintings, television shows, and web videos.

No analysis of length seems to exist that compares the *Noli* with *Nínay.* The coupling is always with its successor, the *Fili,* instead of its predecessor by Paterno. The principal three sentences on the subject are by León Ma. [María] Guerrero in his 1961 biography of Rizal, *The First Filipino* (the adjective alone renders Paterno invisible to posterity), which has been the canonical account for half a century now. Guerrero's analysis, which reappears cited or referenced in later scholarship by Schumacher and others, is as follows:

> The parallel between the two plots is obvious. Berto is Elías in the *Noli;* Carlos, Ibarra; *Ninay* [*sic*], María Clara; Don Evaristo [Nínay's father], Capitán Tiago [María Clara's father]; the ruin of Carlos, like that of Ibarra, is encompassed by a false denunciation of complicity in a rebellion; like María Clara, *Ninay* [*sic*] sacrifices her lover for her father and goes into a convent, believing her lover dead. The bare plot of the *Noli* is indeed reminiscent of *Nínay.* (130)

Despite such correspondences, Guerrero concludes a few pages later, "The resemblance between the *Noli* and *Ninay* is wholly superficial" (135). Pedro Ortiz Armengol adds, "Berto—que será Elías en el *Noli*—. . . Existen grandes diferencias entre *Ninay* (1885) y el *Noli* (1887). En primer lugar por la calidad de los personajes quien en la primera son rígidos y elementales, mientras que en el *Noli* hay no pocos caracteres—no todos—tomados de la realidad, con sus lenguajes propios, sus pasiones" ["Berto—who would be Elías in the *Noli*—. . . There are great differences between *Ninay* (1885) and the *Noli* (1887). This is due in the first place to the quality of the characters, who in the former are rigid and rudimentary, while in the *Noli* there are not a few characters—not all of them—taken from reality, with their own ways of speaking, their passions"] (211). Sometimes the similiarities of the two plots are deemed, as by Schumacher, to be a coincidental result of the profound influence of the contemporary novel *Doña Perfecta* by the Spanish author Benito Pérez Galdós (*Propaganda*, 91). Both Paterno and Rizal would have read Galdós, the leading novelist in Spanish of his time, prior to writing their own novels. And certainly, Rizal would have considered Galdós a far more substantive writer than Paterno. Nonetheless, a sustained comparative exploration of *Nínay* and the *Noli* awaits to be undertaken, as do so many other obvious investigations into Filipino literature in Spanish. Until then, the main pairing of the *Noli* will continue to be the *Fili*.

Despite its grim ending, the *Noli* is noticeably lighter than the *Fili* and rather more accessible. The romantic story-line involving María Clara, for instance, has received innumerable re-creations in the Philippines in all genres. The *Fili* is a much more bitter and overtly politicized book, and its dark criticisms less easily sidestepped. It is a harder read and its details are almost certainly less familiar to the public and academics alike, whether reproduced in written texts or audiovisual media. Nonetheless, the *Fili* stands with the *Noli* as one of the only two indisputably canonized novels of Filipino literature in any language, Western or indigenous. The prolific Ambeth Ocampo effectively underlined this reality in a February 2008 editorial in a major Manila newspaper bemoaning the lack of compliance with the Rizal Law: "Would it help if the 'Noli' and 'Fili' were available as graphic novels or short YouTube video clips? With the continuing decline in English and the nearly extinct reading proficiency in Spanish, how can we make Rizal's novels better known, better read?" Evident in these reflections is the will even now, over a century since the death of Rizal and over half a century since the Philippines gained independence, to employ the novelist in the service of constructing the nation. Literary analysis of his texts per se seems to be of remote importance. To be sure, any number of authors from colonized lands in Africa and Asia have been invoked in similar fashion.

Yet Rizal merits particular attention as one of the first truly globalized authors of the contemporary era.

PLOTTINGS

The *Fili* opens with what is literally and metaphorically, as its narrator metatextually observes, a "nave del Estado" ["ship of State"] that is "genuinamente filipino" ["genuinely Filipino"] (31). It sails forward with a population representative of the islands and distributed vertically according to their relative places in the local sociopolitical hierarchy. *Indios*, Chinese, and mestizos are stuffed below deck among the cargo while friars and secular Spanish elites sit in comfortable chairs above deck, "vestidos á la europea" ["dressed in the European fashion"] and protected from the sun by a canopy (32). As the focus sharpens onto this latter group, their discussion about how the colonial government should proceed with some waterway projects is interrupted brusquely by a strange jeweler. Identified by the narrator as Simoun, the jeweler speaks with "un acento raro, mezcla de inglés y americano del Sur" ["a strange accent, a mix of English and of South American"] (36). When he proposes that the solution to the argument at hand is the construction of an immense canal, the leading journalist of the colony responds, "¡Es un plan yankee! Observó Ben Zayb que quería agradar á Simoun.—El joyero había estado mucho tiempo en la América del Norte" ["'It is a Yankee plan!' observed Ben Zayb, who wanted to please Simoun. The jeweler had spent a long time in North America"] (37).

This opening appearance by Simoun is already unmarked in terms of a Philippine national identity and unstable to specific foreign ones as well. After all, although the conversation is conducted in Spanish, the local imperial language, the jeweler speaks not in Castilian (the hegemonic dialect of Madrid) but in an accent identified confusingly as both English and South American. Furthermore, the plan that he suggests, though characterized as "yankee" (a word spelled in English throughout the *Fili* rather than in Spanish as *yanqui*) by the *peninsular* Ben Zayb, actually associates Simoun not with the North America he mentions (a context that here is tantamount to the United States) but with the Latin American setting of Panama, where French construction of a famous pending canal was a global news story of the 1880s.[16] Simoun thus enters the novel not as a *filipino* (in any sense of that term) but as an American as that word is used in Latin America, that is, as someone from the Americas rather than exclusively the United States. As he will be revealed eventually to be a fourth-generation *filipino* (i.e., creole) as well as a revolutionary, his hybrid American identity seems to be a pivotal metaphorical displacement of the islands themselves.

That American identity is further complicated by successive passages in the opening chapter of the novel. The civil elite Don Custodio is scandalized by the canal proposal because of the deaths of many conscripted *indio* laborers that the plan would require, and so he "volvió la cara para ver si cerca había algun indio que les pudiese oir" ["turned his face to see if there was any Indian near who could hear them"] (38). Of course, the repeated use of the term *indio* is rooted foundationally in the misapprehension of Columbus that the islands that he came upon in 1492 were in Asia. And it requires a tremendous act of imagination *not* to map a furtive conversation among church and Spanish colonial elites about *indios* and forced labor onto the engrained pattern of such phenomena throughout the history of the Americas. Don Custodio himself notes the relationship by pointing out of Simoun, "ese señor, como es americano, se cree sinduda que estamos tratando con los Pieles Rojas" ["that man, as he is American, believes without doubt that we are dealing here with the Redskins"] (40). Further strengthening the identification of Simoun with the New World, Don Custodio sneeringly refers to him as "¡Un mulato americano!" ["An American mulatto!"], adding that he is an "Americano, se lo digo á usted . . . S.E. (el gobernador-general colonial) me lo ha contado; es un joyero que él conoció en la Habana" ["American, I'm telling you . . . His Excellency (the colonial governor-general) has told me so; he is a jeweler that he met in Havana"] (39–40). Here as well, Simoun appears as American in a diverse hemispheric sense. The Philippines whose cause he secretly champions does not seem embodied in him but in enmeshed lands on the other side of the world.

The particular American allusions at play are not internally consistent. Simoun appears to personify Mikhail Bakhtin's analysis that the protagonist of a novel exists in a "zone of contact with an inconclusive present (and consequently with the future) that creates the necessity of this incongruity of a man with himself. . . . An individual cannot be completely incarnated into the flesh of existing sociohistorical categories" (37). First, Simoun appears as an American oppressor of *indios,* of the "Redskins." Don Custodio perceives him to be a wildly procolonial figure entirely willing to sacrifice local laborers. Yet that makes it odd for him to jeer at Simoun as an American mulatto, that is, a person of a mixed white/black parentage and as such a member of a group suffering sustained repression in the United States in the historical era of the *Fili*. If anything, minority status in the Americas would be shared, albeit in different ways, by "Redskins" and mulattoes in the age of Simoun. This fact is recognized inadvertently by Leon Ma. [María] Guerrero, Rizal's principal biographer and translator in English (his version of the *Fili* is the one most Philippine readers have known), through his unfortunate translation of *indio* in this opening chapter as "nigger" and his iterated use of that word (9).[17] How can Simoun seem an exploiter of *indios*/"Redskins" and at the same time a scorned mulatto?

Put another way, in the opening scene of the *Fili*, Simoun is marked as an outsider in the gaze of *peninsulares*, but of what kind? He is a hemispheric American presence of some sort who, in the name of local progress, proposes the subjection of the *indios*, not their liberation. He appears willing to extend the oppressions of the New World to the Philippines—López Jaena saw the Philippines as part of that New World too, although positively—by sacrificing indigenous laborers in a development plan while maintaining his ties to the colonial governor-general. This mirroring of Spanish and "yankee" hegemony onto Asian islands, however, turns out to be a feint, for later in the rather jagged plot of the *Fili*, Simoun confesses that his plan all along has been to aggravate colonial conditions so much that the locals will rise in revolutionary fervor and smash the regime. He also admits to being Crisóstomo Ibarra, the creole hero of the *Noli* who had fled thirteen years previously. Exiled and radicalized, he has returned, resurrected, under a new name. The fact that "Simoun" turns out to be a pseudonym for a revolutionary determined to unify diverse peoples and overthrow Spanish colonial rule suggests strongly that he is a figure meant to evoke Simón Bolívar, the liberator of various South American lands several generations earlier.[18] Although Bolívar was successful militarily, his dream of a single national unification of former Spanish colonies remained, like that of Simoun, out of reach. Onomastically, Simoun in the *Fili* carries with him to the Philippines echoes of Bolívar's dreams and failures alongside all his other American associations: Yankee canals, South American and English accents, *indio* conscripts, "Redskins" and mulattoes and Havana connections. There is no easy one-to-one correspondence of any of this to the imagining of a Philippine national identity. Quite the opposite, the Philippines as a national project appears to be alienated from itself, transplanted in the *Fili* not only into the historical scenes of 1880s Spain (as suggested by Anderson) but also, via the array of mixed allusions and evocations, into the colonial and anticolonial dynamics that have marked the Western Hemisphere ever since Columbus.[19]

The Americas, however, are not the only global region to emerge often and erratically in the *Fili*, for the Middle East too proves to be a player as the plot unfolds. In fact, Simoun makes a habit of orientalizing, notably in the episode of Mr. Leeds that stretches over parts of four chapters at the heart of the novel. This sequence begins amid a reunion of nearly all the same characters (and their corresponding estates) who relaxed together above deck on the ship of state in the opening passage of the novel. There are assorted friars representing the ecclesiastical elite, Don Custodio of the secular upper class, Ben Zayb of the print capitalism sector, and Simoun. The subject arises of the ongoing fair of Kiapò at which "Mr. Leeds, un americano" ["Mr. Leeds, an American"] is exhibiting the head of an alleged sphinx (192). Simoun urges the others to see this curiosity but as they go toward the carnival, he mysteriously disappears. This causes one friar to harrumph about the "americano" and Zayb adds that that "americano" is an "amigo" ["friend"] of Mr. Leeds (199–200).

A fascinating conflation of identities is thus presented here, for whereas Leeds seems at first to be from the United States—the use of "Mr." rather than "Sr." (short for *Señor*) marks him as an "americano" from North America rather than South America—he next appears to be a sort of double for Simoun, likewise dubbed an "americano." The fact that they are friends and that one disappears just before the other appears suggests metonymically that they are essentially the same character, that Leeds in effect incarnates the American presence of the suddenly vanished Simoun. And indeed, Leeds's national identity turns out to be just as hemispheric as Simoun's. He is introduced as "un verdadero yankee" ["a true Yankee"] who "Hablaba bien el castellano por haber estado mucho años en América del Sur" ["Spoke Spanish well for having spent many years in South America"] (201) Like Simoun, this "yankee" is a hybrid phenomenon with associations up and down the Western Hemisphere. It is from these plural American spaces of enunciation that Leeds/Simoun produces next a remarkably orientalized staging for colonial consumption.

This staging involves a private performance of the purported sphinx head for the assembled church and civil elites of the colony. Leeds recounts to them that one day while visiting an Egyptian pyramid, he came upon a mysterious sarcophagus that contained only a box with some ashes in it and a piece of papyrus (203). On his pronouncing a word on the papyrus, the ashes metamorphosed into a mummified talking head (the "sphinx") who would tell a fantastic tale of how it was wronged in the ancient Middle East by a conspiracy of political and religious usurpers; and how one of the involved priests lusted hypocritically after the same virgin as the sphinx. In front of the friars and Don Custodio and Ben Zayb, Leeds conjures forth the talking head and it repeats this tale, which bears an unmistakable resemblance to Simoun's own complaints against Spanish colonial rule and his own biographical story. In other words, Leeds, a double of the absent Simoun, projects (presumably through ventriloquism) Simoun's own litany of anticolonial criticisms through an allegory relayed by another alter ego, the sphinx. Father Salví, a friar who desires the same virgin loved by Simoun, recognizes himself in the story and blanches in terror as the sphinx shouts "¡Asesino, calumniador, sacrílego! . . . te acuso, asesino, asesino, asesino!" ["Assassin, liar, committer of sacrilege! . . . I accuse you, assassin, assassin, assassin!"] (208).

The challenge to dominant classes from this "americano" (a three-headed identity shared by Simoun, Leeds, and the sphinx) is stark. Yet by the time the shaken colonial elites gather themselves and prohibit all further displays of the sphinx, "ya Mr Leeds había desaparecido llevándose á Hong Kong su secreto" ["Mr. Leeds had already disappeared carrying his secret with him to Hong Kong"] (209). Just a few pages later, Simoun reappears at the Kiapò fair "despidiéndose de un estrangero y hablando ambos en inglés" ["saying goodbye to a foreigner, both of them talking in English"] as a passer-by overhears the words "Hong Kong" (215). Although Leeds is not named here nor ever again in the novel, the foreigner is surely him.[20] The import of the whole episode seems clear: anticolonial criticism, unable to be voiced directly under the Spanish regime, has been issued successfully via the sphinx by a conjoined Leeds/Simoun figure of broad but unsettled American identity.

The geocultural projections of the sphinx emerge literally on a Philippine stage but symbolically from a theater on the other side of the world. This is to say that the orientalizing moments of the *Fili* are articulated not from Asia or Europe but from the Americas. This is an "americano" gaze on a stereotyped Orient associated with the Middle East but not with Southeast Asia at all.[21] Furthermore, it is a gaze produced for a colonial elite that aspires to dress itself in all ways, as the first chapter suggests, "á la europea" ["in the European fashion"] (32). Edward Said's influential *Orientalism* is concerned with the complex interactions of power in European discourses on the Middle East, but the case of Rizal offers the additional intricacies of an orientalism mediated by a quasi-nationalist from Southeast Asia who voices a contradictory subalternity from a variably pan-American vantage. The pyramid and sarcophagus and sphinx of Leeds are neither voiced from nor set in the Philippines per se, for the Philippines is essentially absent here despite the Manila location of the Kiapò fair.

Elsewhere in the novel, when Simoun is selling jewels to provincial colonial elites in order to raise money secretly for the revolution, he palms them off as "collares de Cleopatra, legítimos y verdaderos, hallados en las pirámides, anillos de senadores y caballeros romanos encontrados en las ruinas de Cartago" ["Cleopatra's necklaces, legitimate and authentic, found in the pyramids, and rings once owned by Roman senators and gentlemen, discovered in the ruins of Carthage"] (112–13). And when he reveals another collection of jewels, they appear to the ruling class as from "las *Mil y una noches,* los sueños de las fantasías orientales" ["*A Thousand and One Nights,* the dreams of Oriental fantasies"] (114). Such associations of Simoun with an imaginary and typecast but powerful Orient come to a head when he, prepared to detonate a bomb at a party attended by the entire colonial elite, appears "como el genio de las *Mil y una noches* que sale del seno del mar: adquiría proporciones gigantescas, tocaba el cielo con la cabeza, hacía estallar la casa y sacudia toda la ciudad con un movimiento de sus espaldas" ["like the genie of *A Thousand and One Nights* who emerges from the womb of the sea: he acquired gigantic proportions, touched the sky with his head, blew up the house, and shook all the city with a movement of his back"] (353). In short, Simoun, the clandestine *filipino* (but not *indio*) revolutionary, is intent on destroying the colonial ruling class but to do so assumes the persona of an *americano* (in a hemispheric sense) who associates himself with an Orient of sphinxes and genies in order to exert nefarious power over his Europhile enemies.

In this complicated global interplay of metaphorical agencies, what space is carved out for the Philippines as a national project? What imagined communities are implicitly constructed? There are no clear answers. When Simoun, after one of his several sustained disappearances, reenters the novel for the last time, he is immediately marked again by Ben Zayb as a "yankee" even though at no point does his biography place him physically in the United States (345). On the contrary, the last pages of the *Fili* refer again to his past in Cuba (398). Draped in shifting American signs while surreptitiously organizing a doomed revolution in the Philippines, for which he raises funds by promoting orientalist fantasies, Simoun is both Philippine and not, both Asian and American, paradoxically the foundational voice of a nascent national identity even as he is killed off by his author in the final chapter.

At the end of the *Fili*, Simoun has been wounded while leading a guerrilla uprising and subsequently has decided to commit suicide rather than be captured by the approaching colonial authorities. He succumbs to death by his own hands in the house of an *indio* priest, another paradoxical figure representative of multiple sides of colonial society, to whom Rizal gives the final moral of the novel: violent means cannot justify anticolonial ends, no matter how atrocious Spanish rule might be. Rizal thereby rejects the revolution of Simoun and, by extension, the American independence movements his Bolivarian name evokes. A few years later in real life, he would reject as well the independence movement of the Katipunan. This would not save him. In a case of life imitating art, Rizal, like Simoun, would die for his associations with anticolonialism. And this would take place despite his decision to participate in the same Cuban war as his fictional protagonist.

Asia in the *Fili* is seemingly absent. The Orient is present but only via the *americano* persona of Simoun/Leeds.[22] Europe is absent in geographical terms, given that the entire novel takes places in Manila and environs, but is manifestly and allegorically present, via what Anderson denotes as "space-time shifts," among the politics and preferences of the *peninsulares* and *filipinos* who form the colonial ruling class (*Under*, 112). Amid those dominant forces, the revolutionary Simoun is not a particular cause or individual with a fixed identity but a protean array of associations in which he appears as both antihero and hero, *americano* and *filipino*, orientalist and native. This foundational text of the Philippines, as Bakhtin notes of novels in general, "is plasticity itself. It is a genre that is ever questing, ever examining itself and subjecting its established forms to review. Such, indeed, is the only possibility open to a genre that structures itself in a zone of direct contact with developing reality" (39). The flux that Bakhtin signals seems appropriate to the globalized currents of José Rizal, the national hero without a nation who died for patriotic books his patria could not read. As Vicente Rafael has written, Rizal's own "position is split and unstable . . . eccentric to any particular identity and at a remove from any one position" (54).

SUNRISES AT SUNSET

Pedro Paterno was eccentric to particular identities too. He spent years attempting to pass both himself and his first novel as simultaneously Filipino and European. The globalizations of *Nínay* in 1885 presented a swirl of cultural and political powers that, contrary to authorial intent, offered no fixed national identity for the Philippines. Such instability is substantive rather than empty; it is fruitful rather than barren. Twenty-five years later, on the eve of his death and in a Philippines that had undergone an imperial paradigm shift, Paterno returned to writing fiction in order to explore the interrelations of foreign forces in an archipelago that he now lived in and not only wrote about from Spain. In 1910 and 1911, Paterno published a series of "novelas" ["novels"] of varying lengths known collectively as *Aurora social* (*Social Dawn*). Today, readers might differentiate among these texts as novels, novellas, short stories, and legends. It seems likely that the *Social Dawn* rubric was meant originally to apply to just three of the texts but then grew in the mind of Paterno, and subsequently in those of the few scholars who noted the series, to include most of his published storytelling in his final two years. It is not clear what made Paterno decide to revert to fiction so many years after *Nínay* launched a new, if largely unrecognized, novelistic tradition of national, continental, and global dimensions. He had spent the intervening two and a half decades publishing numerous texts on Filipino history and cultural subjects. He also had founded at least five newspapers in the Philippines. Whatever his motivations for the return to *novelas,* Paterno's production of new fiction was prodigious in its rapidity and quantity.

Much had changed since 1885. Paterno was no longer a youthful courter of Spanish high society in Madrid but a mocked, nearly forgotten relic in Manila. Rizal had superseded him completely in prominence, both in life as an author and in death as a martyr. Nearly the entire brilliant generation of Filipino intellectuals who had run the newspaper *Solidarity* in Madrid and Barcelona were now dead or sidelined. The Spanish empire to which Paterno had pledged an allegiance he belatedly retracted was gone. So was the Filipino revolution that he first had opposed and then supported. The United States had crushed both Spain and the independence movement. In correspondence, Spanish, Paterno's principal language of communication, was losing ground in the islands. In the first decade of the twentieth century, as the archipelagic military conflicts dwindled, the U.S.

government solidified its control of the Philippines with a systematic bu-reaucratic and pedagogic regime. Amid this recolonization, vernacular lan-guages such as Tagalog, Cebuano, and Ilocano were allowed to flourish in private spheres and in written media. Periodicals in those languages ap-peared with growing frequency. Meanwhile, in the official public sphere, governmental business was conducted increasingly in English. Many hun-dreds of teachers, known as Thomasites after the S.S. *Thomas* on which the original troop sailed, traveled from the United States to impose a new ed-ucational culture and lingua franca among Filipinos. As their students graduated, English replaced Spanish more and more as the common for-eign language of the island elite. It also penetrated nearly all levels of Fil-ipino society. Spanish never had been widely spoken in the archipelago anyway, so the anglicization of an emergent middle class and of the ex-tensive rural and lower urban classes was a dramatic departure from previ-ous imperial practice. The result of this phenomenon for Paterno was a radically changed readership. The young socialite who had written *Nínay* in Madrid for European readers was now an aging author in Manila with an audience potentially limited to the local speakers of a declining tongue of a dead empire.

Nonetheless, the texts that constitute *Social Dawn* are important. These are considered to be the first Filipino *novelas* to appear in Spanish since the *Fili* two decades earlier and make for compelling counterpoints to the global displacements of Rizal's second novel.[23] After all, America no longer was metaphorically a presence in the Philippines via the persona of Simoun but literally a defining force of the archipelago in the form of the U.S. col-onization. The islands were no microcosm in a symbolic sense but in a very real one as a Western hemispheric regime superimposed itself over rem-nants of the old Europhile classes depicted in *Nínay*. In the early twentieth century, that elite still clung to hispanophone aristocratic identities and so-cial circles even as Filipino languages and English were used increasingly as media for written texts in the archipelago. Once again maps were being re-drawn in the Philippines. And once again, Paterno sought to chart the con-tours of that cartography in his own way. His lifework as an author was dedicated to captaining a Filipino vessel forward, determining its direction around the world. The consequences of his late fictional engagements with globalization, however, escape his control via their inevitable incoher-ences. Even the vague sense of nationalism that pervades most of *Social*

Dawn takes on contradictory implications amid geographic and temporal settings that shift shape seemingly without end.

At the start of 1910, Paterno seems to have planned *Social Dawn* to be a simple trinity of moralizing stories designed to instruct young Filipinas on how to lead their lives. These texts were "La dalaga virtuosa y el puente del diablo" ("The Virtuous Maiden and the Bridge of the Devil"), "La boda moderna" ("The Modern Wedding") (also known as "Boda a la moderna" ["Wedding in the Modern Style"]), and "Maring, amor de obrero filipino" ("Maring, Love of a Filipino Worker"), all published in 1910. In a prefatory letter before the body of "The Virtuous Maiden" that also is printed before "Maring, Love of a Filipino Worker," Paterno writes the following:

De Corazon a Corazon.

Adorables GIRLS *compatriotas:*

A vosotras,[24] corazón de la Patria, gala y encanto de nuestra tierra, os dedico estas cuatro palabras, á guisa de sugestión, para señalaros la nueva orientación social . . . os muestro en esta **Aurora Social,** *colección de novelas cortas,* TRES CAMINOS *para gozar de la gloria:*

1.o El camino de la VIDA RELIGIOSA *consagrada exclusivamente á Dios, para vencer el cerco eterno del diablo, que esto significa:* LA DALAGA VIRTUOSA Y EL PUENTE DEL DIABLO.

2.o El camino, á la última moda, EN VUELO RÁPIDO, *para alcanzar las delicias de la vida. Tal es:* LA BODA MODERNA.

3.o El camino del TRABAJO CONTINUO, *para alcanzar la gloria del matrimonio, así dice* MARING, AMOR DE OBRERO FILIPINO.

Esos y otros caminos están abiertos, escojed. (unnumbered page before title page)

[**From Heart to Heart.**

Adorable GIRLS, compatriots:

To all of you, heart of the Fatherland, glory and enchantment of our land, I dedicate these few words as a type of suggestion to point out to you the new social orientation . . . I show you in this **Social Dawn,** a collection of short novels, THREE PATHS to the enjoyment of glory:

1. The path of the RELIGIOUS LIFE consecrated exclusively to God to conquer the eternal siege of the devil. This is what is meant by: THE VIRTUOUS MAIDEN AND THE BRIDGE OF THE DEVIL.

2· The latest fashionable path, IN RAPID flight, to obtain the delights of life. Thus is: THE MODERN WEDDING .

3· The path of CONTINUOUS WORK to obtain the glories of matrimony. Thus tells MARING, LOVE OF A FILIPINO WORKER.

Those and other paths are open. Choose.]

The tensions within this public epistle are abundant for a trilogy that seems to have as its goal a fairly conservative (if not reactionary) guide to modern life. The somewhat creepy salutation from a man in his early fifties to "Adorable GIRLS," which is what stands out first, hints at the prurient obsession with young female virginity that will mark virtually every text of *Social Dawn.* This virginity will be paralleled explicitly to that of the natural resources of the Filipino landscape, so that the heroes, heroines, victims, and evildoers of all the love stories read allegorically as contests among local and foreign forces for control of the riches of the islands. Of interest expressly sociopolitical in the open letter, meanwhile, is the rendering of "GIRLS" in English and the invocation of them as "compatriots." Taken together, and reinforced by such phrases in the next sentence as "heart of the Fatherland" and "the new social orientation," Paterno evidently conceived of *Social Dawn* as a fundamentally nationalist endeavor struggling to emerge from the recolonization imposed by the United States. Unlike the prolix historical and cultural studies of the Philippines that he produced between *Nínay* and *Social Dawn,* Paterno looks now to the future rather than the past for a collective identity. The premises of whatever foundational fiction Berto and Pilar, the outcasts in *Nínay,* might have promised for the Philippines under Spanish rule were now obsolete, at least in the political particulars, given 1898 and the imperial shift. So too were the specific social conflicts that Rizal engaged in the *Fili.* The priests had been replaced by English teachers. History in the Philippines had begun all over again. What a new dawn of colonization would bring was unknown, but that the future was at hand there could be no doubt. The problem for Paterno, however, is that he was really a man of the past.

Paterno, like globalization, is always out of sync. With justification, Pedro Ortiz Armengol describes him as "inclasificable" ["unclassifiable"] because, at no point, was he one with himself (207). The paradoxes in 1910 of guiding a newly patriotic indigenous identity for the Philippines via fiction in a bygone imperial language could not possibly be resolved. Although Paterno wrote *Social Dawn* in Spanish, as he had *Nínay* twenty-five years earlier, the whole context of navigating Filipino identity forward had changed dramatically. His readership now was not highly literate European adults but barely schooled Filipina teenagers. The dominant discourses at hand were not native to Spain or France but to the United States. The place of publication was not a geriatric imperial center like Madrid but a recently recolonized periphery like Manila. The intended political project was no longer to place Filipinos on a European map of the world, à la Magellan, but to place hispanophone Filipinas on the map of the Philippines themselves, despite the new cartographic drawings by the United States. Rizal had projected the Americas and Europe onto a Filipino stage, but Paterno, having outlived Rizal and the imperial shift, now tried to project the Philippines onto a stage run by Americans with props left over from Europe.

The Philippines in *Social Dawn*, as in *Nínay* and the *Fili*, emerges amid wakes and awakenings. The text that apparently launched the series, "The Virtuous Maiden and the Bridge of the Devil," is subtitled "Leyenda filipina. (novela corta)" ["Filipino Legend. (short novel)"]. The suggestion is of an indigenous tale that bespeaks an earlier oral tradition. Yet also here is a novel, a genre imported from the West. The text of "The Virtuous Maiden" is therefore reducible to neither oral nor written traditions, neither indigenous nor European forms. These irresolutions mark the story from start to finish. For example, Paterno asserts in the very first sentence that modern science has determined that "Filipinas formaba parte del continente asiático" ["the Philippines formed part of the Asian continent"] (5). Though seemingly self-evident, this is actually one of the least likely geographic frames that a Europhile such as Paterno would have stressed in *Nínay* or that Rizal would have underlined in the *Fili*. Paterno then quickly avers that in geological antiquity "separó del Asia nuestro Archipiélago filipino" ["our Filipino archipelago separated from Asia"] and that by ten thousand years ago, Filipinos were monotheistic worshippers of a god named Bathala (9–10). "The Virtuous Maiden" takes place, therefore, in a premagellanic age in which the Philippines was both Asian and not, both proto-Christian (this is how monotheism reads in the context of Paterno's oeuvre) and indigenous. In *Social Dawn*, the Philippines appears geographically and religiously on multiple points of incommensurate matrices.

The heroine of "The Virtuous Maiden," prefiguring all the other heroines in *Social Dawn*, is a "chiquilla tagala, virgen cual sampaga de la selva . . . blanca como un rayo de luna" ["little Tagalog girl, virgin like a *sampaga* of the woods . . . white like a moon ray"] (11). She manages the improbable feat of being white and Filipino at the same time. Her hair is blonde but she is "toda ella, en fin, divina y oriental" ["all of her, in summary, divine and Oriental"] (12). The various descriptions of the breasts of this young innocent and her successors in *Social Dawn* would not be out of place in soft pornography.[25] The bosomy white Filipina virgins who parade through the *novelas*, however, carry national allegories alongside the undisguised Lolita complex of the author. The *sampaga* is a white flower that always stands for the Philippines in Paterno and other Filipino writers, which is why his chapbook of 1880, the first volume of poetry in Spanish by any Asian, was entitled *Sampaguitas (Little Sampagas)*. The Tagalog virgin of "The Virtuous Maiden" is akin to the equally white and innocent national flower and the equally chaste Filipino woods. In Paterno, deflowering the nation and the nubile is always the same thing. The question in his stories revolves around who is trying to exploit whose naturally beautiful body. What appears to be simply a fetishization, consequently, has postcolonial as well as psychoanalytic implications. If the two theoretical approaches are merged, Paterno's fixation on the breasts of many *sampaguitas* in *Social Dawn* could be read as a meditation on potential founding mothers of a repressed national procreation.

In the literal plot of the story, one day while the maiden bathes naked outdoors, a strange creature materializes and swears his love. She tells him to prove it with the impossible task of building a stone bridge on the spot. He does so and she realizes that he is Lucifer. Terrified, the virgin flees to a temple of the indigenous god Bathala. Such moves are typical in Filipino literature in Spanish, where nunneries are sites of refuge from dark events for predecessor virgins such as Nínay and María Clara. The throbbing sexuality of this maiden sets her apart from those characters but not her pale innocence or her religiosity. When the devil pursues her and attempts to sack the temple, the virgin declares herself a priestess of Bathala just in time. The deity carries her home in a cloud and the furious and frustrated devil is converted into an alligator, "abuelo de todos los caimanes que un día inundaron la Laguna de Bay" ["grandfather of all the alligators that one day inundated Laguna Lake"] (31). Paterno concludes the story by telling his "amigo lector" ["friend the reader"] that this is the legend that every traveler will hear aboard the mail steamship in Laguna Lake (33). "The Virtuous Maiden," in consequence, serves the triple function of conveying the importance of religious devotion, the indigenous heritage of the premagellanic Philippines, and the origins of alligators in a particular place.

Despite its apparent simplicity, "The Virtuous Maiden" is unsettled in time and space and ideology. The temporal setting is prehistoric but, given Paterno's readership of "Adorable GIRLS" under U.S. rule, the moral is meant as a guide for the future. The geographic setting is both Asian and not. The heroine is somehow white and blonde and Oriental. The religion involves Bathala, a god native to the Philippines, but also Lucifer, who certainly is not. The legend remains part of an oral tradition (it is told shipboard) but Paterno transmits it through writing. The language of the protagonists is evidently Tagalog but that of the story is Spanish. Paterno still permits himself pseudointellectual asides, particularly at the beginning of the story, but the dramatically changed audience for his narratives has altered all the linguistic stratagems that previously were on the table. For instance, rather than explaining Tagalog words in footnotes, Paterno repeatedly leaves them untranslated. His readership now will understand them as native speakers. The footnotes and appendices of *Nínay* have vanished too along with the symbolic importance of their untranslated French passages and the hypertextual transoceanic jumpings among all the marginalia. Indeed, there is not a single footnote or appendix in any of the ten *novelas* in *Social Dawn* whose texts are known. The global forces in play now appear in the main body of the text. Before 1898, Paterno and Rizal had to conjure the intercontinental dimensions of the Philippines via their awkward positionings as Asian expatriates in Europe. This was a starting point inherently globalized. In contrast, Paterno now writes as a repatriate who does not need to prove that the periphery constitutes a center because, in the arrival of the United States and the displacement of Spain, the center itself has moved manifestly in and out of the periphery.

The second *novela* of *Social Dawn*, "Boda a la moderna" ("Wedding in the Modern Style") is dedicated "A las GIRLS Filipinas" ["To the Filipina GIRLS"] (title page). It is not a reworked local legend but a frontal engagement with modernity, to wit its subtitle "De Manila á Antipolo en Ferrocarril" ["From Manila to Antipolo in Rail-road"]. For a mostly agrarian place like the Philippines, going by railroad to an ancient pilgrimage site amounted to a striking juxtaposition even as late as 1910. Throughout *Social Dawn*, the presence of modernity in the Philippines is tied to the U.S. colonial regime via associations with novelties as diverse as electricity, airplanes, fashion, license plates, and democracy. As Paterno faces a present laden with such a future, he seeks to distinguish Filipino identity on its own terms. This puts him in contrast with the Filipino characters of *Nínay*, who emulate Europeans, and with the Bolivarian persona of Simoun in the *Fili*, who embodies the Americas in an attempt to spur a revolution of transpacific inspiration. Yet in the two passages in "Wedding in the Modern Style" that give name to the whole *Social Dawn* series, Paterno cannot help but convey the paradoxes of the autonomous national identity that he embraces. The *novela* opens as follows:

> *Hoy, que las costumbres filipinas han cambiado, dejando las mujeres su timidez proverbial y humilde resignación cristiana, en que nos educaron los conventos, místicos, para consumir no sólo nuestros bienes, sino también nuestra libertad, nuestro hogar, nuestra patria; hoy, que en todas partes se ansía la nueva* aurora social, *y se vive* á la americana, *hasta en las antíguas romanas Haciendas, hallándose tan de moda el* rapto *entre los novios de la* high life *de Manila. (5–6)*

> [Today, when Filipino customs have changed, with women leaving behind their proverbial timidity and humble Christian resignation in which the convents and mystics educated us, to consume not only our goods but also our liberty, our home, our fatherland; today, when everywhere is desired the new *social dawn* and people live *in the American way,* even in the ancient Roman estates, with *elopement*[26] being so in mode among the young couples of the Manila *high life.*]

This passage is hybrid and global in its confusions. The source of the changes in Filipino customs is not attributed, though evidently the replacement of convents (read Spain) with "la *high life*" (read the United States) is symptomatic. The imperial shift thus correlates to modern times, but does it cause it? Filipinas seem to be leading the change rather than subject to it. Who or what is doing the consuming? Is Paterno criticizing a culture of consumption or not? How can liberty be consumed like material goods anyway, and is that a positive thing? How can a fatherland be consumed? Does Paterno favor such consumption or not? There are no clear answers.

Paterno seems to welcome the social dawn and its emancipated women. And certainly, he always favored the high life whatever his geographic circumstances. But does he invoke Rome to suggest that current debauchery betokens an imperial collapse? Although Paterno writes to promote the dawn of a new Filipino future, a few pages later his narrator critiques "los que pretenden hacernos vivir aún á la antigua, á la *romana decadente*, vida rechazada por las naciones más cultas de Europa como son Alemania, Inglaterra y Francia" ["those who pretend to make us live still in the ancient fashion, that of *decadent Rome*, a life rejected by the most sophisticated nations of Europe like Germany, England, and France"] (10). In the above passage that is eponymous to all of *Social Dawn*, Europe and the United States and the Philippines interrelate in fluid, amorphous, and contradictory ways. In the process, olden epochs in both the European world and the Philippines seem to be relevant once again to the modernity of both. Such unstable macro crashings of space and time are customary in Filipino literature in Spanish and should not be written off as lacks of clarity or consistency. The irresolution is that of a Philippines and a planet that, since Magellan, have never been definable in isolation from each other. "Wedding in the Modern Style," whose alleged aims are simply to show young Filipinas how "alcanzar las delicias de la vida" ["to obtain the delights of life"] is an intervention in globalization by a globalized author from a globalized land.

The plot of the *novela* follows the trip of two strangers, Judit and Don Juan, who meet on a train heading toward Antipolo, the historic Filipino pilgrimage site. They gradually reveal their monied and modern identities to each other. In so doing, markers of national identity are alluded to with pride, such as the 1896 Filipino revolution against Spain. Judit even tells an entire indigenous legend of antiquity. It involves Bathala, which is typical whenever Paterno sets a narrative in prehistory. Amid the usual *Social Dawn* references to virgins and fleeting nudity, the train arrives at Antipolo with the two youngsters in love. They are determined to marry immediately but can locate no priest (the Spanish institutional legacy) or judge (the U.S. institutional authority) to conduct either a religious or civil ceremony. Judit declares that they should marry each other by declaring it to be so "ante el altar de María Purísima de Antipolo" ["before the altar of the Very Pure Mary of Antipolo"] (83). The *novela* ends with the narrator asking Judit if he can publicize the courtship. She replies that it would be a happy sacrifice for her to lose her anonymity, for in that way "por el adelanto de nuestro pueblo, ser yo un martir más *pro patria* ¡qué dicha!" ["for the progress of our people, to be one more *pro-fatherland* martyr, what joy!"] (84). She then exclaims how sweet it is to die for one's country.

The plot, in short, entails a journey in which a Filipino couple comes together via means of modernity (the train) and through national glories running from premagellanic to Spanish times. They are beholden to the institutions of neither former nor present imperial rulers but identify autonomously with a religious tradition running seamlessly from Bathala to the virgin of Antipolo. The story of the free-willed Judit and Don Juan is a parable of nationalism that will advance the Philippines into the future. This, somehow, is a martyrdom as well. Yet the name of Don Juan does not seem Filipino at all, evoking as it does a literary figure strongly associated with various European artistic traditions and a Spanish one in particular. The character of Don Juan originated in a seventeenth-century play by Tirso de Molina and reappears in *El estudiante de Salamanca* (*The Student of Salamanca*), a canonical text of Spanish romanticism by José de Espronceda that Paterno would cite directly in another 1910 narrative, "Leyendas de Antipolo" ("Legends of Antipolo"). In other words, "Wedding in the Modern Style" seems unresolvable into any particular nation or era. And that is precisely the point: Filipino identity cannot be reduced from the world. The inverse is equally true, which is why Filipino literature is critical to assessing globalization itself.

Whenever Paterno plumps for Filipino nationalism (an aim superficially absent in the hispanophile *Nínay* and never quite realized in Rizal's works), he cannot help but enmesh it with the global even as he proclaims autonomy. Such inextricability is evident in a monologue in "Wedding in the Modern Style" that takes up anew the eponymous social dawn that Paterno promised earlier in the *novela*. "Una nueva civilización anima al pueblo de Pasig" ["A new civilization animates the people of the Pasig"], he announces (62). The Pasig is the river that flows through Manila. He adds, "Hoy nuevos caminos, nuevos puentes, nuevas moradas besan las aguas del Pasig y su pueblo se ha despertado con una *nueva aurora social*" ["Today new roads, new bridges, new dwellings kiss the waters of the Pasig, and its people have awoken with a *new social dawn*"] (63). Yet the identity of this nascent civilization is unclear. Despite the pro-Filipino posture, modernity seems to have been introduced from outside, via the imperial presence of the United States, rather than developed from within. This association is avoided nonetheless by Paterno, who next waxes joyous that "Hoy no se quiere ir á Antipolo en banca, ni en hamaca, ni siquiera en carromata ó a caballo: se va en ferrocarril ó en automovil, ¡feliz quien pueda ir en aeroplano en globo volando! Así van, hoy día los filipinos, no quieren caminar como antes, sino correr, y si es posible, volar" ["Today one does not want to go to Antipolo in a dugout or hammock or even in a covered wagon or by horse: one goes by railroad or car. Happy is he who can go there flying in airplane or balloon! Thus go Filipinos today, they do not want to walk like before but run, and if it is possible, fly"] (63). The technology and speed of the *"new social dawn"* is surely indissoluble from the U.S. occupation. The de facto Spanish theocracy running the Philippines for more than three centuries prior to 1898 was hardly known for its futuristic leanings. Yet Paterno does not include the United States or its culture per se in his rhapsodic descriptions. Perhaps as usual he wanted to ingratiate himself with a prevailing power by assimilating to what he perceived to be its most chic elements while not losing his sense of Filipino identity in the process. The role of imperial model in his fiction may have switched from one nation to another, but Filipinos remain in his dramas as leading method actors.

In fact, a few paragraphs later Paterno extols any opportunity to die for the Philippines: "¡Matar por defender la libertad del pueblo!" ["To kill to defend the liberty of the people!"] (65). He adds immediately an indented, unattributed couplet: *"¡Morir por la patria: / qué dulce morir!"* ["To die for the fatherland / how sweet it is to die!"] (65) This, if anything, seems to present a resistance rather than adaptation to the U.S. occupation. It might even hint at a bellicose pan-Asian and anti-Western stance. Paterno cites approvingly the example of the Japanese who now were "respetado entre las Naciones libres y grandes" ["respected among the free and great Nations"] because of their "saber matar, matar muchos blanco rusos y morir por su patria" ["knowing how to kill, to kill many white Russians and die for their fatherland"] (66). The reference here is to the Russian-Japanese war of 1904–5, whose outcome stunned Europe as, for the first time, a militarized Asian power crushed a Western army. Paterno, in asserting a new dawn for the Philippines, thus seems to praise a modernity associated with the U.S. occupiers while decrying foreign domination itself. The message is mixed further: although modern Filipinos might be flying in airplanes in Paterno's head, they were heading to the same place they always did, Antipolo, the historic religious site that for Paterno emerges time and again as an eternal symbol of national identity.

Like Rizal and the *Fili,* Paterno and "Wedding in the Modern Style" are at once seemingly for and against modernity, for and against America, for and against Europe. In the monologue mentioned above, Paterno lauds contemporary Filipina women as strong and independent, unlike those of the old indigenous legends, but he constantly weaves those same ancient stories in and out of *Social Dawn* as a root source of collective identity. He welcomes the life options presented by the new era but gives his schoolgirl readership only three limited paths to the good life, as nuns, wives, or workers. These options correspond to the three installments of the original trilogy. Even his choice of language is inherently contradictory. His decision to write about Philippine modernity in Spanish is an anachronistic gesture given a geohistorical context in which Spanish was demonstrably a language of the past and not the future. The "Adorable GIRLS" to whom he wrote and whom he characterized as modern would be speaking in English increasingly as their lives wore on, not in Spanish.

Such contrasting forces appear also prior to the start of the third text in the original trilogy, "Maring, Love of a Filipino Worker." This *novela*, running over a hundred pages, is both the longest and worst written of all of Paterno's output in 1910 and 1911.[27] It is prefaced by fourteen pages naming all those girls to whom he is dedicating his work. The girls are categorized by their schools, each of which is given a mini-dedication such as "A las dalagas angelicales del LICEO DE MANILA conservadoras del Alma Filipina y adalidades del feminismo pátrio" ["To the angelical maidens of MANILA HIGH SCHOOL, conservers of the Filipino Soul and champions of patriotic feminism"] and "A las preciosas hijas del Pueblo implantadoras de la nueva civilización democrática en Filipinas" ["To the precious daughters of the People, implanters of the new democratic civilization in the Philippines"] (ix, xii). The conservation of the Filipino Soul and the implantation of a new democratic civilization are at odds with each other. Democracy did not characterize either the Spanish or premagellanic era. The idea is obviously an import from the undemocratic U.S. occupation, yet Paterno passes it off as an autonomous concept and endeavor. The original trilogy of *Social Dawn* is again compelling in its incoherence.

LANDSCAPES UNDONE

The exact contents of *Social Dawn* remain to be determined. "Wedding in the Modern Style" actually references at one point a different *novela* by Paterno, "El alma filipina" ("The Filipino Soul") as already having been published (21). This complicates the presupposition of an organic original trilogy. Meanwhile, the back cover of at least one printing of "The Filipino Soul" notes that Paterno has in press four more *novelas* belonging to *Social Dawn:* "Amor de Obrero Filipino," "Las Espureas," "Su Magestad LA

USURA," and "De la cueva 'Dampalit'" ("Love of a Filipino Worker," "The Espureas," "Her Majesty USURY," and "From the 'Dampalit' Cave").[28] The first would seem to be "Maring" under an earlier, shortened title. The texts of the last three, if they did see print, are undiscovered. The only commentary on them seems to be from Teofilo del Castillo y Tuazon and Buenaventura S. Medina, Jr., who claim that they consist of "native romances" and form part of a "collection of tales" known as *El Alma Filipina* (*The Filipino Soul*) (172). There is no known proof of such a collection per se, however, and the title here might be a confusion with that of the extant *novela* of the same name. Meanwhile, "native romances" is a term vague enough to leave in doubt whether del Castillo y Tuazon and Medina actually had seen the texts in question. Another *novela* from 1910, "En el PANSOL de Kalamba: Amor de un día" ("In the PANSOL WATERFALL of Kalamba: Love of a Day"), lists *Social Dawn* as a trilogy that, surprisingly, consists of itself, "The Filipino Soul," and "Wedding in the Modern Style." In addition, "Love of a Filipino Worker, "The Espureas," and "Her Majesty USURY" are noted as being in press. This brings to seven the total number of *novelas* listed at one point or another in 1910 as being part of *Social Dawn,* which various front and back covers subtitle as a "Colección de novelas cortas" ["Collection of Short Novels"]. Three of those *novelas,* however, lack proof of existence. Furthermore, two texts from 1911, "Los últimos románticos" ("The Last Romantics") and "Los heraldos de la raza" ("The Heralds of the Race") are also indicated on front or back covers of other *novelas* as belonging to *Social Dawn.* Of all these texts, the only known editions that have the prefatory "From heart to heart" letter from Paterno are "Wedding in the Modern Style" and "Maring, Love of a Filipino Worker," though it can be presumed that some editions of "The Virtuous Maiden" also carried it.

There are two works of fiction from 1910 by Paterno, "Leyendas de Antipolo" ("Legends of Antipolo") and "La braveza del bayani" ("The Valor of the Hero"), that are not linked explicitly to *Social Dawn* in known editions. "Legends of Antipolo" is also the only fictional text from those years not dubbed a *novela* on its title page. Mojares notes that an alternate title for the same text, "Los amores en Antipolo" ("Loves in Antipolo"), has existed too (*Brains,* 534). As for "The Valor of the Hero," it is one of three *novelas* written in response to literary contests sponsored by a periodical called *El ideal* (*The Ideal*). Its title page notes that it was "premiada con 4,137 votes del publico" ["awarded 4,137 votes by the public"] and was written in accordance with the theme "La Esperanza de la Patria" ["The Hope of the Fatherland"]. Another *novela*, "La fidelidad" ("Fidelity"), composed on the theme of "Mas leal que un perro" ["More loyal than a dog"], received the first prize in a different *The Ideal* contest with 9,156 votes. Although that story was published in 1911, the contest seems to have been held for symbolic reasons on December 30, 1910, that is, on Rizal Day. That year marked the fourteenth anniversary of the 1896 execution. A third *novela* from a *The Ideal* contest, "Haz el bien y no mires á quien" ("Do Good without Considering for Whom"), received 4,650 votes, but, as its text has not yet been found, its theme and year of publication remain unknown.

The overall difficulty of establishing which texts constitute *Social Dawn* has led to inconsistent calculations of Paterno's 1910–11 fictional output.[29] What can be said for certain is that *Social Dawn* may comprise as many as nine titles, only six of which are definitively known to exist and to appear listed at one point or another as part of the collection. Three more *novelas* outside *Social Dawn* were written in response to *The Ideal* contests, but one of them remains unlocated. "Legends of Antipolo" stands alone in a third category. It is also, according to Mojares, the only text in the series with a known translation, a Tagalog version in 1910 (*Brains,* 534–35). There may be additional *novelas* as well whose titles and texts are not yet known. Although the original trilogy was intended for schoolgirls, the anticipated readership of most of the other *novelas* seems to be adults. This would be the case with those written for newspaper contests. In fact, most or all of the *novelas* may have been printed originally, and in some cases only, in periodicals rather than bound books. This makes the recovery of the texts particularly challenging.

The generally poor quality of Paterno's writing in *Social Dawn,* the belated appearance of the *novelas* (Paterno had ceased being of political importance by 1910), the lack of translations, and the physical inaccessibility of many of the texts have left the scholarship on them minimal relative to that on the *Fili* and more or less nonexistent in absolute terms. The graduate theses on Filipino literature in Spanish by Sánchez and San Agustín do not mention *Social Dawn* at all, nor does *Origins and Rise of the Filipino Novel: A Generic Study of the Novel until 1940,* the canonical work by Mojares.[30] In *Brains of the Nation,* also an indispensable text, Mojares seems to allude to the series just once: "In his last years, Paterno . . . wrote undistinguished, Spanish-language plays and novels that became archaic almost from the time he wrote them" (64–65). Elsewhere, Ortiz Armengol adds obliquely, "Falleció en 1911, después de escribir novelas y ensayos diversos" ["He died in 1911 after writing diverse novels and essays"] (213).

One abridged version of "The Virtuous Maiden" appears in Reyes Soriano's 1965 language primer *Cultura Hispano-Filipina* (*Hispanic-Filipino Culture*) for the purposes of teaching Spanish to anglophone Filipinos. A longer but still abridged version appears in a 1976 anthology, *Literatura hispano-filipina* (*Hispanic-Filipino Literature*) designed to teach Spanish reading comprehension to students at the University of the Philippines; this time "The Virtuous Maiden" is followed by ten pedagogical questions about the content of the story. The same abridgment reappears in Edmundo Farolan's 1980 anthology *Literatura filipino-hispana* (*Filipino-Hispanic Literature*); again, albeit with a few footnotes and some minor font and layout changes (and also alongside an excerpt of *Nínay*), in Manuel García Castellón's 2001 *Estampas y cuentos de la Filipinas Hispánica* (*Sketches and Short Stories from the Hispanic Philippines*); and again in the Winter–Spring 2006 issue of the online journal *Revista filipina* (*Filipino Magazine*). No other *novela* of *Social Dawn* seems to have seen print in any form since Paterno died in 1911.[31] Sycip, in her graduate thesis, does spend four pages considering "The Filipino Soul" and "Love of a Day," but her commentary consists of plot summaries plus a few analytical sentences (44–47). A single article by Hornedo, one of the few scholarly texts to address *Nínay* seriously (if disparagingly), offers the only known three paragraphs of analysis of *Social Dawn*. After extensively summarizing the plots of "The Filipino Soul" and "The Heralds of the Race," Hornedo writes that Paterno "merely sees simplistically the political problem as a question of ethical rightness, not as a play of forces . . . his love for the romantic and sentimental plot that is generally so lean it fails to be convincing, is still there. His *costumbrismo* has somewhat faded into mere listing of ill-described places in Manila. But his moralizing has become more marked. He certainly has become nationalistic in a way he was not in *Ninay*" (398). This dismissiveness is understandable, for *Social Dawn* is not accomplished fiction in any aesthetic sense imaginable, but it does seem to miss the complexity of Paterno's attempt to grapple directly with a hybrid and unstable nationalism arising amid global political forces.

All of Paterno's fictional narratives of 1910–11 merit study along any number of analytical lines.[32] Among the most fascinating are "Legends of Antipolo" and "The Last Romantics" for their complicated interweavings of European, American, and Asian geotemporalities. The former stands out for its odd collation of three very different stories that take the concept of "legends" in divergent directions. The first is a legend in the most familiar sense and fits well with similar texts by Paterno. It is set three thousand years earlier in the age of Bathala and tells the story of a boyfriend who defends his girlfriend against a violent suitor. They flee to a magician who in turn recommends them to the lady of Antipolo, who salves them mentally and physically with medicinal waters of her baths. The point of the story is to explain the origins of the baths of Antipolo. The second "legend," in marked contrast, takes place in contemporary times and features a tourist in the provinces who asks his innkeeper for a local guide to a waterfall on a nearby mountain. The tourist, who apparently is from the United States, is spotted by the innkeeper's virginal daughter.[33] They promptly fall in love and hold hands. The guide, who lusts for the daughter, plots with her father over alcohol to throw the tourist off the mountaintop. This happens and the tourist is left for dead. The daughter finds and reanimates him and, as the story ends, they flee to Manila. It is challenging to square this conclusion with that of the preceding story. There a rural, ancient Philippines is invoked as the setting for a foundational indigenous legend that promises Filipino liberty forever blessed by the traditional lady of Antipolo and her healing waters. National identity is rooted in this eternal parable. In the second story, however, rural Philippines and its waters betoken a dastardly crime. Indigenous Tagalogs are drunk murderers, and the local girl runs off with the foreigner to live happily ever after in the modern capital city.

The third legend adds still more apparent incoherence to "Legends of Antipolo." In this metatextual narrative, Paterno himself is a protagonist. The tale begins with his wandering through a forest in search of Filipino revolutionaries with whom he will discuss further the peace, known as the Pact of Biyak-na-Bato of December 1897, that he recently had negotiated as an intermediary between the rebels and the Spanish government.[34] As Paterno pauses in the woods, he hears a murmur akin to fallen leaves and he quotes to himself a quintet from *The Student of Salamanca* by Espronceda, the above-mentioned Spanish poem about a Don Juan figure. Following the rustle of the dead leaves, he comes upon a spectacular crystalline fountain and, suddenly, a military general surrounded by a large number of virgins. The general and Paterno recognize each other from one of the Biyak-na-Bato negotiating sessions. To Paterno's surprise, the general declares that he and his family (all the virgins are related to him) now live in the woods beside a natural wonder. As the general explains:

—*Pues esa es la fuente del agua que rejuvenece y hermosea.*
—*Sonriendo contesté:*
—*Esta es la fuente, entónces, que buscaba Ponce de Leon en América, y no la halló.*
—*¡Cómo la había de hallar si está aquí, entre nosotros, en Filipinas! (47)*

["Well that is the fountain of water that rejuvenates and beautifies."
Smiling, I answered:
"This is the fountain, then, that Ponce de León looked for in America and did not find."
"How could he have found it if it is here among us in the Philippines!"]

Upon this remarkable exchange, Paterno drinks from the fountain and guarantees himself immortality. He also learns that "Las Hadas de Filipinas" ["the Fairies of the Philippines"] favored his work at Biyak-na-Bato and hears the surprising suggestion from the general that the Fountain be destroyed (56). After all, as the general explains, "Por buscar unas aguas semejantes, que rejuvenecen, Ponce de Leon, hizo esclava la Florida, y siguieron sus huellas todos los conquistadores de América; y hoy toda la América es esclava de Europa. Pues, Don Pedro, por estas aguas milagrosas, que hermosean y rejuvenecen, nuestra patria, será siempre esclava de las grandes Naciones; destruyamos esta fuente, para vivir libres sempiternamente" ["In searching for similar waters that rejuvenate, Ponce de León enslaved Florida, and all the conquerors of America followed his footsteps; and today all America is the slave of Europe. Well, Sir Pedro, due to these miraculous waters that beautify and rejuvenate, our fatherland will always be the slave of the great Nations; let us destroy this fountain so that we may live eternally"] (56–57). After thinking it over, Paterno agrees: "En verdad; fuentes de aguas milagrosas, bosques de maderas incomparables, minas en extremo valiosas, de que abunda superlativamente nuestro país, son causa de que gimamos hasta ahora en afrentosa esclavitud colonial" ["In truth; fountains of miraculous waters, forests of incomparable woods, extremely valuable mines, of which our country is superlatively abundant, are the cause for which we moan even now in humiliating colonial slavery"] (57).

This story is impossible to reconcile with itself, much less with the first two legends. In this text from 1910, Paterno fondly recalls his time in 1897 as an important personage when the Philippines belonged to Spain, just before the United States arrived and changed everything. The whole point of his Biyak-na-Bato negotiations was to halt an indigenous revolution and keep the archipelago Spanish, at least for the moment.[35] This was successful, for the pact resulted in a military truce and the departure by the anti-colonial leader Emilio Aguinaldo for Hong Kong. Corresponding to this nostalgia for imperial Spain, the virginal Filipino woods remind Paterno not of a Filipino poet but of a major Spanish author reminiscent of Paterno's own youth. He too had studied in Salamanca and no doubt, amid the autumn of his own life, now dreamed that the dead leaves of his last years would lead him somehow to a rejuvenating spring. Notwithstanding all this, Paterno the protagonist is also anti-Spanish. He empathizes explicitly with the Filipino revolutionaries and the general he encounters in the woods. He sympathizes with the general's point that Spain offered the world a tradition of enslaving conquerors. And in agreement with the profound nationalism of the general, Paterno concludes that the Philippines groans under foreign enslavement.

This marks an anti-American turn in the story, because the current version of that exploiter from abroad is the United States. The protagonists concur that the Fountain of Youth should be destroyed because of the great-power tradition of enslaving the Philippines in order to appropriate its natural resources. Such an argument, however, carries within it a stance that is at once allied with the United States, for the Fountain of Youth is a Floridian ideal that is now transplanted to the Philippines. Such envisioning of the archipelago as historically part of the New World was not unusual among Paterno's generation. An implication of his Fountain of Youth analogy is that Spain attempted to exploit the resources of the future United States as much as those of the Philippines. That is, both lands confronted the same conquerors. Along similar lines, Paterno aligns the Philippines with the New World upon declaring that "all America is the slave of Europe." Factually, how that made sense in the early twentieth century is impenetrable, but even metaphorically and transhistorically it is inconsistent at best. The United States would seem to be part of "all America" and therefore enslaved by Europe, not only now but also historically (thanks to Ponce de León and his successors), but it is the same "great Nation" that Paterno accuses of exploiting the Philippines. As for Europe as an enslaver, the young version of Paterno who wrote *Nínay* and, for that matter, the Rizal of the *Fili* so embraced that continent that they could not even countenance the possibility of archipelagic independence. The assorted implications in "Legends of Antipolo" for and against Spain, for and against an independent Philippines, for and against the United States, for and against antiquity, and for and against modernity create an unstable but vast force field of meaning.

All these paradoxes are true to Paterno and the Philippines and the world over. This is because global whirlpools arise from the wake of Magellan. It makes perfect sense that Paterno would drink from the Fountain of Youth to guarantee immortality and then accede to the logic that the same spring should be destroyed "para vivir libres sempiternamente" ["to live free eternally"]. That is, the promise of eternity must be obliterated so as to make freedom for eternity possible. History is fluid and so contains within itself both current and countercurrent. One reason why Paterno has not been nationalized as a figure like Rizal is that his contradictions in life and literature are far less easy to smooth out. There is no all-encompassing Romantic drama to make a century of citizens overlook Paterno's opposing inclinations as they largely have those of his canonized contemporary. If Rizal had not been executed for a crime he did not commit, if he had not begun his career as a struggling intellectual but as a high-society hopscotcher, then who knows what ambiguous roles he might have played in the post-1898 world? Would he too have drifted off into the popular imagination as an erudite nineteenth-century has-been out of touch with the needs of an agrarian and modernizing country? The entire Filipino population of the last hundred years and more has been exposed in every way imaginable to the *Noli* and the *Fili*, but relatively few people, including generations of local and foreign scholars, have read the novels from start to finish with the aim of lingering on their unresolved internal tensions. Almost no one today considers those novels as fictions that can be interpreted with the full range of analytical tools applicable to all literature. Instead, Rizal's texts have served as collections of fleeting details and subplots to be enlisted in drawing out the character of the heroic, martyred author and the country to which he is deemed metonymic. The whole point of the endless hagiographies of Rizal is to present a coherent picture of the man and the nation he putatively personifies. The unexpected advantage of Paterno is that, unread and unappreciated, his incoherences do not struggle to emerge beneath a larger saintly narrative. Posterity has pressed the *Fili* into the Filipino patria; the task at hand is to unpress it. Paterno, for his part, awaits impressions of all sorts to be made.

This holds true with what seems to be the final *novela* that Paterno composed, "The Last Romantics," about which there is no known scholarly commentary. It is the last narrative included in one of the known listings of the contents of *Social Dawn*. The dedication page is dated February 1911 and Paterno died on March 11 of that same year. He wrote the *novela* inspired by the disastrous eruption in January of the volcano inside Taal Lake, a few dozen miles southeast of Manila.[36] Over a thousand people perished in the calamity but "The Last Romantics" does not mention that mass casualty. The story focuses instead on the romance between the alabaster virgin Chilang and the impetuous journalist Andong, a youth of humble origins who grew up beside the Taal volcano. Chilang's father, who is associated with novelties such as telephones, electric light, and electoral politics, is an assemblyman who detests both journalists and the youth whose attractions have debilitated his daughter to the point of hysteria. The father is a contradictory emblem of modernity, for while he utilizes new technologies and participates in a limited form of democratic governance under the U.S. occupation, he loathes the idea of the critiques of a free press. A fourth character, a spinster aunt who believes ardently in Christian saints and priestly advice, is treated as a caricature of an old-fashioned religiosity obviously inherited from Spain. At one point she remonstrates Chilang for not having wanted to accompany her to church (15). Since the aunt is treated as a weak and comic figure, Paterno seems to satirize through her the legacy of the pre-1898 colonial master.

To escape both the paradoxical U.S. modernity represented by the father and, less directly, the anachronistic and empty devotions of the aunt, Chilang and Andong flee to Taal Lake in order to find refuge in his aged parents' island home and solace in "las viejas encantadas leyendas" ["the old enchanted legends"] of the lakeside (49). As they travel, their successive means of transportation imply a metaphorical trip backward in time toward Andong's indigenous origins: they begin on a train, then transfer to a horse-drawn carriage, and then finally ride over waters in a dugout. Symbolically, they journey thereby to a premagellanic past, an immemorial age untouched by outsiders either from Spain or the United States. This is not a halcyon environment, though, for Andong also describes "aquella pobre islita de pescadores tendida como una triste esclava medrosa á los piés del volcán" ["that poor little island of fisherfolk spread like a sad and fearful slave at the feet of the volcano"] (43).

As the couple arrives at the lake, the volcano is beginning to erupt. Andong's elderly father, who embodies ancient Tagalog understandings of the world, explains that "El volcán está furioso. ¿Sabes? unos americanos han violado su cumbre y se han llevado el *toro de oro*" ["The volcano es furious. Do you know? Some Americans have violated its summit and have carried off the *golden bull*"] (51) This declaration impedes any reading of "The Last Romantics" simply as a tired story of a virgin and a hero on the run. The Spanish word *violado* means "raped" as well as "violated" and so the Americans are, as in "Legends of Antipolo," charged with the aggressive appropriation of resources rightfully Filipino. The reference to the biblical story of the golden calf speaks further to a blasphemous disregard by the United States for the natural wonders of the Philippines while in pursuit of material wealth. The conversion of the calf into a bull perhaps alludes to Spain as the previous imperial power who did the same. The god at hand, though, is not an abstract monotheistic entity, whether Western or Bathalan, but a deified indigenous landscape. Strikingly, Andong laughs at the "ancestrales supercherías" ["ancient frauds"] of the locals (51). Unsettled again, therefore, is whether the heritage of Tagalog folk culture and the Filipino landscape is a solution to a collective identity or antagonistic to it.

The metaphorical rape by Americans of the Philippines appears contrary to the second of the "Legends of Antipolo" in which a U.S. tourist and a countryside virgin flee together toward the good life in Manila. Yet it is in keeping with the similarities between virginal Filipina women and virginal Filipino landscapes in all of the fictions of Paterno. The adjectives that he uses to describe his heroines are often identical to those with which he depicts indigenous flora and geographical features. At issue allegorically therefore is who exploits the paradisiacal natural resources and who does not. The answer, notably, keeps changing. On one level, Paterno's *novelas* read as atrociously sexist texts by a lascivious and untalented fifty-something. On another level, they are extraordinarily complex interventions into fluid spaces and temporalities and discourses that are simultaneously colonial, postcolonial, and precolonial as well.

In the final scenes of "The Last Romantics," the landscape is angry. The Americans have stolen the golden calf. And as the volcano in the middle of the lake threatens to erupt in full, Andong unties a dugout and rows Chilang across the turbulent waves. The canoe runs aground on a mixture of lava and sand. Andong, mad with passion, carries the terrified Chilang up the volcano while kissing her feverishly and stripping off her clothes. A "dulce grito de la virgen" ["sweet shout of the virgin"] is matched by a "grito del volcán" ["shout of the volcano"] and a climactic eruption in gold, pink, blue, orange and silver sparks falls upon them (55). The story, and probably Paterno's lifework as a novelist, concludes with "la isla, violada por el volcán" ["the island, violated/raped by the volcano"] and the two protagonists "sepultos bajo lava de fuego!" ["buried under lava of fire!"] (55)

It is an eerie climax, a suicide mission toward a doomed indigenous heritage. If *Nínay* and the *Fili* end with many potential national heroes dead, at least those characters tried to forge paths to the future. If they are crushed by larger forces, at least their efforts were tinged with promise at one point or another. In "The Last Romantics," however, the hero goes crazy as he attempts to project national identity not to the future but to a precolonial past. He runs away from the U.S. legacy (represented by Chilang's father) and away from the Spanish legacy (represented by the hispanized aunt) in a journey of return to a premagellanic era of old local legends, old local people, and old animistic attributions of divinity to a volcano. Yet these old ways lead him to death. The volcano violates its island just as the Americans violated the volcano. Andong sacrifices himself and a helpless virgin to the volcano for no apparent reason. He indeed is the last of the Romantics, passionate and unlucky and auto-condemned to an inferno. As for the stripped and bound Chilang, her orgasmic shout and that of the eruption once again reveal the female figure and the natural landscape of the Philippines to be the same in Paterno, an Edenic source of national identity that offers simultaneously salvation and death. This is the case with María Clara in Rizal's novels as well.

In the final sentence of "The Last Romantics," Paterno's narrator grieves, "¡Ay" at the fate of his nonfoundational couple (55). There is a profound pathos in this inarticulate ejaculation. As Paterno lay dying less than two months after the Taal eruption, the Philippines could turn neither to modernity nor to antiquity for its identity. It could turn neither to the United States nor to Spain, neither to the Americas nor to Europe, neither to Bathala nor Magellan nor Lapu Lapu nor the priestly orders nor the English teachers nor the Tagalog elders nor the revolutionaries. The Philippines was all these things and none of them too. The era before 1898 had provided but a partial foundation at best for a sense of cultural or political coherence across the archipelago. In that earlier time of Nínay and Simoun, the Philippine nation was not imagined as such. The seeming contradictions of the young Filipino novelists in Europe were therefore apt, for they mirrored those of history. As Alma Jill Dizon suggests of Rizal, his "novels exist as invented memory, helping to shape a sense of national identity that is itself, like any identity, shifting and tenuous yet at the same time powerful" (423). The same could be said of Paterno at the foppish start and forgotten end of his remarkable, and mostly unremarked, writing career. At the end of the day, the nature of the *Fili* and *Social Dawn* is not that of a Philippines or an Asia evacuated of themselves but of an irreducible heterogeneity in which all geopolitical imaginations are inseparable from each other, fused and opposed at once and slipping away the moment they seem to be within definition. Ever since European presences appeared in the Pacific from the Americas, the identities of all the lands involved became necessarily globalized. The authorship of the Philippines by Rizal and Paterno would be shared by many others after them, but the paradoxes they represent, honest to the undeniable hybridity of history, were then as now rightfully unresolved.

CHAPTER THREE

Globalized Isolations: Félix Gerardo's
Justicia social y otros cuentos *(193?–41)*

A yellowed manuscript in Spanish sits in the National Library in Manila. The typewritten pages reveal the author's handwritten corrections amid tiny holes bored by insects long ago. The title of the manuscript is *Justicia social y otros cuentos* (*Social Justice and Other Stories*). Inside is a seventy-one-page novella, "Social Justice," and twenty-two short stories. The author is an unknown writer named Félix Gerardo. The catalog of the National Library gives a date for the manuscript only of 19–, but the title story is date-lined at the end as Cebu City, July 15, 1941. Clues abound in the other narratives in *Social Justice* that indicate a series of composition dates starting in the late 1930s. The July 1941 date was less than five months before Japan bombed the U.S. air fleet in the Philippines. That raid took place just a few hours after the one at Pearl Harbor, another U.S. military outpost located on another U.S. colony in the Pacific. The war would end the so-called Golden Age of Filipino literature in Spanish. In early 1945, the Japanese made their last major stand in Intramuros, the old walled city in Manila where many Spanish-speaking Filipinos still lived. In the fighting, the United States assailed Intramuros relentlessly. Given the global forces at odds, *Social Justice,* though perhaps never read by anyone but the author, justifiably could be canonized as a major marker of prewar literature not only in the Philippines but also in Spain, Japan, and the United States.

The first-person narrator of the *Social Justice* stories consistently self-identifies as a Cebuano. He appears to be an alter ego for an author from that same central Philippine island on which Magellan landed. The recurring folkloric and bureaucratic scenes in the narratives suggest that Gerardo, the author, had a good knowledge of local traditions plus much experience at high levels of Cebuano civil society. The Book of Acquisitions of the National Library notes that *Social Justice* was obtained for four pesos with a batch of other books from the Malacañang Palace Library, probably in 1950 or just before.[1] Malacañang is the executive home in Manila of the national government, the equivalent of the White House. Somehow, after the war, *Social Justice* ended up there. This underlines the likelihood of Gerardo as being a significant player in Cebuano society. But how could Gerardo be completely unknown as an author and yet connected enough to have an unpublished manuscript, written in an old imperial language, arrive at Malacañang?

Prior to the war, pseudonyms abounded among Filipino writers, so probably Félix Gerardo was not actually Félix Gerardo. In 1977, a scholar named Epifania L. Magallon, working at the Cebuano Studies Center at the University of San Carlos in Cebu City, collected all known pen names of prewar local writers and typed them up in a small booklet. Sometime after that, she or another individual added in pencil the name of "Félix Gerardo" next to that of a man named Uldarico Alviola. It was the sixth of seven pseudonyms (five typed, two handwritten) listed for Alviola, a prominent journalist and novelist in Cebu in the first half of the twentieth century. Prior to the summer of 2008, however, he was not known to have written fiction in Spanish. Whether in fact he did currently rests on the two words, "Félix Gerardo," penciled in at some point long after his death in 1966 by an unknown hand.

The anonymity of *Social Justice* should not obscure its global import. At hand is a local writer from a periphery (Cebu) of a periphery (the Philippines) using the language of a former worldwide empire (Spain) to critique the social realities brought about by a new worldwide empire (the United States). This is literature marginalized in every conceivable way—unpublished, unread, unknown—that nonetheless constitutes a complex challenge to centers everywhere. Through its celebrations of persisting indigenous customs, the Gerardo manuscript creates a new center from which to evaluate a staggering breadth of twentieth-century sociopolitical phenomena and their transmutations. The commencement of globalization is at stake as well, for Magellan and Lapu Lapu themselves show up as characters in *Social Justice*, posthumously at that. How does their legacy metamorphose in this last great, if unknown, creative work of the "Golden Age"? How does the anthology reframe hybrid collective identities that are at once parochial and planetary? And what does it mean for world literature when a provincial Filipino writes fiction in Spanish during a U.S. colonization about to be smashed by Japanese occupiers? The questions emerge in waves, amid the international currents that give rise to *Social Justice* and spill over every shore.

The same could be said of 1898 as not a year but as a fluidity that spreads across all fixed spatial and temporal notions of fin de siècle imperialism in Europe, North America, the Caribbean, and Southeast Asia. A notable singularity of the artistic processing of 1898 in the Philippines is that its events and personalities have endured longer there than anywhere else as live subjects for literature. This is true even vis-à-vis Spain, where the tragic victory by fascists in the Civil War of 1936–39 trumped the earlier focus by prominent intellectuals on a presumptive national identity crisis after the loss of Caribbean and Pacific colonies. Yet Félix Gerardo was still writing about the transitions of 1898 past the moment of the Spanish Civil War and up until 1941. The inclusion of *Social Justice* in discussions of 1898 literature would challenge dramatically all existing understandings of the scope and meaning of that year as a global phenomenon. It is not nearly enough to add only the Filipino hero José Rizal alongside the Cuban hero José Martí as some sort of marginal author-martyr to be eulogized before getting back to business with such mainstream Spanish writers as Miguel de Unamuno, Pío Baroja, Azorín, and Antonio Machado. That does not change the basic structure of analysis because it leaves the aftermath in the archipelago outside the conversation. And perspectives from the Philippines are pivotal to revamping prevailing views of a world globalizing anew in the wake of 1898.

Empires thought dead in the supposed metropole usually have lengthy posthumous lives in the supposed periphery. The artistic imaginings around 1898 did not stop shifting form with the deaths of Martí in 1895 or Rizal in 1896, with the battles in Manila Bay and on San Juan Hill in the titular year itself, with the de jure but not de facto independence of Cuba in 1903, with the death of Pedro Paterno in 1911, with the self-classification as the Generation of '98 by Azorín in 1913, with the nationalization of Puerto Ricans as U.S. citizens in 1917, with the advent of World War I, with the death of the warmongering Theodore Roosevelt in 1919 or with the Spanish Civil War. When an East Asian empire arrived to crush a North American occupation of an ex-European colony of seven thousand islands in Southeast Asia, the phenomenon that is 1898 continued and kept changing yet. The story of globalization is therefore incomplete without consideration of how it produced authors like Gerardo. His ideas are remembrances of a bygone era in a bygone language that anachronistically suggest future, mutable, and incommensurate Cebuano and Filipino collectivities. He evokes a provincial, national, and global past whose dynamics of Magellan and Lapu Lapu are unresolvable and which he nonetheless tries insistently to resolve. His *Social Justice* filters the world through Cebu in the most faithful way, by never being one with itself.

The myriad paths of Asian literature in Spanish from the era of Paterno and Rizal to that of Gerardo and beyond remain to be followed at length. The few scholarly texts on the subject, including this one, are all woefully incomplete and replete with errors, mostly of omission. Part of the problem lies in the brutal macroscopic history of the Philippines in the century that followed Paterno's *Social Dawn*. Although the 1920s and 1930s proved to be a comparably peaceful epoch in which the United States made preparations to cede relative autonomy and, ultimately, independence to the Philippines, the advent of World War II changed all calculations of gradualism. Japan occupied the islands for more than three years and slaughtered countless civilians as well as allied Filipino and U.S. troops in the process; the Bataan Death March of captured soldiers, which took place to the northwest of Manila Bay, was one of the lowlights. The unnecessary decision by Douglas MacArthur to fight the main Japanese force in the Philippines rather than Taiwan resulted in the obliteration of Manila and, in particular, its old Spanish town and many Spanish-speaking residents.[2] Among other effects, World War II further globalized an already global country as the Philippines endured the rare distinction of being colonized first by a European empire, then an American empire, and then an Asian empire. This is to say that Filipino history is also Spanish history, also U.S. history, also Japanese history. The oldest university in the United States, to take one example, was not always Harvard. From 1898 until World War II it was the University of Santo Tomás in Manila, a fact evident to those U.S. citizens held by the Japanese military in campus buildings that became internment camps. Harvard University was founded in 1636 but the University of Santo Tomás was launched in 1611, before the Pilgrims arrived in Massachusetts.

The United States allowed the Philippines to become independent soon after the war, unlike Guam and Puerto Rico, which were also possessions taken from Spain in 1898. The new nation struggled in the second half of the twentieth century under the egregious Marcos dictatorship and the massive, continuous corruption of its ruling classes. The country often leads the world in the assassinations of journalists. With a history like that, the conditions for research on Filipino literature in Spanish have not been optimal. Numerous potential researchers and students died in one catastrophe or another. Others were exiled or jailed or murdered. Meanwhile, the financial capital to fund intellectual endeavors has flowed in other directions. The physical plants of university and public and private libraries often have been destroyed, their old books and periodicals in Spanish turned to ashes and dust. Of those that remain, the infrastructure of information technology for both preservation and dissemination is minimal. Important holdings, such as those at the Cebuano Studies Center and the López Library in Manila, are offline and rely on aged card catalogs that have to be consulted in person. Due to lack of consistent air conditioning, many books and theses in the National Library are simply rotting away in the tropical heat and humidity. Rich nations with stable histories do not necessarily afford many research opportunities to scholars, but poor countries buffeted by decades of war and dictatorship are less likely to do so. The Philippines is one such place.

Nonetheless, throughout the twentieth century, scholarly texts on Filipino literature in Spanish were written in isolated moments. Not one of them is in print. All consist primarily of biographical blurbs about authors, plot and style summaries, and short attempts at periodization. As such, they are invaluable as bibliographic resources. Most if not all, however, are guided by imperial nostalgia passed off as patriotism. There is little literary analysis per se. The majority of the texts were not published and reside only in forgotten corners of one Manila library or another. Many have never been seen outside the country. Moreover, the data in much of the scholarship often cannot be corroborated, for Filipino literature in Spanish usually found outlet not in books but in newspapers and magazines that since have disappeared. It is common for the secondary sources to list creative writers of whom there survives no known example of their works. It is also common for publication dates to be inaccurate and for quantitative conclusions to be miscalculated, usually undercalculated. Research in Manila shows, for example, that there were more Filipino novels in Spanish than any extant scholarly text declares. Each of the unmentioned but surviving novels diversifies the understanding of the tradition to date. For instance, the text of the only known Filipino science fiction novel in Spanish, *La creación* (*The Creation*) by Mariano L. De la Rosa in 1959, was found only in 2008. There are certainly more short stories, poems, and novellas than any scholar has documented. Most of these texts circulated in periodicals that have never been methodically searched or indexed. The challenge of discovery is complicated by the reality that these sorts of materials, when held by university libraries in the Philippines, are occasionally dumped into an irregular, obscured, and quasi-random used-book market in the name of creating shelf space for newer books.

Any study of the emergence of Asian literature in Spanish has to take account not only of the inaugurating figures of Paterno and Rizal but also of this bibliographic context in which creative writings will continue to appear as long as anyone makes a point of looking for them. Whole swaths of Filipino literature in Spanish remain to be discovered or, at the very least, acknowledged to exist. A pre–World War II author such as Félix Gerardo, though a late contributor to the cultural phenomenon, is therefore an emergent figure just as much as his pre-1898 predecessors, albeit in a different sense. As the fictional, poetic, and theatrical texts of different twentieth-century writers come to the fore, the history of Asian Hispanic literature will have to be altered accordingly. Among the constant reappraisals that will be necessary is of the idea of a "Golden Age" that surfaced among various scholars who, decades ago, attempted to periodize Filipino literature in Spanish.

ACCOUNTINGS OF APPEARANCES

This presumptive Golden Age started, depending on the critic consulted, around the turn of the nineteenth century and ended with the onslaught of World War II and the Japanese occupation of the archipelago. Such periodizations try to account for an apparently asymmetrical literary history in which Rizal's *Noli me tangere* of 1887 and *El filibusterismo* of 1891 seem to stand alone in space-time as the greatest works of Filipino literature in any language, followed in importance within hispanophone circles only several decades later by a surge of renowned poets. Of those creative writers who were contemporary to Rizal, Paterno tends to be ignored as a novelist even when remembered as a politician. Meanwhile, single-sentence acknowledgments in the extant academic criticism are often the lot, at best, of the Spanish-language poets of the Filipino revolution against Spain and then the United States at the turn of the century. The most esteemed of them, Fernando María Guerrero (1873–1932), was largely forgotten thereafter except via his nephew, León Ma. [María] Guerrero, who became the canonical Rizalian biographer and translator of the second half of the twentieth century.[3] Whether based in Europe or the Philippines, the journalists, essayists, and polemicists of the 1880s and 1890s who wrote in Spanish are always granted in literary histories to be talented prose writers, but the dearth of their fictional, poetic, and theatrical output has relegated their work mostly to scholars in social science fields.

This leaves any periodizer of the Golden Age with the challenge of including in it the *Noli*, the *Fili*, and some of Rizal's poetry, and then jumping to the rather later verses of Claro M. Recto (1890–1960), Jesús Balmori (1886–1948), Manuel Bernabé (1890–1960), Cecilio Apóstol (1877–1938), Flavio Zaragoza Cano (1892–1969), and many others.[4] This acme of Filipino literature deserves study alongside the poetic renaissance of that time throughout the Spanish-speaking world, from Pablo Neruda and César Vallejo in Latin America to Federico García Lorca, Rafael Alberti, Pedro Salinas, Luis Cernuda, Vicente Aleixandre, and others in pre–Civil War Spain. The issue in the local context, however, is that such a Golden Age encompasses more or less the entire run of Filipino literature in Spanish: there is no other age against which to posit a golden one. The other taxonomic option is to dub as gilded only the flurry of accomplished Filipino poetry in Spanish from the mid-1910s through the early 1930s. This was a relatively coherent phenomenon in which the major authors knew and read each other and engaged in live poetic competitions known as *balagtasan*. Yet since there is universal agreement that Rizal's oeuvre dwarfs in talent and importance the output of these later writers, quantity rather than quality, and insularity instead of influence, would become then the unusual hallmark of this particular Golden Age.

In any case, the rubric itself is laced with oddities in a Filipino setting. It is a rare golden age of literature that develops in an increasingly isolated language. Whatever the time span chosen, the period correlates closely to the era of U.S. occupation. As noted in chapter 2, very few Filipinos could read Spanish in the earlier time of Rizal. Unlike in Latin America, the priests in the Philippines made efforts for centuries to suppress the dissemination of their tongue and thereby of the European knowledges that it could convey. When proselytizing and preaching, the friars attempted to use indigenous languages instead. An educational reform law in 1863 finally led to the more widespread teaching of Spanish in the Philippines. Its effects coincided with the new trend of Filipino men such as Paterno and Rizal making their way to Spain. The combined result was a young, generally elite population in the last third of the nineteenth century that was literate in Spanish. Yet just at the moment when this group was beginning to produce a serious artistic tradition in that language, the United States invaded.

Shortly after the imperial shift of 1898, Filipinos began publishing creative works in diverse vernaculars and, eventually, in English, which grew to be a far more widespread tongue in the islands than Spanish ever was. Meanwhile, the generation of hispanophone Filipinos educated between the 1863 educational reforms and the 1898 takeover found themselves being sidelined by history. Their children might grow up speaking Spanish at home but would use English in schools and various official spheres and an indigenous language (Tagalog, Cebuano, Ilocano, etc.) among friends and in sundry informal environments. The children's children would know or utilize Spanish still less. The generation of Filipinos born before 1898 would arrive at maturity inspired to write poetry and novels in a language understandable by a public that literally was dying off. The authors and readers of the Golden Age who were not killed in World War II had few years left in any case in which to sustain a tradition whose productive apex, unusually, occurred at the same moment as its chronological decline. Had it not been for the obliteration of Intramuros, a community of Spanish speakers might have maintained itself for many decades more in Manila and even in smaller cities elsewhere in the archipelago, but the critical mass necessary to ensure the continuous circulation of new creative works in printed media in Spanish was destroyed by the war.[5]

The anachronisms implicit in a Filipino "Golden Age" extend to its evocation of the "Siglo de Oro" ("Century of Gold," usually translated in English as "Golden Age") of Spain. This term traditionally has referred to the wealth of canonical literature, including *Don Quijote,* that was produced in the peninsula after 1492 and upon the conquest of a New World that, perhaps counterintuitively, comprised Magellan and the Philippines as well as the Western Hemisphere.[6] The Siglo de Oro developed at the height of, and in the heart of, the Spanish empire. In contrast, the Golden Age of Filipino literature in Spanish took place several decades after that same empire had collapsed and on the margins of a national history that had moved on definitively to other languages and other concerns. The only Filipino writer who can stand with Cervantes in the sense of an undisputed national author is Rizal. But again, if he is included in the Golden

Age, then the rubric is virtually coterminous with the full sweep of Filipino literature in Spanish.

Despite the limitations of existing scholarship, such efforts offer significant listings of authors and titles. This information is collected nowhere else. Much of it will remain forever the only record of some fiction, poetry, and drama. The surnames and texts mentioned in the assorted graduate theses and language primers and self-published or conventionally published books are a necessary starting point for forthcoming investigations, whether such research is done on foot in the Philippines or in archives around the world. Illustrative here is the case of *81 Years of Premio Zóbel: A Legacy of Philippine Literature in Spanish* by Lourdes Castrillo Brillantes. The annual Zóbel Prize for the most accomplished Filipino literature in Spanish was launched at the start of the 1920s in order to stave off the decline of the language as a written medium in the archipelago. Over the decades, other contests for literature in Spanish were organized by various parties, but the Zóbel became the most prestigious. This is not to say, however, that it survived the century intact. Although the prize was granted in 1922 and then annually from 1924 onward, World War II and its aftermath put an end to the entire contest from 1942 to 1952. The competition resumed in 1953 but from 1967 to 1973 was stopped yet again, this time because there were no longer enough authors to make a Spanish literary contest viable.[7] In 1974, the Zóbel rules were changed so that anyone in the Philippines who promoted the Spanish language could become a potential prizewinner. Among the consequences of this decision was the awarding of the Zóbel in 1993 to Blas Ople y Fajardo, an important senator who did not know any Spanish at all.

As of 2000, the contest was stopped altogether as Georgina Padilla y Zóbel, granddaughter of the contest founder, decided to invest her capital instead in a book commemorating her family and the prize. She commissioned Brillantes, a professor of Spanish at the University of the Philippines who had received the award in 1998, to put together a volume based on material that the Zóbel family had collected over the years (prizewinning texts, newspaper clippings announcing the awardees, and so forth), related documents stored at a private library founded by the family, and information from past recipients and their relatives.[8] The Cervantes Institute, a cultural arm of the Spanish government, helped fund the project, which was published in Spanish as *80 años del Premio Zóbel* (*80 Years of the Zóbel Prize*) in 2000. This first version of the book, notwithstanding its uniqueness, was not put on sale. It thus remained nearly as inaccessible as Padilla y Zóbel's trove of documents, to which only Brillantes has been allowed access.

By contrast, Brillantes's self-translation into English that was published in 2006 is now sold in every major bookstore in Manila. It is the lone source on twentieth-century Filipino literature in Spanish that is readily available to the public. The contents include a history of the Zóbel family and the competition plus biographical and textual details regarding every awardee. Such information is of immeasurable value, particularly the frequent lists of authors and texts that vied for the annual honor and did not receive it. Those names and titles will be the infrastructure of the fuller accounting of Filipino literature in Spanish that remains to be attempted. The book does, however, reflect its origins. The hagiographic tone toward the Zóbel family was probably inevitable, given how the book was commissioned and funded. The data are rich and compelling but also at times a bit inaccurate, again an ineluctable consequence of source materials being restricted to archives overseen by the commissioning family and to documents and interviews offered by award recipients and their families.[9] Scholars will depend on *81 Years of Premio Zóbel* for decades thanks to its availability and thoroughness, but the text fits with the erratic history of earlier graduate theses and self-published books as being worthwhile primarily as a starting point for the construction of analysis rather than as intellectual argument per se.

Most of the contours of Asian fiction in Spanish after Paterno and Rizal are not yet queried. Nor are their connections to the dynamics of globalization begun by Magellan and Lapu Lapu centuries earlier. The Golden Age in particular, if posited to exist, needs to assimilate to its conclusion the unheralded production of Gerardo's *Social Justice*. Paterno's *Social Dawn* of 1910–11 allegedly ended the two-decade long drought of Filipino novels in Spanish that followed the publication of the *Fili* in 1891. The Paterno *novelas* also marked a shift in the place of the production of fiction from Europe to the Philippines. The geographic movement of poetry took place earlier as *Sampaguitas,* the 1880 volume of verse published by Paterno in Madrid, yielded to the works of Fernando María Guerrero and the other poets who, in the Philippines, penned in Spanish during the fin de siècle revolution against Spain and the United States. The early swell of poetry relative to novels was abetted by the macroscopic historical and economic conditions in effect around the turn of the century. The end of the periodical *Solidarity* in 1895 as a general organ of the expatriate intellectuals in

Spain, the deaths of Rizal (who probably would have continued writing novels in one language or another), Graciano López Jaena, and Marcelo H. [Hilario] del Pilar in 1896, the indigenous revolution in the archipelago that contested two empires, the end of the Spanish colonization and the start of the U.S. colonization in 1898, all disfavored the appearance of long, complicated works that might require time, resources, and relative stability to produce. The rapidly changing, turbulent world of Filipinos in the late 1890s and early 1900s seems more propitious to shorter creative forms open to topicality and speed of composition.

This context began to change as the Philippines settled into its neocolonial status under the United States. Although the appearance of *Social Dawn* in 1910 has been ignored by most literary historians, that same year has been accepted anyway as the resumption of a Filipino tradition of novels in Spanish because of the publication of *Bancarrota de almas* (*Bankruptcy of Souls*) by Jesús Balmori.[10] The author would become more famous as a poet and win the Zóbel in 1926, but *Bankruptcy of Souls,* followed by his *Se deshojó la flor* (*The Flower Was Stripped*) in 1915, are widely and inaccurately considered the fourth and fifth Filipino novels in Spanish after Paterno's *Nínay* (1885) and the two Rizal texts.[11] Florentino Hornedo, in his "Notes on the Filipino Novel in Spanish," an article from 1980 of forty pages that is the sole known monograph on the subject, identifies other novelists as Antonio Abad, Estanislao Alinea, Enrique Centenera, Cesar Mercader, Miguel Ripoll, Rafael Ripoll, and Anastacio Teodoro. The remarkable thing about this list, which may be based largely on a 1964 literary history by Alinea, is that as of 2012 there are no known texts of novels by five of those six individuals.[12] The majority of them probably were serialized in periodicals and never appeared as bound books.[13] The exception is Abad, who wrote four novels. He is generally considered the greatest of the twentieth-century Filipino fiction writers in Spanish and, with *La vida secreta de Daniel Espeña* (*The Secret Life of Daniel Espeña*) in 1960, the last major contributor to the tradition. Mariñas considers Abad's *La oveja de Nathán* (*Nathan's Sheep*), a Zóbel winner in 1929, to be "posiblemente, la cumbre de la novela filipina en nuestro idioma y superior por valor literario a las publicadas antes o después" ["possibly the summit of the Filipino novel in our language and superior in its literary value to those published before or after"] (58). This elogium would appear to be the only one in history that considers placing any Filipino novel in Spanish above those by Rizal. Alinea judges *El campeón* (*The Champion*) by Abad to be the "novela máxima del

'Periodo de Oro'" ["greatest novel of the 'Golden Age'"] (95).[14] Abad was from Cebu, like Félix Gerardo, and often wrote in Cebuano, but he is usually identified as a national rather than regional writer because of his many years in Manila. Meanwhile, many novelists whose texts are definitively extant were apparently unknown by Hornedo, including Félix Gerardo. If the texts of *Social Dawn* qualify as novels, which is a position taken by Hornedo, then so does the title narrative of *Social Justice*. Overlooked too have been Mariano L. De la Rosa, various winners and contestants of the Zóbel competition, and probably numerous others.

This history of Filipino novels in Spanish needs to be complicated yet further. Although Paterno dubbed the 1910–11 texts of *Social Dawn* as *novelas*, most are significantly shorter and less multifaceted than that amorphous term usually suggests. Other writers published fiction of at least the same extension and development that circulated among hispanophone Filipinos in newspapers and magazines in the first years after 1898. This continued in the decade after *Social Dawn* as well, when supposedly only Balmori was publishing novels. For example, the monthly magazine *Cultura Filipina* (*Filipino Culture*) announced in its October 1912 issue the results of a contest for novels that it had opened. A jury of prominent Filipino intellectuals explained that three submissions had been received, entitled *El rebelde* (*The Rebel*), *Charito,* and *Los misterios de Manila* (*The Mysteries of Manila*), but that none had quite met the competition criteria of being properly *costumbrista*—in other words, they had not used the plot primarily as a means through which to describe local customs and color—and that therefore no winner would be declared (1–2).[15] They suggested, "sin embargo, ya que no como premio como estímulo á sus autores, que la Dirección de *Cultura Filipina* compensara de alguna manera y con la cantidad que tuviera por conveniente los esfuerzos de los concurrentes" ["however, although not as a prize but as a stimulus to its authors, that the heads of *Filipino Culture* compensate the efforts of the competitors in some way and with the quantity (of money) that they see fit"] (2–3).

Although the texts of the novels submitted for the *Filipino Culture* contest are probably lost forever, the strong likelihood is that both the authors and this particular competition represent but a fraction of the production of the genre during the decades after 1898. The periodicals of the time, many of which survive in libraries in the United States and Spain, await methodical searching. As late as September 1922, there was also *La novela semanal* (*The Weekly Novel*), a periodical that consisted entirely of a new novella or novel at a length of usually around fifty densely typeset pages. *The Weekly Novel* was offered at least fourteen weeks in a row and probably many more. Individual issues of *The Weekly Novel* were on sale at newsstands, bookstores, stamp stores, even bakeries. Alternately, the entire series could be subscribed to for a period of four, six, or twelve months. Most issues remain to be located and so it is not currently possible to determine how long *The Weekly Novel* continued in operation, but of the eight narratives that are known to be extant, one ran as long as ninety-three pages. Early contributors to the series included Balmori and José Sedano y Calonge.

Even if novels are defined to include only fictional texts longer and more complex than those *novelas* submitted for newspaper contests, the case of Sedano y Calonge colors the existing accounts of a tradition that putatively careens from the *Fili* in 1891 to Balmori's novels of 1910 and 1915. Sedano does not seem to be studied in any critical literature to date. Yet the first chapter of his 370-page novel *La madrastra* (*The Stepmother*), whose second edition was published in Manila in 1910, indicates that he wrote the bulk of that novel in 1902 or earlier in Spain but was too listless to impel it into print. At issue in establishing the truth of this description is whether the narrator of the following passage is an entirely invented character who assumes a first-person voice as a literary convention, or whether he is more or less relaying accurately, on behalf of the author, the actual historical context for the production of the novel: "Esta obra debía haberla dado á la publicidad ocho años há: mas no lo hice por apatía hasta hoy que, encontrándome en Filipinas, mi país natal . . . se me ha ocurrido darle cima, añadiéndole algunos tipos y costumbres filipinas que necesariamente tuvieron que rozarse con el principal personaje de mi novela" ["This work should have been made public eight years ago: but because of apathy I did not do it until today since, finding myself in the Philippines, my country of birth . . . it has occurred to me to top it off, adding to it some Filipino people and customs that necessarily would have come into contact with the principal character of my novel"] (5). Even if this account is disbelieved, the fact remains that the unlocated first edition of *The Stepmother* likely appeared prior to 1910 (the odds of two editions in one year seem small) and perhaps much earlier. Such a date would place Sedano, and not Balmori, after Rizal as the first Filipino author to publish a lengthy work of fiction in Spanish in a bound (nonperiodical) form. And with Sedano, Balmori, and Paterno all printing Spanish-language *novelas* of one kind or another in 1910 in Manila, and perhaps with other unknown authors engaged similarly, the second decade of the U.S. occupation seems to be marked by a Filipino tradition of fiction in Spanish that actually was strengthening.

Sedano would go on to become a prolific writer of fiction and other genres up until World War II. Under the name "José Sedano Calonge," in fact, the Library of Congress has microform copies of *The Stepmother* and a 157-page volume of poetry from 1911, *¡Almas de flores!* (*Souls of Flowers!*). An advertisement at the back of his provocatively titled *Soy de tu raza, Castila* [*sic*]: *Recopilación de novelas relámpago* (*I Am of Your Race, Castille: Compilation of Lightning Novels*), a 1936 collection of fifteen short texts, notes that Sedano was the author of two other *novelas* ("La hidalguía del dolor" ["The Nobleness of Grief"], which won some sort of prize, and "Cuando se empeñan ellas" ["When They Strive"]) as well as a book of poetry and prose entitled *Háblame en español* (*Speak to Me in Spanish*), the aforementioned volume of poetry *Souls of Flowers!*, an operetta, a drama, and the full-length novel *Celia* that was in preparation (142).[16] Yet the only acknowledgment in scholarship of his oeuvre seems to be a single mention by Alinea of "José Sedano" in a long list of distinguished poets of the Golden Age (86). Additionally, Brillantes notes that Sedano submitted *Háblame en español* for the 1935 Zóbel contest and another text, *Ya hablo en español* (*I Already Speak Spanish*), in 1941, the last prewar competition.[17] That, however, is it.

The consistency of his published output and the timing of his life would seem to make Sedano one of the most overlooked figures of Asian literature in Spanish. He could be viewed as a bridge between the early era of expatriate fiction in Spain and the emergence of a tradition within the Philippines during the U.S. occupation. The reasons for his invisibility in the critical literature are somewhat mystifying. The most likely answer emanates from the fluidity of Filipino identity in the first place. Although a prerequisite for a Zóbel contestant was Philippine citizenship, it is possible that Sedano was not considered Filipino enough to earn a place in the national literary tradition. In "Mi mala sombra" ("My Bad Shadow"), an autobiographical sketch in *I Am of Your Race, Castille,* Sedano recounts that he was born during the Spanish colonial period in the southern Philippine island of Mindanao to an Andalusian father and a Galician mother (12).

With two parents from Spain but a Philippine birthplace, Sedano would have been considered *filipino* rather than *indio,* or in other words, a creole rather than a native. His parents would have been called *peninsulares,* or Spaniards from Spain proper. Sedano spent some childhood years in Spain but then returned to the Philippines in 1895 as a soldier ("Mi mala sombra,"

14–15). When the revolution broke out the next year, he fought with Spain against the *indios*. This would seem to have solidified his national identity as a Spaniard, yet when "vino América del Norte a regir nuestros destinos, se repatrió al ejército español y dijeron. [*sic*] Los que son filipinos y desean quedarse en su pais se les dará la absoluta y ¡cinco pesos! ¡Y aquí estoy yo, tan fresco!" ["North America came to rule our destinies, the Spanish army was repatriated and they said. [*sic*] Those who are Filipinos and wish to stay in their country will be given absolution and five pesos! And here I am, so full of life!"] ("Mi mala sombra," 17).[18] Sedano cast his lot with the land of his birth. His legal status as a Filipino in the primarily twentieth- and not nineteenth-century sense of the word—that is, as a Philippine rather than a creole—must have been sufficient for him to qualify as a contestant in the two Zóbel competitions more than four decades later. The plasticity of his national identity is representative of the ways in which globalization has been refracted through the archipelago. The appearance of literature in Spanish by Filipinos, therefore, is not only about the emergence of "literature in Spanish." It is also about the emergence of "Filipinos."

The above is true regardless of whether "My Bad Shadow," subtitled as an "Autobiografía" ["Autobiography"], is factually reliable (12). Its data, presented via colorful rhetoric, has to be accepted or not at face value because there is no known way of corroborating it. It is uncertain how its narrative squares with a presumed initial writing of *The Stepmother* in Spain in 1902 at the latest. In any case, Sedano deserves nuanced study because his work points to a larger gap in the scholarly narrative of Philippine literature: the fiction by *filipinos* in the nineteenth century, which is to say, creole novels and short stories. Paterno and Rizal are acknowledged as the first novelists of the country because they are the first *indios* to have published long fiction.[19] There were, however, plenty of previous novels written in Spanish and published in the Philippines by *peninsulares*. These are generally not included as part of the national literary tradition and have received an initial modern scholarly critique by Lilia Hernandez Chung in *Facts in Fiction: A Study of Peninsular Prose Fiction: 1859–1897*, published in 1998. What remains unclear, however, is whether there was a third literary tradition in existence at the tail end of the Spanish colonial period, either inchoate or mature, led by *filipino* (creole) writers. Such individuals would have been the predecessors or early contemporaries of Sedano. Once the U.S. colonial period was under way, many *peninsulares* returned permanently to Iberia and surely numerous *filipinos* made their way there too, often for the first time. The *peninsulares* and *filipinos* who remained in the archipelago, like Sedano, merged with *indios* under the new category of islanders: Filipinos in the contemporary meaning of that term.

CEBUANO CENTRALITIES

By the time Félix Gerardo wrote *Social Justice* in the late 1930s and early 1940s, that is, the same era in which Sedano wrote *I Already Speak Spanish*, Filipinos were definitively Filipinos in the current sense of that word. Yet not all Filipinos were Filipinos in a sociopolitical sense, for the national domination of Manila tended to marginalize all other regions of the archipelago. Nowhere perhaps was this felt more acutely than in Cebu, the central island where Magellan had landed, and the neighboring and smaller Mactan Island, where he died. Gerardo sets his stories in both locales and in so doing orients the eyes of the reader not to the Philippines in general but to Cebu in particular. It was in Cebu where the narrative of an interconnected humanity and its unending intrastruggle began. Gerardo implicitly argues that Cebu has historical primacy in a globalized world, that the Cebuano language and Cebuano culture reside at the root of modernity. For Pedro Paterno, in contrast, Filipino identity means Tagalog identity. All the fictions nested into his *Social Dawn* are of Tagalog characters in Tagalog landscapes. Rizal too foregrounds Tagalog speakers in Manila and its environs. Yet Cebu and Cebuano have an alternate claim to national and international significance. Cebu, after all, is where the story of globalization starts with Lapu Lapu and Magellan. Under the Spaniards, it was also the first capital of the archipelago, a sort of Philadelphia of the Philippines.

Cebuano always has been spoken widely in the central Philippine islands but did not become an official national language because Tagalog predominated around Manila, the seat of the archipelagic government.[20] Tagalog (or, technically, Filipino, which is a standardized version of Tagalog mixed with some words from other idioms) was chosen as the national vernacular only on the last day of 1937, just before Gerardo sat down to compose most or all of the *Social Justice* stories. The fact that this government-approved, formalized Tagalog is known now as "Filipino" is not lost on native speakers of Cebuano, whose language manifestly is not so dubbed. Yet in the time span of 1912 to 1934, according to Erlinda Alburo, Cebuano "had the largest number of speakers in the country," not Tagalog (88). After

1937, Cebuano may have been pushed into a peripheral existence by forces both domestic and international, but it is hardly a minor language. More than fifteen million people today speak Cebuano, far more than well-known European tongues such as Greek, Czech, Swedish, and Danish. Within a Spanish context, the comparisons stand out even sharper. More than twice as many people speak Cebuano as Catalan, more than seven times as many as Galician, and more than twenty times as many as Basque (Euskera). In the Philippines, Cebuano has maintained a strong presence through all the decades since Tagalog was nationally sanctified in 1937. Resil Mojares could still note in 1975 that Cebuano "is the mother-tongue of the greatest number of Filipinos" (*Cebuano*, 1). As late as 1989, observes Paraluman Aspillera, despite half a century of official promotion of Filipino as the national vernacular, 25 percent of all Filipinos were native speakers of Tagalog but a full 24 percent spoke Cebuano. Notwithstanding this negligible statistical difference, the aggressive nationalization of Tagalog through schooling and popular media has marginalized Cebuano inside and outside the archipelago. Many Cebuano speakers now can understand Tagalog but the inverse is not at all true. And beyond the islands, international recognition of the existence of Cebuano is minimal. The encounter between Magellan and Lapu Lapu, however, provides an eternal Cebuano claim to global genesis. Tourists to the city today are thus directed to the monument known as Magellan's Cross and the adjacent Basilica of the Santo Niño, the most important church in the central Philippines, which features oil paintings of the inaugural interactions of Spaniards and Cebuanos.

The significance of Gerardo resides in large part in his writing outside the frameworks of Manila. He challenges notions of globalization from a space that exists beyond the national center and yet can be imagined as foundational to the world. He also writes beyond international centers. Unlike Paterno and Rizal, he did not produce expatriate fiction from Europe. He did not even seek to depict Manila, a capital at least of the margins that Paterno, in the first footnote in *Nínay*, could strive to describe as a microcosm of human civilization. Instead, Gerardo was a provincial writer raised in a provincial language who rewrote the planet from the periphery of a periphery. The world passed through Cebu in 1521 with Magellan and passed through again in *Social Justice* some 420 years later. In the first case, Lapu Lapu parried and vanquished the invading Western mariner. In one *Social Justice* story, the two instead kibbitz in the afterlife. Amid such remarkable scenes, Gerardo demonstrates that globalization, though imposed from without, can always be transformed from within. Whether he himself could captain a Cebuano vessel into the future without his own cause becoming uncontrollable is another matter altogether.

Given the years in which *Social Justice* was composed, the title of the collection resonates with particular national implications. In 1934, a bill known as the Tydings-McDuffie Act that already had passed in the U.S. Congress was approved in the Philippine legislature as well. The law provided for the creation of a transitional Filipino state, the Commonwealth, that would yield to an independent archipelago in 1946. In 1935, Manuel L. Quezon won the election for president of the Commonwealth and launched a set of initiatives known as Social Justice. According to Teodoro Agoncillo, whose *History of the Filipino People* remains a canonized account half a century after its initial edition, "Perhaps no other Commonwealth policy has received as much attention, curiosity, and even, criticism, as Quezon's social justice program. The Constitution of 1935 mandated that 'the promotion of social justice to insure the well-being and economic security of all the people should be the concern of the state.'[21] Social justice was equated with justice to the common man" (355). Frank Hindman Golay finds a later origination than the Commonwealth constitution, writing that after a 1937 trip to North America, Quezon decided to make upcoming "local elections a campaign for 'social justice,' a catchy slogan he had picked up during his brief visit to Mexico. . . . Social justice was also the theme of a special legislative session called by Quezon upon his return from Washington to implement the programs he had agreed to fund with coconut oil proceeds" (365). In electioneering in 1938, says Golay, "Always a sponge for new ideas and slogans, Quezon modified the theme of social justice, which he had shrewdly manipulated in 1937, and . . . campaigned for a 'distributive state'" (367). Gerardo, composing some of the stories in *Social Justice* in the late 1930s and therefore amid the Commonwealth politics of Quezon, would seem to be responding directly to contemporary initiatives of national significance. Yet nowhere in *Social Justice* does he engage Quezon and his policies in any substantive and sustained fashion. For that matter, the Philippines as an entity tends to be bypassed as Gerardo concentrates more narrowly on Cebu and more broadly on global historical forces. If Gerardo is responding in any way to Quezon, he is doing so via allegorical narratives that otherwise seem to stand entirely on their own.

There are four stories in *Social Justice* that are especially relevant to the reconceptualization of globalization that Asian and African literature in

Spanish impels. The first, "La tragedia de un campesino" ("The Tragedy of a Peasant"), opens with the narrator acting as a local tour guide to the reader:

> *Un extranjero o cualquiera persona venida de fuera, que en viaje de estudio y observación o de simple pasatiempo visite la ciudad de Cebú y se interese por ver cosas que amplíen su bagaje cultural . . . facilmente encontrará quien oficiosamente o al incentivo de una propina le conduzca a sitios históricos, tales como, por ejemplo, el lugar donde se celebró la primera misa cuando la expedición comandada por Hernando de Magallanes arribó a estas hermosas playas, o el monumento erigido en el mismo sitio donde aquel célebre navegante cayó muerto en formal duelo con el régulo de Maktang, Lapulapu. (1)*[22]

[A foreigner or any person arriving from outside who, in a trip of study and observation or as a simple pastime, visits the city of Cebu and becomes interested in seeing things to broaden his cultural heritage . . . easily will find someone who, unofficially or with the incentive of a tip, will lead him to historical sites such as, for example, the place where the first mass was celebrated when the expedition commanded by Ferdinand Magellan arrived at these beautiful beaches, or the monument erected in the same site where that celebrated navigator fell dead in a formal duel with the local king of Mactan Island, Lapu Lapu.]

The strain on Gerardo to memorialize the Cebuano heritage of both Magellan and Lapu Lapu is quite evident. The former brings the boons of Catholicism (the mass) and fame to Cebu, while the latter stands as his indigenous equal, a royal worthy of engaging with the famous mariner in "a formal duel." Historically, of course, there was no such one-on-one combat in European fashion. According to Antonio Pigafetta, chronicler of the circumnavigation, Magellan led an assault of sixty men from the shallow waters offshore Mactan Island, forty-nine of whom constituted the military force.[23] Mactan lies immediately next to the much larger Cebu. Lapu Lapu repulsed the invaders with more than a thousand armed individuals, possibly more than three thousand (87, 163).[24] Magellan and his men were driven backward knee-deep into seawater. The foreign captain was wounded by a poisoned arrow in a leg, a bamboo lance in an arm, a javelin in the left leg, and ultimately a flurry of javelins and bamboo and iron lances as he sank face down into the brine (88).[25] It was hardly a mano a mano duel and certainly was not formalized. The advantages of Gerardo's account is that it enables him to sidestep a dialectic of conquest and resistance by claiming and celebrating both sides of the foundational moment of globalization. Lapu Lapu, via the nonexistent duel, is elevated to pseudo-European status akin to that shared by many of the Filipino characters invented by Paterno and Rizal. And yet Magellan and Lapu Lapu cannot be reconciled so easily.

Gerardo takes his time in getting to the main plot of "The Tragedy of a Peasant." After praising the cathedral of Cebu, he lauds the city as "la mas antigua de este bendito archipielago" ["the most ancient of this blessed archipelago"] and thereby grants it another claim to original importance, one that roots itself in a premagellanic epoch perhaps comparable to the age of Bathala evoked by Paterno in his Tagalog legends (1). Next, however, Gerardo notes that there is a place some thirty kilometers away from downtown Cebu that "no figura en el mapa de la Ciudad, sería porque las mismas autoridades desconozcan la existencia de semejante lugar o lo han relegado al olvido. Mas este menguado cuentista lo ha descubierto o mas bien lo crea, con el auxilio de su fantasia, y lo saca a luz para que sirva de base y fondo al relato que va a continuación" ["does not figure in the map of the City, which would be because the authorities themselves do not know the existence of such a place or have left it forgotten. But this diminished storyteller has discovered it or, better said, creates it with the aid of his fantasy and brings it to light so that it serves as a base and backdrop for the narrative that follows"] (1). This geographical fantasy is remarkable for its further complications of the global and the local, intertwining the two so as to render them indistinguishable from each other. Cebu is centered on a worldwide map as the ur-site of globalization and on an archipelagic map as the oldest city and starting point of a hybrid, Catholic national culture. At the same time, "The Tragedy of a Peasant" takes place in a nonexistent village so far removed from Cebu City that urban authorities do not even reckon with it. The story itself, a tale of peasants in the provinces, will be relayed not in the Cebuano the characters speak but in Spanish, a language they probably did not know at all. The highly literate Gerardo, in other words, presents a local and, presumably, predominantly oral culture through written stories in an incomprehensible foreign language whose patron empire had disappeared some four decades earlier.

The dramatic action of "The Tragedy of a Peasant" begins with the premise that once upon a time in the Spanish colonial period, an array of felons and renegades found refuge in the village in the woods (2). Their descendants include an orphaned teenage girl named Matilde and her suitors Kolás and Tatyong, a pair of best friends. The threesome flirt under an imperial flag different from that known by their outcast ancestors, for they live during the U.S. colonial period. The grandfather of Matilde declares that her hand will go to whichever of the two lads obtains a governmental job under the current foreign regime. Kolás promptly travels to Cebu City in search of employment but fails at the task because he is not multilingual. Though articulate in Cebuano, he is stymied by the meaning of signs in English such as "NO VACANCY" and "KEEP OFF THE GRASS" (7). Finally, he returns to the village empty-handed.

Tatyong, in contrast, is conversant in the new imperial language and lands a job as a fireman. As a result, he wins Matilde. Their wedding "fué solemnizada al estilo y usanza del lugar, que consistía en celebrar el acontecimiento con . . . amén de alegres danzas y cantos de que el foklore filipino tiene un nutrido repertorio, acompañados de guitarreos y otros ruidos que los labriegos arman en sus jolgorios" ["was marked in the style and custom of the place, which consisted in celebrating the event with . . . the amen of happy dances and songs of which Filipino folklore has a well-nourished repertoire, accompanied by strumming and other noises that farmworkers use in their merrymaking"] (10). Kolás does not attend the celebration. Instead, he climbs to the top of a mountain and shouts out,

¡Oh, Filipinas, patría de mis amores! . . . ¡ay! en vísperas de tu emancipación, en que te aprestas a vivir libre de toda influencia extraña, como dueña absoluta de tu destino, aún te aferras a una peculiaridad característica tuya, resabio de tu pasada esclavitud, defecto capital que obstaculizará en gran manera la formación de una robusta y recia individualidad autóctona, tan indispensable para ti y para cualquiera otra nación o raza que desee mantener su independencia politica a través de las vicisitudes de su historia. Me refiero a la poca estima en que tienes lo que es tuyo, exclusivamente tuyo, consustancial con tu manera de ser, la voz de tu alma, que es tu dialecto al que has relegado a irrisoria postergación. Y por esto se da el triste caso de que hijos legítimos tuyos, que arden en deseos de servirte en la esfera gubermental, como este humilde labriego, son inhabilitados para desempeñar el puesto mas ínfimo de la administración, por desconocer el idioma anglosajón. Que desventurada eres, patría mía! (10–11)

[Oh Philippines, fatherland of my loves! . . . Ay! On the eve of your emancipation, in which you prepare yourself to live free from all foreign influence as absolute owner of your destiny, you still anchor yourself to a characteristic peculiarity of yours, a bad habit from your historical slavery, a capital defect that blocks greatly the formation of a robust and vigorous autochthonous individuality that is so indispensable for you and for any other nation or race that desires to maintain its political independence through the vicissitudes of its history. I refer to the little esteem in which you hold that which is yours, exclusively yours, tantamount to your manner of being, the voice of your soul, which is your dialect that you have consigned to derisive underappreciation. And from this the sad case results that your legitimate sons who burn with the desire to serve you in the governmental sphere, like this humble farmworker, are rendered unable to fill the lowest post of the administration for not knowing the Anglo-Saxon language. How unfortunate you are, my fatherland!]

The tragedy of a peasant ends with this apostrophe. The plea is provincial and national and global at once.

This utterly unknown story, written by a Cebuano in Spanish on the eve of World War II, should be anthologized around the world. The world, certainly, is inextricable from it in the most complicated and contradictory of ways. At hand is a local writer from a periphery (the fictional village) of a periphery (Cebu) of a periphery (the Philippines) using a former global empire's language, Spanish—an empire that had been dead in Asia for forty years already—to critique the social realities of a new global empire that operated in English. The tragic finale, a call for the retention of indigenous language and culture, is issued in an idiom, Spanish, that betrays the call itself. The immediate national framework is that of the Social Justice initiatives of Quezon and the proclaimed nationalization of Tagalog over Cebuano and other vernaculars, but the implications of "The Tragedy of a Peasant" extend far beyond domestic politics to a world crisscrossed by successive empires. Moreover, the story is foundationally anachronistic in its frame of Magellan and Lapu Lapu and in its mid-twentieth-century use of what is, for Filipinos, a language linked primarily with the nineteenth century of Rizal and his peers. Yet "The Tragedy of a Peasant" is also ahead of its time, anachronistic in a future sense, for it anticipates as impending other decolonizations around the world to which the Filipino case might be instructive. This story set in Cebu was probably written in the late 1930s, an era when the United States was already formally on its way to granting independence to the Philippines but before the liberations of "any other nation or race" after World War II that seem to have been foreseen by Gerardo here.

In "The Tragedy of a Peasant," Gerardo does much more than view the national politics of Quezon and the Commonwealth through a local lens. Instead, he reverses the geographies of empire. He upends imperial hierarchies by displacing the powers of the foreign to the margins of his story. Simultaneously, he centers the various peripheries of which he writes. He does this by beginning with a historical backdrop of resistance to empire, represented with the killing of Magellan. This is followed by the populating of a village by felons and renegades, transgressors of Spanish law who had escaped the disciplinary reach of that system. Gerardo's starting point, therefore, is not a fondness for the religious, political, and linguistic legacies of empire but rather the spaces that those who resist or escape it create for themselves. The love triangle of Matilde, Kolás, and Tatyong generations later is framed as local survival and thereby as a continuum of local community. In other words, Magellan may come, Spain and the United States may come, but through it all, Cebuanos retain the right to the centrality of their own lives by accommodating with the outsiders only so far as necessary. This is why the wedding at the end features not Spanish or U.S. customs but "happy dances and songs of which Filipino folklore has a well-nourished repertoire." The true cause for celebration here is that Tatyong has demonstrated provincial strength by adapting to imperial demands (in this case, fluency in English) without abandoning his own cultural identity. Unexpectedly, he uses English to preserve a traditional Cebuano space. And Gerardo uses Spanish paradoxically to do the same, in his case by relating the lament by Kolás about the imperial suppression of Cebu in the first place. A navigation amid tossing currents, the short story emerges from the dialectic of Lapu Lapu and Magellan unresolvable to either.

In this complicated interplay of agencies and critiques, the most apparently marginal of the marginal—villagers on the fringes of a provincial island ruled by consecutive world powers—utilize knowledges gained in different historical moments to challenge the dominance of the foreign while being undeniably circumscribed by it. In so doing they construct a flexible cultural tradition, one in which they are the subjects and centers of literature rather than its objects and outskirts. It is the U.S. actors in the story who are relegated to the cast of colonial extras. Gerardo foregrounds the Cebuano characters while backgrounding empire. Still, though, it is the old colonial language, Spanish, that provides for a climax in which an illiterate peasant boy gets to issue a searing rebuke of empire. Kolás surely cries out in Cebuano, not Spanish. A major thrust of the story, after all, is that a local language should not have to cede to a foreign one. Gerardo, by writing in an imperial tongue, belies his own protagonist's criticism of the same.

Another story that stands out in *Social Justice* is "El amor de un español" ("The Love of a Spaniard"). Its plot begins in Cebu in 1897, just before the imperial shift, and ends in the late 1930s with news of the Spanish Civil War. Like "The Tragedy of a Peasant," this narrative features a romantic triangle involving two young men and a young woman. Luis is a well-educated product of the traditional Cebuano elite, while Francisco, a foreigner, is a lieutenant in the Spanish civil guard. Both angle for the hand of the beautiful Charito, who is from the same provincial elite class as Luis. This gives him the upper hand until he expresses "los falsos teoremas del Racionalismo . . . por ende, había motivos para sospechar de su catolicismo" ["the false theorems of Rationalism . . . therefore, there were reasons to suspect his Catholicism"] (4). So end his chances for the chaste and devout Charito. The prospects of Francisco, the "joven peninsular" ["young Spaniard"], correspondingly rise. Soon he wins the "cuerpo soberano" ["sovereign body"] of "la 'dalaga' filipina" [the "Filipina 'maiden'"] as Charito agrees to marry him (6, 5). Four days before the wedding, however, these plans are ended by a surge of the Filipino revolution. While Francisco busies himself fighting the rebels, a Spanish ship inadvertently destroys Charito's family home. Once Spain loses to allied Filipino and U.S. forces, Francisco and Charito swear eternal love and he sails back to Iberia. The heroic leader of the revolutionary forces turns out to be Luis, who renews his courting of Charito. She remains faithful to her faraway Spanish love. Over the next forty years, Luis eventually gives up hope for Charito, marries instead a Cebuana from the traditional local elite, becomes a successful lawyer, then provincial politician, then finally a national political star with a populist bent as the Philippines transitions to autonomy under Quezon and U.S. oversight. The story ends in 1939 when the armies of Francisco Franco are finishing off the Spanish Civil War. The aged and still virginal Charito emits a cry of grief upon reading in a newspaper that the first Francisco, now a general in the fascist air force, has died in a tragic air accident (16).

"The Love of a Spaniard" spins in indigenous and imperial currents as multidirectional as those in "The Tragedy of a Peasant." The focus on the upper rather than lower socioeconomic class of Cebu does not alter the message much. In "The Love of a Spaniard," the "sovereign body" of an indigenous Cebuana corresponds again to the sovereign bodies of Cebu in particular and the Philippines in general. This trope of the virginal female as tantamount to the virginal nation, both subject to a competition between indigenous and foreign appropriators, is reminiscent of multiple characters in the fictional texts of Pedro Paterno and of María Clara in the novels of José Rizal. In "The Love of a Spaniard," as in "The Tragedy of a Peasant," male protagonists once again have a choice to make in terms of seeking control of that body. They can place their bet with the old empire or the new one, with history or with the future, with a provincial and/or national identity that is either static or adaptable. Once more appear the epochal violences of 1898 to provide the macrohistorical context for the contest. The characters and the cultural forces they represent again face the need to craft flexible collective imaginaries.

In "The Love of a Spaniard," Spanish colonialism in the Philippines is personified by Francisco, a military figure who, metaphorically, seeks to secure the Hispanic identity of the islands by wedding and bedding the indigenous elite. This attempt at consolidating a cultural marriage is doomed by history. Francisco will become a fascist leader, just like his namesake Franco, and die in the course of fighting republicanism in Spain after having lost in the same reactionary effort in the Philippines. In adopting these postures, he abandons a Cebuana, Charito, who is equally abandoned by history to a sterile and lifelong isolation. Faced with the Filipino revolution and the appearance of the United States, Charito represents a Cebuano elite joined with the old Spanish order on the wrong side of history. Pedro Paterno, a member of a parallel Europhile elite, the Tagalog version, who also lived through the revolution and the U.S. arrival, ran hard after the publication of *Nínay* in 1885 to catch up with the right side of history and never quite did. That is why he looks foolish in retrospect. Rizal too found himself behind the curve of the future despite having propelled it forward with the *Noli* and the *Fili*, novels that never pushed for independence notwithstanding their impact on the popularization of that cause. The story of his martyrdom in 1896 obscures the real possibility that Rizal might have made decisions similar to Charito's if he were in her shoes. After all, when the Filipino revolution broke out, its leaders invoked his name but Rizal himself rejected it and instead signed on to join a Spanish military contingent heading to Cuba to quell anticolonial unrest there. He would have been on the same side as Francisco.

Unlike Charito, Luis, who also is Cebuano, takes advantage of the U.S. regime's relative tolerance for local autonomy and agency. He marries a fellow member of his provincial class and then becomes a republican champion acclaimed by the people. He leads in inaugurating new political roles for Filipinos, albeit under colonial occupation. The U.S. empire, though not a direct presence in "The Love of a Spaniard" as in "The Tragedy of a Peasant," once again implicitly comes off, unlike its Spanish predecessor, as creating a bureaucratic more than military or ecclesiastical regime in which flexible constructions of semisovereign indigenous imaginaries are allowed space to develop. In the two stories, the U.S. occupiers appear only as a backdrop for the more important narratives of how Cebuanos, trying to maintain their cultural autonomy, do or do not adjust to the dynamics of 1898.

Gerardo, writing "The Love of a Spaniard" sometime between 1939 and 1941, forges a memory of how those Cebuanos who adapted to the systemic sociopolitical changes brought about by the new empire proved able to continue marrying each other, symbolically and literally both. They thereby retain indigenous lineages, cultural as well as biological, and produce pliable forms of Cebuano and Filipino identity. Those locals, however, who are unable or unwilling to adapt to the post-1898 landscape are doomed to solitude, sterility, and death, again both culturally and biologically. This is why Kolás does not get the girl in "The Tragedy of a Peasant" and is left lamenting alone atop a mountain, and why Charito is left lamenting alone upon learning of Francisco's fate in Spain. In contrast, Tatyong, like Luis, adjusts competently to the imperial shift and thus gets the job and the Cebuano girl and the profoundly happy wedding.

In these interplays, there is no sharp distinction between the analogues of Magellan and Lapu Lapu. Success derives from navigating adeptly the wakes of both men and not from escaping one of them altogether. That would be impossible in any case. History cannot be resolved, only traversed. This is true of Gerardo. His stories celebrate Cebuano adaptability under a U.S. regime but do so in Spanish. This is the linguistic choice opposite from that his own heroes make. Gerardo pilots a ship of state that arrives where he himself does not. His stories are consequently instructive to the crashing currents of globalization. Those who seek to captain it cannot control its resistances.

IDENTITIES UNRESOLVED

According to the penciled notation by an unknown individual in the unpublished booklet of Cebuano pseudonyms, the totally obscure Félix Gerardo was actually the fairly famous Uldarico Alviola. Further research may bear this out. Certainly, Alviola is a reasonable candidate for Gerardo. Born in 1883, he witnessed firsthand the imperial conflicts in Cebu at an age old enough to be aware of what was happening. The stories of *Justicia social* that have a just-before-1898, once-upon-a-time feel to them correspond to the moment of his own youth and perhaps a resultant nostalgia. A native speaker of Cebuano educated in Spanish, Alviola eventually served as editor of at least four bilingual Spanish/Cebuano periodicals. These included the early and important *Ang Suga,* launched in 1901 and published until at least 1912 (Mojares, *Cebuano,* 57).[26] Evelyn S. Racho describes *Ang Suga* as "the first predominantly Cebuano newspaper . . . [it] was born under the editorship of Uldarico Alviola" (27–28). In 1901, Alviola would have been only about eighteen years old, but apparently he was already deeply committed to processing the shifting climate around 1898 through written media that, radically for the time, invoked the local language.

Alviola would prove to be a pioneering writer of fiction as well as journalism. In 1912, he published *Felicitas,* which is the second Cebuano novel to be published.[27] Alburo regards *Felicitas* as a flat, poorly written novel that "exhibits elements of a medieval morality play" (165).[28] Regardless, the existence of the text at least shows an interest by Alviola in producing sustained fiction in a particular language, in this case Cebuano, when few others were doing so. Racho notes that Alviola also wrote short stories in Cebuano from the first decades of the century through at least the 1920s (46, 49). In her consideration of a subsequent national "Period of Emergence," denominated by Racho as extending from 1936 to 1954, she discusses Philippine literatures in vernaculars and in English but not in Spanish (64, 66–68).[29] At no point, in fact, does she or Alburo mention any fiction in Spanish by Alviola or anyone else, Cebuano or otherwise. This absence does not correlate necessarily to a lack of texts in Spanish by Cebuano authors. Perhaps, simply, neither researcher could read the old imperial tongue and so had to forgo such investigations. Resil Mojares, a longtime leading scholar of Cebu, does work with Spanish texts but also does not know of any fiction by Alviola in that language.[30]

Nonetheless, it is clear that Alviola knew Spanish well. Moreover, Mojares notes that he was a "distinguished writer and lexicographer," so much so that he was considered "The 'dean of Cebuano writers'" (*Cebuano*, 138). His political background was also substantive, including stints as the "Secretary of the municipal council of Cebu" in 1917 and as the "Deputy Governor of Cebu" (*Cebuano*, 138). Such posts dovetail with the implicit background of the narrator of *Social Justice*, who is conversant with a broad range of Cebuano society; and with the protagonist of one of the short stories in the collection, "Ante la bandera" ("Before the Flag"), who is a municipal secretary as well, although of a small town and not the provincial capital.[31] Moreover, Alviola survived through the next imperial shift of the Philippines, from U.S. to Japanese occupation, which also qualifies him as a potential author of the *Social Justice* texts of the late 1930s and early 1940s. Indeed, according to Mojares, he lived long enough to receive a major lifetime achievement award in 1962 for "his contributions to Cebuano culture" (*Cebuano*, 138). Alviola died in 1966 as a man of letters unknown perhaps to most Tagalog scholars in Manila but evidently a central figure in Cebuano literature and society for over half a century. No monograph seems to exist on his creative work, whatever the language in which it was written.[32] In fact, there appears to be only one published paragraph on his entire life, the one by Mojares cited above. The absence of attention to Alviola reflects how much basic research remains to be undertaken on Philippine literature. In the meanwhile, he seems to be a viable candidate for Félix Gerardo. His life and language skills as a writer and civil servant appear to match those of Gerardo and his narrator. Alviola was in his middle to late fifties when *Social Justice* was written, and this too seems to fit well with the chronological vantage of the narrator. Finally, the fact that the unpublished manuscript ended up in the Malacañang Palace Library after World War II suggests that its author might have had direct or indirect political connections with the national government. Here too, Alviola surely could qualify. The literary and political elite of the Philippines often have had close ties, to wit Paterno and Rizal and numerous twentieth-century intellectuals, and frequently have been one and the same.

Whatever the resolution of the identity of Gerardo, the prewar short stories in Spanish that constitute *Social Justice* will not change. And analyzed on their own terms, they are remarkable for their planetary and provincial tensions that remain inconclusive even when most stridently concluded. Such is the case of "Before the Flag," an avowedly patriotic narrative that is nothing of the sort. The ambiguity of the titular flag is notable. For a Cebuano manuscript in Spanish during the U.S. occupation just before the Japanese invasion, there are at least four possible standards: those of Cebu, of the Philippines, of Spain, and of the United States. A fifth that looms is that of Japan and a sixth that appears in the story itself is that of Kamiland, a nonexistent country that also threatens an occupation. "Before the Flag" in its title alone suggests the elasticity of identity in the postmagellanic world. Depending on the frames and parameters chosen to construct a vantage point within "Before the Flag," each of those half dozen flags would alter entirely the relationships of metropole and periphery at hand.

The plot of "Before the Flag" begins with Ismael Terramante, a former municipal secretary in the town hall of Santander, a village on the southernmost tip of Cebu island. Geographically, this community is about as far away as possible from Cebu City, the provincial capital. Like the village in "The Tragedy of a Peasant," the setting therefore lies outside the hub of the island proper. Ismael, who happens to be an orphan, is down on his luck because the mayor who appointed him lost in recent elections to a politician who promptly replaced Ismael with one of his campaign supporters, an inexperienced layabout. Ismael finds himself without a way of making a living, so Mercedes, his "novia" (the word translates as either "fiancée" or "girlfriend") decides that he is a failure and writes him a letter announcing that she is ending their relationship (2). Disconsolate, Ismael strikes out for Cebu City, the nearest metropolis, in search of employment. This endeavor too fails because "en todas partes sólo hallaba un rótulo con esta desalentadora, insultante inscripción 'No Vacancy' (No hay vacante)" ["everywhere he only found a sign with this disheartening, insulting inscription: 'No Vacancy' (No vacancy)"] (3). With his situation dire, Ismael decides to commit suicide by throwing himself off a dock. Just at the moment of his leap into the sea, a passing foreigner grabs him. The benevolent stranger is Elías Levy, a native of the fictional country of Kamiland. Levy asks Ismael about his troubles and, on hearing them, gives him a job in his import business. This arrangement works out well for many years, so much so that Ismael "profesaba un afecto casi filial a su Jefe" ["professed an almost filial affection for his Boss"] (6).

Eventually, Levy decides to retire to his homeland. He offers to take Ismael with him. In the ensuing globetrotting, "Ismael pudo visitar Estados Unidos, las repúblicas iberoamericanas, Egipto, España, Italia, Francia, Inglaterra y varias otras naciones, en un viaje redondo que le fué gratuito enteramente; pues en esta recorrida alrededor del mundo todos los gastos corrieron por cuenta de Elías Levy" ["Ismael could visit the United States, the Spanish-American republics, Egypt, Spain, Italy, France, England, and various other nations, in a round trip that was entirely free for him because in this trip around the world all expenses were paid by Elías Levy"] (6). When they finally settle in Kamiland, Ismael, though longing to return to Cebu, falls for the niece of Levy, named Kate, "aquella muchacha de ojos azules, cabellera rubia y tez de nítida blancura" ["that girl with blue eyes, blonde hair, and clear white complexion"] (7). They wed and Ismael obtains citizenship in Kamiland. Time goes by and then, out of the blue, Kamiland declares war on the "archipielago rizalino" ["Rizalian archipelago"], that is, the Philippines (8). In the harbor of Cebu City, a Kamilandian military transport ship approaches the dock, flanked by the Kamilandian air force. The Filipino air force repulses all the incoming pilots save for one who maneuvers through the bullets toward the Cebuano capitol. The expert Kamilandian pilot then turns around and, utterly unexpectedly, bombs his own country's transport ship. As the narrator explains, the aviator was

> *el ex-filipino Ismael Terramante, quien, al ver la bandera filipina que ondeaba en uno de los mástiles del Capitolio Provincial, se le revivió el amor a la tierra que le viera nacer y que era la patria de sus padres y antepasados. Sintiéndose filipino, como lo era por la sangre que corría por sus venas, los explosivos que llevaba en el aeroplano para emplearles en la destrucción de la Ciudad de Cebu, los arrojó contra el transporte con el resultado que ya sabemos. El desembarco quedó, por tanto, frustrado, habiéndose dado a la fuga los aviadores enemigos excepción hecha de Ismael que aterrizó y se dejo capturar por los defensores de la Ciudad, a quienes contó la hazaña que había realizado, al impulso de su resucitado filipinismo. (10)*

[the ex-Filipino Ismael Terramante, who, upon seeing the Philippine flag that waved on one of the flagpoles of the Provincial Capitol, felt revived in him the love for the land that saw him born and that was the fatherland of his parents and ancestors. Feeling himself Filipino, which he was because of the blood that ran through his veins, he hurled against the transport ship the explosives that he carried in the airplane for use in the destruction of Cebu City, with the result that we already know. The landing was, as a result, frustrated, as the enemy aviators had fled with the exception of Ismael, who landed and let himself be captured by the defenders of the City, to

whom he told the great deed that he had done upon the impulse of his resuscitated Filipinism.]

Such is the moral of the story: Filipinos are Filipinos, come what may. A Cebuano can be taken out of the Philippines but not the Philippines out of a
Cebuano. The only problem with this conclusion is that every detail of the
narrative undermines it.

The fact of the matter is that "Before the Flag" is not a patriotic story because there is no organic patria to uphold at any point. National and other
collective identities ebb and flow throughout the narrative without coher-
ing in Ismael or in the climax or denouement. Despite the explicit conclusion, there is no plot here of a Filipino man who, having traveled the
world, finds his internal "Filipinism" intact and eternal. A sense of such Filipinism was never definitive of his being in the first place, so it certainly
could not be lost and then regained. The story instead is that of a provincial orphan who is transnational even when he seems parochial. The flag of
the title, despite its identification in the climactic scene as Philippine, is no
clearer at the end of the narrative than at the beginning.

The imprecisions and contradictions commence with the opening context of Ismael as a town hall secretary let go by the new mayor. His
identification here is with the government of the remote village of Santander, not with that of the province or its capital and certainly not with
that of the country. As a result, Ismael seems isolated in the beginning from
any complicated national or international dynamics. There is no Cebuano
or Philippine patriotism on the table. He is simply a random local victim of
a patronage system familiar to electoral losers and victors the world over.
But here is where Ismael is intimately related to globalization. After all, the
existence of elections and peaceful transitions of power takes place under
the U.S. occupation. By definition, such democratic activity now is aligned
within the larger political system enforced by the foreign regime. Santander, furthermore, according to websites, was founded in 1898 or at least
reinaugurated in a substantial way in that year.[33] To this extent it is rooted
historically in an era of revolution. To partake in the civil government of
such a place is to function within a context marked measurably by imperial
shift.

The movement from the provincial hinterland to the capital city
heightens Ismael's encounter with globalization and the modernity to
which it is tantamount. The villager, orphaned biologically by his parents

and socially by his fiancée/girlfriend and culturally by his unemployment, encounters all those No Vacancy signs.[34] Like Kolás in "The Tragedy of a Peasant," the abstraction of a U.S. colonization concretizes in English signs and Ismael's inability to secure a job amid the new sociopolitical realities. Yet in his moment of deepest despair, it is not a Cebuano who saves him nor a Filipino of some other ethnic group but a foreigner. This stranger, who carries two suggestive names that are never developed as such—"Elías" is a quasi-nationalistic hero of Rizal's *Noli me tangere,* while "Levy" sounds Jewish and thereby inherently somewhat transnational—preserves Ismael's life, gives him a job in his import business, and takes him on a free trip around the world. The orphaned Ismael becomes the foreigner's symbolic son, the husband of his phenotypically Anglo niece, and his naturalized compatriot. All of these developments are presented as positive. The distraught provincial lad of yesteryear is now a man versed in international capitalism who has circled the globe and gained a new flow of transnational identities.

These constructions of a redefined self did not result from exchanging one set of static collectivities for another. Ismael's early life on the farthest shores of Cebu island was not isolated in an ethnic enclave unchanged from time immemorial but instead tied to vast sociopolitical dynamics from the very beginning. Thereafter, his economic fortunes in the import business depend upon the movement of border-crossing capital. Even his sexual achievement of replacing Mercedes, an indigenous Cebuana, with an Aryan stereotype is not the one-to-one substitution it seems. The moment Ismael meets "la rubia beldad" ["the blonde beauty"] is also the first time that he is depicted explicitly as "filipino" (7). This categorization immediately recurs amid "la pasión que ardía en su pecho con la retórica arrebatadora propia del filipino galán. Kate . . . correspondió en el afecto a su malayo adorador" ["the passion that burned in his breast with the captivating rhetoric proper to a Filipino gallant. Kate . . . requited the affection of her Malay adorer"] (7). The instant he becomes passionate for a Western woman, in other words, is also that in which he is said to be acting as a Filipino and rather robustly at that.[35]

The surprise return of Ismael to Cebu City as a Kamilandian pilot does not quite describe a full circle, as that would have entailed a homecoming to the distant village of Santander. Nonetheless, the military transport ship is heading straight for the docks of Cebu City, a locale last seen when Levy saved Ismael from suicide. This time Ismael arrives as a foreign national himself, intent on inflicting death on others rather than on his own person. Cebu island, meanwhile, now appears as a subset of a national collectivity, the Philippines, a country not mentioned even once in the pre-Kamiland opening of the story. This is to say that Cebu has metamorphosed from a seemingly autonomous collectivity with its own identity to a loyal province in the indivisible "Rizalian archipelago" (8). The invocation of Rizal, a Tagalog always invoked as a national rather than ethnic hero, hints strongly of the conclusion to "Before the Flag" in which any potential Cebuano differences with the domestic hegemony of Manila and Tagalogs are ignored in favor of general patriotic moralizing. Symbolic of the melding of the province and the nation is that Ismael is inspired to act upon seeing the Philippine flag that marks the Cebuano capitol, a hybridization of competing collective identities that is not acknowledged as such. An all-encompassing nationalism prevails. The story ends with a second attempt at suicide by the docks, this one metaphorical, as Ismael kills off his Kamilandian self by bombing a military ship that is not foreign to him in any legal sense, for he is now a Kamilandian citizen. This ritualized purification through violence transforms him, according to the story, back into what he always was, a Filipino. His metamorphosis is not forward into a new being but backward into an old, "resuscitated" one.

Such is the conclusion of "Before the Flag." Yet it is entirely belied by the story proper, a tripartite tale that develops time and again amid amorphous and amendable collective identities. In the first third of the narrative, Ismael is identified with Cebu island at the levels of the remote village and then the capital city. These provincial milieus are inescapably intertwined with the outside world by the ongoing fact of the U.S. occupation and, as an artistic creation, by the Spanish legacy inherent in Gerardo's choice of language. The Philippines as a national context is invisible and irrelevant. Only when Levy takes Ismael around the world and ultimately to Kamiland in the middle third of the story does the protagonist suddenly become identified as a Filipino rather than as a Cebuano. The nordic attractions of Kate are what casts him in oppositional relief both nationally and phenotypically. Yet this same oppositionality is matched by the erasure of his Filipinism via his nationalization as a Kamilandian. When Ismael returns to Cebu as an air force pilot he is both an enemy combatant and a prodigal son, with neither of those two personae capable of being resolved to each other. Although the city defenders celebrate his heroic repulsion of a foreign military force and the manifestation of his innate Filipino identity, neither development would have taken place had a citizen of the invading power not saved Ismael long ago from suicide, rescued him economically, shown him the world, and given him a blue-eyed blonde to romanticize. The Lapu Lapu legacy of sovereign defense cannot be separated from that of Magellan, the attacking imperialist, however much Gerardo wishes it so at the end of this story. Ismael is both the (quasi)circumnavigator who dies in the Philippines and the local hero who does the killing.

A conquest by outsiders arriving by sea to Cebu is averted this time only because a globe-circling traveler of protean identities takes matters into his own hand. This traveler is simultaneously a foreigner and a doubly native son, a Kamilandian and a Cebuano and a Filipino. Meanwhile, he is also made to speak in Spanish by his author and made to live under U.S. rules by his colonizer. His surname is "Terramante," suggestive of *tierra* ("land") and *amante* ("lover"), but the land that he loves is an irreducible multiplicity. At every moment in the story, Ismael must navigate the marginal and metropolitan at once, struggling to stay afloat in an ever-changing push and pull of collective currents and resistances to the same. That is why Gerardo cannot control the consequences of globalization even in a story that appears to offer a particularly nationalistic moral. The celebration of Ismael's resurrected Filipinism does not mark the final coherence of an unconsolidated identity but just one more moment in which that identity is not definitively settled at all. At the end of "Before the Flag," a foreign empire, that not of Kamiland but of the United States, still controls the island and the archipelago. Gerardo still writes of Ismael in the tongue of a previous empire. And unknown to him, another empire is about to attack, that of Japan. The whole story recasts the global dynamics of the middle of the twentieth century into the vantage of a villager on a periphery of a periphery of a periphery. This is why "Before the Flag" is an important text: Gerardo, through it, reorients the world. But its conclusion marks a false remapping, a fall into the Magellanic fallacy. The promotion of a coherent nationalism by Gerardo is transmuted by the successive forces in the story that resist exactly that.

JUXTAPOSITIONS WITHOUT END

A comparison could be made here to an array of short stories in Spanish that was contemporaneous to *Social Justice* and unlike it in virtually every way imaginable: *Ficciones* (*Fictions*) by Jorge Luis Borges. The Argentine writer published his compilation in 1944 but its first half in a separate volume in 1941, the same year in which Gerardo wrapped up his own collection. Probably the most canonized of all short-story anthologies in the history of Spanish, *Fictions* functions as the bizarro *Social Justice*. The fame of the one almost seems to redouble the obscurity of the other. The cerebral, polished, Europhile etherealities of Borges make the emotive, uneven, Cebuano melodramas of Gerardo appear particularly rough and amateurish. Yet much might be learned by reading the two together. For starters, the seductions of Borges into conceptual worlds barely touched by material reality are thrown into sharp relief by the very tangible sociohistorical contexts through which characters in Gerardo have to find their paths. This is true even of Kamiland, as fictional a place as Uqbar in Borges's short story "Tlön, Uqbar, Orbis Tertius" but one whose invasions into the reality of the protagonist do evoke manifestly experienced history rather than theoretical scenarios. The intellectual games in Borges produce captivated readers. The war games in Gerardo produce captives.

The themes of the most famous stories in Borges often resonate with those in Gerardo despite the authors' dramatic differences in aesthetic approaches and political concerns. As the protagonists of "The Love of a Spaniard" find out, the events of 1898 presented alternative possible paths in space and time in which, as in Borges's "El jardín de senderos que se bifurcan" ("The Garden of Forking Paths"), the potential for varying individual choices results in the simultaneous creation of multiple and opposite narratives. The Gerardo text plays out what the Borges story leaves abstract: in the key moment, faced with the same decision, the characters opt differently and so their destinies diverge into discrete planes that run parallel into the future. They could have opted otherwise, however, and the unmaterialized possibilities of their resulting hypothetical trajectories linger manifestly before any reader. This is surely what befalls Charito as she ruminates over the years. Gerardo makes it possible to frame Borges within the Filipino context of 1898. Such analysis, of course, has not been undertaken despite the thousands of studies of *Ficciones* produced since the completion in the late 1930s and early 1940s of both authors' most noteworthy stories.

Another juxtaposition worth considering is with perhaps the most famous Borges narrative of all, "Pierre Menard, autor del Quijote" ("Pierre Menard, Author of the Quijote"). In this story, the titular character copies

Cervantes's masterpiece word for word. Nonetheless, its meaning changes dramatically owing to the passage of time that has altered the original context for reading the novel. For example, an unremarkable custom of rural people that Cervantes might have described in passing could strike a modern reader, envisioning the scene through the lens of the present, as both colorfully archaic and also ideologically powerful as an allegorical argument against contemporary urbanization and cultural alienation. In Gerardo, such theoretical concerns are concretized in his treatment of the material contexts of the 1898 imperial shift. The dancing to traditional Cebuano music at the wedding of Matilde and Tatyong in "The Tragedy of a Peasant" does not mean the same thing under U.S. occupation as it did under the Spanish empire or in premagellanic times. The music may be the same, the lyrics and dancing may be the same, but its import as art is entirely different. The new nuances of the political, ethical, and theoretical implications of the celebration are unique even if a complete repetition of a tradition is presumed. Writing in a land far away from those in which Borges lived, Gerardo grounds Borges and his work. The interwoven abstractions and correspondingly conceptual narratives of twentieth-century world literature—for example, labyrinths in Joyce lead to labyrinths in Borges lead to labyrinths in García Márquez—are worth passing through Philippine earth and water. The other side of the globe is usually far closer than is thought. And labyrinths do originate on islands after all.

And so the last word ought to rest for the moment with *Social Justice,* a collection of fiction finished just months before one imperial era ceded to another. Within the trajectory of Filipino literature in Spanish, Gerardo's anthology can serve, for the moment, as the bookending text to Paterno's chapbook *Sampaguitas* (1880) and novel *Nínay* (1885) some six decades earlier in Madrid. Back then, the world seemed in some senses a far different place. Spain had fought off a major rebellion in Cuba that lasted from 1868 to 1878; the United States had transitioned from its own Civil War epoch to a Gilded Age in which continental rather than international expansion was the order of the day; Japan had begun implementing the industrialization and Westernization policies stemming from the Meiji Restoration; and no tradition of Filipino literature in Spanish existed. The imperial violences of the fin de siècle world remained to come, but at deep levels little would change in 1898 or even by 1941. Navigators would still arrive from across the seas intent on claiming local shores and local people and remaking them in their own image. And the story by Gerardo that seems most fitting

as a temporary marker of the ongoing dynamics of globalization begun by
the encounter of Magellan and Lapu Lapu in 1521 is "El despecho de un
héroe" ("The Spite of a Hero"), in which the vanquished conqueror and the
indigenous king meet in the afterlife on the streets of Cebu City. The resolution of the story, or lack thereof, is in its ambiguity perhaps the most
proper note on which to pause the present exploration of Filipino literature
in Spanish.

At the start of "The Spite of a Hero," the narrator announces, "me pro-
pongo hoy tejer un cuentecito" ["I propose today to weave a little story"]
in which "el lector ya puede barruntar que es pura ficción, producto de mi
fantasía . . . y si por casualidad logro sentar una moraleja, tanto mejor"
["the reader can sense already that it is pure fiction, a product of my fantasy
. . . and if by chance I manage to establish a moral, so much the better"] (1).
With an ambiguous finale thus foreshadowed, the narrator sets the scene of
a séance held in a room near an oil factory of the Visayan Refining Company on Mactan Island. In this setting, as always in Gerardo, multiple times
and contexts overlap. Here, a story relayed in Spanish describes an indus-
trial factory with a name in English—a deliberate nod to the U.S. presence
and all its implications—built atop the small island where Lapu Lapu was
once king.[36] After the lights are turned off, a medium starts channeling the
spirit of the indigenous leader. He asks through her, "¿Ya no se acuerdan del
rey de Maktang, que mató a Magallanes, la primera vez que los españoles
pisaron tierra cebuana?" ["Do you no longer remember the king of Mactan
Island who killed Magellan the first time the Spaniards stepped on Cebuano land?"] (3). Excited, the head of the séance requests through the
medium that "Hermano Lapulapu . . . héroe de la raza" ["Brother Lapu
Lapu . . . hero of the race"] relate why the king now has returned (3). This
invocation of brotherhood implies a direct inheritance, from one Cebuano
to another, of the act of killing Magellan. The result is a familial and transhistorical Cebuano identity based on resistance to outside aggressors. And
indeed, Lapu Lapu proceeds to explain, "Yo maté a Magallanes en la refr-
iega habida con él y sus compañeros de la expedición, porque mi dignidad
de monarca nativo no podía consentir que nuestro bendito suelo fuese hol-
lado por gentes extrañas que venían so pretexto de hacerse nuestros amigos, pero que su verdadera intención ere someternos a su dominación
política" ["I killed Magellan in the skirmish with him and his companions
of the expedition because my dignity as a native monarch could not consent that our blessed earth was set foot upon by foreign peoples who came

under the pretext of becoming our friends but whose true intention was to make us submit to their political domination"] (3).

At this point, the moral hinted at by the narrator seems evident: the Lapu Lapu legacy is what binds Cebuanos, possibly Filipinos in general, across the ages in a spirit of anticolonial collectivity. "The Spite of a Hero" will instruct its readers in a certain nationalism much like "Before the Flag." Yet this does not happen in the former story any more than in the latter. Lapu Lapu, it turns out, was condemned after his own death to wander "errabundo por varios planetas" ["aimlessly among various planets"] for unknown reasons, perhaps, he guesses, as "mi castigo por haber matado a un hombre, que fué Magallanes. Pero al terminar lo que parecía mi expiación" ["my punishment for having killed a man, who was Magellan. But at the end of what appeared to be my expiation"] he is allowed to return to Mactan for what is, unexpectedly, "la experiencia más amarga en toda mi existencia" ["the most bitter experience of all my life"] (3):

Ya no hallé el bosque sombrío que había en la época de la llegada de los españoles. En cambio, se desplegaba ante mis ojos atónitos el hermoso panorama de una población perfectamente urbanizada, con su plaza pública bién cuidada, sus calles anchas y bién pavimentadas, muchas y elegantes casas de materiales fuertes, a diferencia de las que hubo en mi tiempo, que eran pocas y de caña y nipa; los edificios escolares de cemento concreto, la hermosa iglesia, y, por último, la enorme fábrica de la Refining Oil Co., que parecía una colmena de actividad pregonando el progreso material de una población . . . De pronto, experimenté como una sensación instintiva de remordimiento por haberme opuesto a la dominación extranjera, que como he visto, ha traido la cultura y el progreso a mi pueblo. Francamente creí que había errado en odiar al extranjero invasor cuya convivencia con mis compoblanos ha reportado tantos beneficios de que éstos hoy disfrutan; aunque me creí exonerado de toda culpa; pués yo ignoraba entonces lo que era la luz de la civilización. (4)

[I no longer found the gloomy forest that there was in the epoch of the arrival of the Spaniards. Instead, a beautiful panorama unfolded before my astonished eyes of a perfectly urbanized city with its public square well cared for, its wide and well-paved streets, many elegant houses made of strong materials unlike those that there were in my time, which were few and made of reeds and nipa [a type of palm whose leaves were often used for traditional huts]; the school buildings of concrete cement, the beautiful church, and lastly, the enormous factory of the Refining Oil Co., which resembled a beehive of activity announcing the material progress of a city. ... Suddenly, I felt something like an instinctive sensation of remorse for having opposed foreign domination, which, as I have seen, has brought culture and progress to my people. Frankly, I believed that I had erred in hating the invading foreigner whose coexistence with my fellow people has yielded so many benefits that they enjoy today; although I believed myself exonerated of all guilt because I did not know then what was the light of civilization.]

This passage upends the apparent moral of the entire story. Lapu Lapu suddenly is not the native son returned home as conquering hero—after all, he conquered Magellan, not vice versa—and welcomed as such by his transhistorical brethren. Instead, he is a penitent who knew not what he did. The material progress brought by Spain (represented by the church) and the United States (symbolized by the oil company; some things never change) turns out to have been well worth the successive invasions and occupations by foreign aggressors. Killing Magellan was a mistake. The paving of paradise was a good thing. The anticolonial commencement of the story now yields to a procolonial conclusion.

Where is "the most bitter experience" of which Lapu Lapu laments? The above account seems wholly positive. As Lapu Lapu wanders from the "Town Hall"—which Gerardo renders in English—to Cebuano homes and schools, he realizes that he cannot understand the tongue that his compatriots speak (5). He wonders if the Cebuano language has changed so dramatically since his time that he can no longer comprehend it. This possibility reminds him that something similar happened to Julius Caesar (5). The proposed similarity to that Western conqueror is, to say the least, unexpected. Metamorphosing with each paragraph, the dead Mactan king next comes upon the dead Magellan, who "se dirigía a visitar el monumento erigido en su memoria" ["was heading to visit the monument erected in his memory"] (5). Fortunately, the captain is doing well in the afterworld "por haber muerto defendiendo una santa causa" ["for having died defending a holy cause"], that is, Christianity, and he has no hard feelings for Lapu Lapu (6). On the contrary, notes the king, "me saludó afablemente" ["he greeted me affably"] (6). Gerardo has managed the improbable feat of making peace between the two historical figures in the name of a Cebuano collectivity that accepts colonialism as a boon of progress and civilization. The struggle between Magellan and Lapu Lapu is to be resolved this time, apparently, in favor of the former.

Yet this conclusion too proves no more tenable than any other. Magellan explains to Lapu Lapu that the incomprehensible language is English, "lengua de los actuales dominadores" ["language of the current dominators"], and that Cebuanos by and large shun their own tongue and only use it with "sus fámulos o en conversación con personas que no se han educado en las escuelas públicas" ["their servants or when conversing with people who have not been educated in the public schools"] (6). Even in the movie theaters, Magellan observes, English is the idiom of choice (7). Upon delivering this bit of news, the captain bids goodbye and Lapu Lapu bursts into tears. He is overwhelmed by

> la convicción de haber realizado en vano un acto héroico; pués, para nada ha servido para estimular el patriotismo de los míos, que, como se vé, tienen a menos el propio dialecto, que es consustancial con nuestra manera de ser, y esto no significa otra cosa sino que tienen el alma completamente sojuzgada por influencias extrañas; y que, a este paso y si Dios no lo remedia, mi pueblo perderá su individualidad característica y, a la postre, será extranjero en propia tierra. (7)

[the conviction of having realized in vain a heroic act because it has done nothing to stimulate the patriotism of my people who, as can be seen, look down upon their own dialect, which is tantamount to our manner of being, and this does not signify anything other than that they have their soul completely subjugated by foreign influences; and that at this juncture and if God does not remedy the situation, my people will lose its characteristic individuality and ultimately will be strangers[37] in their own land.]

So much for colonialism. Outside domination is now a bad thing, leading as it does to cultural suicide. The killing of Magellan is once again advisable in retrospect, notwithstanding the geniality of the half-circumnavigator's ghost. Meanwhile, the patriotism that Lapu Lapu lauds has nothing to do with the Philippines and everything to do with Cebu. There is not a single mention in "The Spite of a Hero" of the nation or its capital or its official vernacular, Tagalog. The fatherland here is Cebu. The cultural destruction is of Cebuanos and their language. Lapu Lapu ends up as a tragic hero whose lesson of indigenous resistance and survival was ignored by future generations, to their great loss. Of course, not too many moments previously, Lapu Lapu was instead an ignorant primitive happily succeeded by thriving Westernized locals. This lack of a stable resolution makes "The Spite of a Hero" the compelling narrative of globalization that it is. Like everything in Paterno and Rizal and Gerardo, the story is simultaneously of planetary and provincial dimensions and unresolvable to either. Events the scale of the world, events that played out across the globe, from the voyage of Magellan and Pigafetta to the clash of great powers from Europe and the Americas, are reframed and reenvisioned through characters on a small island on the sideline, and at the center, of human history itself.

When Lapu Lapu finishes his monologue of lament, the séance erupts into chaos as a young "entusiasta anglo-parlante" ["English-speaking enthusiast"] bolts up from his seat and accuses the medium of faking the spirit of the indigenous king in order to make all present "creer que Lapu-lapu era opuesto a la hegemonía del inglés en Filipinas" ["believe that Lapu Lapu was opposed to the hegemony of English in the Philippines"] (8). Others rise to the defense of the medium. Amid the hubbub, the narrator serenely announces that the story has ended. The moral foreshadowed at the beginning remains undelineated. The collective welcoming of "Brother Lapu Lapu" has dissolved into a very unfraternal shouting match. Perhaps the only moral to be gleaned is that there is no unproblematized legacy of either Magellan or Lapu Lapu, no resolution of the dynamics they initiated. The modern world began in a Cebuano theater and there is no sign of its ending, no sense of an imminent final act in which one set of forces or another emerges cleanly triumphant. The characters of "The Spite of a Hero" keep shifting their posture toward globalization and toward each other. Local resistances surge forward in righteous waves that fade just as they reach shore, only to be replaced by others. Various Lapu Lapus keep defending their islands against sundry Magellans and those Magellans keep dying and resurrecting only to land once more at Mactan. The captains of globalization cannot control its consequences, its transmutations, its resistances, but their ships of state do keep arriving at Filipino docks time upon time upon time.

The lament of Lapu Lapu that English has crushed Cebuano is betrayed by the language in which the indigenous king is made to speak: Spanish. Contrary to one of the possible points of this and other stories in *Social Justice*, Gerardo too situated himself on the wrong side of history, the Spanish side. As the last writer of the Golden Age, he was in a uniquely valedictory position to invoke the language of a dead empire to critique its successor. Doing so, however, placed him in a paradoxical posture toward the Cebuano culture whose adaptable continuity he commends and bemoans in "The Tragedy of a Peasant," "The Love of a Spaniard," "Before the Flag," and "The Spite of a Hero." His approaches to the global and the modern never harmonize with his postures toward the local and the historic. His attitudes do not harmonize with themselves. This is perhaps inevitable in a work that reframes questions of a global nature by a provincial Filipino writing in Spanish during a U.S. occupation about to be smashed by Japanese occupiers.

Gerardo is simultaneously postcolonial and colonial and, via Lapu Lapu, precolonial too. On the eve of World War II, he is stranded by historical forces in a situation of internal literary exile, his Spanish translating a previous imperial era into a current one for a readership that did not exist. His words circulate in a foreign tongue even as he confines himself to domestic spaces. He negotiates the transoceanic without ever leaving home. His texts travel through time and space, never stopping in either and always circling back, metamorphosed into new forms. From *Nínay* to *Social Justice,* Asian literature in Spanish has been time and again a protean phenomenon that surpasses all attempts to define it as one thing or another. Like Magellan, its circumnavigation remains unconcluded, never quite making it home. The journey is always finished by someone else and then taken up anew by yet another. The waves are where Lapu Lapu made his stand. That is where his legacy survives.

CHAPTER FOUR

The Turn to Africa: Daniel Jones Mathama's Una lanza por el Boabí *(1962)*

Antonio Pigafetta never saw Magellan again. The European survivors of the battle on Mactan Island proposed a trade for the body of the captain but Lapu Lapu refused. The victorious indigenous king declared that "they would not give him up for the greatest riches in the world, but that they intended to keep him as a perpetual memorial" (Pigafetta, 89). The first circumnavigator would be nothing of the sort. Meanwhile, wounded by a poisoned arrow in the forehead, Pigafetta recuperated shipboard while two dozen of his peers were tricked into going ashore on Cebu island (90). Most were slaughtered in an ambush.[1] The remainder of the fleet then had further adventures in Southeast Asian waters and lands, including the Spice Islands, before committing to the radical decision, as Pigafetta understatedly puts it, of "laying course between west and southwest" and entering the Indian Ocean (147). Pigafetta dispatches the long trip back to Spain in just a few bits of prose. Upon reaching Africa, he seems to find little worth narrating. His entire account of the voyage from the Cape of Good Hope to the Cape Verde islands comprises the laconic comment, "we sailed northwest for two months continually without taking any refreshment or repose" and an acknowledgment of the deaths along the way of another twenty-one shipmates (147). He makes no mention of the West African island of Fernando Poo, named for a Portuguese mariner who preceded to the seas his compatriot Magellan. But the turn inward that Pigafetta never makes toward that island, either in prose or water, corresponds inversely to the turns outward that the denizens of Fernando Poo would initiate centuries later in launching a globalized literary tradition in Spanish. Neither Pigafetta on sighting Spanish sands anew nor the empire that launched the fleet of Magellan in the first place would have foreseen that, in the wake of the circumnavigation, Africans would appear one day on Spanish shores as well.

By bypassing in silence western Africa and, in particular, Fernando Poo, Pigafetta left out of the story of the voyage the disparate lands that eventually would form the nation of Equatorial Guinea. Yet just as Pedro Paterno and José Rizal, the first Filipino novelists, would follow Pigafetta to Spain in a twinned trajectory, so too would Guinean intellectuals many decades thereafter. Once again, the arrivals in Madrid and Barcelona of subjects from virtually ignored faraway colonies would create a cartographic conundrum. After all, a nowhere on one map is a somewhere to those whose lives mark it, and when they head to a metropole they never do leave the periphery behind. Colonies and capitals result so intertwined as to become unresolvable to either. Similarly, the life of Pigafetta resounds with the death of Magellan, whose corpse stayed on Mactan Island even as its ghost sailed onward around the world. That circumnavigation continues still, coming to completions now and then but never to conclusions. The twentieth-century Guinean writers who joined the macrohistorical journey to Spain of Pigafetta, Paterno, and Rizal would demonstrate the Magellan fallacy again. The consequences of globalization are uncontrollable, regardless the powers of those who presume to put the whirls of the world in order by pen or by sword. The turn to Africa arrives however the continent is claimed to be constrained and contained, with words or without.

As a transoceanic phenomenon, African literature in Spanish emerges from a discontinuous series of Western absences. These include the Magellanic voyage no longer led by Magellan; the Pigafetta narrative that elides the return route northward toward Spain; the possession on paper by Spain of sub-Saharan lands that was not immediately matched by substantive Iberian presences there; and the persistent African invisibility in the story of 1898 that is still taught throughout the Spanish-speaking world and its corresponding academic departments. In that year, Spain lost in a war to the United States and consequently, by nearly all accounts, its final remaining colonies of Cuba, Puerto Rico, the Philippines, and Guam. The fact that colonies did remain thereafter in imperial control, most notably Spanish Guinea and Spanish Sahara, tends to go unrecognized, as does the protectorate that Spain ran over much of northern Morocco from 1912 to 1956. Redoubled Spanish efforts in the twentieth century at consolidating colonialism in western Africa did little to place on international maps the geopolitical spaces known today as Equatorial Guinea and Western Sahara.

The triumph of fascism in the Spanish Civil War in 1939 caused Spain itself to withdraw into a lengthy international isolation. If Filipino literature is inherently globalized because the world kept arriving on the shores of Mactan and Manila, Guinean literature is inherently globalized because the world kept turning away. The deliberate absences of the rest of the planet are an antipodal constituent of intentionally internationalized appearances elsewhere.

The Philippines and Equatorial Guinea do share the experience of Spanish occupation. This means that both nations coalesced amid its attendant cultural phenomena: influxes of Catholic missionaries, the literal and figurative architectures of administrators (both religious and secular), the creation of a Spanish-speaking indigenous elite, the desultory opportunities available to that elite by a geriatric empire long past the peak of its power, and so forth. This common imperial legacy, however, is somewhat deceptive. The formal Spanish presence in the Philippines ended decisively at the end of the nineteenth century, a moment when the de facto colonization of Spanish Guinea had not yet achieved a critical mass. It was only some decades after the imperial losses of 1898 that Spaniards began heading to sub-Saharan African in significant numbers in search of crops, timber, labor, souls, and other perceived resources of the land. In other words, there is more of a chronological succession than overlap between the lived experience of substantive Spanish colonialism in the Philippines and Equatorial Guinea. By contrast, the Philippines and Mexico maintained important commercial and political ties throughout the centuries following Magellan, with a famous galleon shipping route linking Manila and Acapulco on an annual or biannual basis for some 250 years.

In the middle of the twentieth century, the histories of the Philippines and Equatorial Guinea diverged still more dramatically. The violent colonization of the former by the United States from 1898 to 1946 was interrupted by the still more horrific colonization by Japan from 1942 to 1945. Both imperial invasions testified to the ongoing arrival of global forces in the archipelago. On the other side of the world, the isolated lands of Spanish Guinea experienced no comparable trajectory. Events of global magnitude largely passed them by. Nationalism too was slow to emerge in the colony despite the various militant movements that appeared in much of Africa after World War II. Whereas independence was granted to the Philippines in 1946 by the United States, autonomy of any sort for Spanish Guinea was not even a dim prospect at that point given the strongman rule over Spain itself by Francisco Franco. The colony remained under strict fascist control throughout the 1950s, notwithstanding some anticolonial stirrings among relatively small groups of individuals. This was the same era in which the first two novels by Guineans were written, some seven decades after the inaugural Filipino forays into that genre.

When the possibility of democratization did arrive belatedly for Guinea with nationhood in 1968, an experience of brutal dictatorship instead proved to be around the corner. This does provide a coeval point of potential comparison with the Philippines. The last third of the twentieth century was marked in Equatorial Guinea by the egregious regimes of Francisco Macías Nguema (1968–79) and Teodoro Obiang Nguema Mbasogo (1979–present) and in the Philippines by the autocracy of Ferdinand Marcos (1965–86). The infamy of Marcos, however, including his globally televised fall in the People Power movement headlined by Corazon Aquino, diverges sharply from the obscurity of the Equatoguinean despots despite the latter's rather worse record of governance. The only obvious moment in modern history when the world beyond Spain took note of Equatorial Guinea was when its large offshore oil reserves were discovered in the 1990s. Exploitation of those fields by U.S. interests was quick to follow. Here is another link to the Philippines, where the United States has dominated the extraction of natural resources, assisted as in Equatorial Guinea by the governing local elite, for over a century. The promise of Equatoguinean petrodollars is presumed to be a primary inspiration for a coup attempt in 2004 in which Mark Thatcher, son of the former British prime minister Margaret Thatcher, was implicated. It was also the root cause of an Equatoguinean money-laundering scandal that broke the same year in Washington, D.C., that forced the complicit and hitherto eminent Riggs Bank to close. As of this writing, various U.S. companies continue to drill Equatoguinean waters with the vocal political backing of the U.S. diplomatic mission.

Virtually all the national profits from oil go directly to the small group of individuals centered around President Obiang, who, at the death of fellow despot Muammar Gaddafi or Libya in 2011, became the longest-ruling dictator in all of Africa. The mathematical result of undistributed oil wealth is that, according to the human rights organization EG Justice, although Equatorial Guinea has "a per capita income exceeding that of Italy, the vast majority of its population lives in poverty on less than two US dollars per day" ("The Need").[2] A broad readership with the disposable income to support a conventional literary market is therefore an impossibility. There are very few basic freedoms permitted to writers and their potential audience inside the country in any case. There is no civil society to speak of nor any other non-state spaces in which writers might feel at liberty to express themselves however they might wish. There are no independent bookstores and no publishing houses to support such authors either. A free press, which under more democratic conditions would be a source of information flows to and from the rest of the world, does not exist. There are no independent mass media outlets of any kind.

Despite the many isolations and suppressions of the nation, Equatorial Guinea shares with the Philippines the primary marker of the world since Magellan: the instability of any attempt to contain the forces that constitute it. The country is inherently out of sync with itself, innately irreducible to its tired imperial overlays, to its archetypal dictatorships, to its tragically elusive petrodollars, to its poignant intellectual ideations that almost exclusively have been developed by authors in exile. Nor is the country definable as the sum of its ethnic heterogeneities, which, as in the Philippines, never have synthesized into a national polity. Even its geographic makeup is disjointed beyond any chance of cohesion. Equatorial Guinea, cut and pasted into a country by forces entirely foreign to it, features the island once known as Fernando Poo, now named Bioko. It is the historic home of the Bubi people and of an ethnic group of nineteenth-century origins, the Fernandinos. The largest region of Equatorial Guinea, however, named Río Muni, is a distant and completely artificial rectangle of land on the African continent proper. The Fang people and some smaller groups, such as the Ndowe (or Combes), traditionally have lived in Río Muni. A scattering of tiny islands, including faraway Annobón, where a Portuguese creole language is spoken, makes up the rest of the country.

During colonial epochs, Bioko, that is, Fernando Poo, received most of the attention and attempts at development. It is the seat of the national capital, Malabo, which was known before independence as Santa Isabel. Although Fang society emerged on the mainland over many centuries and is culturally foreign to Bioko, both dictators and the overwhelming preponderance of the ruling class of Equatorial Guinea have been Fang. The only place where Fang, Bubi, Fernandino, and Annobonese individuals seem to cohere in a sustained sense of a common nationality is, corollary to the paradoxes of the postmagellanic planet, in exile. The Macías regime of 1968 to 1979 was genocidal in its pursuit of intellectuals, so young Guineans who had gone to study in Spain before independence had little choice but to stay abroad during the decade-long tyranny. The ensuing Obiang dictatorship has allowed some writers and thinkers to live inside the country but nearly the entire surviving generation of authors who grew up prior to 1968 continues to invent the nation textually in writings composed outside its physical borders. As in the case of the early Filipino writers such as Paterno and Rizal, the narrative production of Guinea via prose and poetry in Spanish is geographically alienated in large part from the homelands of the authors. And like Paterno and Rizal, who therefore also navigated a ship of state outside the state itself, the exiled Equatoguinean authors have been foiled by the unexpected betrayals and irreducibilities of their own texts.

Given the persisting obscurity of hispanophone Africa, Guinean literature in Spanish may seem to be among the most parochial of written traditions to emerge in the middle of the twentieth century. Its authors are virtually unknown, its texts virtually inaccessible. Yet its appearance is deeply enmeshed in the dynamics of globalization that have defined the world since Magellan. In restless flows and uncertain orientations, Guinean literature in Spanish reaches out to other shores despite all the absences that have characterized it from Pigafetta to the petrodollars. Centuries of robust oral literatures in the Bubi, Fang, Ndowe, and other local languages do precede the incipience of all African Hispanic literature, but modernity emerges precisely in the unsettled nature of local and foreign interactions rather than in the relative geocultural coherence of artistic traditions of precolonial origins. Diverse indigenous oral traditions inform richly all written Guinean literature in Spanish, and to be sure, if any inverse influence exists, it is negligible. But it is the antigenealogical admixture of the local in unresolved tension with the foreign that lends the seemingly provincial nature of the Guinean corpus a manifestly global import.

The affirmative incoherence of many early African texts in Spanish, as in their early Asian counterparts, their inability to ground themselves either here or there, or to assume any form without simultaneously metamorphosing into another, is the hallmark of a transoceanic literature. Yet such fluidities often go unrecognized by academic projects invested in identifying unfamiliar artistic traditions. If the aspiration of such efforts is to bring to the fore a marginal national canon in order to recognize it as such, the effect is to ignore the fundamentally nonperipheral nature of the periphery. The attempt to open eyes leads instead to myopia. Guinean literature is certainly compelling by itself, but it also offers the opportunity to revamp multiple vantages on mainstream texts from Latin America and Spain. And when the center is viewed from the margins, instead of vice versa, the whole question of what is central and what is marginal begins to implode altogether. The underlying impossibility of constraining Guinean literature within Guinean narratives is what makes the tradition a globalized one and therefore of theoretical importance the world over.

INITIAL INSCRIPTIONS

The first African novel in Spanish, *Cuando los Combes luchaban* (*When the Combes Fought*) by Leoncio Evita, appeared in print in 1953 only because its Spanish editor, Carlos González Echegaray, wanted to show that "nuestros negros" ["our Negroes"] were successful colonial products of the fascist Francoist state ("untitled prologue," 5). He asserts in his preface that an "indígena evolucionado" ["evolved indigene"] like Evita "le merecen el carácter y la colonización de los españoles" ["deserves the character and colonization of the Spaniards"], with the novel a clear demonstration of the civilizing prowess of Spain ("untitled prologue," 6). The assumption behind its promotion and publication was that *When the Combes Fought* would serve as a useful anthropological novelty for the fascist government. The proof that a colonial subject could write a novel seemed to González Echegaray and his ideological cohort as an implicit defense of the Spanish imperial project as a progressive current in an African backwater. Such a self-congratulatory narrative contrasted sharply with those of the anticolonial movements that simultaneously were emerging ever stronger throughout other European territorial holdings in Africa. The idea that the novel by Evita, in terms of aesthetic or political achievement, was anything more complicated than a quasi-competent sketch of indigenous customs and comportment was inconceivable to González Echegaray. Decades later, when a few literary critics began to comment at last on *When the Combes Fought,* a corresponding consensus emerged despite the general anticolonialism of the new scholarship: the novel was routinely characterized as a local curiosity of mostly ethnographic interest. That is, in the half-century since publication, the politics of its reception had shifted dramatically but not the reception itself. The novel, recuperated but not reimagined, still today appears in nearly all accounts as a profoundly parochial artifact.

When the Combes Fought, however, is not a text at one with itself. It cannot be contained within the apparently limited boundaries of a minority ethnic society of a minor colony. For instance, the editorial intrusions and censorship by González Echegaray converted the text into a hybridity whose extent of forced hispanizations is unknown. The original manuscript by Evita is lost to history; all that remains is the version circumscribed and "corregido" ["corrected"], perhaps greatly bowdlerized as well, by the Spanish prologuist (González Echegaray, "[untitled prologue]," 5). The novel, far from an organic product by an isolated Guinean individual, is effectively coauthored in both visible (the prologue) and invisible (the corrections) ways. Moreover, it was published in Madrid, where Evita himself is not known ever to have been. The text, alienated from its author geographically, appeared and circulated far from the confines of the society that it depicted. Consequently, the novel was consumed by Spaniards, not Combes. The hypothetical alternative of publication within the colony would have been estranging in any case to most Combes, many of whom surely did not know Spanish or were not literate enough to read a novel even if it were available. In other words, no reading public of fellow Combes (or Bubi or Fang or Annobonese, for that matter) existed in Spain for *When the Combes Fought* and probably not in Spanish Guinea either. The genre alone was foreign to indigenous cultures of orality. If only for all these reasons, *When the Combes Fought* is a text so fraught with fragments of authorship and readership that it does not fit neatly within the prevailing presumption of a narrow tale ensconced in an equally narrow local space.

Like Evita, Pedro Paterno of the Philippines published his groundbreaking novel in Madrid. That text, *Nínay,* appearing in a metropole so distant from the people it describes, also escapes entirely its facile reduction to a product of the periphery. Paterno, however, at least lived and wrote his novel in the same place where he published and publicized it. He did not have to deal with a suppressive figure like González Echegaray. And he knew his novel would be read by fellow Filipino expatriates in Spain. To these extents, he was less alienated from its mode of production and distribution than his Guinean counterpart. Neither author, however, can be abstracted within a simplistic opposition of imperial center and colonial fringe. Time and again, each eludes the restrictions of any binary tensions that are stable in their assumptions of antipodality. Paterno does so by aligning the Philippines culturally and intellectually with Europe in common contradistinction to an uncivilized global South. Evita does so by re-

situating metaphorically the Spanish-American War of 1898 into the West
African lands of the Combes (Lifshey, *Specters*, 90–116). His protagonists include Protestant missionaries from the United States and military adventurers from Spain who have run away from anticolonial rebellions in Cuba.
The 1898 war, even without its figurative displacement to Africa by Evita,
was a conflict of extraordinary geographic dimensions in which North
American and European powers fought both each other and local revolutionaries in Southeast Asia and the Caribbean. The transposition by Evita
globalizes the conflict further by extrapolating it to his homeland in Africa.
His novel is therefore no more limited by localism than is Paterno's *Nínay*
and the postmagellanic world as whole. Though regarded by its procolonial
editor and later anticolonial critics alike as a rough artifact of ethnic dimensions, *When the Combes Fought* is actually a fluid phenomenon at all
levels of production, reception, content, and interpretation. It consistently
transgresses borders of colonial, national, and imperial import, unborder-
ing them in the process and offering instead shifting international signs
whose interrelations are never as stable or as easily defined as first appears.

The histories of hispanophone literature in Equatorial Guinea and the
Philippines are thus similar in their production of surpluses, for all attempts in the first novels to confine cultures and colonies within clear
boundaries come up short. Slippages and trespasses without end characterize *Nínay* and *When the Combes Fought*. In terms of quantitative output and
qualitative reception, however, Evita was no Paterno. The slim novel of the
former, an amateur writer with few if any pretensions to fame, stands in relief against the prolixity, prolificacy, and pomposity of the latter, a professional author. And Daniel Jones Mathama, the second African novelist in
Spanish and a forgotten forebear, is no José Rizal, the second Asian novelist in Spanish and a national hero. Evita and Jones Mathama only published one novel each and launched no consistent tradition, literary or intellectual or political or otherwise. Apparently, they were not aware of each
other's texts, which vanished into the void. Neither author left a lasting impression of any kind in either Spanish Guinea or Spain. Paterno and Rizal,
in contrast, knew each other personally and moved in overlapping circles
and social networks. They and their fellow Filipino expatriates in Europe
are hailed as the founding fathers of the Philippines. To this day, Rizal is a
posthumous institution at the center of the Filipino national imaginary.
And Paterno, though consigned by scholars of the Philippines to a consistently contemptuous place among the coauthors of the country, is still rec-

ognized at least as a minor, if ridiculous and occasionally traitorous, figure of a key generation of Filipino intellectuals. History and historians may have sidelined him, but Evita and Jones Mathama are isolated altogether. They are not associated with any national movements, minor or major, nor with any national sense of self. And though both Evita and Jones Mathama lived abroad for long stretches, unlike Paterno and Rizal they did not participate in the world of expatriate print journalism like *Solidarity*, the remarkable Filipino newspaper published in Barcelona and Madrid. They could not, in any case, for no Guinean equivalent existed.

By currently prevailing accounts, Paterno and Rizal were not succeeded immediately in Spanish by compatriot novelists. Supposedly, the third Filipino to publish a novel in that language, Jesús Balmori, did not do so until 1910, nineteen years after *El filibusterismo* by Rizal had appeared in 1891.[3] Similarly, twenty-three years passed after Jones Mathama's *Una lanza por el Boabí* (*A Spear for the Boabí*) of 1962—"Boabí" refers to a local leader—before the third and fourth Guinean novels were published in 1985. This parallelism of discontinuity, however, is somewhat misleading. In 1899, just three years after the death of Rizal and at the start of the U.S. colonial era, the first Filipino novel in Tagalog was published (Mojares, *Origins*, 169–70). Hundreds more appeared in the immediately ensuing decades (Mojares, *Origins*, 195). Creative texts in other Filipino languages also saw light soon after the imperial shift of 1898, with inaugural novels published in Pampangan and Hiligaynon in 1907, in Ilocano in 1909, and in Cebuano in 1912 (Mojares, *Origins*, 170). In other words, the hispanophone lineage was seemingly uneven in the years before and after the turn of the century, but in the meanwhile the written corpus of Filipino fiction in general grew increasingly polyglot. Eventually it would include novels in English as well. By contrast, when the two Guinean novels of 1985 were printed, *Ekomo* (the title refers to one of the lead characters) by María Nsue Angüe and *El reencuentro: el retorno del exiliado* (*The Reencounter: The Return of the Exile*) by Juan Balboa Boneke, no indigenous tradition of novels in any language had filled in the chronological gap that stretched from *A Spear for the Boabí* more than two decades earlier. As of 2011, in fact, no novel had yet appeared in Bubi or Fang or Annobonese. Whereas Rizal, despite composing in Spanish, remains acknowledged as the primary initiator of a written and multilingual national literary tradition, there is little sense that Evita and Jones Mathama are the forerunners of any such thing.

Likewise, the abundant and eclectic literary production by Paterno from *Sampaguitas* (the first Asian book of poetry in Spanish) and *Nínay* onward has no counterpart as of yet in Equatorial Guinea.[4] Few people today, including in the Philippines, are aware that Paterno wrote fiction, but in his time he could anticipate some sort of audience for many of his texts. His midcareer output, particularly his histories of the Philippines, was derided by his compatriot intellectuals as apocryphal and poorly executed, but erudite derision also is a form of reception. Moreover, Paterno wrote several of his late short stories for literary contests in Manila newspapers. These texts received thousands of votes from readers. Such a response by an approving public was denied to Evita and Jones Mathama because they had no public in the lands they wrote about in the first place. Indeed, there is not a single known contemporary comment on the publication of either *When the Combes Fought* or *A Spear for the Boabí*. Yet given the distance between the former prominence of Paterno and his current oblivion, the abyss into which his texts have fallen is arguably more profound than that which swallowed up the African authors. Their novels originally made no impact at all. Furthermore, a recuperation of Evita, though not of Jones Mathama, seems to be vaguely under way. The growing research into Equatoguinean literature by academics in Europe and North America, plus the writings of an active coterie of exiles in Spain, has led to some readings of the two novels of the colonial era. Such reception is almost certainly wider and more appreciative (at least in the case of Evita) than that which took place at their moments of publication. It is certainly greater than that bestowed upon Paterno today, for his fiction has next to no audience at all.

As for Rizal and his canonized novels, poems, and essays, there is no equivalent figure or corpus in hispanophone Africa. The absence of a national author-martyr-patriot and all corresponding mythologies is far and away the primary distinction between Asian and African literature in Spanish. Every Filipino child is required by law to read Rizal in the public school system. As a result, with Spanish de facto dead as a national idiom, the country is filled with translations of his writings into English and various vernaculars. But even if bookstores and libraries existed freely in Equatorial Guinea, a parallel law would be inconceivable because there is no sense that Evita and Jones Mathama are intertwined with a national identity in any way. Although a number of languages circulate in Equatorial Guinea, indigenous and European as well as creoles and pidgins, most people do speak Spanish and so, in theory and if sufficiently literate, could read the early novels. Neither one, however, is in print or readily available, though *When the Combes Fought* reappeared briefly in a second edition in Madrid in 1996. The lone issue of *A Spear for the Boabí* dates from half a century ago, and not a single copy of it may exist today in all of Equatorial Guinea. Moreover, no translation of it or of *When the Combes Fought* has been published in any language. In practice, the vast majority of Filipinos may not have read the Rizalian oeuvre any more than the vast majority of Spaniards have read the entirety of *Don Quijote*. Public and private forces of literary promotion are one thing and the realities of readership are another. Today, the primary consumption of both Rizal and Cervantes may be mediated instead through repackagings and rearrangements in other media such as films, television shows, websites, songs, school plays, and the like. Nonetheless, there endures in both Spain and the Philippines an intellectual and popular sense that the national literature and the national identity revolve in large part around a towering foundational author. This is not the case with Equatorial Guinea.

That disjunction between nation and literature is liberating. The apparent absence of any direct interpersonal or intertextual connection between Evita and Jones Mathama, plus the fragmented linkages among the communities of which they write, plus the utter artificiality of the nation into which those communities were yoked in 1968, is evocative of the unlimited limits of the postmagellanic world. The manifest lack of a tradition *is* a tradition: a tradition of discontinuity. The publication of a novel that has no public to read it *does* have a reception: a reception of absence. And Jones Mathama, the second novelist of hispanophone Africa, is as complex a figure as Rizal, the second novelist of hispanophone Asia. But *A Spear for the Boabí*, free of a narrative imposed by its own canonization or that of its author, avails itself to an array of interpretations beyond the type of a priori and overemplotted inclinations that guide, consciously or otherwise, so many readers of the Rizalian corpus. In its uniquenesses and distances of multiple kinds from Guinea, *A Spear for the Boabí* may seem to be an unrepresentative example of indigenous writing. Of the postmagellanic planet, however, there is nothing more representative than a literary text out of sync with itself and its conceded cultural context. Such is the mark of all African literature in Spanish and, in particular, the mark of novels from Guinea. If novels appear some day in Bubi or Fang or Annobonese, they still will emerge from a national antigenealogy that is consistent in its inconsistencies. The Guinean novel, at the moment, remains the Guinean novel in Spanish, yet still published entirely in Spain, still removed linguistically and physically from many, perhaps most, of those who appear in its pages.

When Rizal published his first novel, *Noli me tangere,* he knew that Paterno had published *Nínay* two years previously. For that matter, he knew Paterno. So did, apparently, every other Filipino in Spain as well as much of the Spanish elite, for Paterno was a remarkable self-promoter and high-society hobnobber. But Jones Mathama, unaware (like nearly everyone else) of Evita, found himself in a position of authorial isolation. Consequently, *A Spear for the Boabí* was advertised as a novelty when it appeared on the Spanish market. Published in Barcelona in 1962, the novel announces on its title page that it is the product of the "Primer autor de la Guinea Española" ["First author of Spanish Guinea"].

This claim is misleading, and not just because of the fact of an unknown predecessor. The African locus that is indicated, for example, is arguable. While it is true that Jones Mathama was born a colonial subject in Spanish Guinea and that the plot develops there, key elements denote that *A Spear for the Boabí* emerges from elsewhere: its publication in Catalonia, for instance, and the narrator's explicit positioning of himself as "aquí en España" ["here in Spain"] throughout his many metatextual musings (51). Furthermore, the question of whether the text is a novel in the first place is disputable. No other genre exists by which to classify its three hundred pages, but *A Spear for the Boabí* reads more like a failed attempt at imitating a foreign form than anything else. It is a bildungsroman whose structure repeatedly breaks down as the narrative digresses time and again away from the apparent protagonist, a boy named Gue. The fact, nonetheless, that the novel is not the first of Spanish Guinea, nor published there, nor conceived from there, nor perhaps even a novel, makes it compelling in its nonconformities. The text, inaccurately dismissed by scholars as collaborationist, reveals through its equivocations and ambiguities the hesitations of an indigenous and colonial author who believes he is launching a national literary tradition in harmony with empire. Yet his failures at metropolitan mimicry, both of ideology and form, are the true successes of his novel. These failures are the reason for the relevance of *A Spear for the Boabí* to theorizations of colonial and postcolonial literatures in other languages and regions of the world.

Readers of canonical Latin American literature long ago came upon references to the island setting of *A Spear for the Boabí* even if they did not recognize it as such. For example, "Danza negra" ["Black Dance"], an often anthologized poem by Luis Palés Matos of Puerto Rico and a key antecedent of the Afro-Cuban verse of writers such as Nicolás Guillén, begins as follows:

Calabó y bambú.
Bambú y calabó.
El Gran Cocoroco dice: tu-cu-tú.
La Gran Cocoroca dice: to-co-tó.
Es el sol de hierro que arde en Tombuctú.
Es la danza negra de Fernando Poo.
El cerdo en el fango gruñe: pru-pru-prú.
El sapo en la charca sueña: cro-cro-cró.
Calabó y bambú.
Bambú y calabó. (51)

[Calabó and bamboo.
Bamboo and calabó.
The Great Cocoroco says: tu-cu-tú.
The Great Cocoroca says: to-co-tó.
It is the iron sun that burns in Timbuktu.
It is the black dance of Fernando Poo.
The hog in the mud grunts: pru-pru-prú.
The toad in the pond dreams: cro-cro-cró.
Calabó and bamboo.
Bamboo and calabó.][5]

The eponymous sixth line implicitly links the rhythms of Afro-Caribbean culture to those of Fernando Poo, that is, the Guinean island now known as Bioko. Long after Palés Matos, Jones Mathama would become the first novelist originally from that island to portray life on it at length.[6]

The island of Fernando Poo also makes a brief appearance in a canonical text closer in time to Jones Mathama, *Biografía de un cimarrón* (*Biography of a Runaway Slave*) of 1966 by Miguel Barnet. This text is perhaps the primary prototype of the testimonial genre later made globally famous by the indigenous Guatemalan activist Rigoberta Menchú and her anthropologist collaborator, Elizabeth Burgos. Barnet based the biography on his interviews with Esteban Montejo, an Afro-Cuban centenarian who recalled his time as a slave in the late nineteenth century. In the text, Fernando Poo is described as a sort of penal colony to which recalcitrant slaves are banished by Camilo Polavieja, a Spanish governor of Cuba in the 1890s: "Una vez le dio por mandar negros a la isla de Fernando Poo. Aquello era un castigo fuerte, porque esa isla era desierta. Era una isla de cocodrilos y tiburones. Ahí soltaban a los negros y no se podían ir. A Fernando Poo mandaban a ladrones, chulos, cuatreros y rebeldes" ["One time he decided to send blacks to the island of Fernando Poo. That was a severe punishment because it was a desert island. It was an island of crocodiles and sharks. There they let the blacks go and they could not leave. Sent to Fernando Poo were thieves, pimps, rustlers, and rebels"] (85). This image of Fernando Poo is not altogether accurate, as it was by no means "desert." Quite the contrary, the island long had been home to the Bubi people who appear in *A Spear for the Boabí*. In other words, the emptying of an insular indigenous presence in Barnet is not remotely present in Jones Mathama. As a trope, however, the Fernando Poo in *Biography of a Runaway Slave* is richly suffused. On one hand the island is barbarism incarnate, with savage animals ready to assault slaves deemed equally unfit for human society. On the other hand, those slaves have achieved a kind of offshore return to an ancestral continent and a certain liberty of action and speech unthinkable in Cuba. They bear on their bodies the brand of subversion of empire as well, for Barnet notes that all Cuban slaves sent to the island were marked with a tattoo that was a "señal de rebeldía contra el gobierno español" ["sign of rebelliousness against the Spanish government"] (85).

The interviews that formed the basis of *Biography of a Runaway Slave* took place in 1963, just after the publication of *A Spear for the Boabí*, so Barnet could not have served Jones Mathama as any type of influence. Nonetheless, the history of slaves condemned to freedom on Fernando Poo in the late nineteenth century would seem a potent social and temporal context, one of many that the Guinean author either ignores or does not know about. In fact, *A Spear for the Boabí* at first glance seems to be a chronologically and intertextually limited novel. Jones Mathama does not mention any historical episodes prior to the temporal framework of his plot, which begins with the birth of Gue on May 17, 1913, and ends with a denouement upon his leaving the island for Lagos in 1923 (14, 284). In the very brief final section of the novel, entitled "Conclusion," Gue heads to Europe in 1925 (308). Virtually all subsequent history, individual and social as well as African and European, is then elided by the passing remark that Gue returns to Fernando Poo upon the death of his father after "muchos años transcurrieron" ["many years passed"] (308). In short, the internal time span of the plot of the novel is seemingly unlinked to major historical phenomena before or after it.

A Spear for the Boabí also appears ungrounded by any traditions of written literature before it. Jones Mathama makes no reference either to Palés Matos of "Black Dance" or to Leoncio Evita, the only predecessor novelist from Spanish Guinea. And so uncontextualized, Jones Mathama struggles constantly to affirm his right to an authorial existence given the writerly vacuum in which he senses himself situated. The successive opening frames of his text, including the book cover and an advertising ribbon that surrounds it, the inaccurate title page, a prefatory remark, an introduction, an epigraph, and the commencement of the first chapter, constitute in the aggregate a desperate attempt to establish his legitimacy in an authorial space so undefined as to allow him no stable grounds from which to write. The prefatory mark, for instance, reveals his acute awareness of transgressing a boundary simply by daring to publish:

> *Acaso sea innecesario, pero me veo obligado a dar una corta explicación antes de iniciar mi breve e histórico relato. En la actualidad, la mayoría de los autores ponen sus fotos en el anverso o en el dorso de sus libros, y como quiera que esta costumbre se va generalizando, no quisiera apartarme de la corriente; pero tampoco quiero que la gente me juzgue de antemano siguiendo la célebre frase 'La cara es el espejo del alma'. Porque sé positivamente que si me tuviesen que juzgar de acuerdo con la mencionada frase sería condenado sin discusión alguna. (5)*

[Perhaps it is unnecessary, but I find myself obligated to give a short explanation before initiating my brief and historical story. Currently, the majority of authors put their photos on the front or on the back of their books, and since this custom is becoming general, I did not want to stray from the trend; but I also do not want people to judge me beforehand by following the famous phrase, "The face is the mirror of the soul." Because I know positively that if they had to judge me in accordance with the mentioned phrase, I would be condemned without any discussion.]

That a portrait photo on a book cover would render an author "condemned without any discussion" is hardly common. That such an author would produce a thoroughly collaborationist text in the subsequent pages—and this is the consensus verdict of the scarce existing scholarship on *A Spear for the Boabí*—seems even less likely. Jones Mathama shows himself here to be extremely cognizant of the tensions involved in putting a photo of a Guinean on his text. His readers in Spain, he suspects, literally will judge the book by its cover. A physically black face, he implies, will be taken immediately as a reflection of a metaphorically black soul. Consequently, it is risky for him to join the "custom" and "trend" of metropolitan authors no matter how much he desires to do so.

The concerns voiced in the prefatory remark are discordant with the cover that did appear on the lone edition of the book. It features a snapshot, the size of a passport photo, of the author in a suit and tie. The author's eyes focus to the right of the reader, as if looking ahead. The photo is inset amid a much larger sketch of a black man wearing only a loincloth and holding a red spear against a green, presumably sylvan backdrop. His profile opposes that of the photographed author in that the sketched figure is seen only from behind and facing to the left of the reader, as if into the past. In this sense, the professional Western dress and gaze of the author explicitly contrasts with the signifying stylings of the sketched figure. It also contradicts the prefatory remark that suggests that there will be no such photo. Jones Mathama is so unsure of where he stands that all presumed pairings dissolve into neither parallels nor binaries: the geographic (the European site of publication and the African mise-en-scène of the narrative), the aesthetic (the visual signs of the cover and the verbal message of the prefatory remark), the technological (the photograph and the sketch), the temporal (the future and the past), the sartorial (the suit and the loincloth), even the phallic (the necktie and the spear) all overflow with signification. Apparently opposing signs play against each other but remain unresolved into one or another, much less joined in some sort of synthesis. There is no functioning dialectic here because the implicit theses and antitheses are too unstable to exist coherently unto themselves in the first place. The cover covers nothing because the inside of the book spills over to the outside that in turns spills back inside. Everywhere there is surplus and supplement. The subjectivity of the author settles in a fluid nowhere that is at once a fluid everywhere. And this is the paradoxical phenomenon that is the postmagellanic planet: the limitlessness of all borders and therefore of all self-definitions within them. Jones Mathama is a colonial subject willing to imitate a hegemonic model but consciously unable to do so. His text resists assimilation in its pervasive efforts at embracing it. These tensions brim over the book before the text that it only seems to contain even begins. The metatexuality of the prefatory remark and the semiotic stresses of the cover and title pages allude to an authorial voice and project that wavers over the edges of viability.

GROUNDINGS UNGROUNDED

The little background data available on Jones Mathama may seem to offer clues for a more traditional contextualization of the dissonances of the novel. Jones Mathama was a Fernandino, an ethnicity of disparate and relatively recent origins on Fernando Poo. Sources do not entirely agree on the historical constitution of this group, though all coincide in placing its ethnogenesis as rooted in multiple international arrivals to the island in the nineteenth century. In that era, writes T. Bruce Fryer,

> *la isla estaba poblada por esclavos liberados de los barcos negreros por los ingleses, por criollos angoleños liberados y por braceros procedentes de Sierra Leona y Nigeria. The Baptist Missionary Society instalada en la isla en 1841 también empezó a hacer venir colonos de Jamaica, los cuales junto con los esclavos libertos e inmigrantes de Sierra Leona formaron una clase comerciante llamada los 'fernandinos'. Actuaban como intermediarios y empresarios en el negocio del aceite de palma entre los españoles y los bubis. (6)*

[the island was populated by slaves freed from slave ships by the English, by freed Angolan creoles, and by seasonal workers arriving from Sierra Leone and Nigeria. The Baptist Missionary Society established in the island in 1841 also began to make colonists come from Jamaica, who with the freed slaves and immigrants from Sierra Leone formed a commercial class called the "Fernandinos." They acted as intermediaries and businessmen in the trade of palm oil between the Spaniards and the Bubi.]

Justo Bolekia Boleká says that arrivals from Liberia, Cuba, and Germany also merged into the Fernando Poo population as Fernandinos, who were "considerados menos negros por parte de los colonizadores, actuaron de intermediarios para que éstos se fueran adentrando cada vez más en las tierras bubis, fang, etc. . . . llegaron a aconsejar a la autoridad militar el uso de métodos violentos para poder así doblegar a los Bubis, siempre contrarios a ser contratados como braceros" ["considered less black by the colonizers.

They acted as intermediaries so that the colonizers went ever deeper into the lands of the Bubi, Fang, etc. . . . They reached a point where they advised the military authority on the use of violent methods in order to crush thereby the spirit of the Bubi, who were always opposed to being contracted as seasonal workers"] (86). Susan Martin-Márquez describes the Fernandinos as "descendants of the English-speaking free blacks who rose to prominence on the island of Fernando Po beginning in the late nineteenth century" (281). Annette Dunzo says that along with freed slaves and creole individuals from Sierra Leone, the group included "men from Lagos, Krumen from Liberia, Luso-Africans, Fantis from southern Ghana; together they constituted a kind of economic and cultural creole *élite* known as Fernandinos" (321).

All scholars, however differently they specify the demographic creation of the ethnicity, concur that as an intermediary class between Spain and the older indigenous societies of the colony, the Fernandinos came to enjoy access to capital and legal rights denied to the Bubi, the Fang, the Ndowe, and the Annobonese. Ibrahim Sundiata, however, whose 1972 dissertation appears to stand even now as the only lengthy monograph on the Fernandinos, emphasizes that their uniqueness lies not in their moments as ethnic middlemen so much as in the transient historical era that was the last third of the nineteenth century. At that point, European power on Fernando Poo, and specifically its urban center, was mostly nominal, and a largely autonomous Fernandino bourgeoisie arose: "The significance of Fernando Po and the Fernandinos is that on that island a class of black plantation owners was allowed to develop to an extent unknown in most other areas inhabited by black freedmen. Fernando Po is striking in that it is the one area in which a class of highly Westernized black landowners were able to temporarily gain a dominant place in a colonial economy" ("The Fernandinos," iv).

Whatever the originary and subsequent components and roles of the Fernandinos, the ethnicity is clearly a direct product of globalization. Transcontinental and transatlantic movements of capital, both monetized (the palm oil trade) and human (the slave trade), are inextricable from the history of the Fernandinos. Their ethnic essence is their ethnic nonessence, their primordial roots utterly modern. European, African, and American cultures interweave in an unsteady mix that, if the above accounts are to be believed, must have incorporated dialects of Spanish and English from variegated sources on three continents as well as German, Bubi, Fang, Angolan variants of Portuguese, and African languages from Nigeria, Liberia, Ghana, and perhaps elsewhere. The mediating and sometimes exploitative role that the Fernandinos purportedly played often in Guinean economics and politics between the Spaniards and indigenous populations also necessarily would have left them with an ill-defined place in any inchoate sense of a national community and identity.

Put another way, Jones Mathama did not emerge from an ethnic group that could attempt to claim territorial or cultural roots on Fernando Poo or elsewhere in Spanish Guinea from time immemorial. The "Jones" of "Jones Mathama" is evidently a legacy of an anglophone forebear and as such a marker of the extraterritorial roots of all Fernandinos, not just his own family. Donato Ndongo-Bidyogo, writing about mid-nineteenth-century Fernando Poo, offers a hint that the Jones family may even be of U.S. origins: the island "atrajo a los negros libertos que los Estados Unidos estaban enviando a Liberia y Sierra Leona. Así llegaron a Fernando Poo los primeros King, Jones, Dougan, Atkins y Collins" ["attracted the freed blacks that the United States was sending to Liberia and Sierra Leone. Thus arrived to Fernando Poo the first individuals named King, Jones, Dougan, Atkins, and Collins"] (*Historia*, 29). As a member of an ethnicity at once dramatically foreign and uniquely Guinean, Jones Mathama cannot be smoothly claimed as "the first author of Spanish Guinea" not only because of the erroneous indication of primacy but also because he writes from a community space that arguably is not, at several levels, quite "of Spanish Guinea" either. He may have been born on Bioko but neither he nor the Boabí turns out to be Bubi. He is not Spanish either, at least not from a normative Spanish perspective. And he can no more assimilate his text to a paradigm of the colonizers than to a paradigm of the colonized. The history and relative wealth of the Fernandinos in general destabilize any easy imagining of Jones Mathama as a national or protonational voice for an oppressed and local people.

As an individual, however, Jones Mathama is no more reducible to his ethnic group than anyone else. No man is an archetype. But the few details that have been published of his own life also complicate his authorial position. According to Mbaré Ngom, the titular Boabí of the novel "no es otro que un esbozo de Maximiliano C. Jones, el padre del autor, una de las autoridades locales más representativas y 'respetadas' por las autoridades coloniales por su adhesión a la política de España" ["is none other than a sketch of Maximiliano C. Jones, the father of the author, one of the local authorities most representative and 'respected' by the colonial authorities for his adherence to the policies of Spain"] ("La literatura africana," 413).[7] Jones was the richest and most powerful of the Fernandinos and a man with a hazy and internationalized background of his own. He does not seem to have been raised on Fernando Poo, perhaps not born there either. Popular opinion held that he was of Nigerian descent and arrived on Fernando Poo toward the end of the nineteenth century (Nkogo). The eponymous passage of the novel, however, says of the Boabí that "se veía que era oriundo de la formidable raza de los zulús" ["it could be seen that he was a native of the formidable Zulu race"], which would place his origins in southern Africa (222). Max Liniger-Goumaz, whose biographical blurb on Jones may be the most detailed in publication, does not identify a birthplace or childhood environment but notes that the future patriarch was "Protestant, but educated at a Jesuit school in Spain" (222). Subsequently, Jones rose to become a unique figure in early twentieth-century Guinean history. According to Liniger-Goumaz, Jones "opened a printer's shop" in Fernando Poo in 1900, "advised the Spanish troops in their repression of the Bubi revolt against forced labor" in 1910, and "was the only African among the 10 largest planters of the island" in 1920 (222). Sundiata writes that Jones's father was a prominent trader and that his mother was from Freetown in Sierra Leone and that, by 1907, Jones's "position enabled him to ingratiate himself with the Spanish administration by freely granting lands to the town of San Carlos for its expansion. Jones practically owned the town; the inhabitants having to depend on him for certain building supplies" ("The Fernandinos," 345).

In correspondence to such wealth, various formal and informal powers kept accruing to the family. Liniger-Goumaz notes of Wilwardo Jones Niger, son of Maximiliano and elder brother of Daniel, that "Around 1945 he became the most important native planter of Fernando Po" and that "He won the municipal elections of June 1960 in Santa Isabel [present-day Malabo] and became the first African mayor to be elected in Equatorial Guinea" (222–23). That political triumph, in other words, took place about the same time at which his younger brother in Barcelona probably was completing A Spear for the Boabí. Liniger-Goumaz adds that in 1970, shortly after national independence, Spanish coup plotters apparently intended to install Wilwardo Jones Niger as the new president (223). The putsch, like most others in subsequent years, was not realized. Two sons of Jones Niger also sought and/or held political office (223). Furthermore, Sundiata points out that Maximiliano's "affluence enabled him to send two of his sons, Daniel and Adolfo (Adolf), to Spain for training, the latter being trained as an electrical engineer. This skill was no doubt useful in 1925 when Maximiliano constructed a thermal electric generating plant in the capital. The daughters of the family, Clara, Mabel, and Juana (Joan) completed their education in Barcelona; Mabel's wedding in Barcelona in 1921 was a social occasion of great importance for the Fernandino community" ("The Fernandinos," 346). In short, the Jones family was a singular phenomenon in Guinean history. Launched by the economic and political heft obtained by Maximiliano Jones and shaped by sundry extraterritorial trajectories over several generations, the family does not offer a particularly representative and rooted set of protagonists for a novel that ostensibly features traditional life in Spanish Guinea.

As for Daniel Jones Mathama himself, the hybrid geographies of his life transcend even those of the rest of his family. According to Ndongo-Bidyogo, Jones Mathama was born on Fernando Poo in 1908 as "el menor de los hijos reconocidos por Maximiliano Jones, el exponente más representativo de la burguesía fernandina" ["the youngest of the children recognized by Maximiliano Jones, the most representative example of the Fernandino bourgeoisie"] (*Literatura de Guinea Ecuatorial,* 455). Spanish Guinea, however, was the setting only of Jones Mathama's childhood, for as Ndongo-Bidyogo adds, he then studied at Oxford College in England, moved to Barcelona in 1931 to study medicine, then switched paths and "fundó una de las primeras academias de inglés de la Ciudad Condal, que alcanzó enorme prestigio, siendo elegida para la educación de los hijos de la burguesía catalana" ["founded one of the first English academies of Condal City. It became extremely prestigious and was the school of choice for the education of the children of the Catalan bourgeoisie"] (455–56). Among the students was Juan Antonio Samaranch, the future president of the International Olympic Committee (456). Jones Mathama thus wrote what was promoted as the first novel from Spanish Guinea only after spending nearly three decades in Barcelona. In addition, if not an anglophile, he was at least an individual heavily invested in the anglophone world. Ndongo-Bidyogo notes that Jones Mathama even published some English grammar texts and an anthology of children's stories in English (456). Annette Dunzo writes that Jones Mathama "authored several short stories in English, which, he claims, were printed in Irish newspapers. One of them, entitled 'I Denied my Father' (1968), deals with a political incident that occurred during the Spanish Civil War" (325). These literary products complicate the assumption that Jones Mathama should be considered a novelist of or from Guinea. He did not obtain his higher education there nor make his career there nor spend his adult life there. The only reason he is not considered a Spaniard is because the mythologies of Spanish national identity have no discursive space for immigrants. Indeed, modern Spain is built on historic notions of expulsion and exclusion, such as of Moors, Jews, and Romani, hence the conceptual impossibility of marketing Jones Mathama, decades after he left his colonial birthplace behind, as anything other than Guinean.

The descriptions by Ndongo-Bidyogo and Liniger-Goumaz seem to be the source for virtually all later published references to the lives of Maximiliano Jones and Daniel Jones Mathama.[8] Such is the isolation of early Guinean literature and any contemporary commentary on it, however, that there may be texts buried in archival holdings that yet can enter debates with substantive new information and so change existing frameworks of interpretation. An essay from 1965 by Manuel Castillo Barril, for example, that is cited on occasion by linguists but apparently not by literary scholars, offers data that contradicts and complements that in Ndongo-Bidyogo. Castillo Barril says that Jones Mathama was born on May 17, 1913, not in 1908, and then in 1923 "fue enviado por sus padres a Lagos, Nigeria" ["was sent by his parents to Lagos, Nigeria"] (61). These details, if true, would be critical to any biographical reading of the novel for indicating that the author was born the same day as Gue, the protagonist, and left Spanish Guinea for Lagos in the same year. Castillo Barril also gives 1929, not 1931, as the time when Jones Mathama arrived in Barcelona and adds that "En 1933 contrajo matrimonio con una bella dama catalana, de ojos azules y de sonrisa dulce" ["In 1933 he married a beautiful Catalan lady with blue eyes and a sweet smile"] (61). In terms of the literary production of Jones Mathama, Castillo Barril offers a report repeated nowhere else. First, he says that the initial publications of Jones Mathama were "cuentos en inglés" ["short stories in English"], a primacy not indicated by Ndongo-Bidyogo or Dunzo (61). Second, he identifies the title of an English grammar book published by Jones Mathama as "Our Friends" (62). Third, and most important, is that Castillo Barril writes "Tiene otra novela inédita, 'Etapas', y en la actualidad prepara otra, 'Las dos razas'" ["He has another, unpublished novel, *Stages,* and currently is preparing another, *The Two Races*"] (62). That is, there very well may be three or even four Guinean novels from the colonial era, not just *When the Combes Fought* and *A Spear for the Boabí*. Somebody needs to start searching Barcelona to see whether the manuscripts of *Stages* and *The Two Races* remain in the possession of some relative or are preserved in a local archive. Jones Mathama was evidently a fairly well-known figure in certain Catalonian circles and, vis-à-vis Spanish Guinea, a member of the most powerful family from the colony. It is entirely possible that his unpublished novels survive somewhere.

If an analysis of *A Spear for the Boabí* is going to take into consideration extratextual questions, that is, the biography of the author, his familial and ethnic context, his geographical and historical moorings, and so forth, then the significance of Jones Mathama as a protonational novelist is that the nation in question is unbordered within his own person to the extent that no local, regional, continental, or hemispheric frame constrains it. Jones Mathama was a man who no doubt moved fluently among at least four languages (Catalan, Spanish, English, and the Fernandino creole) and many shores.[9] His timeline in Spain is itself marked by one of the landmark twentieth-century international events, the Spanish Civil War of 1936–39, in which he must have taken part in one fashion or another given the tumultuous centrality of Catalonia. No resident, particularly not an intellectual by profession, seems likely to have remained a complete bystander to the events and atmosphere that drew writers such as George Orwell and Ernest Hemingway to Barcelona. It is quite possible that Jones Mathama read those authors in the original, perhaps even taught excerpts from them at his English school. When he died in Barcelona in 1983, some two decades after *A Spear for the Boabí* had appeared and disappeared in obscurity, Jones Mathama still must have believed that he stood as the first and only Guinean novelist. But what it means to be a Guinean novelist more than fifty years after having left Guinea is another issue altogether.

However the shifting international history of the Fernandinos in general and of his family in particular are deduced to contextualize Jones Mathama, he perceived himself with *A Spear for the Boabí* to be entering political, economic, and literary markets hitherto closed to his kind, whatever kind that is. The contours of those markets before him overlapped various national, subnational, and supranational boundaries that ranged from a Spanish state tightly consolidated by the Franco autocracy, to suppressed Catalan and Bubi drives for autonomy, to the persisting Euro-African stretch of the Spanish empire itself. Jones Mathama is not a new novelist attempting to break into a stable terrain because the grounds from which he writes are themselves fluid. And the permutations of his positionalities are probably what led him to seek security from a governing body that could sanctify his right to speak from wherever it was that he spoke: the selection committee of the Nadal Prize, a prestigious annual literary award in Spain. Previous winners had included many authors whose texts now form the canon of midcentury Spanish literature, including Carmen Laforet, Miguel Delibes, Carmen Martín Gaite, and Ana María Matute. Strikingly, some if not all of the copies of *A Spear for the Boabí* were encircled by a red strip of paper that announces "OBRA SELECCIONADA EN EL PREMIO NADAL 1960 por el primer autor de la Guinea Española" ["SELECTED WORK OF THE 1960 NADAL PRIZE by the first author of Spanish Guinea"].

This declaration is deceptively simple. Jones Mathama is not "the first author of Spanish Guinea." But that mistake is understandable given the ephemeral presence of *When the Combes Fought*. More interesting than the error of the epithet is its presence per se as a marketing device. It was intended no doubt to pique the curiosity of any bookbuying Spaniard who otherwise might look past an unknown novel with an indecipherable title by an unknown author. Yet the very quality that makes Jones Mathama marketable, his advertised Guineanness, is that which undercuts his ability to stand for a national prize as a literary figure in the first place. It is inconceivable, for instance, that the Franco dictatorship, determined to repress all regional drives for autonomy, would permit a native Barcelonan author to be highlighted as writing from Catalonia rather than from Spain. But Jones Mathama is publicized as hailing from a geopolitical subset of the state instead of from the nation proper. His claim to discourse is based directly on his lack, as a colonial subject, of a claim to discourse.

Coincident with that contradiction, the marketing moniker ignores entirely the reality that by that point Jones Mathama had lived outside Spanish Guinea for three and a half decades and wrote from a space fully embedded in the Spanish state, his Catalonian context and anglophone profession notwithstanding. The tagline of "the first author of Spanish Guinea" is therefore an intricate mixture of multiple suppressions and conversions.[10] The fact that Jones Mathama did not win the Nadal Prize but was merely "selected" for it—an ambiguous achievement of uncertain significance—also leaves him in the gray zone of an author who both is and is not authorized to write by a nation and a national literary committee. Castillo Barril says that *A Spear for the Boabí* came in "el honroso décimo lugar" ["an honorable tenth place"] in the competition. Whether the

qualifier "honorable" here is meant condescendingly or not—either interpretation is possible—the fact remains that the producers of the advertising
ribbon chose not to specify exactly how low, or how high, the novel ranked
for this prestigious prize and thus how validated was the voice that issued
forth within it (62).

Jones Mathama's own introduction to *A Spear for the Boabí*, notably,
suggests that he senses that his right to discourse is so questionable as to
raise the issue of whether his readers would consider him sane. "Primero he
de aclarar," announces Jones Mathama, "que según dictamen facultativo,
soy un ser bastante normal, y mis amigos y conocidos lo corroboran"
["First, I must clarify that according to medical report, I am a sufficiently
normal being, and my friends and acquaintances corroborate that"] (7).
This unusual need to affirm the legitimacy of his own existence, and therefore of his right to articulate that existence via the production of a text that
inscribes it, should be located in its unacknowledged roots: his mistaken
understanding that he is the first Guinean author to enter the world of
Spanish letters. Dominant discourses, by definition, set the rules of nor-
malcy. Excluded voices that seek inclusion, therefore, have to first and foremost prove that they belong within the definition of the normal. Yet this is
a paradoxical and doomed endeavor because exclusion a priori implies
anormalcy and any of its devastating sociopolitical variants: barbarism,
madness, oneiric delusion, and so on.

Subsequent musings by Jones Mathama on how "[le] asaltan extrañas
ideas" ["strange ideas seize him"] reveal the nature of the task before him,
such as when he confesses that "A veces me veo convertido en un Tarzán
de pie sobre un elefante blanco y dando órdenes a una manada de pro-
boscídeos y paquidermos" ["Sometimes I see myself converted into a
Tarzan standing atop a white elephant and giving orders to a herd of pro-
boscideans and pachyderms"] (7). The dream of becoming Tarzan is that of
inverting his relationship to the very darknesses he knows his readers
dread, those that lie beyond and therefore oppose and define their own systems of knowledge. Here in a virtual space, this African author suddenly
does have a portrait photo that will not condemn him. He is a white man
taming the jungle, representing it for the armchair colonialist back home.
This is to say that he deserves to be included in the discursive systems that
exclude him. There is a deep pathos in this yearning by Jones Mathama to
become Tarzan. It is a dream destined to failure.

The unreality of the Tarzan conversion is manifested further by the rapidity with which it succumbs to other equally unstable imaginings. As Jones Mathama writes in the next sentence, "En ocasiones, también me veo montado a caballo al frente de numerosos soldados, guerreando y conquistando ciudades y naciones contra un enemigo desconocido. En otras me veo cargado de cadenas, sudando y sangrando bajo el látigo de un implacable carcelero" ["On some occasions, I also see myself mounted on a horse in front of numerous soldiers, warring and conquering cities and nations against an unknown enemy. On other occasions, I see myself weighed down with chains, sweating and bleeding beneath the whip of an implacable jailer"] (7). Conquistador one moment and slave the next, he then promptly refashions himself as "sentado sobre un trono, con el cetro en la mano, dictando leyes y dando órdenes a unos ministros que se mantienen en pie con las cabezas inclinadas en señal de respeto y sumisión" ["seated upon a throne with the scepter in hand, dictating laws and giving orders to some ministers who remain standing with their heads bowed in a sign of respect and submission"] (7–8). What kind of an introduction is this? The purpose of any prologue is to guide the reader on how to interpret the text to follow; the exercise is at once pedagogical and affirmative. In the nested opening frames of *A Spear for the Boabí,* however, Jones Mathama ricochets from inaugural author (allegedly) to material nonentity (the absent photo that appears nonetheless) to conqueror to slave to king, none of which has anything to do with the text at hand and everything to do with his own metatextual position as author. This position is so precarious as to collapse constantly and without end. Jones Mathama seeks to explain away his diverse imaginings with "¿Acaso no podría ser un sueño lo que la gente llama realidad?" ["Perhaps what people call reality is but a dream?"] and situates this rhetorical conjecture in a Christian episteme (8). The true reality, he says, is not the tangible world but the spiritual sphere of Christ. Yet the religious argument is unconvincing. For an indigenous author seeking inclusion in a foreign discursive system, the difference between "what people call reality" and the worlds of dreams, insanity, and barbarism is all that which separates metropole from periphery.

FAILURES AS SUCCESSES

Most scholars have dismissed *A Spear for the Boabí* as a straightforward defense of the Spanish colonizing project. Mbaré Ngom has argued repeatedly that "En definitiva, la novela de Daniel Jones Mathama justifica la situación colonial . . . lo cual la sitúa . . . dentro de la literatura de consentimiento" ["All in all, the novel by Daniel Jones Mathama justifies the colonial situation . . . which situates it . . . within the literature of consent"] ("La literatura africana, 413).[11] He adds that *A Spear for the Boabí* offers the author's praise-filled vision of the colonial situation, whose benefits he describes in Spanish Guinea. Nor does he miss any opportunity to cast a critical eye upon the indigenous populations and to denounce them as 'savages'" ("African Literature," 589). Jorge A. Salvo, one of the few researchers to attempt an analytic overview of early Guinean prose, has implied that *A Spear for the Boabí* is not worth studying at all because of its procolonial sentiment. Although only five Guinean novels were published prior to 1990, the upper time limit of his study, Salvo argues that excluding *A Spear for the Boabí* from interrogation is justifiable on ideological grounds: "Por pertenecer a la llamada literatura de consentimiento, que hace la apología del colonialismo, se descartó la novela de Jones Mathama" ["For belonging to the so-called literature of consent, which serves as an apology for colonialism, the novel by Jones Mathama was ruled out"] (2). This decision is striking given the paucity of Guinean novels and the title of Salvo's investigation, "La formación de la identidad en la novela hispano africana" ("The Formation of Identity in the Hispano-African Novel"). It seems certain that in a text of some three hundred pages that is a unique artifact of world literature, there must be any number of possible analytical endeavors worth undertaking. Yet up until now only a few short studies have focused on *A Spear for the Boabí* and sought to unpack its complications.[12] The bulk of all references to the novel are brief and committed to the conclusion that it is ideologically collaborative.

Such verdicts are rooted in the many times that Jones Mathama lauds the Spanish colonial presence. The titular Boabí is the leader of a local community on Fernando Poo, a wise and mature man who evidently deserves his position and who is great friends with the Spanish imperial authorities. "Siempre luchó en pro de la justicia," explains the narrator. "Tanto es así, que el mismo gobierno de S.M. Alfonso XIII, y más tarde el de la República, supieron distinguirle merecidamente" ["He always fought for justice, so much so that the very government of His Majesty Alfonso XIII, and later that of the Republic, knew to honor him deservedly"] (92).[13] Gue, the Boabí's son, is born in the opening pages of the text and proceeds through a series of coming-of-age experiences that allow the narrator to explore various local landscapes and customs. In the final pages, Gue heads to Europe to be educated. In other words, *A Spear for the Boabí* sets itself up for the charge of procolonialism by tracing the trajectory of a Fernando Poo father-and-son tandem who prove able to assimilate to Western orders.

It would be a disservice to exclude *A Spear for the Boabí* from discussion even if it presented a case of clear-cut collaborationism. After all, as Benita Sampedro Vizcaya notes, "The inclusion of Africa in intellectual discussions of Spanish imperial and colonial history and criticism remains a largely unexplored path. It is a path that must be pursued" ("African Poetry," 202–3). And Ngom himself suggests that "African literature in Spanish is a cultural project that has received very little critical and theoretical attention. . . . African literature in Spanish may be considered the most conspicuous absentee in the literary debate on Hispanic and/or African literatures" ("African Literature," 584). Surely even an allegedly procolonial novel is worth examining at length given the dearth of relevant primary and secondary literature, particularly a text that claims to be launching a particular cultural tradition in the hispanophone world. After all, praise of power is rarely absent of implied tensions. A panegyric from the periphery is usually not quite what it seems.

A periphery, from all appearances, is indeed Jones Mathama's subject in *A Spear for the Boabí.* He indicates as much as the novel proper begins with an epigraph and the initial lines of the first chapter. These are the final frames that position his reader before the plots and characters are introduced. The epigraph is the first of many that will precede the chapters to come. Each of them is a curious construction. Although the epigraphs are usually portentous and vaguely moralistic, they often seem to bear no direct relationship to the chapter that follows. Furthermore, they are always signed by "El autor" ["The author"]. This belies the basic purpose of epigraphs, which is to inform the subsequent text with the legitimizing declaration of a third party. As a result, Jones Mathama materializes in them at a distance from his own literary production. He cites only himself in the epigraphs as the authorizing inscriber, which suggests again that he is an isolated figure whose book is precariously situated outside the realm of the discourses of other people. Moreover, the dubious relationship of the epigraphs to their associated chapters unsettles further the organizing principles of the novel. The first chapter, for example, begins with the following epigraph: "Al asomarme al exterior quedé asombrado ante tanta belleza, pero más adelante aquel asombro se tradujo en horror ante la monstruosidad de hombres y bestias. El autor" ["Upon leaning outside, I was amazed before so much beauty, but later that amazement translated itself into horror before the monstrosity of men and beasts. The author"] (11). The main body of the chapter, however, commences with "En un apartado rincón del mundo, sembrado por la Naturaleza y cultivado por manos invisibles, crecen las más variadas especies de vegetales. Tal es la abundancia y espesura que no hay pluma capaz de describirla" ["In an isolated corner of the world, planted by Nature and cultivated by invisible hands, grow the most varied species of vegetables. Such is the abundance and undergrowth that there is not a pen capable of describing it"] (11). Perhaps the "exterior" ["outside"] of the epigraph can be linked to the "Naturaleza" ["Nature"] of the opening sentence, but the sinister, almost Gothic quality of the former bears no resemblance to the lush marvel of the latter. A segue does appear, nonetheless, in the shared metatextual expression of an inability to articulate. Whether the narrator gapes in amazement and horror or notes the impossibility of describing the scene before him, a commonly frustrated attempt at expression befalls him. This is to say that Jones Mathama begins this (presumed) inaugural representation of Spanish Guinea with a doubled acknowledgment that his own marginalization has left him incapable of speaking.

All the peripheries that surround *A Spear for the Boabí* as a literary project—all the scriptural borderlands that are the cover, the advertising ribbon, the title page, the prefatory note, the introduction, the first epigraph and the first words of the first chapter—are paralleled by those of Spanish Guinea itself, an "isolated corner of the world" and a colonial project of equally tenuous frames and frontiers. On the opening page of chapter 1, the narrator refers to Africa as "aquel continente" ["that distant continent"] and thereby seats himself in the metropole, far away from the inarticulable land he will seek uncertainly to represent (11). He repeats both his vantage point and his verbal incapacity shortly thereafter: "Lamento de veras no poder describir adecuadamente la incomensurable grandiosidad y exotismo de lo que he visto en aquellas tierras" ["I truly regret not being able to describe adequately the incommensurable grandiosity and exoticism of that which I have seen in those distant lands"] (11). The fundamental failure at mimicry that marks *A Spear for the Boabí* is already evident, for the narrator admits here that his testimonial experiences in "those distant lands" of "exoticism" cannot be communicated. He wants to depict the colony but cannot, for it exists beyond the realm of metropolitan discourse. He positions himself in Spain and writes in the Spanish tongue, all with the aim of serving as a willing author of empire, yet this intention is condemned at the start by the unrepresentability of a space so far away in kind as well as geography as to be inexpressible within the imperial episteme he has chosen. As Jones Mathama writes later in the novel, "Difícil, por no decir imposible, sería explicar o dar a entender a un europeo lo que ocurría en aquel poblado, porque lo tomaría por un 'cuento africano'" ["It would be difficult, not to say impossible, to explain or make understood to a European what happened in that distant village because he would take it for an 'African tale'"] (189).

This is the paradox of *A Spear for the Boabí* and the larger implication at hand: the attempt to confine a colony within the discourse of the colonizer is doomed even when a colonial subject seeks to achieve as much. The *différance* of a colony frustrates the most avid attempt to yoke it within familiar frames. Its discursive existence is ever deferred into difference when an imperial pen is dedicated to define it. Consequently, all remaining efforts by Jones Mathama in his initial chapter to force the alterity of Spanish Guinea into models familiar to Europeans result in the creation of a very different ideological thrust than the collaborationist impulse noted by scholars. Specifically, a surprisingly robust defense of Guinean traditions, comportments, and landscapes appears and even overwhelms the apparent aim of the author to craft a pro-Western story. Instead of the assimilation of the African into the European that the narrator proposes frequently and that supports the charge of colonial consent, the reverse often takes place in the novel. The narrator, that is, repeatedly draws European customs and Europeans themselves into Guinean cultural spheres. This is a critical point overlooked by those who would portray the text as an unproblematized acceptance of empire.

For instance, a description of Guinean food in the first chapter begins with the narrator noting that "Existen dos clases de desayunos: el fernandino y el bubi. El primero se parece bastante al de estilo europeo" ["There are two types of breakfasts: the Fernandino and the Bubi. The first resembles a lot the European-style breakfast"] (19). At first glance, this comment seems like a minor attempt at narrowing the cultural space between colonized and colonizer. If something as quotidian as breakfast is experienced by Fernandinos almost in the same way as by Europeans, perhaps the former assimilate to the latter in other ways as well. Simultaneously, the alignment away from the Bubi may appear to be synecdochical to a subtle ongoing ideological agenda of defining a middle ground for Fernandinos as less African than their fellow islanders. Yet the subsequent description of Bubi cuisine is quite effusive in its details. And it is followed by a depiction of the shellfish of Fernando Poo as "de exquisito sabor ["of exquisite taste"] and of local land crabs as "también un plato estupendo" ["also a fantastic dish"] (19). The underlying logic of these gastronomic passages moves from apparent Europeanization by the Fernandinos toward an overall vindication of island foods.

On the next page, the narrator depicts how Guineans allow dried meat to become infested with worms and stresses a cultural equality with the West: "Esto de los gusanos me hace recordar el queso Roquefort, en el cual se ve a éstos moverse y saltar y, sin embargo, causa la delicia de muchos europeos" ["This matter of the worms reminds me of Roquefort cheese, in which you see them move around and jump and, nonetheless, delights many Europeans"] (20). Again, the perspective of the narrator subtly undercuts the manifest Eurocentrism. The ideological impetus of the passage is not that of an Africa that should become like Europe but a Europe that turns out to be a version of Africa. The Roquefort cheese appears as a European referent framed by African gastronomy rather than vice versa. Along similar lines, the narrator concludes the overview of Guinean foods by noting that "Muchos son los europeos que se acostumbran a estas comidas y les gustan" ["Many are the Europeans who accustom themselves to these foods and they like them"] (21). This statement reverses the gambit of how a Fernandino repast "resembles a lot the European-style breakfast," for now it is the Europeans who end up adapting to African culture and not the other way around. The original impulse to assimilate the colonized to the colonizer is successively turned on its head by the praise of Guinean seafood, the framing of the wormy Roquefort, and, finally, the conclusion of how Europeans become successfully Africanized.

This sort of autodeconstructive process pervades *A Spear for the Boabí* as it tacks against its own procolonial currents. Another such example is when the Boabí is introduced to the reader as the "reyezuelo o gran jefe" ["local king or great chief"] of the island who reports a local conflict "a su gran amigo el gobernador general de los territorios de la Guinea Española" ["to his great friend the governor-general of the territories of Spanish Guinea"] (16). The governor-general promptly issues a solution to the conflict. Here the stances of the Guinean author and leader seem evident: the Boabí is an underling of the colonial superstructure who happily allows the Spanish to perform their rightful role as imposers of law and order. The procolonial patina of the passage seems palpable. Yet such a reading misses virtually everything that is significant about it. First, the conflict at hand is actually caused by Spanish and other foreign sailors who exploit local workers: "Tanto fue el abuso y los actos de violencia, que los nativos elevaron sus quejas al hombre más influyente en toda la isla, o sea el gran boabí" ["There was such abuse and acts of violence that the natives raised their complaints to the most influential man on all the island, that is, the great Boabí"] (16). Second, the governor-general's solution of jailing and then repatriating the Spanish miscreants does not succeed, as "desgraciadamente, la semilla del mal ya se había sembrado entre los propios nativos" ["unfortunately, the seed of evil had already been planted among the natives themselves"] (16). In short, the Guineans have been corrupted by Spaniards rather than being deemed, say, inherently barbaric.

Third, the narrator concludes by noting that "La selva es el albergue de las fieras y a nadie le extraña encontrar en ella leones, gorilas, elefantes y toda clase de animales dañinos, pero tampoco nadie debe dudar que en las ciudades existe cierta clase de animales bípedos mucho más perjudicial que sus selváticos hermanos" ["The forest is the home of wild beasts and no-body thinks it strange to find there lions, gorillas, elephants, and all kinds of harmful animals, but neither should anyone doubt that in the cities there exists a certain class of bipedal animals who are much more harmful than their brothers of the forest"] (16). The urban bipeds in question are clearly Europeans, a population "much more harmful" than the savage beasts whose home is the jungle. The heart of darkness is in Europe, not Africa. As in the gastronomic passages, the apparent assimilation of the colonized upends into a counterhierarchy in which the colonizer huddles at the bottom. The Boabí is not a bootlicker nor the Spanish governor-general a Solomon, for the conquerors caused the conflict, not the conquered. That is why the local leader charges the representative of the imperial power with resolving it. But this the governor-general cannot do. His powers are too limited to deal with the insidious influence of the "bipedal animals" who are his fellow foreigners. Those who call the African forest their home may be dehumanized, but not nearly so much as those of the concrete jungle in Europe. Guineans here are neither aspiring Europeans nor, for that matter, any other trite trope of colonial discourses about indigenous peoples. They are not noble savages, wholesale barbarians, prelapsarian innocents, or anything else but individuals with a unique and legitimate existence of their own.

Such rhetorical gestures that undermine seemingly obvious ideological hierarchies tend to pass unperceived amid all the explicitly Europhile prose. An instance of acclaim for empire is the penultimate page of the novel, which features the rousing sentiment of the author that "lo considero un deber ineludible proclamar por todo lo alto la gran labor que España está realizando en aquella isla" ["I consider it an unavoidable duty to proclaim for all to hear the great work that Spain is doing in that distant island"] (309). Ngom cites this line as a prime example of the procolonial ideology of the novel ("La literatura africana," 413). It is followed by the bullish proclamation that Spanish institutions are "dotando a la isla de un sin fin de beneficios y mejoramientos sobre todo en lo que se refiere a la enseñanza y religión" ["providing the island with a great many benefits and betterments, above all with regard to that which concerns teaching and religion"] (309). But these unqualified encomia are not the servile acceptances of inherent European superiority that they seem.

Rather than framing Spanish imperialism as the triumph of civilization over barbarism—a facile dialectic altogether too familiar to readers of Latin American literature—Jones Mathama casts it as concretizing universal human fraternity and equality. The legator of such broad brotherhood is given as the Christian god, but the spirit is in some implicit sense that of the best of the French Revolution. Unlike many texts that portray indigenes in Latin America, *A Spear for the Boabí* does not promote either the extermination or absolute assimilation of the people of Fernando Poo. The former prospect is never on the table and the latter is belied by the extensive and positively engaged depictions of local customs by the novelist. Instead, the Guineans are to benefit by colonialism because it will help consolidate their innate equality before heaven and earth. The argument is proimperial but the egalitarian premise is hardly conservative. Jones Mathama is no proponent of a return to Guinean autonomy either politically or culturally, this much is certain. He accepts fully both Spain and Christianity as twin evangelical projects. But he also sees both, however naively, as forces for fulfilling a common human brotherhood.

Consequently, the culminating praises of imperialism in the novel are replete with the presumption that the glories of Spanish rule on Fernando Poo reside in their recognition of racial and ethnic equality: "Por doquier se veía el progreso, el bien estar, las escuelas, el magnífico hospital y la asistencia en todos los centros docentes sin discriminación de ninguna clase" ["Everywhere there could be seen progress, social welfare, the schools, the magnificent hospital, and attendance in all the educational institutions without discrimination of any kind"] (309). Similarly, Jones Mathama insists that in Spain, "Aquí en esta bendita tierra, no existe diferencia en el color de la piel. Os hablo con la verdad que brota desde el fondo de mi corazón" ["Here in this blessed land there exists no difference according to skin color. I speak to all of you with the truth that wells from the bottom of my heart"] (310). And when summarizing Gue's educational experience in Iberia, Jones Mathama declaims that "todos sus compañeros sólo vieron en él a un nuevo condiscípulo sin importarles el color de la piel. En esto reside la razón del triunfo y la verdadera vida social que siempre ha reinado en España" ["all his companions only saw in him a new classmate without regarding his skin color as important. In this resides the reason for the triumph and the true social life that always has reigned in Spain"] (308–9). This description of Spanish history and society is absurdly inaccurate but not slavishly colonial. In *A Spear for the Boabí,* Guinean culture in general is subject to hispanizing forces generally portrayed as positive. And this is tantamount to an assimilationist stance by the author. But the changes afoot in Spanish Guinea, according to Jones Mathama, develop in the service of the larger humanistic dream of universal equality. That his belief is inspired by Christian religious doctrine does not condemn it necessarily to fundamental conservatism any more than the dreams of liberation theologians.

The epigraph of the final section of the book (entitled "Conclusion") reads as revelation but parses as revolution: "La verdad es unicolor y solo tiene un nombre, PUREZA, al contrario de la mentira cuyo único calificativo es, IMPUREZA, y para engañar a ingenuos se disfraza con colores llamativos" ["The truth is monochromatic and only has one name, PURITY, in contrary to the lie whose only label is IMPURITY, and which to trick naifs is disguised with bright colors"] (308). No human by virtue of his color has claim to the truth, implies Jones Mathama, and those deceived by the connotations of language (e.g., blackness associated with impurity, whiteness with purity) are but fools and simpletons. In linguistic terms, Jones Mathama recodes here the signified of the colonial signifier. He asserts that Europeans are no more inherently human than Africans because the value of all before the order of heaven is equal.

The same holds true before the order of earth, to wit the final scene in the last full chapter of the novel in which Gue, on the deck of a ship heading to Europe, is asked by a foreign girl to light her cigarette. He is "extasiado" ["made ecstatic"] by the moment "porque jamás estuvo en semejante situación con una muchacha que no fuera de su raza" ["because he had never been in a similar situation with a girl who was not of his race"] (306). Jones Mathama proceeds to lavish the girl with praise: she is "aquella beldad" ["that beauty"] and "la hermosa muchacha" ["the beautiful girl"] with "sonrientes labios" ["smiling lips"] and "una risa cristalina" ["a crystalline laugh"] (306). Gue is so awestruck that the match burns down to his fingers. Once again, an unproblematized procolonial hierarchy seems apparent; and once again, such a reading proves wrong. The scene (and this final chapter) ends with the girl turning to Gue and requesting the following:

> —*Dame tu brazo para bajar al comedor.*
> *Al entrar en el amplio salón, uno de los comensales dijo medio en broma medio en serio:*
> —*¡Miren, ahí llegan Africa y Occidente!*
> *Sonrientes, y por primera vez, los dos se juntaron para cenar. (307)*

> ["Give me your arm so that we might go down to the dining room."
> Upon entering the spacious hall, one of the guests said half-jokingly, half-seriously,
> "Look, there arrive Africa and the West!"
> Smiling, and for the first time, the two came together to dine.]

If the subsequent epigraph proclaims that moral truth knows nor color, here neither does society. A black boy and a white girl, "Africa and the West," join and eat as equals. True, the ship is bound for Europe all the same, but it does not leave Africa altogether behind. Gue deserves a seat at that table, alongside a pretty European girl no less. And proposing such a union in the late 1950s, when the novel probably was written, is radical. Gue and the girl are not only given as equals in rights but, none too subtly, as potential sexual partners as well. *A Spear for the Boabí* is not a call to arms amid an era of militant decolonization movements in Africa, but neither is it a sycophantic and wholesale submission to European dominance.

These tensions that worm through the text and upturn it—these constant conversions of colonial kowtowing into something rather more upright—manifest themselves within the structure of the book as well as its content. The first chapter appears to initiate a conventional bildungsroman in which the newborn Gue will little by little come of age. In the third chapter his mother dies, a point at which Gue is only five years old. This development isolates the paternal line as a narrative axis. Myth criticism might provide ample analytical frameworks for what happens next as the child passes through a series of adventures while marked as the heir to the Boabí. The problem, however, is that the bildungsroman just never quite comes together. First, Gue is repeatedly described as devilish and barbaric, as a sort of antihero more than anything else. For instance, within the span of a few representative paragraphs he is depicted as "aquel pequeño salvaje" ["that little savage"] and "aquel diablo de muchacho" ["that devil of a boy"] (68). Reading the novel as a transparently autobiographical roman à clef, with Gue standing for Jones Mathama and the Boabí for his father, seems problematic in part because of the unlikelihood of authors describing their younger selves as infernal.

Moreover, the title character of the novel is the father, not the son. This disjunction creates the contradiction of a bildungsroman whose protagonist is somehow alienated from his own story. Indeed, in considering the biographical element at play in the text, Ngom inadvertently reveals this instability: "Relato autobiográfico, la obra de Jones Mathama también defiende la ideología colonial y, como tal, cae dentro de la literatura de consentimiento. Esa es la razón por la cual la figura de Maximiliano C. Jones, el Boabí, personaje prominente de la colonia y padre de Gue el protagonista, ocupa el primer plano en casi todo el texto." ["An autobiographical story, the work by Jones Mathama also defends colonial ideology and thus falls within the literature of consent. This is the reason why the figure of Maximiliano C. Jones, the Boabí, a prominent person in the colony and the father of Gue the protagonist, occupies center stage in nearly all of the text"] ("Algunos aspectos," 93). That is, Gue is "the protagonist" even though his father paradoxically "occupies center stage." The reality is that the Boabí makes only scattered appearances in the long text that bears his name, even if the references made to him in absentia by other characters are included in the tally. The confusion over identifying the main character suggests that *A Spear for the Boabí* is a bildungsroman more in intent than achievement.

The generally dominant focus on Gue also does not provide a fundamental coherence to the text. Jones Mathama does not sustain a unifying structure any more than an ideologically consistent content. For instance,

Gue and his adventures often disappear before a wealth of *costumbrismo*—that is, the foregrounded description of local environments and behaviors—that needs no human character, much less a colonial David Copperfield, to exist. More important still is the fact that Gue's adventures abruptly break off in the middle of the eighth chapter when an entirely separate story begins. The abruptly inserted narrative continues for over eighty pages, or more than a full quarter of *A Spear for the Boabí*. This novella of sorts, which details how a hypnotist temporarily turns village women into sex slaves, contains a set of characters who appear nowhere else in the text. Additionally, apart from its brief references to the Boabí, the novella bears no apparent relationship to the rest of the plot. The bildungsroman featuring Gue, such as it is, simply vanishes and reappears equally unexpectedly. Furthermore, the conclusion that would seem to impel it forward, the climactic trip by Gue to Europe and his resulting imperial education, is postponed throughout the book. Three times in the text Gue is positioned to leave for Europe. Three times this does not happen. The European experience, however, seems to be the implicit prerequisite for Gue to take his rightful place one day as the successor to his father. And this destiny remains repeatedly deferred. Why can Jones Mathama not bring himself to move Gue off the island? The final pages in which this transferal does take place are but cursory. The multiple narrative structures established in the novel are never truly realized.

Scholarship that focuses only on the plentiful procolonial statements in order to dismiss *A Spear for the Boabí* as unworthy of serious attention ignores that the novel is manifestly uncomfortable with itself. This is a text published in the imperial homeland, narrated from there as well, written in the imperial language and in a particular form (the bildungsroman) of a genre (the novel) of Western origin. But despite all these frames and all the assimilations of empire they imply, the novel as an artifact at one with the colonial project never does emerge. The tensions of empire are never relaxed. The author is unsure of his right to speak in the first place, indeed, uncertain how to present himself in any media. When he finally does commence the main of his text, he cannot abide by the integrationist ideology he stakes out nor by the foreign literary structures he seeks to assume. The abundant *costumbrista* passages alone lend copious space to the unique existences of Guinean culture and flora and fauna, all phenomena that cannot be reduced to imperial mimicry and that, as in the case of the wormy meat and cheese, often reverse in subtle ways the frames through which Africa

and Europe envision each other. Jones Mathama fully desires the progress
for Spanish Guinea that he believes Spain represents, but at no point does
he call for Guinean subjectivity itself to vanish. Quite the opposite, when
discussing Bubi youths who have been sent to Spain for education, he ad-
monishes them for trying to shed their ancestral culture: "De entre vosotros,
incluso hay quien está avergonzado de que sus padres sean bubis y tengan
la cara cortada: *I say shame on you a thousand times, and may God pity your
damn ignorance*. (Mil vergüenzas caigan sobre ti, y que Dios compadezca tu
maldita ignorancia). ¡Al diablo con vuestras estúpidas presunciones!"
["Among yourselves, including he who is ashamed that his parents are Bubi
and have cut faces: *I say shame on you a thousand times, and may God pity your
damn ignorance*. (I say shame on you a thousand times, and may God pity
your damn ignorance. To hell with your stupid pretensions!") (252).[14]

   A Spear for the Boabí is therefore a procolonial text that encourages the
maintenance of African subjectivities while praising the adoption of the religious and material progress attributed to the colonizing power. Although
Jones Mathama frequently denigrates Gue and some local customs, his belief in the universal equality of all human beings as ordained by Christianity and upheld by Spain—again, the accuracy of his beliefs is beside the
point—forces him to level constantly the hierarchies that he himself has established and that divide metropolitan from colonial subjects. Thus, while
talking about "las virtudes y los vicios de la humanidad" ["the virtues and
vices of humanity"], the narrator proposes that "en aquella minúscula isla
de Fernando-Póo suceden las cosas como en todas partes. Hay gente buena
y gente mala que allí se divierte, son felices, sufren y mueren, y la virtud y
el vicio impera como en cualquier otro lugar" ["in that distant minuscule
island of Fernando Poo, things happen as they do everywhere. There are
good people and bad people who enjoy themselves there, who are happy,
who suffer and die, and virtue and vice rule as in any other place"] (229).
And in a passage in which the narrator, opining from "aquí en la Penín-
sula" ["here in the (Iberian) Peninsula"], denounces polygamous customs
on Fernando Poo, he again ultimately equates the situation in Guinea with
that in Europe:

> *esta situación de la poligamia es una de las más graves y peligrosas enfermedades
> no sólo en Africa, sino en todas partes del mundo. Todos sabemos que en Europa
> son muchos los que viven en secreto una doble vida . . . lo que sí puedo afirmar es
> que las debilidades y las miserias humanas no se localizan sólo en Africa, sino que*

está extendida en todas partes, y aún me atrevería a decir que el refinamiento y por tanto la corrupción y las costumbres licenciosas, tienen su cuna precisamente en los países más civilizados. (275)

[this situation of polygamy is one of the most grave and dangerous sicknesses not only in Africa but in all parts of the world. We all know that in Europe there are many who secretly live a double life . . . what I can affirm is that human weaknesses and miseries are not located only in Africa but are found everywhere, and I would even dare to say that refinement and therefore corruption and licentious customs have their cradle precisely in the most civilized countries.]

Once again, an unproblematized reading of the text as procolonial is difficult to sustain. The moral backwardnesses of Guinea, like the worms in its food, turn out to be similar to those of Europe. Indeed, metropolitan culture suffers perhaps even greater from the ills of the world. Again in the novel, an ideological equalizing of Guinean with Spanish subjects is either achieved or the expected imperial hierarchy is reversed.

As an extraordinary instance of world literature, *A Spear for the Boabí* should be read. It is, after all, only the second African novel in Spanish and the last published novel of colonized Guinea.[15] As an artwork that succeeds in its insufficiencies, it should be studied and taught. The same can be said of the first Asian novel in Spanish, Pedro Paterno's *Nínay,* and its more polished and influential successors by José Rizal, *Noli me tangere* and *El filibusterismo.* The three Filipino texts are also rife with discourses that deconstruct the presumptive binaries of metropole and colony, North and South, center and periphery. The anxieties of classification so evident in Jones Mathama, the sense of a perpetual inability to belong either here or there, is applicable to his early Asian counterparts as well. Indeed, it is precisely this taxing of the taxonomic that makes Guinean and Filipino literature in Spanish so important to the broader study of Hispanic literatures. If one day global literature in Spanish becomes a recognized rubric, then the duality of Iberia and Latin America will have dissolved into the dust it deserves. That persisting binarism in which careers are made, tenures are awarded, courses are taught, graduate students are hired, and undergraduates are trained, is actually an ideological mechanism so intellectually impoverished that its underpinning assumptions are almost never acknowledged as such.

APPROACHES AND ESCAPES

A whole field of comparative Asian Hispanic and African Hispanic literary studies awaits its first researchers. Without reducing early Filipino and Guinean fiction in Spanish to facile alignments, scholars and students could take as a starting point the colonial commonalities of indigenous authors who write and publish their books while making their home in the metropole. More profoundly still, the challenges of starting a national literary tradition in the absence of a national language, a national readership, and for that matter a nation, beset both the first Asian and the first African novelists in Spanish. Jones Mathama, like Paterno and Rizal, tries to stand on many shores simultaneously and as a result stands on none stably. The grounds keep shifting beneath all their feet, whether those grounds are geographic in nature or ideological or aesthetic. These men—and all, notably, are men, an unstressed fact in this book that leaves entirely open a vast range of gendered analyses not broached herein—intend in different ways to imitate European voices and styles and genres and yet succeed most when they fail at doing so. The multiple and miscellaneous gaps between what they attempt to accomplish and what they actually do are the most substantive hallmarks of their literature. And their diverse struggles to articulate coherently what it means to speak from their protean subject positions provide clues to the postmagellanic problematics of other indigenous literatures in Western tongues throughout the world.

At the same time, the contrasts between Jones Mathama and the Filipino writers also demand further investigation. In *Nínay*, for example, Paterno does move his protagonist off his home island. That plot sequence proves central to positing the Philippines as part of the global North and in antipodal distinction to the global South. In *A Spear for the Boabí*, however, Jones Mathama defers repeatedly the opportunity for Gue to leave his own home island. How do the different authorial decisions resonate with the ideological disparities of the two novels? On another tack, when Paterno inadvertently offers as his heroes a marginalized and hypothetical couple of Berto and Pilar who survive, perhaps to flourish, beyond the last page of his novel, are there any similarly radicalized characters whose futures are hinted at beyond the final paragraphs of *A Spear for the Boabí*? Would the potential offspring of Gue and the Western girl in the dining room be able to transcend or upend prevailing power structures in both Spain and Guinea? Or are their linked arms tantamount to a foreclosure of such a history to come? Additional potential foci for comparative discussions include the divergent ways in which Paterno and Jones Mathama employ *costumbrismo* in the service of defending cultures and comportments indigenous to their homelands. The extent and kinds of auto-orientalizing in their texts also merit interrogation.

Filipino juxtapositions aside, a way to integrate African literature in Spanish into broader studies is to intertwine a text such as *A Spear for the Boabí* with canonical fictions from Latin America and Spain. This might be the most practical first step, given the widespread lack of knowledge of Asian Hispanic traditions. A viable initial approach would be to take particular chapters from Jones Mathama and read them alongside texts from the prominent Latin American literature known as the Boom that was produced by such contemporaneous authors as Carlos Fuentes and Gabriel García Márquez. The year in which *A Spear for the Boabí* appeared is the same in which Fuentes published *Aura* and *La muerte de Artemio Cruz* (*The Death of Artemio Cruz*), both still widely read and taught half a century later. The magic realism of the former and the fractured, reverse bildungsroman of the latter (the protagonist's life is relayed from his deathbed) would make for compelling conversations if paired with relevant passages in *A Spear for the Boabí*. The Guinean novel too features surreal and hyperbolic elements and a jagged structure for the life story of its main character. The whole debate in Latin American literary studies regarding how to define magic realism and its associated notion of *lo real maravilloso* ("the marvelous real") put forth by the Cuban writer Alejo Carpentier, whether exemplified in *Aura* or still more famous texts such as García Márquez's 1967 *One Hundred Years of Solitude,* would take on new nuances if worked through the African environments and belief systems in *A Spear for the Boabí*.

Another line of inquiry could begin with the many renowned Latin American novels of the 1960s, including Julio Cortázar's *Rayuela* (*Hopscotch*) of 1963 and Mario Vargas Llosa's *La casa verde* (*The Green House*) of 1966, that achieved canonization in large part because of their structural innovations. These texts were the products of extraordinarily deliberate efforts by highly professionalized authors. Jones Mathama, though an amateur novelist, offers a fragmented and jumpy text that challenges any definition of the genre of the novel as much as do those of his contemporaries from across the seas. His own structural originalities, of course, may be seen as an accidental result of an imitative failure of metropolitan models. And in a larger sense, they could be viewed as a natural outcome of any attempt to force indigenous content into foreign form. But either way, reading *A Spear for the Boabí* alongside *Hopscotch* or *The Green House* would raise complex issues of why certain deconstructions of literary genres are elevated and capitalized while coeval others are entirely ignored.

Those scholars who would approach Jones Mathama from the frame of the literature of Spain could consider where his novel might fit in with and perhaps amend the traditional histories of fiction during the 1939–75 period of the Franco state. Casualties of the preceding civil war included generations of active or potential Spanish writers, many of whom either died in the struggle or went into exile. Those who stayed in Spain were not able to develop their craft freely in the ensuing decades. Meanwhile, the fascist regime kept the nation largely isolated from international currents of all sorts. Collectively, these factors led to a noticeably enervated and provincial Spanish literary canon of the mid-twentieth century, notwithstanding the rise to prominence of Camilo José Cela (who in 1989, long after Franco had died, won the Nobel Prize for Literature) and other accomplished prose stylists such as Ana María Matute, Miguel Delibes, and Carmen Martín Gaite. Considerations of Jones Mathama as both a Guinean and a Catalan writer operating within and against this larger national literary context would diversify in disparate senses any broader conceptualization of the fictional discourses that appeared under Franco. For example, Matute's depictions of Spanish villagers and small-town life, if matched against those in Jones Mathama, might initiate illuminating rereadings of both writers and of the belletristic and political potentials of the genre of *costumbrismo*. Similarly, an analysis of *A Spear for the Boabí* against other nominees for the 1960 Nadal Prize could make for a compelling monograph that would open new arguments about why the aesthetic architects of fascism select certain material as foundational and others as insulation.

A Spear for the Boabí also deserves study by all scholars specializing in African literatures in Western languages. To date, no investigations of that ilk exist owing to the language barrier, for such Africanists would be trained in French, English, or Portuguese. There remains no translation of the novel. Yet Jones Mathama, by virtue of his many uniquenesses, may prove to be a pivotal case in the ongoing debates over the choice of idioms by authors from the global South. Apparent outliers can test the coherence of any graph. In defending the composition of African literature in indigenous African languages, Ngugi wa Thiong'o, the well-known Kenyan writer and scholar, has suggested that "A writer who tries to communicate the message of revolutionary unity and hope in the languages [i.e., African] of the people becomes a subversive character" (453). The anti-imperial impulse of deliberately using a language of local rather than European origin to create African literature is self-evident. But can an African author who employs a European tongue in order to produce procolonial literature somehow also be subversive?

The sole published novel of Daniel Jones Mathama would seem to suggest yes. Here is an author who consciously launches (or so he believes) a literary tradition with a text that fully welcomes the Spanish presence in Guinea, religiously and politically as well as linguistically. As a culminating gesture, he sends his apparent protagonist off to Spain to be educated in European ways. *A Spear for the Boabí,* from its content to its form to its language, shows a persistent effort by Jones Mathama that is the opposite of what Ngugi proposes: a willing embrace and imitation of the metropolitan. And yet every step of the way, from his hesitations to his upended hierarchies, Jones Mathama does not satisfy the structures that he sets up for himself. His ideology self-destructs as it autodeconstructs and in so doing undercuts all charges of colonial consent. The failures of his text show the impossibility of willful mimicry of the metropolitan even by a colonial author entirely in step with the march of empire. By extension, this incommensurateness indicates as well that the postmagellanic world is dissonant with itself, that empire never can be resolved into either the victory of some thesis or its fusion with some antithesis.

There is no Lapu Lapu figure in the history of Spanish Guinea, no real or imagined local antagonist to a mythohistoric foreign invader. Nor is there a Magellan by some other name, no other world-historical character. Fernando Poo, the only possible candidate, is more noteworthy as a toponym than as a traveler. There is no foundational drama of Spanish Guinea like that on the shores of Mactan Island and there is no foundational death. Yet the Magellan fallacy is committed time and again by all parties to *A Spear for the Boabí.* The text continuously escapes all those who try to contain it, from the author who attempts to situate it on maps unfamiliar but on beaches approachable, to the publicists who seek to impel it as a new current, to the aesthetic autocrats who assign it the place of also-ran in a fascist award, to the scholars who designate it a dismissable dead-end.

Daniel Jones Mathama himself cannot captain *A Spear for the Boabí* within recognizable geoliterary or artistic or ideological borders because Spain and Spanish Guinea, despite their asymmetrical powers, are unresolvable to any particular shores. Antonio Pigafetta, though he sailed without a word past what would become Spanish and then Equatorial Guinea, left in the wake behind him a world forever arriving and departing in the winds.

CHAPTER FIVE

Beginnings at the End: María Nsue Angüe's Ekomo *(1985) and Juan Balboa Boneke's* El reencuentro: el retorno del exiliado *(1985)*

One hundred years after Pedro Paterno left the Philippines for Europe, the arc of Asian and African literature in Spanish seemed to have come to an end. The once robust tradition in the Philippines had sputtered out of existence, apparently forever, so much so that the annual Zóbel Prize for the best Filipino literature in Spanish closed down in 1967 for a lack of enough writers left to compete for it.[1] On the other side of the world, in the new country of Equatorial Guinea, national independence in 1968 was followed by the rapacious dictatorship of Francisco Macías, during which execution and torture were meted out to anyone who raised a voice. As a result, African Hispanic individuals who survived in exile faced a traumatic reality back home and profoundly uncertain possibilities in their own futures abroad. This was not a position conducive to devoting much time or energy to composing creative texts. The scarcity of output was so acute that the 1970s came to be known in Guinean studies as the "Years of Silence."[2] Antonio Abad's *La vida secreta de Daniel Espeña (The Secret Life of Daniel Espeña)* of 1960 and Daniel Jones Mathama's *A Spear for the Boabí* of 1962, both of which appeared and disappeared with very small readerships, seemed destined to be the last Asian and African novels published in Spanish.[3] In the case of Abad, a national novelistic trajectory of nearly eight decades was ending, but Jones Mathama remained perched on the verge of initiating a Guinean tradition that apparently would never come to be. In 1971, four and half centuries since the forces of Lapu Lapu killed Magellan and Pigafetta sailed home to tell the tale, and one century since Paterno arrived in Madrid from Manila, there was effectively no fiction in Spanish still being produced by Asians or Africans. The prospects of global literature in Spanish seemed dead.

EXTERNALITIES AND INCONSISTENCIES

The most prominent fictional representation of Equatorial Guinea that circulated in the 1970s was not published by an African nor written in Spanish. It also was not, on the surface, about Equatorial Guinea. *The Dogs of War* by Frederick Forsyth, an author of worldwide fame thanks to his 1971 thriller *The Day of the Jackal*, was a 1974 novel that detailed the staging of a coup d'état by a handful of mercenaries against the dictator of a fictional West African country named Zangaro. Forsyth lived in Malabo for two years while writing the novel, which contains hints—not that a mass Western readership could be expected to recognize them—that Zangaro was in actuality a version of Equatorial Guinea, then ruled by Macías, the post-independence tyrant. In the novel, for instance, the capital of Zangaro is called Clarence, one of the colonial names for present-day Malabo. Also, the protagonist likes to whistle the song "Spanish Harlem," thereby evoking a vague image of hispanophone presence within the West African setting. British newspapers of the time gave credence to rumors that Forsyth, in the course of conducting research for *The Dogs of War,* had hired a mercenary force in an unsuccessful bid to topple the Macías regime. Forsyth's alleged goal was to see how the episode would transpire so that he could lend more realism to his novel. Forsyth denied that he had participated in such a plan.[4]

Foreign fictional representations of Guinean spaces also circulated in the 1970s outside the country in venues less bound than the pages of a novel. Around the time Forsyth was in Malabo preparing *The Dogs of War,* press coverage in Washington was following a homicide involving the only two diplomats of the United States in Equatorial Guinea. The case ultimately reached a federal court of appeals over the question of which court has jurisdiction over a "murder committed by an American official at a Foreign Service post" (Shurtleff, 54). The circumstances of the crime remain somewhat unclear. According to George Gedda in an Associated Press article entitled "'Heart of Darkness' or a Challenge?" that appeared two decades later, there was an incident there years ago worthy of Agatha Christie. On a steamy late August day in 1971, amid signs of a homosexual relationship gone sour, a U.S. diplomat plunged a pair of scissors into a colleague inside the Embassy compound, killing him. The full explanation as to why Alfred J. Erdos, 46, murdered Donald Leahy, 47, has never come to light. But some officials believe the appalling circumstances at that time in the tiny country, run by one the [*sic*] world's most ruthless dictators, were at least partly to blame. (A39)

The idea that Equatorial Guinea was at fault apparently lay at the core of Erdos's legal argument, though the diplomat had lived in the country for only four and a half months prior to the homicide (Erdos, 44). As Gedda concludes, "The prosecution said Erdos and Leahy were lovers whose relationship had gone bad. Erdos, a career diplomat, denied the allegation, citing the 'heart of darkness' theory in his defense. In effect, he contended that life in Equatorial Guinea had driven him insane, at least temporarily" (A39). In terms of discourse analysis, whether Erdos really was disoriented by Equatorial Guinea is not as germane as his assumption that such rhetoric would justify his action. The "heart of darkness" trope, as with the Agatha Christie reference in the Associated Press article, is essentially novelistic, as if the only way to make the Macías years understandable is through fiction. A 2008 article by Chris Erdos, son of Alfred, that offered new information on the case, was also entitled "Heart of Darkness" (43). Len Shurtleff, who was the first U.S. diplomat to see Alfred Erdos after the murder, did not use the "heart of darkness" phrasing in his 2007 recollection of the case but did describe the murder as "a legendary Foreign Service tale, often embellished in the retelling" that took place in "steamy tropical backwaters" on a "fateful day" (51). This is the rhetoric of imperial pulp fiction.

Had Equatorial Guinea offered in the 1970s a context in which its own literature was being articulated and disseminated, perhaps foreign narrators like Forsyth, Alfred Erdos, Chris Erdos, and Shurtleff, disparate though otherwise they were, would not have depicted that space through metaphors so easily imported from colonial narratives. The frequent use of "heart of darkness" and similar phrases weighted with racism and conquest is unfortunate at best. Yet there is no question that the Macías years, hyperbolic in their atrocities, are hard to represent in the modes of traditional realism that usually characterize documentary journalism. Chris Erdos, emphasizing the horrific environment of the time, notes that one day before the murder of Leahy, "The police took the cook, a woman whom my parents considered a friend as well as an employee, across the street to the courtyard in front of the prison. They removed her clothes and staked her to the ground, in full view of the residence. They then proceeded to strip the skin from her body. The woman screamed for two days before she finally died" (46). How to describe such an event properly is an unanswerable question, but the adoption here of a tone of concise and objective reportage is as artificed a rhetorical strategy as anything by Forsyth or Shurtleff. It is an approach clearly chosen for its implications of trustworthiness. There is no reason to think that the brutal murder of the woman did not happen, but Chris Erdos was two years old at the time and hardly in the position of reliable witness that his journalistic mood implies (45). And in the Years of Silence, with no local individual based in Malabo besides Macías with the power to fill in a national narrative space, the circulation of tropes of Equatorial Guinea was left almost entirely at the disposition of foreigners who could evoke them for whatever the purpose.

Certainly, the reemergence of Guinean literature in Spanish in the mid-1980s and its proliferation since has not meant the end of foreigners who set fiction in the nation. In recent decades there has been more regrettable literature produced about Equatorial Guinea by outsiders, including two novels featuring mutant apes. One of them, Robin Cook's *Chromosome 6* of 1997 features a Westerner in Equatorial Guinea who duly laments, "And what good is being rich when I have to be out here in the heart of darkness?" (45).[5] Robert Klitgaard, a neoliberal economist with World Bank ties who spent two and a half years in Equatorial Guinea in the mid-1980s, stopped just short of the "heart of darkness" trope when entitling his memoirs of his time there as *Tropical Gangsters: One Man's Experience with Development and Decadence in Deepest Africa*. This text was cited by the *New York Times Book Review* as one of the six best nonfiction books of 1990 ("Editors' Choice"). The title, however, is suffused with troublesome metonymies. Equatorial Guinea is in no geographic sense in "deepest Africa," consisting as it does of islands and a coastal mainland. The word "deepest" therefore only can refer to images of the "heart of darkness" kind. The deliberate opposition of "development" to "decadence" (the former obviously associated with the civilized West, the latter with degeneracy and barbarism) underlines the "deepest Africa" rhetoric.

It would not be desirable, of course, notwithstanding the production of foreign texts that carry neocolonial overtones, to limit representations of a country to its own nationals. In the postmagellanic world, this is not possible in any case, and the particularities of Guinean history mean that the question of who is a foreigner to begin with is irreducibly complex. But at the very least, since the appearance of an anthology of Guinean writers in 1984 edited by Donato Ndongo-Bidyogo and the publication of the two 1985 novels that marked the resumption of Guinean contributions to that genre, *Ekomo* by María Nsue Angüe and *El reencuentro: el retorno del exiliado* (*The Reencounter: The Return of the Exile*) by Juan Balboa Boneke, foreign accounts have had to compete for discursive space with more local products.

As always, however, the concept of "local" in a Guinean context is acutely problematic. The novels by Nsue Angüe and Balboa Boneke were both published in Spain, not in Equatorial Guinea.[6] Moreover, the authors are both individuals who had lived in Spain for years and whose books obtained a circulation restricted almost entirely to Europe. The extent to which the novels are Equatoguinean is questionable conceptually at the state level as well, for "Equatorial Guinea" as a nation was created only in 1968, long after the authors' respective childhoods. Upon independence, the country was commandeered by a despot who transformed all intellectuals into either cadavers or exiles. Whatever mutual experience of nationhood that might have inspired Nsue Angüe and Balboa Boneke to write their novels therefore could only have developed in exile, a paradox in itself. Their distinct ethnic and geographic provenances also provide little common ground for a preindependence sense of (proto)nationalism. Nsue Angüe is of Fang background and was born in Río Muni (the swath of territory on the continental mainland), whereas Balboa Boneke is of Bubi heritage and was raised on the island of Fernando Poo (now known as Bioko). The disjointed senses of time and space in their novels, texts in which Equatorial Guinea as a concept just about disappears in a welter of precolonial, colonial, and utopian signifiers, is a natural outcome of this fragmented geohistorical context.

Discontinuity, in fact, is the primary continuity of the early literature of Guinea, where the local always twines jaggedly with the foreign until any clear distinctions evaporate. Virtually all studies of Equatoguinean literature today, however, frame the texts in a space either tribal, national, binational (i.e., vis-à-vis Spain), or continental. This is a mistake. The novels that emerge in the mid-1980s are of much broader and complex implication. The indissolubility of the local from the foreign in Equatorial Guinea, the paradoxes of nations that are nonexistent in all but name and yet produce literatures deemed national, is not particular to this small region of West Africa but characteristic of the world over ever since Magellan. Unlike the Filipino case, it is true, there are no world-historical moments in Guinean space. No figure comparable to Magellan met his demise there, no writer of planetary import like Pigafetta appeared as its chronicler, and no imperial deathmatch like that between Japan and the United States in World War II bloodies its history either. Yet the marginalized are not necessarily marginal. The reemergence of African literature in Spanish in the mid-1980s is a globalized phenomenon as much as the emergence of Asian literature in Spanish in the mid-1880s. The primary marker of that globalization is not only the instability of the self-definition of the local and seemingly peripheral, now interwoven inextricably with the foreign, but also the instability of the self-definition of the foreign and seemingly metropolitan, now interwoven inextricably with the local. The uncontrollability of all Guinean signifiers in the novels by Nsue Angüe and Balboa Boneke is the manifestation of this postmagellanic reality.

In relaunching the Guinean novel a decade and a half after Equatorial Guinea was itself launched, Nsue Angüe and Balboa Boneke evoke a national space whose nationality and spatiality are prominent primarily for their incommensurability with themselves. The novels depict local worlds that are no longer conceivable as such, for the only way to write of the local is to write of all that escapes endlessly from and to it: flows of a here and now that is always a there and then, with all temporal and geopolitical projections simultaneously tending backward and forward, inward and outward. In lieu of the obvious unviability of Equatorial Guinea as an organic entity, Nsue Angüe and Balboa Boneke work diligently to will a strong tribal and continental presence into existence in their texts. That is, they privilege an identity at once subnational and supranational instead of prenational in colonial times or national in the postindependence era. Yet this project disintegrates as it consolidates. Guinea, in either its Spanish or Equatorial version, cannot be separated from its constituent ethnicities or the African landmass beyond, but nor can these from an array of Western forces that are seemingly discrete from the entities of tribe and continent. All identitarian discourses in these novels spill beyond their apparent boundaries.

In other words, readers and scholars may turn to Nsue Angüe and Balboa Boneke as the inaugurators of a specific and constrained novelistic tradition, that of Equatorial Guinea, but national coherence is absent in both *Ekomo* and *The Reencounter*. So too is an autonomous indigenous tradition or ethnic sense of social self. These are supracontinental texts of subnational texture and continental aspirations, despite their common reception as national markers. They are, in short, macro in their micro, global in their local, transnational in their national. It is not that the center of Guinea cannot hold in these texts; it is that there is no center in the first place. Things do not fall apart in *Ekomo* and *The Reencounter;* things are so thrown together as to be incoherent at the start. In these novels, there are plenty of laments at sundry foreign dominations of Guinean spaces, but such protests are belied by simultaneous and contrary assimilations by the authors and texts of cultural elements that originate outside Guinea. The external and the internal prove in no sense to be definable without each other. Indeed, Nsue Angüe and Balboa Boneke could be viewed convincingly as Spanish authors more than Equatoguinean, with their novels participating in a boom of innovative Spanish culture that followed the collapse of fascism not in Malabo but in Madrid, not of Francisco Macías but of Francisco Franco. They redefine Spanish identity by evoking its social margins as much as, say, their contemporary Pedro Almodóvar. Such transnational arguments are rarely if ever advanced, however, for antidictatorial scholars tend to be as dedicated in practice to the concept of national histories as prodictatorial politicians. Yet in *Ekomo* and *The Reencounter,* as in the Guinean novels of the colonial era *When the Combes Fought* and *A Spear for the Boabí,* and as in the Asian fictions in Spanish stretching from *Nínay* to *Social Justice,* every conclusion that draws a line between the local and the foreign is subverted in the process by the postmagellanic unsustainability of both concepts.

The specific event inside Equatorial Guinea that led most to the resurgence of African Hispanic literature in Spain was the fall of the Macías regime in 1979. The dictator was eliminated by his nephew, Teodoro Obiang Nguema Mbasogo, who as of this writing holds the unfortunate distinction of being the autocrat longest in power in all of Africa. Not all strongmen are created equal, however, and the egregious baseline established by Macías—the murder of a tenth of the population and the flight of a third, all in a context of omnipresent torture and fear—was not hard to improve upon. In the years after Obiang took power, a number of Guineans who either had made Spain their home before Guinean independence in 1968 or survived there in exile during the Macías regime felt free enough to travel back to the country for visits of varying stays. These included the poet Raquel Ilombé and the scholar Donato Ndongo-Bidyogo as well as Nsue Angüe and Balboa Boneke.[7] *The Reencounter,* in fact, is dedicated to the new ruler: "A S.E. T. Obiang Nguema: En prueba de mi sincero afecto y consideración. EL AUTOR" ["To His Excellency T. Obiang Nguema: As proof of my sincere affection and consideration. THE AUTHOR"] (dedication page).[8] In the Iberian context, meanwhile, new cultural and political openings also presented a backdrop as Spain emerged from the stultifying somnolence of the Franco years and began its own sundry liberalizations.

To produce the first anthology of Guinean literature, Ndongo-Bidyogo literally went knocking on doors in 1981, just two years after the regime change, to collect whatever examples of literature he could find in the country from whichever persons might have been able to retain their work. Since possession of papers easily could have proved fatal under the Macías tyranny, the publication of the anthology in 1984 in Madrid represented a seminal triumph. Ndongo-Bidyogo's labors overlapped in time with those of Nsue Angüe and Balboa Boneke, whose novels appeared the following year in Madrid. Ndongo-Bidyogo, who eventually would go into exile again, this time forced at gunpoint as the Obiang regime worsened, would contribute in 1987 the first of his three novels, *Las tinieblas de tu memoria negra* (literally, *The Darkness of Your Black Memory,* translated into English in 2007 as *Shadows of Your Black Memory*), also published in Madrid. As of this writing he remains in exile, living in the Spanish city of Murcia but occasionally teaching at the University of Missouri–Columbia, which positioned itself in the 1990s as a central institution of Guinean studies.

Of the 1984 anthology and the 1985 novels that constituted the first published books of Guinean creative writings since Daniel Jones Mathama's *A Spear for the Boabí* of 1962, *Ekomo* is the most commented by scholars and most disseminated among readers in general. It was the first Equatoguinean novel to be translated, with a French version appearing in 1995, and the third to be republished in Spanish, with a new edition unveiled in 2007.[9] Moreover, *Ekomo* remained for two decades the only published Guinean novel by a woman; the second and third would be Guillermina Mekuy's *El llanto de la perra* (*The Cry of the Bitch*) (Barcelona, 2005) and *Las tres vírgenes de Santo Tomás* (*The Three Virgins of Saint Thomas*) (Madrid, 2008).[10] The gender of the author, matched inside the text by the lone female narrator in twentieth-century Guinean fiction, continues to garner *Ekomo* special interest.[11] The quantity of attention to the novel exceeds that on any other Guinean literary text save for the probable exception of Ndongo-Bidyogo's *Shadows of Your Black Memory,* which has been republished twice in Spanish and translated into French and English. In contrast, *The Reencounter* has been mostly ignored since its appearance. Given the paucity of scholarship in general on Guinean literature, however, *Ekomo* remains very much an understudied text. In fact, the most extensive and provocative examination of it to date is a 2009 undergraduate thesis from Mount Holyoke College.[12]

The prestige of *Ekomo* relative to *The Reencounter* is due not only to the issues of gender that are foregrounded inside and outside the text but also to its apparently more complex belletristic and sociological attempts at conveying the sensibilities of an oral and traditional culture into the written and foreign genre that is the novel. The plot of *The Reencounter,* in which an exile returns to Equatorial Guinea after the fall of Macías and visits a succession of individuals in order to learn about the state of the country, seems forced and dry by comparison. Furthermore, Balboa Boneke's preference for the tones of ostensibly objective reportage and overt editorializing probably has made his text less attractive to literary scholars who, after all, tend to privilege those creative discourses that are themselves privileged in the university machinery that accredits literary scholars. Yet *The Reencounter,* no less than *Ekomo,* technically initiates in 1985 the national novelistic tradition of Equatorial Guinea and takes up in equally complicated and unrealizable ways, and with no less underlying literariness, a project of identity formation that a postmagellanic planet has rendered impossible. At the very least, *The Reencounter* should be seen alongside *Ekomo* and the two novels published in the colonial era as nearly completing the inaugural forays into the genre that originated among each of the main constitutent ethnic groups of Guinea: Balboa Boneke writes of the Bubi, Nsue Angüe of the Fang, Jones Mathama of the Fernandinos, and Leoncio Evita, the first Guinean novelist, of the Combes (also known as the Ndowe).[13]

But it is *Ekomo* that continues to attract readers and circulation. A translation into English of the first chapter was published in 2003 in the anthology *Daughters of the Diaspora: Afra-Hispanic Writers.* A translation into English of the entire book is appearing as well and, as a result, its reach keeps growing as it enters its fourth decade of existence. This seems rare for a late twentieth-century novel. And if popular audiences and scholars approach it as the first postindependence novel of Guinea, they might naturally expect it to address themes of a young and unique nationhood. Nsue Angüe, however, skips over the entire national era and sets her plot in amorphous moments during the colonial period. Dorothy Odartey-Wellington notes that "La única referencia histórica en *Ekomo* es un presagio de la muerte de Patrice Lumumba. Esta referencia nos hace ubicar los acontecimientos de la novela entre los años cincuenta y sesenta" ["The only historical reference in *Ekomo* is a portent of the death of Patrice Lumumba. This reference makes us situate the events of the novel between the 1950s and 1960s"] ("La necrosis poscolonial," 148). Yet this is a very fleeting historical marker that probably would pass unrecognized by most Spaniards and most readers of *Ekomo* in the era of its plot, in its moment of publication, and still now, leaving the chronological setting of the novel de facto imprecise.[14] Amid this vagueness of the temporal setting and the absence of the nation proper, the title character represents the dying cultural memory of a Fang society and, by extension, of all of Africa. Guinea, as a colonial or national entity, is mentioned just once in passing in the novel and only when the lead characters are put under great duress. The collective cultural memory at hand is evidently being lost at tribal and continental levels, not being gained within a nascent national context.

The cause of the loss is seemingly identified in *Ekomo* as the intrusion of European influence into traditional Fang life. Those characters who spend time in Europe or in African spaces impacted by European culture end up detraditionalized and doomed. Scholars trained in postcolonial methodologies therefore tend to read the novel through a dialectic of the local and the foreign in which the former gives way, with dire social consequences, before the latter. Such readings are in keeping with the superficial flow of a novel that, in seemingly positing Afro-Euro hybridization as the problem, also seems to suggest the tribe and the continent as theoretical alternatives to the absent nation as sources for a collective identity, even if those options in reality are now rendered impossible by the fact of European cultural presences in Africa. The issue with this conventional interpretation, however, is the ultimate incoherence in *Ekomo* of both the tribe and the continent when offered implicitly and explicitly as identitarian substitutes. For starters, "Africans" could not be imagined as constituting a continental community until "Europeans" arrived and the twinned concepts developed in mutual self-referentiality. The broad invocation of Africa as such, instead of a colonial or independent Guinean polity that would include not only Fang but also Bubi and Fernandinos and Ndowe

(Combes) and Annobonese, is also, along with nationhood, a move steeped in modernity, not ancestral tradition. It is inconceivable that a village community would see itself as metonymically continental prior to the penetration of European phenomena. As for the tribe as a more specific and micro locus of identity, *Ekomo* is self-contradictory about the very cultural hybridization it mourns. Nnanga, the narrator/protagonist and a sympathetic figure, is a Christian and professes to be so even at the end of the novel (170, 191).[15] That is hardly a traditional Fang affiliation. Plus, the primary symbol in *Ekomo* is a tree sacred to the Fang that, in material reality, is not sacred to the Fang. And if extraliterary elements are to be taken into consideration, questions of authorial anchoring complicate matters further. Nsue Angüe does not have a straightforward relationship with Fang culture, having spent her formative years in Spain and having been unable to speak Fang until studying it. In a 1998 interview with Teobaldo Nchaso, she acknowledged,

> *Yo siempre, para los guineanos, he sido como el patito feo y esto, en gran parte, porque he estado mucho tiempo fuera y en Guinea se me ha visto siempre como la mujer que no sabe cosas de sus país, la mujer que no habla fang, que desconoce algunas cosas de la tradición y eso, quieras o no, de alguna manera te marca, ¿no?* (*Lewis, 136*)

> [I always, for the Guineans, have been like the ugly duckling and this, in large part, is because I have been outside for a long time and in Guinea have been seen always as the woman who does not know things of her country, the woman who does not speak Fang, who is unfamiliar with some things of the tradition and that, whether you want it so or not, in some way marks you, no?]

The tribe in *Ekomo,* much like the continent, is therefore a projected collective identity rife with postmagellanic problematics. So too are the issues of nationhood, virtually invisible in a text that nonetheless is commonly hailed as the first national novel. An authorial or academic embrace of syncretism does not explain this welter of phenomena, for there is no coming together in *Ekomo* of disparate cultural forces into any totality unified in its heterogeneity. There is no coming together and there is no falling apart. There are only powers and resistances crashing among each other in all directions, and narrations of the same that escape all controls as a consequence.

Oddly, early critics did not take the obvious first step of reading *Ekomo* as regretful of anything at all involving the presence of Europe, via Spain, in Guinea. Cues were probably taken from the neocolonial remarks of Nsue Angüe's editor and prologuist, Vicente Granados, who prefaces *Ekomo* by referring to Guinean Spanish as "una lengua artificial" ["an artificial language"] full of "errores de dispersión del sistema vocálico" ["errors of relaxation of the vowel system"] and other "innumerables confusiones" ["innumerable misunderstandings"] (11).[16] Granados is convinced of both the inherent superiority of Castilian Spanish and the lack of anything in Nsue Angüe's novel that might contest Spanish colonialism and its legacies. He suggests that "no hay en la novela el más mínimo resentimiento, ni trata ninguna cuestión política de carácter panfletario, porque la obra cumple una de las características de la literatura guineana escrita: la ausencia de sentimientos anticolonialistas" ["in the novel there is not the most minimal resentment, nor does it address any political question in a demagogic way, because the work fulfills one of the characteristics of written Guinean literature: the absence of anticolonial sentiments"] (13). This conclusion is demonstrably counterfactual. Nevertheless, the verdict of Granados is in keeping with most scholarly views of not only *Ekomo* but all early Guinean literature.[17]

Just prior to the publication of *Ekomo*, in the introduction to his groundbreaking 1984 anthology, Ndongo-Bidyogo asserted that "La ausencia de estridencias anticolonialistas podría, desde luego, llegar a ser una singularidad permanente de la literatura guineana, que daría así al resto de las literaturas africanas un tono nuevo caracterizado por la serenidad, sin voces quebradas por el llanto ni indignaciones retrospectivas" ["The absence of anticolonialist stridency could, therefore, become a permanent singularity of Guinean literature, which thereby would give to the rest of African literatures a new tone characterized by serenity, without voices broken by cries or retrospective indignation"] ("El marco," 29).[18] The text of *Ekomo* rebuts both Granados's neocolonial self-satisfaction and Ndongo-Bidyogo's hypothesis that "serenity" might enduringly mark Equatoguinean literature. An explicitly nationalistic message of anticolonial protest may be lacking in the novel, but that absence in no way elides the author's profound sorrow for a collective memory that is collapsing on both tribal and continental scales. The colonial context of Spanish Guinea and of Africa in general is clearly implicated in Nsue Angüe's multiple ideations of collective memories that are in the midst of being extinguished.

INTERNALITIES AND DISJUNCTURES

The plot of *Ekomo* begins in a Fang village in Río Muni (that is, mainland Guinea) and radiates outward as a quest. The novel is narrated by Nnanga, the wife of the title character, who is a young man suffering a persistent illness in his leg.[19] After the death of the tribal elder and various flashbacks to her childhood, Nnanga sets out with Ekomo on a journey whose ostensible goal is curative (they search for someone to heal his sickness) but whose allegorical purpose is spiritual and educational: Ekomo, who is versed in indigenous oral traditions, explains these histories and stories to Nnanga. The journey itself thus articulates a collective indigenous memory. Yet this memory is mostly conveyed at the climax of the journey, with Ekomo on the verge of death, as he and his leg are decomposing even in life. Ekomo, like the collective cultural memory he represents, no longer has anything to sustain him. As maggots emerge from his body, his journey in all senses, including the metonymic one of his tribe and continent, terminates in solitude and tragedy. Throughout the novel, whose episodes are less linear in the early village scenes than in the culminating quest sequence, the point of view is consistently that of Nnanga. She filters the world around her as Ekomo and other characters move in and out of her personal life. The foregrounding of her psychological and material experiences from childhood through widowhood plainly make her, and not her husband, the protagonist of the novel. Ekomo himself is more of a metaphor whose import Nnanga and the reader try to grasp rather than a human character in his own right.

When the novel opens, the tribal elder is sitting in judgment of a case of adultery in the village. The elder explains the reasoning for his sentence by noting "Todos recordaréis que se dijo en la antigüedad: 'No busques a la mujer de tu hermano'" ["You will all remember what was said in antiquity: 'Do not search out your brother's wife'"] (18). This convocation of tribal memory by the elder, however, is followed by a bad omen. In a sky described as "ceniciento" ["ashen"], a black cloud appears in the shape of a tombstone (19). The elder interprets it as "la señal del Africa antigua, la lápida de los poderosos. Cada vez que veáis esta señal dibujada en el cielo, habréis de entender que un poderoso va a morir en Africa . . . Esta señal que aparece hoy en el cielo se aparecía a los antiguos, cuando Africa era Africa. Y cuando en Africa sólo se adoraban los dioses africanos" ["the signal of ancient Africa, the tombstone of the powerful. Each time that you see this signal drawn in the sky, you will have to understand that a powerful man is going to die in Africa . . . This signal that appears today in the sky appeared to the ancients, when Africa was Africa. And when only African gods were worshipped in Africa"] (19). The elder thus draws upon his own knowledge of tribal and continental memory in order to interpret an omen that paradoxically makes an appearance in a collective context that no longer exists. Africa, he suggests, is no longer Africa. The continent is no longer commensurate with itself. But was it ever? Only tautological reasoning could conclude that a Fang community rooted in a small forested locale had a primeval sense of belonging to a vast continent whose geopolitical or cultural dimensions they could not possibly have known. Only contact with people who were not denominated as African and who came from various elsewheres could lead to the creation of Africa as a continental imaginary. Modernity did not bypass Africa; modernity produced it. Moreover, this sign that appears in the sky actually suggests the opposite of what the elder says. The ominous symbol of the present moment is the same as that which appeared in ancient times, with the same meaning and the same foreboding powers. Africa evidently still indeed is Africa, with the regime of the olden gods still able to produce its codes and disciplines. In contradiction, however, the elder suggests that Africa is no longer Africa as well.

According to María Zielina Limonta, "El término lápida pues adquiere connotaciones simbólicas, convirtiéndose en imagen estructural del pacto que va a desaparecer, romperse, enterrarse" ["The term 'tombstone' thus acquires symbolic connotations, converting itself into a structural image of the pact that is going to disappear, break apart, bury itself"] (95). The forecasted death of "a powerful man" deepens this implication. The elder adds rhetorically, "¿Quiénes son los poderosos de la tierra? Porque habréis de entender que, cuando hablo de la tierra, hablo de Africa y, no lo digo por decir, ya que hace mucho tiempo que los africanos abandonaron a Africa y Africa a los africanos. En Africa ya no hay poderosos" ["Who are the powerful of the earth? Because you will have to understand that when I speak of the earth, I speak of Africa, and I do not say it just to say it, for long ago Africans abandoned Africa and Africa the Africans. In Africa the powerful are no longer"] (20). The elder, a link to all previous generations, is certain that a collapse of immense social proportions is under way due to the mutual alienation of Africa and Africans. The coherence of the latter concept is questionable, however, for if Africans have abandoned Africa then they would seem to be no longer categorizable as Africans. A personified Africa without African people could be conceived—ecologies and geographies would remain, perhaps even gods—but, inversely, could Africans exist without Africa? The elder speaks with the premise that two essentialized identities, one continental and one human, have disintegrated and yet remain who they are. This is untenable. A more fluid sense of the forces that conditionally bring "Africa" and "Africans" both into and out of being seems the only way out of the contradiction.

The framework presented at the start of *Ekomo* is of a paradoxical continental death in progress that is perceptible from a local vantage. The tombstone in the sky is soon followed by another grim sign when the sacred ceiba tree at the spiritual center of the village suddenly collapses, dragging a "una rama joven y robusta" ["a young and robust branch"] along with it (26). This ceiba, according to Nnanga,

> guarda el totem de la tribu, pues en sus raíces están enterradas las venturas, desventuras, las epidemias, el hambre y la abundancia de la tribu. En la ceiba está la muerte, la vida, la salud y la enfermedad. Por ello, los miembros de la tribu saben guardar las normas establecidas por los antepasados desde hace siglos para que no lleguen a nosotros los estragos. La ceiba sagrada ha anunciado que van a morir dos hombres: Un gran jefe y un hombre joven. *(25–26)*

[safeguards the totem of the tribe, since in its roots are buried the good fortune, ill fortune, epidemics, hunger, and abundance of the tribe. In the ceiba are death, life, health, and sickness. The members of the tribe thereby know how to safeguard the norms established by the ancestors centuries ago so that destruction does not arrive upon us. The sacred ceiba has announced that two men are going to die: a great chief and a young man.]

Nnanga's narrative voice here is at once individual and collective, for it functions as a tribal voice as much as her own. Similarly, the death of the ceiba augurs the personal fatalities of not only a "great chief" (symbolized by the tree itself) and a young man (symbolized by the "robust branch") but also of the tribal collectivity that they represent. Thus Zielina Limonta argues that "la ceiba ha sido derribada indirectamente por todos, por aquellos que, bien por el escepticismo o por la indolencia, han permitido que el mundo de sus antepasados se resquebrajara, fuese desapareciendo" ["the ceiba has been felled indirectly by everyone, by those who, whether because of skepticism or indolence, have permitted that the world of their ancestors split asunder, that it disappear away"] (98). It is at this moment that Ekomo appears in the novel in person for the first time. He has returned to the village from a city, emblem of modernity and Western intrusion into African space, where he was busy committing adultery. There is something wrong with his leg. The suspicion grows in Nnanga that Ekomo may be the young man whose fate has been signaled by the fallen limb.

The choice of a ceiba as the central symbol of the village is noteworthy, since according to Granados, the editor and prologuist, the ceiba is "un árbol ajeno a la tradición fang, porque el árbol sagrado de esa tribu es el oveng" ["a tree that is alien to Fang tradition, because the sacred tree of that tribe is the oveng"] (11). With his will to produce in Nsue Angüe's text his own sense of narrative coherence, this time on a symbolic rather than linguistic level, Granados adds, "Puesto que *Ekomo* se mueve dentro de la cosmogonía fang, sugerí a la autora que cambiara el árbol, y me contestó tajante: la ceiba es el árbol del bien" ["Since *Ekomo* moves within Fang cosmogony, I suggested to the author that she change the tree, and she responded sharply that the ceiba is the tree of good"] (12). This interchange is complicated at several levels. Granados, as the editor, exercises a disciplining role over the novel, one that Nsue Angüe here rejects. Elsewhere, however, she apparently accepted such interventions from the Spaniard, who in his prologue lauds her attempts to edit out the local versions of Spanish that he deems "errores" ["errors"] and "confusiones" ["misunderstandings"] in need of correction (11). Yet it is also Granados who advises her to replace the ceiba with a more authentic symbol of what is presumably her culture. She, in turn, rebuffs him by maintaining the choice of an authentic symbol of what presumably is *his* culture. The attempt by Granados to control the consequences of colonialism, that is, Nsue Angüe's familiarity with biblical motifs, backfires on him. He wants her to be both less and more Fang according to circumstance. He likes indigenous cultural color just so long as it does not challenge the intended inviolability of his own sense of identity. A transculturated version of Spanish and of Genesis are "errors" and "misunderstandings" in need of reclarification. Yet when Nsue Angüe deliberately selects a Western allegory ("the tree of good") as a parable of Fang identity, she demonstrates that that allegory has ceased to be so Western, that the line between center and periphery has become irremediably blurred. Despite producing the novel under the gaze of Granados, she still manages to claim narrative space for herself where she can, in this case by paradoxically insisting upon the inclusion of a Western metaphor at the symbolic heart of a story of a traditional African village.

The great chief whose death the ceiba foreshadows turns out to be none other than the tribal elder who had opened the book by convoking ancestral memory to justify his punishment of the adulterers, and who had used that same memory to read the tombstone in the sky.[20] On his death, Nnanga reflects, "Me di cuenta que acababa de morirse el último superviviente de una época que había acabado hacía tiempo. La época del abuelo (i.e., el gran jefe) había acabado antes con él" ["I realized that the last survivor of an epoch that had ended long ago has just died. The epoch of the grandfather (i.e., the great chief) had ended before with him"] (41). These lines echo the seeming contradiction offered earlier by the elder himself about the imminent death of a powerful African in an Africa already dead. The continent cannot be dead and the olden epoch over if predictions based on ancestral knowledge are still coming true. Nnanga then adds that the elder "marcaba con su muerte el fin de un Africa y daba comienzo a otra . . . al africano de hoy le interesan otras cosas. Tiene otros problemas, otros dioses, otras creencias, y va abandonando lentamente su tradición" ["marked with his death the end of one Africa and launched another . . . The African of today is interested in other things. He has other problems, other gods, other beliefs, and he slowly abandons his tradition"] (42). Here again, a personal fate is merged with a temporally incoherent collective one, as the elder personifies a dying local and continental memory that nevertheless already has perished. Nnanga regrets the passing of the elder and the indigenous traditions he represents, but this sadness is difficult to reconcile with her own acceptance of a foreign faith—she is Protestant—and her own decision at the end of the novel to violate one of the most basic beliefs of her society by touching the cadaver of her husband.

With the elder dead, Nnanga and the whole village wait for the second half of the prophecy to be fulfilled: a young man must perish. The worsening leg of Ekomo makes him the likely candidate. Meanwhile, a great lethargy and uncertainty pervades the society, for the traditional world seems to have expired along with the elder. Even the natural environment of local life seems no longer comprehensible. As Nnanga notes, "La naturaleza se había apartado del hombre, formando un mundo ajeno, insensible a los hombres y sus acontecimientos" ["Nature had separated itself from man, forming an alien world, insensitive to men and their events"] (59).

Amid this alienation, the narrative turns to Nfumbaha, a young man who recently had returned from Europe, where he had acquired some Western education and belief systems. Although the tribal elder had forbidden any villager to enter the forest during a certain period after his death, Nfumbaha decides to defy that ban. On seeing him disappear into the woods, Nnanga notes, "Nfumbaha había estado mucho tiempo en Europa, y había perdido el respeto a la tradición. Podía salvarse quizás del embrujo de la selva, porque era ya medio blanco. 'Quizás . . . '" (ellipsis in original) ["Nfumbaha had been in Europe a long time and had lost respect for tradition. Perhaps he could save himself from the bewitching of the forest because he was already half-white. 'Perhaps . . .'"] (60). The village waits a long time for Nfumbaha to come back, yet he does not. Search parties are sent out but to no avail. Salvation from violating the taboo, apparently, will not be gained by Nfumbaha despite his metaphorical whitening in Europe. Again in apparent contradiction to the lament by the elder that Africa is no longer Africa, powers steeped in tradition remain potent.

Now that a second member of the society is presumed gone forever, Nnanga reflects that "Nfumbaha, el africano de hoy, hombre del mañana, tras estar dos lluvias en Europa, dejó su tradición encerrada entre los libros; dejó allí su personalidad y sus creencias africanas, y el ser sin continente regresó a su pueblo con un disfraz del europeo sin el europeo dentro. Con una máscara de Europa pero sin su rostro en ella. Medio blanco, medio negro" ["Nfumbaha, the African of today, man of tomorrow, after being in Europe for two rainy seasons, left his tradition enclosed among books; he left there his personality and his African beliefs, and as a being without a continent returned to his village with a European costume but without the European inside. With a European mask but without his face inside it. Half-white, half-black"] (85). His sanction for betraying his village and his continent, for obtaining a hybrid ethnic sense of self, is evidently his disappearance in the forest. But that fate demonstrates the enduring power of the dead elder and of the allegedly dead traditions. The prohibition by the great chief, transgressed by Nfumbaha, still results in punishment. The novel implies that this is just, given the cultural treason. Yet the lament against Nfumbaha for having left "his tradition enclosed among books" runs directly contrary to the fact that his own story is being relayed to the reader in, after all, a book, one whose European costume could be viewed as its language, whose European mask as its genre. If Nfumbaha the character is "half-white, half-black," so is *Ekomo* the novel and so, of course, is María Nsue Angüe the author.

This conclusion goes utterly against the superficial thrust of the Nfumbaha sequence, which continues with the grief of his mother: "Las lágrimas de la madre son las del Africa y sus lamentos se esparcen alargados por el aire hasta los confines de la tierra por todos aquellos hijos perdidos y no hallados . . . cada vez que cae uno de sus hijos, Africa llora personificándose en cada una de las madres del Nfumbaha" ["The tears of the mother are those of Africa and her laments scatter extended through the air until the ends of the earth for all those sons who have been lost and not found . . . each time that one of her sons falls, Africa cries, personifying herself in each of the mothers of Nfumbaha"] (85). Again here the novel suggests that the loss of a cultural memory by one man, in this case Nfumbaha, is tantamount to the loss of a continent. Nfumbaha's mother is "madre Africa" ["mother Africa"] and the personal and tribal tragedy is continental in scale (85). As before, any possible protonational or national context is bypassed altogether, while the collectivities that are the village and all Africa are inextricable. Once more, the micro and the macro stand for each other without any intermediaries. Not only are Spanish Guinea and Equatorial Guinea absent as explicitly invoked concepts but so too is Spain or any other particular foreign nation or power. At hand, therefore, are dynamics of global resonance. It is Europe and the West in general that is evoked as corresponding inversely to Africa and the village, not specific foreign governments or polities or people. But the varied presences of Europe and the West in the village space are what makes possible the extrapolation of the local society to the vastness that is Africa. The grief of the mothers of Africa is a lachrymose rebuttal to Europe, but it is Europe that allows for the imagination of Nfumbaha's mother as synecdochical to her continental peers in the first place.[21]

ITINERANTS AND IDENTIFICATIONS

If extratextual considerations were to enter analyses of *Ekomo*, such interdefinition of the local and the foreign could be seen even more so as constantly escaping from all attempts to reduce the novel to a tribal or national or continental fiction. In fact, the frequently contradictory performance in the novel of a doomed tribe and continent would be viewed further as almost as consciously artificed into existence as the national idea that it ignores. Although *Ekomo* commences in Río Muni, where Nsue Angüe was born, the history of the author and her text is in no sense restricted to an isolated regional environment. Any of the numerous critics, beginning with the prologuist Granados, who frames the novel as a fundamentally local product is not considering the many displacements of its extratextual origins as well as intratextual projections.

Regarding the author, for example, Nsue Angüe moved to Spain as a young child, returned to Guinea as a young adult, and has moved back and forth ever since. With her formative years spent entirely in Spain, the case could be made that she can be considered just as viably a Spanish as a Guinean author. In fact, she noted in a 1993 interview in Madrid, "Pienso en Español, sueño en Español y hablo en Español la mayor parte de tiempo de mi vida . . . ¿Qué argumento utilizaría usted para afirmar que robo una lengua que siempre ha sido la mía, si cuando llegué a España tenía ocho años y ni siquiera sabía decir tres palabras en Fang?" ["I think in Spanish, I dream in Spanish, and I speak in Spanish the better part of the time in my life . . . What argument would you use to affirm that I steal a language that always has been mine, if when I arrived in Spain I was eight years old and did not even know how to say three words in Fang?"] ("María Nsué Angüe," 117). In the same interview, she cites her principal literary influences as Rosalía de Castro, Carmen Laforet, Ana María Matute, Santa Teresa de Jesús, the Brontë sisters, and, her most recent favorite, Toni Morrison. This is a list of canonical women writers from Spain and the anglophone West that contains not a single African author (115). When asked about cultural creation in Equatorial Guinea in the 1980s, the decade in which *Ekomo* was published, Nsue Angüe adds, "He estado muy poco tiempo en Guinea y, desde luego, tengo muy poco contacto con sus actividades" ["I have spent very little time in Guinea and therefore have very little contact with its activities"] (118). *Ekomo*, a novel that appears to be a local story about local people, a novel that seems to defend a Fang society and all of Africa from European intrusion, is the product of an individual who could not speak Fang and who had lived mostly in Spain and who wrote consciously within the Spanish literary tradition. This does not make Nsue Angüe any less African or Guinean or Fang; it is quite possible to be all three things and also European and Spanish. She herself has recognized as much in asserting, "soy cincuenta por ciento puramente africana en cuanto al modo de ver las cosas y actuar, y otro cincuenta por ciento española" ["I am 50 percent purely African regarding my manner of seeing things and acting, and another 50 percent Spanish"] (113). The investment by both procolonial and anticolonial commentators in the presence of an essentialized local in *Ekomo* is less flexible than the self-perception of its author.

One of the primary distinctions between Asian and African literature in Spanish is simply that many of the major writers of the latter are alive and so can be queried about their work. It is possible to speak with Nsue Angüe directly at the occasional public appearances she makes in Europe or North America or by catching a plane to Equatorial Guinea—thanks to the discovery of oil offshore in the 1990s, flights are readily available via Madrid and Paris—and dropping by the cultural center in Malabo where she works sometimes as a teacher of Fang percussion and as a storyteller. Nsue Angüe has said recently that she has studied the Fang language and so probably speaks it well by this point, but her decades in Spain have given her Spanish as the most native of her languages. She is a particularly eloquent speaker in it at that. Yet her relative accessibility can result in misleading critical appraisals on several counts. One issue, for instance, is that the small world of scholars interested in Guinean literature tends to know personally the small circle of Guinean writers. This carries some advantages that specialists in, say, the texts of the nineteenth-century Filipino novelist José Rizal, do not enjoy, but friendships among critics and the authors they discuss can limit in sundry ways the range of evaluations that ultimately reach publication. For example, Gloria Nistal writes in her prologue to the second edition of *Ekomo* in Spanish that "me ha resultado difícil mantener la objetividad, porque admiro mucho a la escritora María Nsue y me siento muy cercana a la amiga María" ["it has turned out to be difficult to maintain objectivity because I much admire María Nsue the writer and I feel very close to my friend María"] (14).

In addition, unquestioning reliance on pronouncements by writers about the meaning of their texts is an extremely limited interpretive approach that has been anachronistic among literary theorists for half a century or more. This is particularly the case with an author who has had to negotiate survival through three dictatorships so far (those of Franco, Macías, and Obiang) and who continues living in a country where freedom of expression is circumscribed at best and fatal at worst. The apparently self-contradictory discursive maneuvers of Nsue Angüe in her prose and in her person may be part of a larger strategy of remaining elusive enough to

prevent anyone, autocrats and academics alike, from locating her anywhere. Even basic facts about her, such as the year of her birth and the year
in which *Ekomo* was published, appear differently in various sources.[22] If
such objective data are difficult or impossible to pin down, so much more
so is the validity or viability of more subjective or unverifiable truth-claims
made by the author about her novel. Nsue Angüe has said, for instance,
that she based the character of Nnanga on a prostitute whom she met in
Yaoundé, Cameroon; that the figure of Nfumbaha reappears anonymously
as an alleged "loco" ["crazy person"] in a chapter involving a medicine
man; and that Nnanga the narrator really would like to be a woman like her
grandmother, also named Nnanga.[23] What to do with this information is
an open question, as hard textual proof cannot be adduced for any of it. As
a larger theoretical matter, orienting a definitive interpretation around any
authorial statement is problematic even with those writers whose biographies are clear matters of documented public record and who issue consistent and declarative statements about their works.

Nsue Angüe is not such a writer in any case. Brief details of her life are
advanced in miscellaneous publications and often presented without explicit evidence. Miriam DeCosta-Willis says that she was born "in a prison,
where her mother had been incarcerated for her political views. Her family,
who were devout Protestants, had a decisive influence on her religious and
intellectual development" (286). Ndongo-Bidyogo seems to suggest that
her father was an activist in an independence movement and eventually
was assassinated, but whether by the regime of Macías or Franco is unclear;
he adds that she studied in a Madrid high school run by nuns and later regularly appeared on television in Malabo ("María Nsue Angüe," 99–100).
Mendogo Minsongui Dieudonné writes that Nsue Angüe attended a university in Madrid (210). The back cover of the French translation of *Ekomo*
avers that she is a "journaliste, un moment membre du gouvernement de
son pays au Ministère de la Femme, écrivain, auteur d'œuvres pour le
théâtre et la télévision" ["journalist, at one time a member of the government of her country in the Ministry of Women, writer, author of works for
the theater and television"], but leaves unspecified where or for whom or
when the journalism took place, the actions Nsue Angüe undertook when
in the Equatoguinean government, and when or whether any of the theatrical pieces have been staged or any of the television works enacted and
broadcast. Max Liniger-Goumaz, author of a standard reference on important figures in Guinean history, notes that her deceased husband, José Nsue

Angüe Osa, had been an early minister of national education under Macías but then, "Named ambassador to Ethiopia in 1973, he had been poisoned by Macías' sbirros at the end of 1976. In March 1981, his widow, María, was appointed technical director of the State Secretariat for Women's Affairs. However, by December of that year she was relieved of the post. Thereafter, she went to Madrid to study journalism" (321). DeCosta-Willis indicates that at one point Nsue Angue worked in Ethiopia after studying journalism, but for that to be correct the studies in question had to have been significantly earlier in her life than those that Liniger-Goumaz mentions (286). Anna Mester writes that Nsue Angüe is a Spanish national (90). Whichever elements of this biography are accurate, one thing is certain: María Nsue Angüe is not, like Nnanga, a woman whose life has been circumscribed within the parameters of a village in a forest.

As for her literary production, Nsue Angüe has said that she wrote *Ekomo* while living in Malabo; that she has written seven novels and some 150 short stories that she deliberately has not published; that she wants to break into the market for African-American literature; and that she does not want any film version of her work to be made.[24] All of this may be true to different degrees or in the entirety, but even so these statements hint at contrary tensions: prolific output versus a readership that cannot access it, desires to enter new realms of circulation while deliberately abstaining from the same. The corroboration of any of her declarations about her literary career, however, would not affect the demonstrable fact that *Ekomo* was published in Madrid and thus at a great geographic gap from Equatorial Guinea. Given that distance and the reality that the primary ties of Equatorial Guinea with the outside world link to the capital city of Malabo, on the island of Bioko, it seems probable that relatively few original copies of *Ekomo* made it to the relatively few potential readers in Río Muni, where the novel is set. Certainly, there are no Guinean characters in *Ekomo* other than the ill-fated Nfumbaha who would have been able to read this novel about their own lives, given their general illiteracy and their likely unfamiliarity with Spanish. *Ekomo,* in short, is an artifact alienated in a number of significant ways from the culture it depicts. This raises the question of the identity of the culture to which it predominantly pertains. The first edition of the novel was primarily consumed in Spain and by Spaniards, not in Río Muni and by Fang villagers such as those projected in its pages.

That circulation widened internationally with the publication of the French translation in 1995. The existence of this edition effectively recontextualized the novel for a different European readership that, unlike the public in Spain, was long familiar with traditions of African literature in an imperial language.[25] *Ekomo* was slotted as publication number 140 of the francophone African series Encres Noires (Black Ink) of L'Harmattan, a major publisher of such literature. Nsue Angüe was billed on the back cover as "une image de l'africaine d'aujourd'hui, représentante passionnée de son pays et de ses racines" ["an image of the African woman of today, passionate representative of her country and her roots"]. Smoothing the way for easier metropolitan intake are the addition of subtitles to the chapters and to the novel itself. The text is now called *Ekomo: Au cœur de la forêt guinéenne* (*Ekomo: In the Heart of the Guinean Forest*), evoking yet again the hoary "heart of darkness" trope. The translation is unnecessarily liberal in that, among other questionable tactics, it uses standard French expressions to override various local words that Nsue Angüe originally left untranslated into Castilian and therefore unexplained to the Spanish reader except via the implications of context. The overall result of these changes is to lessen the potential strangenesses of the novel to a francophone public while drawing Nsue Angüe and *Ekomo* into the comforting confines of Parisian views of Africa.

Also in the mid-1990s, a few scholars throughout the West gradually began commenting on *Ekomo* in print. Yet it seems unlikely that such secondary texts are disseminated inside Equatorial Guinea. The appearance of a full English translation of the novel, like the French edition, will broaden its orbit again outside the country, more or less exclusively. Nonetheless, despite the extensive external environments in evidence all around, *Ekomo* is still routinely framed as the first novel of the nation of Equatorial Guinea. This description seems accurate only at the most literal, chronological level. There is no national imaginary in the novel. And if extratextual factors are taken into account, the loss in *Ekomo* of a Fang tribal heritage and a continental African memory is complicated acutely by the diverse expatriate origins and circulations of both the author and the text.

Inside the novel, however, such complications are already evinced by the many paradoxes of Fang identities projected with and within non-Fang elements, including the contradictions emergent from the stretch of narration centered upon Nfumbaha. When that sequence comes to an end, halfway through the novel, dramatic tension would seem to have reached its resolution: the prophecy of the fallen ceiba has been fulfilled with the deaths of the village elder and Nfumbaha. Yet the health of Ekomo has de-

teriorated further in the meanwhile. Amid the time that passes during the
Nfumbaha passages, Ekomo's leg continues to swell and his limp grows
more pronounced. Furthermore, Nnanga notes that Ekomo was Nfumbaha's best friend and his "amigo-hermano" ["friend-brother"] (86). Ekomo
is therefore marked by association and metaphoric consanguinity with the
fate of Nfumbaha. This perhaps marks him for death as well. As Ekomo and
Nnanga leave the tribe in search of a doctor for his leg, the village setting
of the first half of the book is replaced by an archetypal journey in the second half. This voyage seems predestined to fail.

The journey that Nnanga and Ekomo undertake is a quest for a cure,
but a cure for what? Ekomo's leg would seem to stand for all that Nnanga
has witnessed decomposing in Africa. On the journey outward from the village, his limb is already emitting a foul liquid that streams onto the floor
and attracts the attention of flies. Nnanga and Ekomo make their first call
to a famous medicine man who lives in a distant region of the forest.
Nnanga is hopeful that this man can help her with her sterility as well as
Ekomo's leg, since she badly wants a child. Symbolically, the two health
problems are matching, with infertility and decomposition implying cor-
poreal inabilities at the personal and, by metaphoric extension, continental scale to regenerate life. The chapter involving their stay with the medicine man is replete with tradition and its signs, from fertility rituals and
beliefs to narrated genealogies of the founding families of Africa, accounts
of the birth of voodoo, and so on. The medicine man, therefore, represents
in his memory of ancestral knowledge the last opportunity for Nnanga and
Ekomo to find a salve in African sources for that which ails them. At the
end of the chapter, the medicine man operates on Ekomo and extracts a
gruesome, tentacled, and alive foreign growth (128). Like much else in the
novel, the precise cause of deterioration, whether personal or cultural or
political, remains somewhat indistinct, but the ghastly growth that at-
taches itself fatally to Ekomo resonates with the other vague foreign forces
that throughout the plot seem to be dismembering local entities in one
form or another.

The operation by the medicine man does not help Ekomo. In this failure disappears the last turning to African remedies for an African disinte-
gration. Ekomo and Nnanga decide to continue their journey to a city with
a Western hospital staffed by white doctors. Given Nfumbaha's fate, however, the West and its institutions seem unlikely to provide alternative salvation. Ekomo, like his "friend-brother" Nfumbaha, has been exposed to

Western urban presences before and that was hardly wholesome or regenerative. The novel, after all, commences with his committing adultery in a city. Significantly, reaching anew such a locus of modernity leads to the lone moment in the novel in which Guinean identity as a concept is mentioned. As Ekomo and Nnanga make their way toward the city, they are suddenly stopped by francophone border guards who request their documentation (153). The couple struggles to understand not only the French words directed at them but also the request for identifying papers. Ekomo, dying and impatient, retorts, "En nuestro país, nadie nos da esas cosas. Nadie se preocupa allí de saber si hemos de salir o entrar, si tenemos papeles o no. Es más, podría asegurar que nadie los tiene" ["In our country, nobody gives us those things. Nobody bothers themselves there with knowing if we have to leave or enter, if we have papers or not. More than that, I can assure you that nobody has them"] (153). Whatever the conceptualization here of "our country," it is strictly produced in negative opposition to that which, as evidenced by the French-speaking border guards, is somebody else's country. Like an imagined continental Africa vis-à-vis an imagined continental Europe, "our country" has no existence in its own right. The absurd request for documentation is based on an empty fiction.

Ekomo then adds, "*Somos guineanos*. Estoy enfermo. Me han dicho que allá hay un médico que quizás pueda curar mi mal. Dejadme pasar, hermanos, nadie le pregunta a un perro a dónde va o de dónde viene y nadie se preocupa de darle papeles" ["*We are Guineans*. I am sick. They have told me that there is a doctor there who perhaps can cure my illness. Let me pass, brothers, nobody asks a dog where it is going or where it comes from and nobody bothers to give it papers" (153). The italicization by Nsue Angüe emphasizes the alienation of the concept of "*Guineans*" from the very people it is meant to designate. Ekomo summarily dismisses the national marker as meaningless before the fact of his putrefying leg. Being Guinean is as relevant to his identity, he observes, as it would be to an animal. The bureaucratic modernity of papers that supposedly confirm his Guinean identity is followed by a second cultural standoff, this time with the white doctor whom he and Nnanga visit when they reach the city. The physician takes one look at the leg and says that immediate amputation is requisite. Ekomo rejects that plan instantly and he and Nnanga set off once more.

The death of Ekomo is now assured. So, by extrapolation, is that of all Africa. It is at this moment of certified death that the travelers reach a sacred river, an arrival that occasions a series of collective memories initiated by Nnanga but then recalled aloud by Ekomo. Nnanga associates the river with foundational stories she had heard as a girl from her nanny, such as one that begins,

> *Mucho tiempo atrás, antes de que llegase la raza blanca a estas tierras, nuestros antepasados, hombres nómadas, viniendo desde el bajo Egipto a través del gran continente, llegaron a las orillas de un río grande, al que pusieron el nombre Ntam, que significa gracias o buenaventuranza, porque vieron que sus tierras eran buenas. Y habitaron en sus orillas durante muchos siglos. (158)*

> [A long time ago, before the white race arrived at these lands, our ancestors, nomadic men, coming from lower Egypt through the great continent, arrived at the shores of a great river, which they named Ntam, which signifies grace or good fortune, because they saw that its lands were good. And they lived by its shores for many centuries.]

When Ekomo learns that Nnanga is remembering fragments of these stories, he immediately becomes the voice of the continental past: "Aquí," he tells her, "nacieron hombres de muchas de nuestras tribus. Aquí, muchas de nuestras costumbres tradicionales y en estas orillas, muchos de nuestros héroes recordados hasta hoy. Este río es histórico" ["Here, men of many of our tribes were born. Here, many of our traditional customs and by these shores, many of our heroes who are remembered to this day. This river is historic"] (158–59). Ekomo proceeds to relate a long sequence of traditional stories of which Nnanga is ignorant. These include how the ancestors sought a promised land, how the Fang emerged from a complex genealogy of ancestors, how the custom of dowries was established, how the pygmies once disappeared into a tree trunk, how albinos exist because of an ancient case of incest, and how different languages emerged. Nnanga frequently interrupts this story-cycle to ask questions about it. She herself does not know the oral tradition of tribe and continent, so she prompts Ekomo to provide the collective memory that she does not possess. As the narrator and protagonist of the novel, Nnanga is the medium through which Nsue Angüe conveys present and past Fang culture, yet the character herself is unfamiliar with the traditions that are supposedly her own.

While Ekomo is talking, the thought occurs to Nnanga that in their journey together they were "recorriendo quizás la misma ruta de los hijos de Afrikara [el patriarca de Africa], aunque en dirección contraria. ¿Llegaríamos hasta los orígenes?" ["traveling perhaps the same route of the children of Afrikara (the patriarch of Africa), although in a contrary direction. Would we arrive at the origins?"] (163) Metaphorically this indeed is the case, for through Ekomo's memory, Nnanga is actually moving backward in time and space toward the start of a collective cultural tradition. This reencounter with origins, however, is a climax of remembrance that is also a definitive death. Once the story-cycle concludes, Ekomo and Nnanga reach a Protestant mission, their final destination (167). As maggots breed inside his leg, and after debating whether to be baptized, Ekomo dies. Since he cannot be buried on the mission grounds because he had not converted, Nnanga inters him beneath "Una ceiba, como aquella otra sagrada" ["A ceiba, like that other sacred one"] that fell at the beginning of the novel (182). An epic memory of tribe and continent apparently expires with Ekomo, symbolized nevertheless by a tree not ancestrally totemic but culturally imported. Such distancing from indigenous tradition is underlined when Nnanga violates a long-standing taboo by touching the corpse of her husband in the course of burying him. Alienated from all orders social and divine, she ends the novel with the tragic lament, "¡Qué tremendamente sola estoy!" ["How tremendously alone am I!"] (194). This heartrending finale counters Ndongo-Bidyogo's suggestion in his anthology, published just a year before *Ekomo*, that Equatoguinean literature might be marked permanently "por la serenidad, sin voces quebradas por el llanto" ["by serenity, without voices broken by weeping"] ("El marco" 29).

Nowhere in the novel, then, is memory really an individual concept. Certain people, like the elder and Ekomo, possess a dying collective memory that is projected as tribal and continental in nature, though never protonational or national, and they pass on fragments of that memory to any villagers who will listen. Yet those who transmit the remnants of collective memory are themselves slated for death, a fate that is not so much individual as social. In other words, the novel relays the incomplete transmission of a dying collective memory by dying men. Dorothy Odartey-Wellington rightly stresses that there is a fundamental issue of gender alienation involved here too, that the personal and vicarious sufferings of Nnanga from patriarchal powers make her voice representative of the lot of women in particular. Yet Odartey-Wellington's analysis that the final lament of Nnanga "no se hace en nombre de todo el pueblo sino específicamente en el de las mujeres" ["is not made in the name of all the people but instead specifically in that of the women"] cannot account sufficiently for the larger social collapse in evidence ("Entre la espada y la pared," 174).[26] The events in *Ekomo* transpire in an extended apocalyptic moment that is well on its way toward the postapocalyptic, a temporality that goes beyond gender issues. Ekomo and Nnanga's final journey, although it hearkens back to creation stories as told by an aggressive man to the woman he betrayed, is socially broad in its eschatologics.[27] For these reasons, the novel does not support the assertion of Vicente Granados, the Spanish editor and prologuist, that "la obra cumple una de las características de la literatura guineana escrita: la ausencia de sentimientos anticolonialistas" ["the work fulfills one of the characteristics of written Guinean literature: the absence of anticolonial sentiments"] (13). While it is true that the text does not assail explicitly the dominant colonial classes of Spanish Guinea, its protracted mourning for the death of indigenous orders amounts to criticism of those external forces whose presences coincided with and seemingly caused this cultural collapse. That the novel is more a dirge than a diatribe does not make it devoid of "anticolonial sentiments."

There is no unproblematized turn in *Ekomo* to ethnic essentialism, however, notwithstanding the claims of successive Spanish prologuists. Carlos González Echegaray, who in 1953 put forth a racialized preface to the first Guinean novel in Spanish, reemerged in 1989 to declare that *Ekomo* is "la primera novela escrita con mentalidad africana y por un africano en lengua española. . . . Su expresión es trabajada para no perder la autenticidad fang" ["the first novel written with an African mentality and by an African in the Spanish language. . . . Its expression is designed so as to not lose Fang authenticity"] ("La novela," 45). The simplistic use of concepts such as "African mentality" and "Fang authenticity" do injustice to the complex maneuverings of the text and author at all levels. For example, in the traditional stories narrated by Ekomo before his demise, it may appear that the novel attempts to promote the survival of those indigenous ideas and narrative forms that are endangered. Perhaps nowhere else in the text does the premise of an "African mentality" and "Fang authenticity" seem to be on such solid ground. Yet these stories are relayed in entirely nontraditional Fang media—the novel and the Spanish language—and in isolation from the communal contexts in which they are usually told. Moreover, at the level of content, the stories now resonate as counternarratives to those of the West. The exact same creation story told before the arrival of Spaniards in Guinea takes on a completely different charge when told afterward. Any invocation to tradition now reads as cultural resistance to the foreign, with the presumptive "African mentality" inextricably defined against, and therefore by, that which it presumptively is not.

Any conclusions contrary to those of Granados and González Echegaray about the presence of essentialism in *Ekomo* may be deepened for some readers by considerations of Nsue Angüe's own background as a frequent expatriate to whom the Spanish language and Spain were in substantive ways far closer than the Fang language and Equatorial Guinea. In an interview apparently conducted in or just before 2000, Nsue Angüe went so far as to say that "El ser africana no tiene que ver nada en mi vida. Me sentiría igual siendo India, europea, asiática o árabe" ["Being an African woman has nothing to do with my life. I would feel the same if I were an Indian, European, Asian, or Arab woman"] (N'gom, "Novelística," 102). In the same interview, nonetheless, she adds, "Doy gracias a Dios por ser negra y africana para poder confundirme con África y compartir su sentir desde una óptica diferente a los nativos, al mismo tiempo que compartir su sentir desde la óptica africana. La simbiosis es mi fuerza y me alegro de ello" ["I give thanks to God for being black and African in order to be able to blend myself with Africa and share its sensibility from a point of view different from that of the natives, and at the same time to share its sensibility from the African point of view. Symbiosis is my strength and I am happy for it"] (102).

The constant slippage in Nsue Angüe's sense of self-identity echoes in the intermixing of Western and African cultures in *Ekomo*, but in no sense do the two exist on equal planes in the novel as perhaps they do in Nsue Angüe's conception of her own life. In *Ekomo*, indigenous worlds disintegrate as foreign forces ascend, however amorphous that ascension may be behind the foregrounded individual trajectories of Nnanga and Ekomo. The collapse of traditional Africa signaled at the surface level of the novel stands as cultural commentary on a continent in a way that is patently recriminatory. The narrative of Nnanga and Ekomo does not achieve the positive symbiosis that Nsue Angüe says she enjoys in her own life. As Lola Aponte-Ramos writes, "La lucha interior por localizar en un espacio en fuga entre los rituales cristianos y fang, sólo subraya la imposibilidad de la protagonista de asediar su realidad partir [*sic*] de las categorías que ambos espacios epistemológicos proponen" ["The interior struggle to locate in a space of escape between Christian and Fang rituals only underlines the impossibility of the protagonist of surrounding her reality starting from the categories that both epistemological spaces propose"] (112). There emerges in the novel no mutually beneficial interrelationship of the local and the foreign, the Fang or African and the Spanish or European. Nor do these identitarian forces compose a larger unit that functions as a totality of any kind. The forces are themselves incoherent, escaping as they do all efforts to retain them within definitive boundaries.

In Nnanga's solitude at the end of the novel there lies a pathos profound beyond the loss of her husband, for she has lost much more than him. She also has lost a tribe and a continent that are now alienated from her forever. That, at least, is the superficial message. A closer read shows that she did not know the tribal stories to begin with, that she herself embraced a foreign faith, that Africa for her was but a metaphor that only gained currency once a figure like Nfumbaha went to Europe and continental binarisms could be conceptualized. Her sorrow at the end of the novel, like that of Nfumbaha's mother when her son disappears, is for all Africa, but the continent is ideated only at its moment of loss. Such paradoxes reappear in the visible representation of what little collective memory has been imparted to Nnanga, which is a version of her story that is in a tongue not her own, in a form she would not recognize, in a material object distributed in a land she has no hope of ever seeing. In other words, the novel itself becomes the repository of the vanishing collective memory that has been passed on orally by the tribal elder and Ekomo, both now dead. Readers are left with the further alienations of Nnanga to which there is no possible resolution, as her projection of a disappearing local and continental heritage is relayed, and therefore preserved, only in a Western genre and a Western language and Western libraries and bookstores. Although Nsue Angüe fills her novel with traits of oral narrative, such as the repetition of key phrases, there is a melancholy implicit in the nontraditional conveyance of Nnanga's memories via a literary product inaccessible to her at so many levels. Tellingly, the most poignant moment of the text comes before it even starts, in the dedication by Nsue Angüe: "A Nnanga, mi amiga vieja. Lástima que no sepa leer" ["To Nnanga, my old friend. What a pity that she does not know how to read"] (7).

NONCIRCULATIONS

The protagonist of *The Reencounter: The Return of the Exile,* unlike that of *Ekomo,* does know how to read, but such education makes him no more or less commensurate with his ethnic or national or continental identity than does the orality of Nnanga with hers. This other Equatoguinean novel of 1985, written by Juan Balboa Boneke, has been sidelined by scholars and yet is equally remarkable for its simultaneous embrace of and resistance to foreign and local forces that are, in fact, irreducible from each other. The incoherence of the text is a postmagellanic one, betraying time and again the manifest will of its author to identify himself with a local culture, in this case the Bubi, from which he is a priori alienated. His reintegration into indigenous society and tradition proves to be nothing of the sort. As in *Ekomo*, this attempted reencounter with an essentialized past and a degraded present unfolds amid a quest of the kind that an archetypal critique would highlight. Whereas Nnanga travels in search of a cure for Ekomo's leg and all that its putrefaction symbolizes, Juan, the protagonist of *The Reencounter,* bypasses such an allegory and travels explicitly in search of a cure for the putrefied state of Equatorial Guinea. He is an intellectual who goes back to his homeland after the Macías years in order to assess the damage done by the dictatorship, interview survivors in different towns, and promulgate a harmonious vision for the national future. The novel opens with his arriving on an airplane from Spain and closes with his voluntary return to expatriation a short time later. Along the way, Juan engages in a series of stilted conversations in which either he or his interlocutor keeps suggesting the same tonic for the cultural and political decay evident all around. At the national level, that remedy is the promotion of dialogue, goodwill, and a common commitment to the rule of law among all the constituent ethnic groups of Equatorial Guinea. At the subnational and supranational level, that is, with respect to Bubi and African identities, the solution entails a return to ancestral roots and customs and language, albeit with the suppression of those "atavismos" ["atavisms"] that a modern country could do without (passim).

The frames and presumptions of *The Reencounter* are therefore in many ways similar to those of *Ekomo*, notwithstanding the obvious differences in the gender, education, and worldliness of their protagonists. Both novels feature journeys in search of cures for large social ills, implicitly or explicitly, and both are voiced in the first person by narrators who gain understandings of their supposedly own ethnic culture along the way. Both quests, notably, end in irresolution, with the protagonists/narrators not really able to process what they have experienced and heard. The plot lines virtually dovetail, with the journey of Nnanga culminating where that of

Juan begins, with an aural education into ostensible roots. Thematically, both novels include elements that are readily comparable: an array of symbolic trees (some of which fall), totemic violations, and laments for the demise of ancient ways. And with sentiments reminiscent of the elder in *Ekomo*, Juan notes, "en épocas pasadas nuestras ceremonias eran puras, se respetaba totalmente las leyes de nuestra tribu. Hoy ya no" ["in past epochs our ceremonies were pure, the laws of our tribe were totally respected. Today no longer"] (169). He adds, "vivimos la muerte de nuestra cultura" ["we live the death of our culture"] (170). Both novels also offer nested stories that are relayed from autochthonous oral traditions, pedagogical depictions of local customs and environments that are designed to inform the reader (i.e., the genre known in hispanophone literatures as *costumbrismo*), occasional uses of indigenous language (i.e., code-switching), scattered footnotes (a feature atypical of novels in general), and so forth. Yet not all foundational narratives are the same, nor are their oral origins necessarily yoked into a written genre like the novel in analogous ways or within equivalent matrices of power. And not all *costumbrismo* and code-switching function to identical ends. The ideological and aesthetic implications of all these phenomena in the two novels of 1985 merit sustained interrogation.

Perhaps the most striking unison of the novels, however, is manifest by its absence: Macías is not mentioned in either text, though the end of his heinous reign is what made the voicings of Nsue Angüe and Balboa Boneke possible. In a national context, the underlying importance of *Ekomo* and *The Reencounter* is that they forced the definitive break in fiction with the Years of Silence, fissured the previous year with the publication of the anthology edited by Ndongo-Bidyogo.[28] In so doing, Nsue Angüe and Balboa Boneke reinitiated the Guinean novelistic tradition in a way that would prove permanent. But by setting *Ekomo* in a preindependent Guinea, Nsue Angüe avoids the Macías cataclysm altogether. Balboa Boneke likewise cannot bring himself to name Macías directly, referring to the fallen regime only with a vocabulary of natural catastrophes: the tyranny was a "tétrica tempestad" ["dismal tempest"], a "vendaval" ["gale"], and so on (55, 59, passim). As with Nsue Angüe, Balboa Boneke aims to assess the state of society, an objective that makes their decision to not name its single most significant phenomenon all the more complex. The effect of the evasion in both cases suggests almost a sacralizing of the horrific, of something that is totem and taboo and so tests the limits of the representable. In this sense, the Years of Silence continue even in these texts that give Guinean creative discourses new spaces in which to operate. One novel details life among the Fang in Río Muni, the other among the Bubi on Bioko, but these differences pale before their shared unvocalization of recent terror. This silence, too, calls for analysis.

As yet, however, there is no study that compares the two texts. This absence is a subset of the larger invisibility of *The Reencounter,* which does not seem to have a single monograph of any length dedicated primarily to it. Fleeting summaries in the occasional published survey of Guinean literature are virtually the only mentions available. *The Reencounter* has received sustained attention solely via commentary threaded through a dissertation by Jorge Salvo and in an article of which the present chapter is tangentially an extension.[29] The reasons for the great discrepancy between the reception and influence of *Ekomo* versus that of *The Reencounter* is related in all likelihood to the apparently unliterary pretensions of the latter. What seems to be at hand in Balboa Boneke is an awkward, thinly fictionalized account of an expatriate intellectual who parachutes into Equatoguinean space and then parachutes out, preaching all the while (or having other characters preach for him) a type of utopian abstraction as the solution for people so traumatized by the Macías years that they appear to exist in an extended state of stunned disbelief. Regardless of the conversations that take place in the novel—interlocutors range from a former Spanish colonist to sundry relatives to random children met on the street—Juan the protagonist and his authorial namesake always seem to be talking to themselves. None of the beautiful prose so compelling in *Ekomo* seems to make its way into *The Reencounter,* nor is any appeal of the narrator/protagonist achieved on emotional grounds. Juan, like Nnanga, feels desperately alone and uncertain amid the social degradation around him, yet in the case of *Ekomo* this reads as tragedy. In *The Reencounter,* it reads as narcissism.

A closer evaluation, however, suggests that the de facto consensus dismissal of *The Reencounter* as a text worth studying and teaching is a judgment in need of redressing. From a literary perspective, although the novel is not as belletristic as *Ekomo,* privileging as it does learned disquisition over rich imagery, it is no less artificed into fiction. In fact, an excerpt of an earlier, unpublished version of *The Reencounter* appears in the 1984 anthology of Ndongo-Bidyogo and is notably different from the text that was printed the following year. That discrepancy reveals an extremely worked novel and not at all the straightforward pseudoautobiography that its few readers probably assume it to be. Plus, *The Reencounter* offers many of the structural tropes that are commonly mentioned in assessments of *Ekomo*. For example, scholars often take note of the frequent repetition of phrases by Nsue Angüe such as "Entre un poco de sol y un poquito de sombra" ["Between a little bit of sun and a very little bit of shadow"] (17 et al.). This opening line is repeated five times on the first page of chapter 1 alone. Its recurrence seems to be a significant marker of orality and of diverse indigenous cyclicalities (temporal, symbolic, etc.) and concepts of narrative. *The Reencounter*, however, also offers a slate of verbal reiterations, most notably a vocabulary of temporality in which *ayer* ("yesterday"), *hoy* ("today"), and *mañana* ("tomorrow") are constantly juxtaposed to indicate the status of the nation in successive historical moments. The repeated question to Juan the protagonist of whether he has returned to Equatorial Guinea to stay likewise functions cyclically. The net result is an endowment of rhythm and meter to *The Reencounter* that approximates that in *Ekomo* but which is never met with the same scholarly acknowledgment, much less approbation.

Additionally, many of the major differences of the two novels are complementary. Balboa Boneke continuously speaks to the ethnic plurality of the country as the grounds upon which a national identity should be constructed, whereas Nsue Angüe keeps her focus on one ethnic group and raises national identity as an issue only at the moment her lead characters are forced into doing so. Regarding familial contexts, the protagonist of *The Reencounter* leaves his spouse at home before setting out on his quest, while the protagonist of *Ekomo* embarks upon her journey with her spouse and because of him. As for gender, its construction in *The Reencounter* is as ignored by scholars as it is highlighted about *Ekomo*, yet surely the former is just as telling as the latter. By any conventional definition of what makes for good literature, *Ekomo* is without question much better written, but the time should long be past when novels are read, studied, and taught primarily on the basis of which ones are more pleasing. Entertainment value is one thing—tragedies have entertained humanity for millennia—and the diversity of cultural production is another.

An extratextual reason that might account for the lack of interest in *The Reencounter* may be a comprehensible distaste for any book dedicated to a dictator.[30] When Balboa Boneke prefaced the body of *The Reencounter* by announcing his "sincero afecto" ["sincere affection"] for Obiang, the autocrat was half a decade into a rule that would last more than three times as long as that of his uncle, whom he toppled and executed in 1979 (dedication page). In retrospect, at the very least, the dedication does not ring well.

Moreover, according to Max Liniger-Goumaz, Balboa Boneke at one period "wrote poems in praise of Macías" before fleeing that regime and seeking "asylum in Spain" (46). Under Obiang in the mid-1980s, adds Liniger-Goumaz, Balboa Boneke

> became president's counsellor for information, tourism and culture . . . In October 1990, he became minister for employment and social security. The opposition considers him one of the regime's barking dogs. . . . He did not hold any post in the December 1993 government, but he did become the president's cultural advisor. . . . In May [1994], he was accused of writing defamatory articles against the government . . . and was forbidden from flying to Spain to participate in the 1st symposium on Afro-Hispano-American studies at the University of Alcalá de Henares. The US ambassador J. Bennet denounced the fact that Balboa had been publicly interrogated on television. In February 1995, Balboa Boneque [*sic*] again sought refuge in Spain (Valencia). (46–47)

Whatever the truth of the "barking dogs" comment, two facts seem indisputable about the author of *The Reencounter*. First, like other surviving Guinean intellectuals, he served dictatorship at high levels and yet repeatedly had to go into exile.[31] Ndongo-Bidyogo and María Nsue Angüe also seem to fall in this category. Second, like most of the early Asian and African novelists, his fictional representations of his homeland emanated from long and repeated removals from the same. The result is once again a forced projection of geopolitical markers rather than a novel with defensible claims to organic origination in the lands it portrays.

The affirmations made by Balboa Boneke about his own life are replete with contradictions. For instance, his jointly subnational, national, and supranational identity is never more evident to him than when he lives in Europe. In a 1994 interview, he stated that "Desde España, ya en el exilio, me descubrí a mi mismo como *bohobe* (bubi), como guineoecuatoriano y como africano" ["From Spain, already in exile, I discovered myself as a *bohobe* (Bubi), as an Equatoguinean and as an African"] ("Juan Balboa Boneke," 92). A number of years later, he reiterated, "a mí me ocurre que empiezo a conocer mi país en el momento en el que me encuentro fuera de Guinea Ecuatorial" ["It occurs to me that I begin to know my country in the moment in which I find myself outside Equatorial Guinea"] (Hendel, 437). The jumbled logic of these statements is entirely in keeping with the

modernity launched by Magellan and Lapu Lapu. But the possibility that
Balboa Boneke is (also) Spanish and European, that he gains these identities by virtue of his long exile or even that he acquires them, as counter-
intuitive reasoning would suggest, when inside Equatorial Guinea, does
not seem to be considered at all. If Nsue Angüe's condemnatory description
of Nfumbaha, the Europeanized intellectual who returns to Guinea, were
applied, Balboa Boneke too would be dismissed as "half-white, half-black"
and therefore doomed (*Ekomo,* 85). As with Nsue Angüe, his admitted ignorance of the traditions and language of the ethnic group he says is his
own stands as proof of that.

With respect to his own literary background, Balboa Boneke noted in
the 1994 interview that "De autores africanos apenas he logrado leer" ["I
have scarcely managed to read African authors"], citing as his major
influences the Spanish poets León Felipe, Antonio Machado, and Juan
Ramón Jiménez (94). He attributes his unfamiliarity with African authors
to the dearth of translations into Spanish (99). But he also admits that he
has never read the first Guinean novel, Leoncio Evita's *When the Combes
Fought,* which was written in Spanish (97). It seems likely that Balboa
Boneke was also unfamiliar with the other, more obscure Guinean novel
from the colonial era, *A Spear for the Boabí* by Daniel Jones Mathama. Since
Ekomo was composed at the same time as *The Reencounter,* Balboa Boneke
apparently wrote in isolation from any Guinean novel and from the works
of virtually any African writer. The early to mid-twentieth-century poetic
tradition of Spain seems to be his dominant literary context. M'bare N'gom
says that Balboa Boneke, "por medio de su práctica cultural y política, sub-
vierte y convierte la dolorosa experiencia del exilio en plataforma de re-
sistencia, y en instrumento de recuperación de la realidad guineana frag-
mentada, dislocada y alienada" ["through his cultural and political
practice, subverts and converts the painful experience of exile into a plat-
form of resistance and an instrument of recovery of the fragmented, dislo-
cated, and alienated Guinean reality"] ("Memoria," 46). Yet the history of
Balboa Boneke and his novel suggests that "resistance" and "recovery" in
this case are riven concepts at best.

Nowhere inside *The Reencounter* is the productive incoherence of the
postmagellanic planet more evident than those moments when the narrator effectively admits that the eponymous "reencounter" with his Bubi
roots is more of a first-time encounter. His repeatedly expressed desires for
"reintegración" ["reintegration"] into his ethnic, national, and continental

"realidad" ["reality"] are demonstrably artificed efforts at integration into a reality that does not exist for him and never did (passim). For example, prior to his arrival in Equatorial Guinea by air, Juan describes his plight as an exile as a loss of identity: "He vivido la ausencia de todo lo que me define como pueblo y cultura. Así, cada jornada era uno más del lento y paulatino alejamiento de nuestra realidad afroguineana y, sobre todo, de nuestra esencia bôhôbe" ["I have lived the absence of all that defines me as a people and a culture. Thus, each day was one more slow and gradual removal from our Afroguinean reality and, above all, from our Bubi essence"] (13). But on the very next page he acknowledges that he does not know the Bubi language well, nor has two Bubi parents, nor grew up in a Bubi environment:

> *Lengua que durante mi infancia no logré dominar, dada mi condición de "é-bobé", circunstancia por la cual me vi desgajado, desde mi temprana edad, del ambiente del poblado y del seno de la familia materna. Residí en la capital, "Ripotó" (ciudad o pueblo de extranjeros), con lo que mi alejamiento del imprescindible y añorado mecanismo de aprendizaje de la historia, filosofía y simbología de nuestro pueblo, fue un hecho. Estaba inquieto por el inminente evento de mi reintegración a mi mundo. (14)*

> [A language that during my childhood I did not manage to learn well, given my condition of "é-bobé," a circumstance due to which I found myself torn away at an early age from the village environment and from the bosom of my maternal family. I lived in the capital, "Ripotó" (city or town of foreigners), with which my removal from the essential and yearned-for mechanisms for learning the history, philosophy, and symbolism of our people was a done deed. I was worried about the imminent event of my reintegration into my world.]

This "reintegration," in short, is an illusion of such. There is no return here to a previous essence. A footnote explains that an "é-bobé" indicates someone whose paternal family line is of foreign descent. It turns out that Juan is actually half-Fernandino, an ethnic group originating in the nineteenth century and constituted by "los esclavos libertos de la costa africana que hallaron en el suelo bôhôbe su nuevo hogar" ["the freed slaves from the African coast who found on Bubi soil their new home"] (14).[32] Balboa Boneke the author is also half-Fernandino, but extratextual information is not needed to flag how *The Reencounter* escapes the control of its captain. By the account of Juan the protagonist, his formative years were spent not speaking Bubi, not raised in Bubi traditions, and not surrounded by his Bubi maternal family. Plus, he is of foreign descent on the paternal side. And all this is before he finds himself exiled for a decade in Spain. Significantly, the exact same word, "alejamiento" ["removal"], is used to describe his alienation from Bubi culture when living in Spain and from Bubi culture when living in Guinea (13, 14). Notwithstanding his claims, expatriation did not distance Juan from a "Bubi essence" (13). His life did that, from birth onward. As for his "Afroguinean reality," if it is conceded to exist as a viable concept, there is little more typical of it than exile. In Spain, Juan did not experience "the absence of all that defines me as a people and a culture" (13). On the contrary, he lived that absence to the fullest. For an intellectual who survived Macías, there is nothing more common to a putative "Afroguinean reality" than expatriation.

Juan may be fully Bubi by consent but he is half-Bubi by descent and far less than that by actual life experience within Guinea and without. His years in Spain alone have given him the gaze of an outsider. This empirical fact is manifested in *The Reencounter* through his repeated rhetoric about the need to follow the best of what Spain has to offer, such as national unity through the harmonious interrelationships of plural polities and languages. Catalans and Castilians as Spaniards, for example, provide him with a model for Fang and Bubi as Equatoguineans. His perspective from abroad also appears via phrases flush with orientalizing that would be lambasted as colonial claptrap if written by a foreign national. Guinean women and nature, for instance, are routinely depicted in *The Reencounter* as "exótica" ["exotic"]. And the Guinean landscape is frequently portrayed as a deflowered Eden. It is "nuestro fértil jardín" ["our fertile garden"] that has been violated by Macías, including, for example, a road that once was a "paradisíaco rincón. . . . La virginidad, pureza, colorido y sabor tropical de Mangro Road y la libre inocencia que antaño envolvió el velo verdoso de sus raíces, es hoy una historia" ["paradisiacal corner. . . . The virginity, purity, colors, and tropical taste of Mangro Road and the free innocence that yesteryear enveloped the greenish veil of its roots, is today history"] (48–49). The rape by Macías was preceded, however, by that of Spain when "el cuerpo extraño del colonizador profanó nuestros sagrados lugares, prostituyó nuestra primitiva virginidad penetrando, sin contar con nuestra opinión, en nuestro tejido social" ["the foreign body of the colonizer profaned our sacred places, prostituted our primitive virginity penetrating, without taking into account our opinion, our social fabric"] (51). This may seem like a momentary anticolonial stance on substance—Juan's attitude toward the colonial legacy varies throughout the novel—but even so, it partakes fully in colonial rhetoric by invoking the same deleterious discourses of primitivism and virginality that mark centuries of Western literature about expansion into indigenous lands all over the world.

Often in *The Reencounter,* those scenes in which Juan seems closest to Bubi tradition and thus closest to achieving his supposed reintegration with himself are those in which his distance from an essentialized Bubi identity is most profound. For instance, the maternal side of his family is the source of his Bubi claims, yet when he arrives at one village he fails to follow the custom of entering first the house of a maternal relative. He makes this mistake out of ignorance of the same practices that he insists are his own: "No tenía idea de esto" ["I had no idea about that"], he admits (128). And he is frustrated in his efforts to communicate with the older generation who are the main link to what he sees as true Bubi culture: "Dialogar con nuestros ancianos no es una tarea fácil, máxime en mi caso, dado el problema del desarraigo que me condiciona y la circunstancia del poco dominio en la realidad de mi lengua" ["Dialoguing with our elderly is not an easy task, maximally so in my case, given the problem of uprootedness that conditions me and the circumstance that is the little control that I have of the reality of my language"] (167). Of course, "my language" is not, in fact, his language. He speaks Spanish. To solve the communication problems, Juan recommends, of all things, the "método socrático" ["Socratic method"] (167). Such is his turning to ancient paths to knowledge.

Passages that are incommensurate with themselves flourish in *The Reencounter.* The inscription of an isolated identity in which foreign arrival and indigenous resistance are not mutually definitive proves again to be a postmagellanic impossibility. At once, Balboa Boneke (and through him, Juan the protagonist) plays the roles of Magellan and Lapu Lapu and Pigafetta: the arriving Western conqueror and the local sovereign who defeats him, the Western navigation nonetheless proceeding apace, the narration marked forever by globalized forces due to which no side is any longer identifiable only on its own terms. *The Reencounter* thrives on such dynamics. "Cual planta de tallo trepador," explains Juan, "me quiero aferrar a mis raíces y a mi origen. Despertar el sentimiento bôhôbe que anida en estado de hibernación en el fondo de mi ser. Así, juntos y hermanados, mi yo bôhôbe y africano y mi yo europeizado, caminarán decididamente al reencuentro con su realidad" ["Like a climbing vine, I want to anchor myself to my roots and my origin. Awaken the Bubi sentiment that nests in a state of hibernation in the depth of my being. Thus, together and united as brothers, my Bubi and African self and my Europeanized self will walk resolutely to the reencounter with their reality"] (34). He is akin to a plant that goes up, but that is because he seeks his own depths. He is a brother to himself, split amid an ethnicity that he pertains to primarily by force of desire and amid two continents that inform each other. He heads toward a reencounter with a reality that is not a reality he has ever known and thus is not a reencounter. The paradoxes are productive. The Magellan in him and the Lapu Lapu in him remain irreconciled and, in those tensions, irruptive. The Pigafetta in him is the wayfarer who chronicles and comments it all.

As in *Ekomo,* there is no ultimate syncretism in *The Reencounter* that unites the disparate into a totality. All attempts to define the cultural dynamics in play within any bounded space fail amid surpluses and supplements and escapes. On just his third day in Equatorial Guinea, for instance, when a woman says that Juan does not appear to have come from Spain, he reflects, "Si fuera esto cierto, no por mi aspecto físico, sino en mis actos y en mi quehacer cotidiano, se palparía en todo momento mi ser africano y bôhôbe. Esto indicaría que estoy logrando por completo mi reinserción en el tejido social de mis ancestros. Siempre que esa reinserción no conlleve la pérdida de todas las cosas positivas adquiridas en Europa, en España" ["If this were certain, not because of my physical appearance but in my actions and my daily routine, in every moment my African and Bubi being would be felt. This would indicate that I am achieving completely my reintegration into the social fabric of my ancestors. As long as that reintegration does not carry with it the loss of all the positive things acquired in Europe, in Spain"] (98). The rapidity of the desired transformation is breathtaking. So soon after arriving on Bioko after years of exile, Juan is tantalized by the prospect of already "achieving completely" a wholesale reintegration into an ancestral environment. This would be preposterous even if the context of post-Macías Equatorial Guinea were indeed ancient, which it was not, and even if he had been integrated in it in the first place, which he had not. The force of will toward realizing, allegedly anew, an ethnic and continental identity is astonishingly powerful but also astonishingly weak. After all, the regaining of that essentialized subnational and supranational sense of self is acceptable only if it does not entail losing newly acquired and foreign senses of self, namely "all the positive things acquired in Europe, in Spain."

There is no union here of the ancient and the modern, the local and the foreign, the reencountered and the recently encountered. There is no symbiosis. There is only a welter of times, spaces, abstractions, and experiences that crash against each other in currents unending and uncontainable. Immemorial ages and millenarian futures tumble into more immediate yesterdays, todays, and tomorrows. Cultural conquest from the alleged abroad is both rejected and accepted, while cultural constructs from the hypothesized home are both essentialized and caveated. These contradictory declarations of Juan are not particular to a lone search for identity, however, nor to the Bubi or Equatorial Guinea or Africa, nor to Castilians or Spain or Europe, nor for that matter to Tagalogs or the Philippines or Asia. It is the state of the world after Magellan died, after Lapu Lapu celebrated, after the inaugural circumnavigation continued nonetheless, after Pigafetta, like Juan on the last page of *The Reencounter,* returned to Spain and began to tell his tale of continents circled and the blood strewn along the way.

There is nothing more material than that blood. Any fundamentally decent deconstruction of the emergence of Asian and African literature in Spanish must conclude with that. The instability of identities in a globalized world is neither a simply ludic matter nor an empty intellectual exercise in the name of a liberating incoherence. There are no liberations at hand, there are only processings of punishments. The facts are these: Spain conquered the Philippines as long as it had the power to do so. The United States crushed Spain and then the Filipino independence movement. Japan routed the United States and the Filipino resistance movement until it could no longer. Spain conquered Guinea as long as it had the power to do so. Macías pulverized the country; Obiang continued the devastation. The result of Spanish imperialism, U.S. imperialism, and Japanese imperialism, of homegrown dictatorships, is, most materially of all, dead Filipinos and Guineans. No trip around world literature must ever obscure that. Identitarian quests, however fraught, are one thing. Routinized murder is another.

A passage by sea and a passage of text have much in common. Both terminate the self that started them, and both continue on nonetheless. Both, too, are premised, always premised, on endless streaks of blood, no matter that the scarlet may no longer be seen, no matter that the crimson may be congealed beyond the most careful of considerations. That maroon must always be mourned. But passages do offer as well vague hopes that not all has been destroyed, that there are new voyages that can be undertaken per-haps informed by those that have come before, by the wanderings writ in wakes, that the paths ahead might somehow bring the world closer with-out, this time, the spilling of ink chronicling the spilling of yet more blood.

Magellan sailed the ocean blue but never made it home. That may now be the lot of all of us. The least we can do is talk with those whom we meet along the way, listen to them, for they too are but travelers in motion, even if they never leave home, though now very often they do, and as later we tell their tales to others, we should remember that they too will be telling of ours. The consequences of globalization cannot be controlled, whoever the captain, but as we, strangers all, break bread together and exchange sto-ries of seas traveled, we can always search in those narratives for the hu-manity that condemns and conjoins us all. Bounded only by this blue planet, we are met now to follow all currents wherever they lead, if only to see what emerges on the other side, for the truth of all circumnavigations will be proven once again: that there is no other side, that if you travel around the world you are forever heading home. And when the currents are adverse, when the flows all head in one direction and threaten to engulf all, we must strive against them as we can. To commit anew the Magellan fallacy is to believe that coherence can be conquered into existence. It is much better to be free.

CHAPTER SIX

The Passages Ahead

The emergence of Asian and African literature in Spanish is a global phenomenon. The tradition is atraditional in its endless escapes from the controls and coherences that delimit particular genealogies and geographies. The cultural, biological, and theoretical inheritances at issue are open spaces that open yet other spaces. Nothing is closed and nothing, in consequence, is foreclosed. The unboundedness of the tradition was set in motion by Magellan, Lapu Lapu, and Pigafetta and continues to this day. However marginalized in its heyday, Filipino literature in Spanish is global in heft. However ignored in its incipience, Guinean literature in Spanish is metropolitan in import. The peripheral is not on the periphery when it reimagines the center by the fact of its existence. The seemingly parochial is the most cosmopolitan of all, for it is only in the processing of the putative limits of the center that the farthest reaches of its influence are created, re-created, and rendered differentially. In such shifts of the sources of cultural production from an ostensible hub to an apparent rim, power is rearranged, resistance is reformulated, and hierarchies are revealed to be but the contingent justifications for might that they always are. The regional defines the capital. The outside defines the inside. All autonomies destabilize as a result and the terms of the debate themselves collapse into indistinction. Such implosion does not deny the blood that has spilled across oceans. But it is liberating, or at least has the potential to be so. The anarchy of amorphousness does not negate the brutality of the postmagellanic planet. But it does offer a space for freedom. That is why people read and write in the first place. There are few other places to be free.

To speak of Asian and African literature in Spanish, to refer to it as a tradition, as an emergence, is to be contradictory and hopeful at once. One country cannot be tantamount to a continent, nor are continents reducible as such but definable only vis-à-vis others so denominated. More specifically, the Philippines is not Asia; Equatorial Guinea is not Africa; and Asia and Africa are not themselves. "Literature," moreover, is a term far more polyvalent and inclusive than the short stories and novels that wend through these pages. The most conventional definitions would include at least poetry as well, a genre of notable importance to successive generations of Filipinos and Guineans. The sustained undertakings of journalism and historiography that mark the careers of these writers deserve extended analysis too, as do their forays into various theatrical genres. More profoundly, there is no reason to restrict "literature" to the written word at all, for the entirety of cultural production intertwined with the Spanish presence and legacy rightly merits a place in this study: local contributions to colonial architecture, postcontact innovations in oral storytelling and dance and music, hybridizations in the visual and graphic arts, technological appropriations leading to videos made for television and cinemas and the Internet, and so on. As for the concept of a single Asian and African "tradition," the jagged trajectories of Filipino and Guinean literature barely can be argued to achieve that individually, much less as a joint phenomenon. As for "emergence," the suggestion is of a beginning, but there have been many beginnings by these texts, chronological and thematic and linguistic, none of which is resolvable to any other, some of which disappear in their moment of appearance and so in truth may be said to commence nothing at all. Many beginnings double as endings.

These are the contradictions. But they are, in their paradoxes, productive. They create spaces. They allow hopes for future freedoms because they force into existence new questions and, with them, the tentative potential for new answers. Starting from the premise that Asian and African literature in Spanish is a tradition, one of a profoundly postmagellanic nature at that, opens up every single accepted understanding of cultural production in the Hispanic world for theoretical and textual reformulation. The point of reading authors from Paterno to Balboa Boneke and beyond should not be to assert that such writers deserve a slot in the last chapter of a textbook or in concluding words by a professor on the day before a semester closes. Nor should the aim be admission into the machinery of pedagogy and mainstream academic inquiry in some spirit of inclusionary diversity. The goal should be to reorient that pedagogy and inquiry altogether. What would happen if the labor by everyone in academic life from elementary school students through full professors began to attempt apprehending the world not from centers but from peripheries? What would happen if what Thomas Pynchon has called "the Primary Questions" are asked from the starting point of Manila and Malabo and, if need be, from Madrid, but not the Madrid of common conception but the true Madrid, the real one, the historical and demonstrable one, the Madrid that in fact exists only by virtue of Manila and Malabo? (68)

The phrase "Filipino literature in Spanish" runs the huge risk of predetermining a national, and seemingly negligible to most non-Filipinos, framework of inquiry; the phrase "Guinean literature in Spanish," even more so. These are countries whose histories and geographies and cultures are, it is safe to say, utterly unfamiliar to nearly all individuals who ever have specialized in the literature of the hispanophone world. And appealing for charitable acknowledgment of the seemingly irrelevant and parochial does no favors to anyone, not to Rizal or Nsue Angüe, not to high school students trudging past irregular verb conjugations to that page at the end of the chapter on the Day of the Dead in Mexico or bullfighting in Spain or the drinking of mate in Argentina. It does no favors to hiring and tenure committees who want to make sure someone is going to teach that canonical survey class (again) nor to graduate students who know that unless they pick a supposedly important country for a dissertation topic they are dramatically increasing their chances of having to waitress through their thirties and forties as well as their twenties. By contrast, "Asian and African literature in Spanish," conceived continentally as such, offers enormous potential for growth because of the abstract weight that the Philippines and Equatorial Guinea lack. "Asia" and "Africa" stand shoulder to shoulder with "Europe" and "the Americas." Perceived as major continental imaginaries rather than minor national constructs, they offer compelling points of departure for students and teachers alike to interrogate globalization and all the principal issues of the modern world. This is not force of mere projection, however. Europe and America (whether Latin, North, South, or as the Americas) exist by virtue of the blood and treasure of Asia and Africa. Their self-definitions, and those of the nations marked out within them, are a product of Asia and Africa rather than vice versa. The tradition of Asian and African literature in Spanish does not, in one sense, exist. In all other senses, the world does not exist without it.

How would understandings of modernity, and of its hispanophone spaces in particular, be reconfigured if the role of Magellan were to substitute for that of Columbus? What would happen, say, to analyses of the literature surrounding 1898 if scholars were to start from Paterno and Rizal in Madrid rather than Miguel de Unamuno in Salamanca? What would happen if a graduate student trained to parse colonial discourses were asked to read the narratives not only of Spanish explorers and functionaries in the Caribbean and Mexico and Peru in the fifteenth and sixteenth centuries but also of those in Fernando Poo (present-day Bioko) in the nineteenth and twentieth centuries? What would happen to undergraduate comprehensions of the Spanish-speaking world if syllabi for survey courses began with Filipino essayists and Guinean novelists and only then moved on to Argentina, to Colombia, to Guatemala, to Cuba, to Spain? What kinds of questions would be raised then about the more familiar spaces and cultures and nations? What would happen to theoretical conversations about postcolonialism and orientalism among teachers and students of anglophone and francophone lands if they were to be made aware of literature in Spanish produced in Europe by individuals from West Africa and Southeast Asia? What would happen to reflections on the national identity of the United States if middle school students were to learn that Asian literature in Spanish was produced by American subjects? What would change if readers of texts in Spanish and Spanglish by Nuyorican poets and Chicano essayists and Dominican American novelists were to learn that the existence of such traditions outside the putative boundaries of the Spanish-speaking world was not singular, that a redefinition of Latin America northward to include Latino writers in the United States could be complicated more richly and deeply still by a conceptualization of global hispanophone literature that included Asian and African writings?

These questions can extend further. What approaches to the literature of the entire Spanish-speaking world need to be developed to account for the energetic and impressive Chilean literature appearing in Canada for decades now? And for rap songs and local media and other cultural expressions being produced by the tens of thousands of Chileans in Sweden? And for the spaces of salsa clubs in world cities from Paris to Tokyo and everywhere in between, in any direction? What would happen if Asian and African fiction in Spanish, isolated by a language barrier from study by scholars of colonial literatures in French and English and Portuguese, led off new discussions on the planetary panorama of marginalized literatures in major tongues? The attempt should not be to read Asian and African literature in Spanish through categories and paradigms imported from elsewhere. Doing so inherently reaffirms impoverished notions of metropoles and peripheries, centers and margins. Reimagining, say, the literary traditions of Spain through the work of Filipinos and Guineans, however, amounts to an inversion of hierarchies of the most potentially illuminating sort. After all, if there is any heart of darkness, it surely is that of the imperial center.

Probably the only exposure to Asian and African literature in Spanish that most Western scholars have is the analysis in Benedict Anderson's *Imagined Communities* of the opening scene of Rizal's *Noli me tangere* as an example of how nations are conceived. As Anderson implies therein, the Philippines can stand not only at the center of any discussion of nationalism but also of the nexus of postcolonialism and modernity. The same is true of Equatorial Guinea. Yet the vast majority of the critical questions have not been asked, much less possible responses proposed. And it seems certain that if textbooks and reading lists in Spanish departments were to start with literature from Asia and Africa and only then proceed to cultural figures and artifacts from Iberia and Latin America, then many innovative educational approaches and interventions would arise immediately. The entirely artificial ethnic amalgams of the Philippines and Equatorial Guinea, for example, could convey how cobbled together are the more familiar nations whose existences, rather than contingencies, are almost always taken as frameworks. The Filipino and Guinean writers in Spanish negotiated homelands whose geographical contours were as arbitrary as history allows and whose constituent peoples—Tagalogs, Cebuanos and Ilocanos, Fang and Bubi and Annobonese, and the list goes on—had nothing inherently in common. But rather than being dismissed as preposterous national polities, the Philippines and Equatorial Guinea could be seen as keys to analyzing "Spain" and "Mexico" and "Bolivia" and "Costa Rica" as equally absurd concatenations. The mere naming of those nations overdetermines a spectrum of critical understandings of literature and history and culture, no matter how much issue is raised in some quarters of the distinct cultural and geopolitical claims of Catalonia and the Basque country, of Chiapas and the Yucatan, of highlands versus lowlands or Caribbean coasts versus landlocked cities.

If, due to a spirit of noblesse oblige by Western academics, Asian and African literature in Spanish were ultimately recognized to exist by scattered university departments but only as anthropological or archaeological curiosities, it would limit severely how Filipino and Guinean writers offer ways to think the world anew. Such authors merit study in their own right, of course, and do not need to be justified on utilitarian grounds any more than Honduran or Panamanian or Venezuelan authors ought to be read only insofar as they inform Europe or North America or the rest of Latin America. But awarding a primacy to Asian and African literature in Spanish, acknowledging that revisions of the rest of the hispanophone world could follow from its expressions, would be upending the hierarchies that have condemned consistently the same people and places to oblivion and worse.

The comparative project of reading Asian and African literature in Spanish alongside Latin American and Iberian literature could be a worthy one as well at levels more thematic than theoretical. These could include respective treatments of standard literary topics such as the representation of indigenous people, the tradition of the dictatorship novel, the legacy of colonialism, the turn to aesthetics of naturalism and realism, the use of *costumbrismo*, the borderland interactions of Christians and Muslims (the Philippines, like Spain, has a history of southern Islamic populations called *moros* and is also separated by a bit of sea from an Islamic nation, in its case Indonesia rather than Morocco), the creation of continental imaginaries, and so on. No less a figure than Gabriel García Márquez began his Nobel Prize speech in 1982 by proclaiming the travelogue of Antonio Pigafetta to be a "libro breve y fascinante, en el cual ya se vislumbran los gérmenes de nuestras novelas de hoy, no es ni mucho menos el testimonio más asombroso de nuestra realidad de aquellos tiempos" ["brief and fascinating book in which the seeds of our novels of today are already visible. It is nothing less than the most astonishing testimony of our reality of those times"] ("La soledad de América Latina"). García Márquez thereby locates the descriptions by Pigafetta of Latin America at the start of a continental tradition that ultimately would include his own *One Hundred Years of Solitude*. The narrative of the first circumnavigation of the world would launch a continental tradition across the Pacific as well.

Within Latin American and North American studies, the question of emergent national literatures long has been a major space of inquiry. The determination of nineteenth-century literati throughout the Western hemisphere to forge collective identities through the production of fiction and poetry is clearly relevant to Paterno and Rizal. Yet many questions must arise whenever a novel deemed national is produced, as in the Philippines and in much of Latin America, that most members of the supposed nation could not access due to their illiteracy in general or their particular illiteracy in Spanish. Matters of the material unavailability of books,

renowned or otherwise, are critical too, whether that nonexistence is due
to reasons of censorship or circulation or, if published and sold abroad, the
basic lack of money and technology and freedom needed to acquire a text
from across an ocean. These issues are not unique to the Philippines and
Equatorial Guinea. In the 1880s and 1890s, José Martí created a large swath
of Cuban national identity through poetry and prose he wrote from New
York, but few Cuban peasants in his era were likely to have had both frequent access to his chronicles and the ability to read them. It is not a coincidence that the nationalized verse of Martí survives maximally not in his
printed volumes but in the oral tradition of "Guantanamera," a song that
includes lines from different Martí poems. Another comparison could be
with contemporary Chilean identity, much of which was penned into existence by exiles after the coup against the Allende government in 1973.
Their work often circulated back home only clandestinely, beyond the
reach of the subsequent dictatorship. Furthermore, extraordinary numbers
of African and Afro-Caribbean thinkers working in French have created national and continental spaces from Paris, the metropole of the empire that
they wrote within and against. How to think Cuba and Chile, as well as
more internally stressed states around the world, from the cultural tensions
of the Philippines and Equatorial Guinea is a project whose first attempts
remain to be undertaken.

The Martí angle is a particularly good place to start. Standard accounts
of modern Latin American literature take the poetry and essays of its two
fin de siècle stars, Martí and Rubén Darío of Nicaragua, as marking a reno-
vation of Latin American letters that continues to this day. Rizal, their contemporary, also changed the arts in his country and continent forever. Indeed, he has a greater claim than any other author in the whole of the
hispanophone world to be the innovator of both a nation and a national
literature. The analogy to Martí, whose landmark essay "Nuestra América"
("Our America") was published the same year as Rizal's *El filibusterismo*, is
often noted but rarely developed substantially. Martí perished at Spanish
hands in his colonized homeland just a year and a half before his fellow essayist and poet in the Philippines was executed by the same empire. Their
deaths as well as their lives crystallized national imaginations. Since all
Latin Americanists are familiar with Martí and his work, an extension to
Rizal studies would be a reasonable initial step for many.

Compelling, therefore, would be a comparatist and transoceanic interrogation of the links between intellectuals and state formation in the hispanophone world, particularly in early epochs of national consolidation. Paterno and Rizal, among others, wrote their nation into existence from Europe. Both of them also participated directly (albeit posthumously, in the case of Rizal) in its protogovernments and inchoate governances, while Félix Gerardo was evidently well connected at elite strata as well. The first three novelists of Equatorial Guinea, Nsue Angüe, Balboa Boneke, and Ndongo-Bidyogo, each served one or both of its dictatorships at high levels for periods of time.[1] This intertwining of the Guinean literary and political elite continued in the second decade of the twenty-first century with Guillermina Mekuy, the second woman novelist of the country, serving as a culture minister under Obiang. Yet all the governmental experiences of the early Equatoguinean novelists ended with exile in Spain. This pattern inverts that of the early Asian novelists, who began their adulthoods with literary careers in Europe and only subsequently became national political figures back in the Philippines. The import of these mirroring phenomena remains to be considered for larger theorizations, relevant far beyond the supposed margins of the former Spanish empire, of how and when an intellectual elite that is expatriated, whether de facto or de jure, turns to the production of fiction and so convokes, intentionally or not, a fractured non-state into existence.

Within the hispanophone world, Asian and African literature in Spanish casts the facile binarism of Spain and Latin America into sharp relief. Asian and African hispanophone literary studies does not need Iberian or Latin American studies to legitimate its existence. Rather, these latter fields are in acute need of perspectives from the Hispanic spaces of Asia and Africa. From high school textbooks to doctoral programs worldwide, the Spanish empire is wrongly and routinely premised as having ended in 1898. African literature in Spanish shows the dramatic error of that. From Latin America to North America to Europe, there is probably not a university anywhere that asks its students to read in the original the most patently foundational novel in the hispanophone world, Rizal's *Noli me tangere*. Asian literature in Spanish shows the dramatic error of that. A fundamental reason to study Asian and African literature in Spanish together before turning to texts from Latin America and Spain, or to other traditions in Asia and Africa, is because doing so necessarily forces the forging of new ways of thinking, new foci, new currents, and new wakes. The ripple effects are global.

OTHER CONTINENTAL LITERATURES

"Asian" and "African" literature in Spanish allow for internal inclusiveness via the sheer linguistic momentum of the terms. The rubric of "Asia" rather than "the Philippines" suggests the need for primary research into the possibility of creative texts in Spanish from other former imperial possessions in what once was known as the Spanish East Indies. These places, whose statuses and affiliations and degrees of sovereignty have varied considerably since the nineteenth century, include Guam, the Northern Mariana Islands, Palau, the Federated States of Micronesia, and parts of present-day Malaysia and Indonesia. Even a bit of Taiwan was briefly in Spanish possession, though probably for too short a period of time for any local people to have learned enough of the language to write in it. On another tack, a promising possibility over the long run is literature potentially emerging out of new Latin American immigrant communities in Japan and Australia. "Literature" in this case may demand initially a broad definition so as to include radio programs geared to Spanish-speaking audiences, community newspapers in Spanish, hispanophone web pages intended for local individuals, oral and informal narratives of migration from Latin America to Asia, and so forth. The branches of the Cervantes Institute in Tokyo, Sydney, Beijing, and New Delhi would be reasonable starting points for connections to local Hispanic environments, notwithstanding the overtones of imperial nostalgia that any project launched from those spaces unavoidably carries with it.

Similarly, the wide frame offered by "African" literature in Spanish rather than "Guinean" also could impel investigation into hispanophone prose and poetry across a vast region and thereby avoid a national framework as a sine qua non for study. According to Guillermo Pié Jahn, "el estudio de la literatura hispanoafricana se puede abordar en su magnitud continental, tal y como se hace con la literatura hispanoamericana" ["the study of Hispanoafrican literature can be considered in its continental magnitude, just as is done with Hispanoamerican literature"] (203). Unlike the Asian case, African literature in Spanish in the familiar forms of published fiction and poetry from other continental lands, such as Western Sahara, Morocco, and Cameroon, is already known to exist. If oral accounts were included under the rubric of African Hispanic literature as they surely ought to be, then the stories of tens of thousands of Equatoguineans living in Gabon also should be considered as an important wing of the continental panorama of hispanophone narratives.

At the beginning of the twenty-first century, the first two anthologies of Western Saharan poetry in Spanish were published. Both appeared on the outskirts of Spain rather than in Madrid or Barcelona: *Añoranza: Imágenes del pueblo saharaui* (*Nostalgia: Images of the Sahrawi People*) of 2002 from the Balearic Islands, off the eastern coast of the country; and *Bubisher: Poesía saharaui contemporánea* (*Bubisher: Contemporary Sahrawi Poetry*) of 2003 from the Canary Islands, which straddle waters opposite the northernmost coast of Western Sahara and the southernmost shores of Morocco.[2] These collections emerge from the long and difficult history of the indigenous Sahrawi people, whose modern travails commenced when Spain was awarded their lands at the infamous Berlin Conference of 1884–85 in which European powers parceled out Africa among themselves. The ongoing Sahrawi struggle against Spanish colonization shifted in 1975 to struggle against a subsequent Moroccan (and, briefly, Mauritanian) colonization that endures still. A referendum on the final status of Western Sahara was supposed to be overseen by the United Nations in the early 1990s but never was held. As of this writing, Morocco occupies the western half of the country and has built a landmined wall of some sixteen hundred miles, stretching between the northeast and southwest corners of Western Sahara, to maintain that position. Meanwhile, much of the Sahrawi population remains in the Algerian refugee camps to which they fled in the mid-1970s. Sahrawi literature therefore stands out among other African Hispanic traditions as emanating from a geopolitical context not postcolonial but persistingly colonial. Western Sahara is the only nonindependent land remaining in the entire continent.

The early publications of Sahrawi poetry in Spanish were followed by the concretization of a cluster of writers who came together as "La Generación de la Amistad" ("The Generation of Friendship") in Madrid in 2005. Proclamations of generational groups are common in Spanish literary history, but the Generation of Friendship may be the first to have self-consciously developed itself through Internet media such as blogs and streaming video. Its de facto manifesto (also a frequent feature of literary innovators in the hispanophone world) reads in part as follows:

> *Nos definimos como escritores saharauis en castellano en reivindicación de ese rasgo que nos distingue como el único país árabe que habla, piensa, sueña y siente en español . . . Nos hemos marcado una meta, un objetivo primordial: hacer llegar la voz de los saharauis a todos los rincones del planeta a través de la poesía. . . . Nuestros versos son las reivindicaciones y las aspiraciones de todos los saharauis.*

Nuestros versos están obligados a mancharse de la sangre de nuestros hermanos y hermanas en las zonas ocupadas. Nuestros versos están a la disposición de los saharauis que llevan más de treinta años soñando con volver a sus casas. . . . Por el sendero de la no violencia transcurren nuestras andanzas en pro de la independencia; nuestras armas son la palabra, la poesía, ese arma cargada de futuro, que, con el permiso de las musas, seguirá siendo nuestro instrumento de lucha predilecto. Sin más preámbulos, pues, permitamos que batallen las palabras. ("Presentación")

[We define ourselves as Sahrawi writers in Castilian to vindicate that characteristic which distinguishes us as the only Arab country that speaks, thinks, dreams, and feels in Spanish . . . We have set a goal, a primordial objective: to make the voice of the Sahrawis reach all corners of the planet through poetry. . . . Our verses are the vindications and the aspirations of all the Sahrawis. Our verses are obliged to stain themselves with the blood of our brothers and sisters in the occupied zones. Our verses are at the disposition of the Sahrawis who have been dreaming for more than thirty years of returning to their homes. . . . Along the path of nonviolence transpire our adventures in favor of independence; our arms are the word, poetry, that arm charged with the future which, with the permission of the Muses, will continue being our favored instrument of struggle. Without further preambles, then, let our words do battle.]

This proclamation diverges sharply from those of authors and critics of early Guinean literature who almost unanimously depict that phenomenon as relatively unpolitical. Any forthcoming theorization of African literature in Spanish will need to account for the implications of this contrast in attitudes and intents between Guineans and Sahrawis, along with the obvious differences in cultural and religious contexts among the authors of the two countries. Similarities of the writers include a high interest in poetry, issues of exile and expatriation, and a recent surge in artistic production. They also seem to share a primary affiliation with Spanish rather than Latin American traditions. The description of poetry as an "arm charged with the future" is a direct quote of the title of a famous poem by the Spanish poet Gabriel Celaya, known for his protests against the Franco dictatorship. Within half a dozen years of the manifesto, a dozen or so more books by the Generation of Friendship appeared in print, including short stories.

New literature is continually made available on their website adjacent to announcements about the activities of the group.

Regarding Morocco, its hispanophone elements are far older than those of both the Saharan country it occupies and Equatorial Guinea. According to Lotfi Sayahi, Spanish "ha formado parte del panorama sociolingüístico de la región [el norte de África] de manera continua desde finales del siglo XV" ["has formed part of the sociolinguistic panorama of the region (the north of Africa) in a continuous fashion since the end of the fifteenth century"] (195). The seminal year here is 1492, when Spain expelled much of its Jewish population and conquered the Moorish kingdom of Granada, thereby putting an end to more than seven centuries of Islamic power in Andalusia. The twin events sent hispanophone refugees across the Straits of Gibraltar, whereupon they resettled throughout northern Africa. More recent, however, was the protectorate that Spain imposed upon parts of Morocco from 1912 to 1956. The current tradition of Moroccan writing in Spanish began in this period, most notably with the work from 1942 onward of the prolific Mohammad Ibn Azzuz Hakim (Oubali; Bouissef Rekab, "Después"). More than two dozen Moroccan authors in Spanish have appeared since. A collection of fiction, *Antología de relatos marroquíes en lengua española* (*Anthology of Moroccan Stories in the Spanish Language*) was published in 1985, the same year as *Ekomo* by Nsue Angüe and *The Reencounter* by Balboa Boneke and just one year after the groundbreaking Guinean anthology by Ndongo-Bidyogo. The title of the collection is somewhat misleading, for of the sixteen writers anthologized, twelve are Spaniards and only four are Moroccans. Still, the publication marked the start of an important new development in African Hispanic letters. Moroccan authors of fiction and poetry in Spanish could anticipate thereafter the possible distribution of their work via books, a more durable medium than the local periodicals that, decades earlier, had offered an outlet and that, apparently, had ended for the most part in the 1950s in correlation with the termination of the Spanish protectorate.[3]

As with Equatoguinean literature, the 1990s proved to be a pivotal decade for the Moroccan tradition in consolidating a continuous production of hispanophone work. Additional anthologies plus individual texts in various genres increasingly saw print, a phenomenon that led to the inaugural Coloquio sobre la Escritura Marroquí en Lengua Española (Colloquium on Moroccan Writing in the Spanish Language) held by the Depart-

ment of Hispanism at the University of Fez in 1994 (Bouissef Rekab, "Hispanistas"). A few years later, in 1997, the Asociación de Escritores Marroquíes en Lengua Española (Association of Moroccan Writers in the Spanish
Language), known as the AEMLE, was founded as "la primera Asociación de
escritores en lengua española de Marruecos, del mundo árabe y de África.
. . . Queda claro que nuestro primer fin es el de llegar a hacernos conocer en
España, que se sepa que hay marroquíes que escriben en la lengua de Cervantes y que con el tiempo deben hallar un sitio en el seno de la cultura española" ["the first Association of writers in the Spanish language in Morocco, the Arab world, and Africa. . . . It is clear that our first objective is
that of making ourselves known in Spain, so that it is known that there are
Moroccans who write in the language of Cervantes and who in time should
find a place in the heart of Spanish culture"] ("Creación de la AEMLE"). The
headquarters of the AEMLE is in Tangier. Apparently the most formally
constituted group of hispanophone writers ever to appear in Asia or Africa,
the AEMLE issued a fairly elaborate internal governing statute in 2005 that
affirmed, for example, a policy of political nonaffiliation, a requirement for
members to have published in Spanish, a three-year wait for new members
for full enfranchisement, the cost of association dues, and ground rules for
the expulsion of any member from the group and for the dissolution of the
association itself ("Estatuto").

The creation of the AEMLE and its online presence thus precede those
of the Generation of Friendship, but unlike the Sahrawi poets, the Moroccan writers do not seem to conceive of themselves as a generation in the
longstanding taxonomic sense of Spanish letters. Superficial similarities between the two groups, such as an Arabic heritage and a desire to make their
voices heard in Spanish, seem to pale before their diverse differences. The
Sahrawi authors are avowedly political; the Moroccan writers are avowedly
not. The goal of the former is to liberate their country through poetry,
while the aim of the latter is to disseminate hispanophone arts and studies
in an already autonomous national culture and so enrich it. Of course,
from a Moroccan governmental point of view, the Sahrawi writers are
themselves Moroccan writers, since Morocco claims Western Sahara for itself. In addition, the Moroccan authors work in an intellectual space in
which both Arabic and French are dominant languages, with Spanish a minority option at best. The Generation of Friendship does not operate
within the context of a second imperial language such as French, so Spanish stands alone as a linguistic link to European arts and knowledge. Most

importantly, the Sahrawi writers compose from exile, as do most of their Guinean peers, whereas the Moroccan authors can develop freely their literature and literary scholarship in Tangier and Rabat and Fez. A number of Western and Moroccan scholars have followed the emergence of Moroccan literature in Spanish and commented on it in an expanding range of publications and academic conferences.

As for Cameroon, a neighbor of Equatorial Guinea by virtue of bordering Río Muni to the north, its literature in Spanish stands out for a double distinction from the main parameters of the rest of hispanophone Asia and Africa: there is no local history of colonization by Spain and therefore no sense of Spanish as a locally imposed language. Like all Filipino and Guinean authors, Cameroonian writers are polylingual, but as Guillermo Pié Jahn noted in a 2007 overview, "Un grupo de autores cameruneses escribe también en español, una lengua no materna para ellos pero que dominan y han elegido libremente como vehículo de expresión artística. Se trata de una mujer y cinco hombres. . . . El corpus de su literatura en lengua española, de varios miles de páginas, abarca todos los géneros literarios: narrativa, teatro, poesía" ["A group of Cameroonian authors also write in Spanish, a language that is not maternal for them but which they control well and have chosen freely as a vehicle for artistic expression. There is one woman and five men. . . . The corpus of their literature in the Spanish language, some thousands of pages, spans all the literary genres: narrative, theater, poetry"] (212). The delinkage of any Spanish colonial context from the production of African literature in Spanish unsettles dramatically all customary theoretical possibilities for analysis. Once again, the Cameroonian authors, like their Filipino and Guinean counterparts, are an elite and cosmopolitan minority who have had access to extraordinary educations and who often are connected formally to academic institutions. This time, though, Spanish actually offers a liberating escape from the weight of colonialism. Cameroon too experienced imperial occupation, but the principal foreign powers in its case were France and Great Britain. The inherited European lingua francas were correspondingly French and English, not Spanish, a language that avails itself to Cameroonians who have learned it as a major international idiom unmoored in local history and culture and therefore free of potentially limiting associations. Early postcolonial theorists posited often that African authors used European languages to write back against the societies that colonized them, but hispanophone Cameroonian authors step outside this dynamic altogether, at least explicitly.

In terms of published Cameroonian literary production in Spanish, texts have appeared such as *Equinoccio: poesía hispanocamerunesa* (*Equinox: Hispano-Cameroonian Poetry*) of 2007 and its companion anthology of prose, *El carro de los dioses* (*The Chariot of the Gods*) in 2008. As with their Guinean, Sahrawi, and Moroccan peers, the Cameroonian authors seem to be predominantly influenced by Spanish rather than Latin American authors (Pié Jahn, passim). Once again, 1985 seems to be a pivotal year for African literature in Spanish, with the Cameroonian author Mbol Nang writing his first novel, *El hijo varón* (*The Male Son*) at that time (Pié Jahn, 231). That was the year that also saw the publication of the first two postindependence Guinean novels and the first anthology that included Moroccan Hispanic authors. The small academic world interested in Guinean literature only recently has begun to take note of the Cameroonian phenomenon. For instance, proposed themes for scholarly talks at the II Congreso Internacional de Estudios Literarios Hispanoafricanos (Second International Congress of Hispanoafrican Literary Studies), held in Madrid in 2010, included both Cameroonian and Moroccan literature in Spanish. Also in 2010, the anthology of academic essays *De Guinea Ecuatorial a las literaturas hispanoafricanas* (*From Equatorial Guinea to the Hispanoafrican Literatures*) included two texts that directly focus on literature from Cameroon in Spanish.

A counterpoint to Cameroon, Gabon, the country that borders Río Muni to the south, does not yet have any formal literature in Spanish despite having perhaps the largest expatriate Guinean population in the world, on the order of sixty thousand people or more.[4] This discrepancy represents the greatest potential new source for African Hispanic literature. Most of the Guinean Gabonese population fled the Macías dictatorship in the 1970s or are the children of those refugees, but there are more recent immigrants as well who have arrived for economic as well as political reasons. According to Jeremy Rich, the border between the two nations is porous despite dividing members of the same Fang language and ethnic group, who often have intermarried ("Nous," 117). Although no published hispanophone literature by the immigrants currently exists, a series of oral migration stories, recollections of the Macías years, accounts of life in Gabon, and transnational "Narratives of loss and redemption" are included in a 2009 article by Rich that is the only study of the Guinean Gabonese to date ("Nous," 121).[5] These individual emplotments of personal and national histories are highly literary in nature and deserve to be supplemented with additional interviews of Guinean Gabonese informants. Their stories are as valuable and legitimate as any printed prose or poetry and are a key to a fuller understanding of the range of African Hispanic literature. Such work is usually parceled out in the academy to anthropologists, but disciplinary territoriality is as artificial as the invisible line between, say, Gabon and Equatorial Guinea. Since only one person so far is doing the necessary navigating, all available hands ought to head for the deck.[6]

In terms of larger postcolonial inquiries, Guinean literature in Spanish challenges the tendency of studies of European impacts in Africa to concentrate on anglophone and francophone spaces and thus overlook certain complexities inherent in the exceptionalisms of Spanish colonialism. For example, Great Britain and France were democracies at home when they decolonized; Spain, on the contrary, was a fascist state. In fact, a principal Francoist institute of propaganda was the publisher of the first Guinean novel. The fascist factor could modify macroscopic analyses of the purpose and interpretive possibilities of early African fiction written in European languages. The relative belatedness of Guinean independence compared to those of francophone and anglophone colonies might also suggest rethinkings of the relationship of chronological context to postcolonial literatures. Lusophone countries in Africa present a closer case in this sense but still, differences abound. The fall of fascism in Portugal in 1974 resulted in the independence of Portuguese-speaking countries such as Mozambique and Angola. The nearly simultaneous end of fascism in Spain, occasioned by the death of Franco in 1975, did lead directly to altered sovereignty contests in the colony of Spanish Sahara (now known as Western Sahara), but the independence of Equatorial Guinea preceded that transition by half a dozen years.

African literatures in European and African languages, meanwhile, could be scoured for representations of Guinean space and read alongside texts from Bioko and Río Muni. *Une vie de boy* (*Houseboy*) by Ferdinand Oyono, for example, a well-known Cameroonian novel from 1956, opens in Spanish Guinea before recounting the fictional autobiography of Toundi, a young boy growing up amid repressive European priests and landholders. The opening of the novel and the final flight of its protagonist, both set in Guinea, frame *Houseboy* within relatively unfamiliar and obscure geocultural parameters even as the plot otherwise takes place in Cameroon. The opening paragraph reads as follows:

C'était le soir. Le soleil avait disparu derrière les hautes cîmes. L'ombre épaisse de
la forêt envahissait Akoma. Des bandes de toucans fendirent l'espace à grands
coups d'aile et leurs cris plaintifs moururent peu à peu. La dernière nuit de mes va-
cances en Guinée espagnole descendait furtivement. J'allais bientôt quitter cette
terre où nous autres "Français" du Gabon ou du Cameroun venions faire peau
neuve quand rien n'allait plus avec nos compatriotes blancs. (7)

[It was evening. The sun had disappeared behind the high summits. The
thick shadow of the forest invaded Akoma. Flocks of toucans split the space
with great beatings of their wings and their plaintive cries died little by little. The last night of my vacation in Spanish Guinea descended furtively. I
was soon going to leave this land where we other "Frenchmen" of Gabon or
Cameroon came to shed our skin when we could not cope any more with
our white compatriots.]

Night is falling furtively, thick shadows spread over the forest, the toucans
issue dying, plaintive cries. The murky atmosphere of Spanish Guinea, a
strange space in the region for its particular linguistic and imperial context,
is potent. Momentarily present in this environment are the "other 'Frenchmen'" (black Africans, hence the quotes Oyono felt compelled to put
around the national identity) from neighboring Gabon and Cameroon
who come to the isolated hispanophone place as a refuge from the
colonists in their own francophone lands. Tropes suggestive of a heart of
darkness, therefore, are not all negative in this case, since they create a positive possibility of escape from the normative rules and regimentation of
white colonial society. If Guinean texts were juxtaposed to such descriptions of Guinean spaces in the literature of Gabon and Cameroon, a number of insights might result. The University of Yaoundé in the latter, in fact,
already has had graduate students who have completed theses on Guinean
writings.

Some scholars of Guinean literature have begun attempts to link it to
better-known Afro-Hispanic texts from Latin America. Institutional support and contextualization for such efforts has been provided, for example,
by the *Afro-Hispanic Review* and the Afro-Romance Institute of the University of Missouri–Columbia. This approach may seem a promising way out
of the irrelevance to which Guinean texts are currently consigned. Yet here
the opportunities for engagement seem unnecessarily self-restricting. With
the exception of one or two authors, Afro-Hispanic literature tends to be

treated in the academy as a marginal category unto itself. Moreover, the assumption that the natural connection of Equatorial Guinea to the rest of the hispanophone world is via Afro-Hispanic literature carries racialized undertones of the negritude sort that seem theoretically dated at best. A hypothetical parallel with Filipino literature in Spanish suggests as much. So far there seem to be no attempts to link that tradition to Asian Hispanic texts from Latin America, such as poetry and fiction by the huge Japanese Brazilian population or cultural expressions of the various Chinese communities in sundry South American capitals. But such links would be premised on a shared Asian racialism that is so obviously dubious that it challenges the latent and active assumptions of endeavors to align Guinean literature with that of the non-Guinean African diaspora in the Americas.

A narrower transatlantic interweaving of Guinean literature in Iberia or Africa with that in the Americas is effectively not possible because of the relative lack of a Guinean population in the Western Hemisphere.[7] In the transpacific context of diasporic ties, comparisons of Filipino literature in Spanish with that in English of the large Filipino American community in the United States would seem more viable. Over a century ago, because of nativist restrictions on immigration from China and Japan, namely the Chinese Exclusion Act of 1882 and the Gentlemen's Agreement of 1907, the United States needed a new source of cheap labor from Asia. The consequences of the war of 1898 provided it. Filipinos arrived in significant numbers on the West Coast in the first half of the twentieth century, a period that overlaps with much or all, depending on definitions, of the Golden Age of Filipino literature in Spanish. Out of this migration, the novelized autobiography *America Is in the Heart* was published in 1943 by the Filipino American immigrant Carlos Bulosan. This text detailing the lives of migrant laborers in the 1930s has become canonical in Asian American literary studies. Its composition is contemporaneous with *Social Justice* by Félix Gerardo, the Cebuano Hispanic writer. Plus, the opening third of *America Is in the Heart* describes life in the Philippines in the 1910s and 1920s, that is, during the U.S. occupation and a few years after the time when Paterno was publishing *Social Dawn* in Manila. Potentially, therefore, *America Is in the Heart* and other early Filipino American narratives could make for interesting juxtapositions to post-1898 Filipino literature in Spanish. Such comparisons along transpacific or diasporic lines have yet to be developed. But travel from Manila to Seattle was not requisite to the creation of a Filipino

American sensibility. As subjects of the United States, Paterno after 1898 and Gerardo before 1946 (when the Philippines became independent) were inescapably Filipino Americans too despite never crossing the ocean eastward. As Oscar Campomanes, the forerunner and mentor of a generation of Filipino American scholars, has argued, "to be Filipino is already, whether you move to the United States or remain where you are, to be American. The term 'Filipino American,' in spite of its anchorage in a history of U.S. identity politics, can be a signifier just as descriptive of the modern and U.S. colonial period formation of Filipinos as it is of an emergent and self-empowering political subject in U.S. multiculturalism" (Tiongson, 42).

With respect to Southeast Asian postcolonial studies in general, analyses of Filipino literature in Spanish produced during the U.S. colonization would diversify understandings of how local individuals still under imperial duress appropriate foreign media of expression after a previous empire has fallen. The closest parallel context might be that of Vietnam, particularly its southern regions. There, U.S. power from the late 1950s onward replaced a longstanding French colonization that had resulted in the creation of an indigenous elite that spoke French and knew Paris personally and, via idioms inherited from that preceding imperial experience, created literary and visual arts in both Europe and Asia. Indeed, the post–World War II substitution of the United States for France in Vietnam as the dominant foreign country followed not long after the end of its direct colonization of the Philippines in 1946, which in any case did not terminate its still ongoing military presence throughout the archipelago. The similarities are not exact, for the United States' governance (directly and via proxies) over Vietnam was always less realized than its earlier and longer control over the Philippines. The cultural impositions of the United States in Vietnam were more weakly implanted than in the Philippines as well. Nevertheless, theorizations of francophone Vietnamese literature and arts from, say, 1954 (the fall of the French garrison at Dien Bien Phu) to 1975 (the fall of the U.S. embassy in Saigon) vis-à-vis Filipino literature in Spanish produced from 1898 (the fall of Spanish forces in Manila) to 1942 (the fall of U.S. forces on Corregidor island to Japan) would open important new spaces for argument and reflection. And beyond such a potential Vietnam comparison, Filipino literature in Spanish could impel other transnational inquiries into diverse Asian cultural expressions in Western idioms: Indian novels in English, Cambodian poetry in French, Indonesian voicings in Dutch, East Timorese speeches in Portuguese, and so forth. Yet the Filipino tradition remains unconsidered by specialists in nearby countries, doubtless in large part because Southeast Asianists, along with sinologists and japanologists and koreanists, are not trained in Spanish even as they may be in other Western languages of impact in the region.

Within Hispanism, a somewhat dated term that denominates the study of Spanish-language cultures, Spanish is never acknowledged as a globalized literary language the way English, French, and Portuguese are. In fact, whereas the terms "anglophone," "francophone," and "lusophone" are widely known among literary scholars in general to refer to colonial literatures created outside the original imperial hubs of England, France, and Portugal, "hispanophone" is extremely uncommon. Latin Americanists do not use it, nor do peninsularists, that is, specialists in Spanish culture. The premise is that there is Spain and there is Latin America and that is it. The idea that Latin American literature is but part of a global production of art by former Spanish colonies is so weak that the word that would be used to characterize the phenomenon virtually has no currency whatsoever. In Spanish departments, the Philippines and Equatorial Guinea are still not on the map despite all the centuries since Magellan. Moreover, literature in Spanish and Spanglish from the United States, Canada, Europe north of the Pyrenees, and many other places around the globe also is nearly invisible in Spanish department cartographies. An obvious example is that Chicano studies and Latino studies in general have been assimilated decisively by English, American studies, and ethnic studies programs. It is the unusual Spanish department that formally structures its graduate exams and reading lists in a way that automatically includes literature by North Americans of Hispanic origins, immigrants or otherwise, that is produced in Spanish, Spanglish, or English.

Meanwhile, the vibrant tradition of Canadian literature in Spanish analyzed by Hugh Hazelton in his book *Latinocanadá* of 2007 does not have any institutional home in the United States or Europe. Much of that literature is by the generation of expatriate Chileans and their children whose international migrations commenced in flight from the 1973 coup of Pinochet and whose creative writings have surfaced since across the world. The overview by Hazelton appeared almost simultaneously with those by Lourdes Castrillo Brillantes and Marvin Lewis that are the only books in English dedicated, respectively, to Filipino and Guinean literature in Spanish. Though these three publications are entirely independent of each other, it seems evident that a historical turn in global literary criticism is taking place in which the full breadth of the hispanophone world is finally being acknowledged. How contemporary Canadian literature in Spanish might be read with its Asian and African counterparts is a subject not yet posed. The issues and anxieties perhaps inherent in producing literature in Spanish in spaces not commonly known to have such traditions might recast texts and aesthetic assumptions arisen in more canonical countries of the Spanish-speaking world. But critical questions of any kind about the global production of literature in Spanish have not been asked.

THE POSSIBILITIES OF CHABACANO

A phenomenon such as Filipino literature in Spanish, however, does not require comparative resonance to be meaningful. It stands on its own as a worthy object of study. And Filipino literature in Spanish is continually resistant to attempts by outsiders as well as insiders to organize it. To begin with, and as noted elsewhere in this book, even the phrase "Filipino literature in Spanish" contains multiple and mutable ambiguities that cannot be controlled without caveats of temporal and spatial import. The complications of defining "literature" alone are evident. As for "Filipino," that term meant something rather different through most of the nineteenth century than it did but decades later and today. In the era of *Nínay* and the *Noli* and the *Fili,* individuals like Ismael in Gerardo's "Before the Flag" were known as *indios* because they were of ancestry indigenous to the archipelago. This appellation also could designate many people, including Paterno and Rizal and a broad swath of the elite, who had Chinese as well as local forebears; "mestizo" was employed specifically to include such individuals of multiple heritages. "Filipinos," in contrast, were born in the Philippines into families of entirely Spanish origin. The fact that Ismael is referred to as a "Filipino" would likely have led Rizal to conclude that he descended from European predecessors, not from Cebuano villagers. Indeed, if a "Filipino" in the initial sense of the word, Ismael might have looked quite a bit like his blue-eyed wife.

Linguistically, the term "Filipino literature in Spanish" is problematic for two additional reasons. The first is that "Filipino" is the governmental name for the particular idiom based on Tagalog that is officially a national language along with English. In this sense, Filipino literature literally cannot be in Spanish or any tongue other than Filipino. The second issue is the case of Chabacano (also known as Chavacano), a creole language derived from Spanish and assorted vernaculars such as Cebuano, Hiligaynon (also known as Ilonggo) and Tagalog. Currently, Chabacano is spoken mostly in the noncontiguous coastal cities of Zamboanga and Cavite. Zamboanga is located on the western tip of Mindanao, a large southern island near Indonesia; Cavite is just a few miles southwest of Manila. Well into the twentieth century, there were other varieties of Chabacano that flourished in disparate locales, notably in Ermita, an urban area now absorbed by greater Manila.

The origins of Chabacano are debated in the details, but scholars generally agree that it arose around different Spanish littoral outposts in the seventeenth and eighteenth centuries as foreign soldiers and bureaucrats came into daily contact with indigenous Filipinos of various ethnic and linguistic backgrounds. In Zamboanga City, home of the most numerous Chabacano population and of the dialect known as Zamboangueño, the roots of the language stretch back to the construction of a Spanish fort in 1635. As of 1990, according to Orlando B. Cuartocruz, half a million speakers lived there (4). In 1995, owing to a difference perhaps of definitions, Emmanuel Luis A. Romanillos wrote that the figure was "about 214,000 . . . or a little less than 50% of the total population," with about another hundred thousand speakers of Chabacano scattered elsewhere in the Philippines (12). In 1942, adds Romanillos, there were "some 18,000" speakers of Caviteño, the Cavite dialect of Chabacano, but the 1990 census showed only 3,405 speakers (22). As for Ermitaño, the dialect of Chabacano in the capital region, Keith Whinnom cites an earlier scholar, a Professor Beyer, who estimated that it was spoken in 1942 by twelve thousand people (13). Ermita was annihilated in World War II and with it an entire linguistic community. Whatever microcontexts may have survived for Ermitaño after the Japanese defeat were promptly overrun by the postwar domestic hegemony of Tagalog and English and their fusion, known as Taglish.

Modern linguistic studies of Chabacano have a genealogy that dates from Whinnom's *Spanish Contact Vernaculars in the Philippines* of 1956. Various professional explorations of the grammar and history of the language have since appeared in Europe, North America, and the Philippines, including by distinguished scholars such as John M. Lipski and Antonio Quilis. Although Whinnom and other early observers forecast that Chabacano was likely to disappear altogether within a couple decades, the opposite turned out to be true: the language has surged in Zamboanga and linguistic papers have followed suit.[8] Publications of Chabacano literature, however, are another matter entirely. The number of speakers of the language seems sufficient to have produced significant written traditions, yet none really has consolidated. There does not seem to be a single novel, for example, composed in any dialect of Chabacano.

Archival investigations intent on revealing otherwise are challenging today for an outside researcher to conduct, given the violence of an ongoing civil war throughout Mindanao between Islamic separatists and the national government. Indeed, in August 2008, the Philippine government nearly signed a treaty that would have partitioned Mindanao and left much of the Zamoboanga Peninsula in an autonomous region controlled by the rebels of the Moro Islamic Liberation Front. Until the political situation stabilizes or investigators (foreign or Filipino) are willing to brave it, studies of Chabacano literature from Zamboanga will have to rely on a small handful of existing compilations of local oral and written texts. Speakers of Caviteño and their literary output are much more accessible, given the short distance between Cavite and Manila and the lack of major military engagements in the region, but the population in distant and troubled Mindanao that communicates in Zamboangueño is vastly greater and far more likely to develop a lasting and broadbased literary tradition.

Filipino literature in Chabacano is much less familiar than even Filipino literature in Spanish, but several leading novelists and poets did work with both languages. Rizal, for instance, nested a short conversation in Chabacano into a scene in the *Fili* between a store owner and a student. According to Romanillos, "Doubtless, Rizal's purpose in including it in his work was to inject local color in the narrative through the Chabacano dialogue" (81–82). This would be a *costumbrista* rationale. Romanillos also remarks that Rizal sent a postcard to Paterno in 1888 that was entirely written in Chabacano, the text of which is as follows:

Ñol. Aquí está nisós con ñol Iriarte. Yo di andá na Londrés, di pasá por Estados Unidos. Pronto di visitá con vos. Ya mandá nisós expresiones con el mga capatid y otro pa suyo.
Adiós, ñol Maguinoo. (83)

[Sir. Here I am with Mr. Iriarte. I will be heading for London after passing through the United States. Soon I will visit you. Send my regards to the brotherhood and I send them to you as well.
Goodbye, Sir Tagalog Lord.][9]

Rizal's motivation for writing the postcard in Chabacano is unclear, as is whether he was fluent in the language or merely daytripping in it for parodic purposes (the valediction suggests a lightheartedness of tone). Regardless, he evidently felt that Paterno would have no difficulties understanding the message and that Chabacano was as viable as Castilian for communicating at least certain types of information.

Jesús Balmori, who succeeded Paterno and Rizal as the third Filipino novelist in Spanish (at least by common acknowledgment), utilized Chabacano on a more regular basis.[10] Whinnom notes that Balmori wrote a daily column of poetry for *La vanguardia* (*The Vanguard*), a Manila newspaper, that sometimes used the Ermita dialect of Chabacano (23). In April 1917, Whinnom adds, Balmori also published "Na maldito arena" ("In the Accursed Sands"), a short story in a refined, literary version of Ermitaño, in *The Philippine Review* (23).[11] Also in 1917, according to Romanillos, Balmori published three sonnets in Ermitaño in *Revista filipina* (*Filipino Magazine*) (198).[12] A methodical searching of various periodicals of the era might turn up additional examples of Chabacano literature composed by Balmori and his peers. In Zamboanga today, new texts in the language continue to appear. In 2008, Antonio Quilis and Celia Casado-Fresnillo noted that "En la actualidad, la prensa en inglés incluye artículos en Chabacano por ejemplo: *Daily Zamboanga Times, Morning Times, Prensa Zamboanga, South Herald,* etc." ["Currently, the English-language press includes articles in Chabacano, for example: *Daily Zamboanga Times, Morning Times, Prensa Zamboanga, South Herald,* etc."] (27). In 2012, four directors showed their short films in Chabacano, all shot in Zamboanga, at the Cervantes Institute in Manila. Currently, the longest single example of a written text in Chabacano seems to be *El nuevo testamento*, a 999-page long translation of the New Testament published in 1981 by the New York International Bible Society. The largest bilingual edition of any Chabacano text is apparently *The Lady of the Fort / El Señora del Fuerte,* which appeared in 2002. The English original, written by Grace Rebollos and Angel Calvo, is followed by a seventy-eight-page translation into Zamboangueño by the authors and three others. For autodidactic study of the language, the best resource is *Chavacano Reader* of 2009, a remarkable collection of forty-five texts in diverse genres plus accompanying English translations, glossaries, grammatical explanations, and cultural notes.[13]

Since Asian literature in Spanish should be developed, like all fields, as inherently liberal and flexible in its contours, oral and written and filmic traditions in Chabacano ought to be included within it. The stories and verse in that language are roughly accessible to anyone with a good grasp of Spanish and a willingness to consult a couple of vernacular dictionaries, so specialists in any branch of hispanophone literature might move to study Chabacano much as they might explore creative expressions in other Hispanic or Hispanic-contact idioms such as Galician and Catalan in Iberia, Garífuna in Central America, and Spanglish in the United States. Studies of poetry, prose, and music in Spanglish are far more prevalent and developed at this point than those of Chabacano arts and would make for a compelling counterpoint. The argument that Spanglish is a legitimate medium for literature, however, tends to confront implicitly or explicitly the opposite premise that linguistically hybridized writings are a degradation of those in more prestigious codes such as Castilian or Standard English. Bypassing such parameters by directly juxtaposing prose and poetry in Spanglish with that in Chabacano may be a liberating move that allows for new theoretical interventions by eliding debates over language purity altogether. The Chamorro language of Guam, which is highly influenced by Spanish, remains another possibility to explore as a medium for Asian Hispanic literature; Guam is the overlooked fourth Spanish colony of 1898 to be transferred to the United States. Linguists have forged ahead in Chabacano studies. The time for literary scholars to make their own paths is now. With Spanish rarely written today in the Philippines, Chabacano may prove eventually to be the enduring medium of Asian Hispanic literature.

SEARCHES TO COME

With Chabacano verse, videos, and narratives included among the subjects of study of Asian Hispanic literature, the field may grow to match reality. Meanwhile, its interior scope depends largely on a much needed endeavor of textual recovery for all poems and short stories and serialized novels in Spanish that appeared in periodicals inside the Philippines from 1898 to the 1960s. Since the defeat of Spanish forces in Manila, Rizal and his peers have been researched and depicted with relative frequency. Most of their literature produced in Europe, including their journalism, essays, and academic works, is both known and available through standard library mechanisms in North America and, a bit more erratically and depending on the text, in the Philippines. On the contrary, much and possibly most of twentieth-century Filipino literature in Spanish is currently immaterial, that is, unknown or lost or inaccessible, which amount to the same thing, at least for the moment. Thanks to the bibliographic efforts over the course of the twentieth century of a succession of isolated individuals in the archipelago, a number of them graduate students, lists of hundreds of authors and titles are extant. Tracking down the surviving texts to which they refer, however, and making them available to be read and studied, is a process virtually uncommenced. The overwhelming majority of Filipino literature in Spanish appeared in periodicals of diverse types (magazines, newspapers, weekly novella subscriptions, etc.) that may not have made it across the seas to archival safety in either Europe or North America. Such physical movement was key, for those texts that stayed in the Philippines had to survive a century that included obliteration by Japan, the Marcos dictatorship, and the enduring tropical humidity and heat that could wreak havoc with perishable media in a land where libraries and private collections often may not maintain climate-controlled environments.

The easiest way to begin the archaeological effort of unearthing and gathering the corpus of Filipino literature in Spanish and, ideally, putting it all up in one site on the Internet—copyright restrictions should be irrelevant at this point, with the deaths of all authors in question so long ago— is twofold. For starters, someone should amass a metalist of all known Filipino authors in Spanish. Doing so would require consulting not only the few published anthologies but also a handful of graduate student theses whose sole known copies are shelved in university libraries in Manila. These invaluable texts include, for example, a 1950 survey by Araceli Pons García, *Filipino Writers in Spanish and Their Works: Historico-Bibliographic Study,* that names 144 authors, classifying 35 of them as "Major Writers" and 109 as "Minor Writers" (ii–vi). A metalist, once compiled, could be used as a guide for methodically searching Google Books and all online North American, Spanish, and Philippine libraries for surviving titles. Meanwhile, someone should begin combing the contents of all hispanophone Filipino periodicals that have been preserved, often on microform, in Western libraries, and extracting and indexing their literary contents and putting their full text up on the Web. Such periodicals are sometimes monolingual in Spanish, sometimes bilingual or trilingual with any combination of Spanish, English, and a Filipino language. The best chances for textual recovery here are probably in the Filipiniana collections of the Library of Congress, Cornell University, the University of Michigan (Ann Arbor), the University of Wisconsin (Madison), and the National Li-

brary of Australia. A sustained effort at making available some Asian Hispanic texts can be found online already at *Revista filipina,* edited by the Filipino Canadian author Edmundo Farolán, but a larger and systematic project of discovery, especially of the earliest twentieth-century texts, is much
needed.

As for research within the Philippines, parallel efforts are requisite but
their realization is impeded by a number of issues. First, the physical and
technological infrastructure for research is very poor. Library holdings can
be thin and often not online. The ability to search catalogs even from com-
puters inside library buildings is frequently limited. The unpublished text
of Gerardo's *Social Justice* was discovered by the very old technique of eye-
balling shelves in person and pulling out books with unreadable spines.
One example of the state of things is the National Library in Manila, whose
browsable collection is exceedingly small and whose reading room, of pro-
portional size, is filled entirely with chatting teenagers on school assign-
ments. Furthermore, the best arrays of Filipino literature in Spanish, almost
certainly in the world, are in the hands of private collectors and elite families and are not listed anywhere, much less available to be perused. The
elite families, who still count among their number native Spanish speakers
and who have survived the successive turmoils in the archipelago since the
1890s, maintain probably the richest literary archives but also the most
guarded. It seems unlikely that their troves will be made broadly available
in any form in the foreseeable future. Perhaps that will change someday. If
so, insider connections almost certainly will be required. Meanwhile, the
descendants of writers from Paterno to Gerardo and beyond need to be located and asked if they possess any of the old papers, including unpublished manuscripts, and would be willing to share them. Such sleuthing
may yield some surprising successes.

Issues of textual recovery of African literature in Spanish are germane
but less acutely so. Unlike the Filipino situation, there do not appear to be
potentially thousands of poems and narratives remaining to be unearthed.
For instance, other than the currently lost manuscripts of Daniel Jones
Mathama that are mentioned in the article by Manuel Castillo Barril, it
seems likely that no other novel was produced by a Guinean during the
colonial era or, for that matter, that any sizable quantity of fiction or poetry
was composed in the immediate postindependence years that is not already known. It is hard to imagine that anyone today could discover much
extant literature written before the early 1980s beyond what Ndongo-

Bidyogo located in his door-by-door search of the country that resulted in his 1984 anthology. There may be texts that will surface now and then in old colonial archives or in hiding places that date from the 1970s, but by and large the material availability of Guinean literature is a question of achieving and sustaining circulation of all those works produced since the mid-1980s. The authors of these texts are often alive but their books are generally out of print. Their publishing houses tend to be small-scale operations in Spain that do not maintain large back catalogs or vigorously operate international distribution networks. As a result, Guinean books may circulate more by hand-to-hand cash transactions directly between authors and readers in North America and Europe than through any standard commercial mechanisms. Inside Equatorial Guinea, still under strongman control and still unwelcoming of free communications, Guinean creative writings do not circulate much at all. One of the saddest lines in *The Reencounter* is when Juan, the protagonist, says to a group of young boys, "Cuando se normalice la situación del país, cuando haya librerías deberéis leer mucho" ["When the situation of the country normalizes, when there are bookstores, you should read a lot"] (68) A generation later, there are still no bookstores in the country.

Textual recovery, especially in Asia but also in Africa, raises the serious question of academic neocolonialism. The fact of the matter is that Filipino scholars of literature, almost across the board, do not know Spanish and therefore are not in a position to read and analyze the local texts for which they might search. Moreover, funding from their institutions for research efforts is scarce. On top of that, the teaching loads of professors in the Philippines tend to be much heavier, and therefore more time-consuming, than those of colleagues at Western universities. In consequence, it is mostly foreigners who are likely to have the combination of Spanish language skills, access to funding, leaves from regular work, and overall institutional and technological backing that would make a massive, multiyear search for unknown texts sustainable. This reality can raise all sorts of problematic politics even with regard to the most well-intentioned of researchers from Spain or the United States who show up, like their imperial predecessors, in Manila or Cebu. Meanwhile, it is mostly Filipino scholars who are the best navigators of the polyglot context of the archipelago and of the social networks that allow access to unpublished or otherwise out-of-sight texts, including those held at libraries whose collections are supposed to be open to the public, paying or otherwise. Transoceanic collaborative work is therefore needed profoundly. Yet foreign academics must take as many steps as possible to avoid reperforming a dynamics of power that recalls, however tenuously, those of the former Spanish and U.S. empires in the islands.

This is a challenge at best; eliding the echoes of history is perhaps impossible.[14] In general, apart from the relatively few Filipino and Filipino American scholars who are native speakers of both English and a vernacular and who have been trained in Spanish, there is almost nobody with the broad set of skills needed to really unveil and interrogate the range and context of Asian Hispanic literature. Many narratives and poems in Spanish in the early twentieth century appeared in bilingual or trilingual magazines that reflected an audience at the time ready to read in both English and an archipelagic language too, so the whole immediate context of the texts in Spanish is lost without scholars able to understand at the most basic, linguistic level such periodicals in their entirety. One way to mitigate the acuity of academic neocolonialism in any textual recovery effort while simultaneously making various comparative studies feasible would be for foreign scholars of Filipino literature in Spanish to learn how to read, at a minimum, Tagalog or Cebuano.

The globalization of Asian and African literature is on ongoing story, however, not at all confined to archival diggings in dusty shelves and their microfilmed equivalents. Engaged studies of power and its permutations are not abstract thought games but potential impactors on the postmagellanic paths of the twenty-first century. Freedom of expression, particularly via written literature, must be radical in the best of senses, else its practitioners would not so often be meted out torture and death by regimes that fear it. The execution of Rizal for two novels that he wrote at the end of the nineteenth century resonates with the gun barrels that forced Ndongo-Bidyogo into exile at the end of the twentieth century and the grim fate that could await him should he return to his birthplace now. Equatorial Guinea remains a very dangerous place to write literature, while the Philippines, though nominally a democracy, often leads the world in the assassinations of journalists. Newspapers and related periodicals are where a generation of hispanophone Filipino intellectuals in Madrid and Barcelona made great contributions in the 1880s and 1890s, where Pedro Paterno published a number of his stories in 1910 and 1911, and where today their heirs in the archipelago are, in particularly bad years, less likely to stay alive than anywhere else on earth. Power is refracted through reportage, whether that storytelling is done through narrative realism or allegorical conceit or lyrical evocation. To study Asian and African literature in Spanish is to allow for alternative voices and visions in a variety of structures with vested interests in suppressing both. This holds true despite the elite class backgrounds of most of the authors and the elite class leanings, particularly in the Philippines, of much of their output.

To read these texts is also to revise globalization. Asia and Africa are interwoven with Europe and the Americas and have been ever since Magellan, yet this longstanding reality is often unknown or ignored as globalization is treated as a strictly contemporary phenomenon. For nearly five hundred years now, new players have appeared all the time on unexpected shores the world over, and sometimes old players have showed up guised in novel ways. This continues unabated. People from the purported peripheries keep making their mark in the supposed centers, and metropolitan forces keep arriving in the most apparently parochial of spaces. As but one example, the U.S. missionaries who protagonize the opening scene of *When the Combes Fought,* the first African novel in Spanish, have been succeeded in Equatorial Guinea by oil corporations from the same country that push neoliberalism rather than Christianity. But this is no structural rigidity in which only the content changes as a Spanish empire in Africa and Asia is replaced by a U.S. empire, yielding eventually to the internally coherent nations of Equatorial Guinea and the Philippines. As the novels by Nsue Angüe and Balboa Boneke show, Equatorial Guinea as a nation barely can be acknowledged to exist in any sense other than a bureaucratic one. It is this and that tossed up by a stormy world whose currents shift and swerve and never achieve any ultimate definition. Equatoguinean novelists register these ricochets and redirect them, consciously or not. Meanwhile, Chinese investments in Gabon today seemingly mark a new turn in globalization and yet are folded into existing narratives told there by Equatoguinean refugees to one another. The marginal does not merely bear the brunt of force majeure. It produces new forces in response, many of which lie outside metropolitan ken.

Asian and African authors in Spanish do not simply emerge from sequences in which prominent powers conquer distant lands. They are not passive objects produced by macrohistorical processes, individuals acted upon and little else. They are, instead, highly subjective agents who work from the hearts of empire, which is wherever empire situates itself, who revise empire in their rewriting of it. As Neferti Tadiar suggests, "The specific

modalities of social life in a seemingly peripheral social formation such as
the Philippines do not merely demonstrate the localization or vernacular-
ization of global forms, as many accounts of alternative modernities would
have it. Rather, these modalities of social life provide hermeneutic elements for understanding the productive dimensions of local, cultural activity and, by extension, the unrecognized productive forces of globalization itself" (20). Asian and African literature in Spanish is not only about
the legacy of the Spanish occupations of Asia and Africa. It is also about the
legacy of the Asian and African occupations of Spain.

   Benita Sampedro Vizcaya writes of "this artificial and unbounded construct that we have come to call Equatorial Guinea" ("Theorizing," 16). The
same description could be applied to the Philippines and also, perhaps unexpectedly, to Spain and the entirety of the Spanish empire. This is not just
because of the variegated Iberian entities that famously have claimed different degrees of nationhood over the centuries, namely Catalonia and the
Basque Country and Galicia, or other regions with pretensions to autonomy such as Andalusia, but also because antipodal writers always have appeared in the center of empire and produced literature whose very existence denies their fundamental antipodality. Paterno and Rizal and
Gerardo and Jones Mathama and Nsue Angüe and Balboa Boneke all wrote
texts that rework the identities and constructions not only of the Philippines and Guinea but of Spain too, of Europe, and of the world. These are
not binational or bicontinental dynamics at hand. There is no binarism in
the first place. The tradition of Asian and African literature in Spanish
defies all definitions of nations and continents. Consequently, the subtitle
of this book is but a heuristic device, for as a rubric alone it is meaningless.
Due to the existence of Asian and African literature, Europe is not Europe.
It too is incommensurate with itself, as much as is the United States, which
is a globalized throe of forces, not a geopolitical entity.

   This is not in any way to affirm that on the postmagellanic planet, all
powers are somehow fused or equalized and therefore voided of responsi-
bility. No, there are those who shed blood and there are those whose blood
is shed. On occasion they can be the same people, but the record of history
is quite clear: some Magellan does most of the killing, some Lapu Lapu
scores the occasional defensive victory, the ship of the foreigners proceeds
around the world anyway and Pigafetta, some Pigafetta, writes it all up and
disappears forevermore. His text stays behind. A new Magellan then raises
his sword, a new Lapu Lapu parries, a new Pigafetta puts to paper what the

next Magellan will read before raising his sword again. Lapu Lapu may never sustain a win in this sequence, and he will never be the same for the blows, but Magellan will never be himself again either. He will be defined forever by Lapu Lapu. This is some sort of story worth telling, whether from Manila or Malabo or Madrid, whether from Washington or Tokyo or anywhere in between, heading west or east, south or north.

We are all Magellan and Lapu Lapu and Pigafetta, teachers and readers and critics alike. These are roles intimately tied to our work every time we process Asian and African literature in Spanish one way or another, and we play more than one of them at a time. That is because they are not distinct from each other but mutually interdefinitive. The same is true of all these authors. None can contain the globalized slippages of their texts any more than the scholars or students who approach them, wherever it is that each of us makes a stand, whatever the shore. The identities sought in these texts, whether by those who write them, those who rewrite them, or those who read them—here too are three common roles—are never the identities gained, for categories of any sort escape the control of everyone who tries to make them coherent, tie up the loose ends, close off the circle, circumnavigate the world. Magellan keeps getting killed off halfway there, or often before. Lapu Lapu keeps proclaiming victory in a moment that at once is necessarily of defeat. Pigafetta keeps rounding the final turn to pronounce the last lines in Europe, but the lines are anything but last and the turn anything but final. Today, one out of every ten Filipinos scrapes out a living abroad under contracts arranged by governmental and private interests. They are designated as Overseas Filipino Workers or, sometimes, Global Filipinos. Several thousand of them labor in Equatorial Guinea, apparently often in the petrochemical industry. More than a quarter of the merchant seamen in the world are from the Philippines (Cabuag). They work on the waters. One wonders what Lapu Lapu would think.

This book attempts to be but a beginning about beginnings. And as Herman Melville writes in *Moby-Dick,* "small erections may be finished by their first architects; grand ones, true ones, ever leave the copestone to posterity" (127–28). The final stone may never be laid, though. Such is not possible in the arts, architectures included. At the end of the day, the day never ends. It merely moves around the world. Meanwhile, the heirs of Mactan Island are all of us, all humanity, and the Magellan fallacy, our ongoing fall in the waves. The next time we travel around the earth, which is right now, we would do well to remember the hubris that has made us think that here is here, that there is there, that we are ourselves. The blood spilled in wakes and turned into ink never ceases to flow through us all. Let us make our stand by the shores of Lapu Lapu, exploring new old ground and writing of it, but this time without striving to make anyone and anything coherent in our image. That may be a quixotic hope, but now and then (and now is always then) there is yet a dream to which it is worthy to cling.

Notes

Introduction

1. See Sundiata for twentieth-century population statistics in Guinea (*Equatorial Guinea*, 32).

2. See *Origins and Rise of the Filipino Novel* by Resil Mojares for the canonical account of written vernacular literature in the Philippines prior to the appearance of the first texts that are generally considered novels, all of which were written in Spanish. See *Frontier Constitutions* by John Blanco for a recent contestation of the categorizations and genealogical logic of Mojares (188–90).

Chapter 1

1. Some sources list the publication year of *Sampaguitas* as 1881. In 2008, Manuel García-Castellón wrote that he had discovered a book of verse entitled *Flores filipinas* (*Filipino Flowers*) by Miguel Zaragoza that antedates the publications by Paterno and his successors. According to García-Castellón, "Nada conocemos de este misterioso Miguel Zaragoza, cuyos versos constituyen, nos atrevemos a decir, el primer libro de poemas escrito y publicado en castellano por un filipino. Tal es *Flores filipinas*, que Zaragoza dedicaba a su novia en la contraportada y que veía la luz en Madrid en 1864. . . . Podemos considerar a este Zaragoza, pues, como primer literato fil-hispano" ["We know nothing of this mysterious Miguel Zaragoza whose verses constitute, we dare to say it, the first book of poems written and published in Castilian by a Filipino. Such is *Filipino Flowers*, which Zaragoza dedicated to his fiancée on the back page and which saw light in Madrid in 1864. . . . We can consider this Zaragoza, then, as the first Fil-Hispanic literatus"] ("Miguel Zaragoza"). If this conclusion is accurate, then the chronological primacy always awarded to Paterno for *Sampaguitas* needs to be revised, but otherwise the story of the emergence of Filipino literature in Spanish would seem to remain effectively the same. All accounts of the trajectory of that tradition, both those contemporary to Paterno and ever since, have taken *Sampaguitas* as its starting point in terms of published books of Filipino creative writing in Spanish. Perhaps further investigations will concretize the

identity of Zaragoza and show that *Filipino Flowers* was indeed known by later writers and that the putative beginnings of Filipino literature in Spanish merit a substantial modification.

2. Teofilo del Castillo y Tuazon and Buenaventura S. Medina Jr. concur that Paterno "was the first Filipino poet in Spanish to publish his poems in book form" but note that two earlier nineteenth-century Filipinos, Don Jose de Vergara and Don Juan de Atayde, occasionally wrote verse in Spanish as a hobby (135–37). Some individual poems in Spanish by contemporaries of Paterno also appeared before the publication of *Sampaguitas* in 1880, with Ben Cailles Unson even affirming that José Rizal's "oda, 'A la juventud filipina,' publicada en 1879, la primera obra hispanofilipina de realce, marca el nacimiento de la verdadera literatura filipina en español" ["ode, 'To the Filipino Youth,' published in 1879, the first Filipino-Hispanic work of significance, marks the birth of the true Filipino literature in Spanish"] (275).

3. John Schumacher and Resil Mojares both conclude in their various texts that the general goal of Paterno in all his sociohistorical writings was to show the premagellanic indigenous cultures of the Philippines as essentially proto-Christian and proto-Spanish. A comparison awaits to be developed here between Paterno's histories of the pre-Hispanic Philippines and those of El Inca Garcilaso de la Vega of Peru, whose ideological goals in *Los comentarios reales* (*The Royal Commentaries*) of 1609 and *La historia general del Perú* (*The General History of Peru*) of 1617 were approximately the same. Like Paterno, Garcilaso was the first mestizo author of his land to channel his education in both European and indigenous culture into written histories of the latter. Garcilaso was born to an Incan mother and Spanish father; Paterno was of Tagalog-Chinese heritage, which is considered mestizo in the Philippines.

4. Torres lauds Paterno as an underappreciated founding father of the Philippines whose example could be of continuing relevance: "Hombres de su carácter son los que hoy necesita el mundo turbado por la gigantesca lucha entre el Comunismo y la Democracia" ["Men of his character are those who are needed today in a world disturbed by the gigantic fight between Communism and Democracy"] (5). This posthumous use of Paterno as an unlikely standard-bearer for Filipino anticommunism surfaces as well in the only other known text to praise him hyperbolically, a high school or possibly college language textbook entitled *Español 4-N: La literatura filipina y su relacion al nacionalismo filipino* (*Spanish 4-N: Filipino Literature and Its Relation to Filipino Nationalism*) by Remigia Pérez and six others that was designed to teach Spanish to Filipinos via exercises that extol the Spanish heritage of the archipelago. It was apparently published in 1978, that is, during the dictatorship of Ferdinand Marcos, when anticommunism served the purposes of an autocratic state. The eleventh lesson is dedicated to a fill-in-the-blank passage; students are supposed to write in the parenthetical spaces an English translation of the preceding word or phrase in Spanish. The passage criticizes those "historiadores contemporáneos que intentan menospreciar (. . .) la actuación cívica, social, diplomática y patriótica de Pedro Paterno" ["contemporary historians who try to look down upon (. . .) the

civic, social, diplomatic and patriotic actions de Pedro Paterno"] (95). The textbook then adds that "Estos radicales, que hacen el papel (. . .) de 'historiadores'
modernos del país, tienen un odio implacable (. . .) contra nuestros hombres
ilustres del pasado por la sencilla razón de que la mayoría de ellos eran, como
Paterno, acomodados. La influencia del comunismo y la falta de conocimiento
(. . .) que tienen en torno a la verdadera cultura de Filipinas, la cultura urbana y
literaria de Filipinas, son los factores que les hacen tomar esa postura antípatica
frente a la mayoría de nuestros héroes y grandes hombres del pasado" ["These
radicals, who play the role (. . .) of modern 'historians' of the country have an
implacable (. . .) hatred against our illustrious men of the past for the simple reason that the majority of them were, like Paterno, well-to-do. The influence of
communism and the lack of knowledge (. . .) that they have regarding the true
culture of the Philippines, the urban and literary culture of the Philippines, are
the factors that make them assume that antagonistic posture toward the majority of our heroes and great men of the past"] (96). For the record, a second language textbook exists with virtually the same title, plus a striking subtitle: *Texto
para español 4-N: La literatura filipina y su relacion al nacionalismo filipino (Revisado): Un Análisis de la Evolución de la Nacionalidad Filipina a Traves [sic] de su
Literatura. Con los Comentarios, Vocabularios, Ejercicios Gramaticales y Cuestionarios Adecuados* (*Text for Spanish 4-N: Filipino Literature and Its Relation to Filipino
Nationalism (Revised): An Analysis of the Evolution of the Filipino Nationality
Through Its Literature. With the Appropriate Commentaries, Vocabularies, Grammatical Exercises, and Questions*). The relationship between the two textbooks is uncertain. Although they share the same title and although the author of the latter, Guillermo Gómez-Rivera, is one of the seven authors of the former, the
contents are different. The listing of the second textbook as a revised edition
does not clarify the relationship because it was actually published in 1972, before the first textbook. Gómez-Rivera is the grandson of a prominent author,
Guillermo Gómez Windham, who in 1922 won the first Zóbel Prize for the best
Filipino literature in Spanish. Gómez-Rivera received the 1975 Zóbel "in recognition of his efforts to preserve the Spanish language and culture in our country" (Brillantes, *81 Years,* 241).

5. Eugenio Matibag suggests that there is an explanation for the similarity of
the Pasiám to customs in Europe, for the former is "the Filipino version of the
Catholic *novena,* or nine-day prayer for the welfare of the soul of the departed
loved one" (45). This may be true, but Paterno does not make the direct connection himself.

6. E. F. du Fresne, the English translator of *Nínay,* dares even less. He skips
over those ellipses and consistently weakens allusions to sexuality throughout
the novel (61 and passim).

7. Guerrero is a complicated figure in his own right. See chapter 2 for a discussion of his work as the principal translator and biographer of Rizal in the
second half of the twentieth century.

8. The paucity of individuals who publish on Filipino literature in Spanish,
along with the lack of virtually any texts translated from that tradition apart

NOTES TO PAGES 41–43

from those by Rizal, has resulted in a type of intellectual cul-de-sac in which scholars of Filipino literature in other languages (English, Tagalog, Cebuano, Mandarin, etc.) who do not read Spanish are forced to rely for background on the same scattering of comments in the same few sources. The isolated passages cited in *The Magellan Fallacy* by Mojares, Schumacher, and Guerrero are reprinted or summarized frequently elsewhere, as there is almost no other secondary literature available with which to dialogue. As but one example, Caroline S. Hau in *Necessary Fictions: Philippine Literature and the Nation, 1946–1980,* leaves her consideration of *Nínay* entirely in citations from Schumacher and Guerrero amid a larger discussion of Rizal in which Mojares figures prominently (63). Portia L. Reyes, in turn, cites Hau and Schumacher and offers English translations of excerpts from *Nínay* that are not from the Spanish original but from the heavily abridged and distorted Tagalog translation (101–2).

9. Similar comments can be found by del Castillo y Tuazon and Medina, who suggest that *"Ninay,* as a novel, is difficult to understand; it is full of detours and extraneous matters. . . . Its artistic value is slight" (172); and by F. Licsi Espino Jr., who writes that the story of Nínay and Carlos "is told in a sentimental manner which detracts from what little literary merits the novel may have . . . written by Paterno when he was only 23, *Ninay* is sheer juvenilia, filled with digressions and written in florid Spanish" (14). Danica Salazar adds that "la primera novela filipina es un fracaso como obra literaria . . . Pero son los cuadros de costumbres que el autor ha pintado tan cuidadosamente lo que hace de la novela una indispensable lectura para cualquier filipino o filipinista que desee conocer las Filipinas de finales del siglo XIX" (the first Filipino novel is a failure as a literary work . . . But it is the descriptions of customs that the author has painted so carefully that make the novel an indispensable reading for any Filipino or Filipinist who wants to know the Philippines of the end of the 19th century"] (114).

10. Regarding the polyglot abilities of Nínay, she speaks "el chino y el inglés además del tagalo y el español" ["Chinese and English besides Tagalog and Spanish"], which makes her voice quite globalized in its own right (48).

11. Oddly, the author is listed as Alejandro Paterno. "Alejandro" was his middle name. The English and Tagalog translations of the novel give the author as Pedro A. Paterno and all criticism refers to him as "Pedro" and not "Alejandro."

12. The ephemeral Cavite Mutiny of 1872 in the Philippines had been crushed summarily by Spanish forces. Whether this isolated military revolt could have developed otherwise into a larger push seems unlikely, but the execution of some of its alleged leaders ultimately would politicize Rizal and others. In Cuba, however, an anticolonial movement led in part from New York by the essayist and poet José Martí was both active and longstanding. In 1885, when *Nínay* was published, Cuba was momentarily in between major wars of resistance.

13. Schumacher describes *Sampaguitas* as follows: "The verses make only occasional mention of the Philippines, and are mostly slight romantic lyrics. Nevertheless, the book is of some significance as perhaps the first attempt to project

a Filipino national personality and to present to the public the work of a Filipino, specifically as such. Paterno himself and others better endowed would carry out this program" (*Propaganda*, 25). Elsewhere Schumacher writes, "Neither in its first edition nor in the subsequent enlarged editions will we find more than mediocre lyrics. They are not great literature nor even good; their significance is in the fact that this was the first conscious attempt to create a *Filipino* literature" (*Making*, 120). Ma. Elinora Peralta-Imson suggests that *Sampaguitas* was "intended to be truly and uniquely Filipino in theme and tenor" (9).

14. The image can be seen readily on the full-text copy of *Nínay* available on Google Books.

15. Mojares notes that Paterno "did not write in Tagalog (it is said that he could not even passably speak the language)" and as a result had to have his own theatrical works translated from Spanish into Tagalog for performances (*Brains*, 38).

16. At the start of the century, William McKinley appointed Taft as the first civil governor of the new U.S. colony that was the Philippines. By the time of the publication of the English translation of *Nínay*, however, Taft had not served in that capacity for several years nor continued to live in the islands.

17. Mojares dubs Pardo de Tavera one of the "Brains of the Nation" along with Paterno and Isabelo de los Reyes, the last a subject also of *Under Three Flags* by Benedict Anderson.

18. Whether Paterno authorized the Tagalog as well as English translation of the novel is unclear. It seems likely.

19. See Edgar C. Knowlton Jr.'s "Philippine and Other Exotic Loan Words in Paterno's *Nínay*" for lists of words in various Asian languages, including Filipino vernaculars, Chinese, Japanese, and Tamil and various other Indian idioms, that Paterno also utilizes in the novel. The effect of their inclusion is likewise to imply his claim to a uniquely broad knowledge base.

20. "Visayans" may refer either narrowly to Cebuanos, a single ethnic group from the important, central island of Cebu who speak the Cebuano language, or broadly to an array of societies from the geographically middle part of the archipelago who live on various islands and speak sundry related languages.

21. Tik is not entirely accurate here, as slavery exists in her own community already. She is concerned, apparently, with the enslavement of all those on the island not already obliged to fan her.

22. This writer seems to be the famous Filipina actress and orator also known as Delfina San Agustín de González whose career spanned much of the twentieth century. As of 2011, a number of recordings of her reading poetry in Spanish by such luminaries as José Rizal and Rubén Darío were available on YouTube.

23. An abridged version of this dissertation is available elsewhere as *Literatura filipino-española* (*Spanish-Filipino Literature*) by Mercedes Conchú de Sánchez.

24. This text consists of two volumes whose page numbers partially overlap.

25. For the record, Federico's father dies of corruption and, apparently, memories of having led an evil life (202).

26. Matibag notes too that "The whole of *Nínay* is an extended act of mourning" (45).

27. In this scene, Carlos rushes heroically to rescue his girlfriend from the brigands but appears ridiculous in doing so: "Carlos resplandecía con su traje blanco como un cisne real cerniéndose en diferentes direcciones" ["Carlos shone in his white suit like a royal swan flapping his wings in different directions"] (190). When Berto recognizes his old friend, they chat for a bit. On learning that Nínay is Carlos's beloved, Berto orders her freed.

28. Perhaps in context, "lemon" makes more sense as a translation than the literal "lime."

29. Pilar's wealth includes her inheritance of her father's money and holdings, which she will receive when she comes of age, and the comforts of being adopted de facto by Nínay's father.

30. In comparison, the aforementioned Cuban novel *Sab* by Gómez de Avellaneda ends with none of its marginalized characters alive and in a position to effect social change. The title character, a slave with a heart of gold, is dead, as is the woman who represents the indigenous heritage of the island, as is the quasi-adopted girl who acts as a metaphorical sister to the virginal daughter who is the novel's heroine. That heroine, unlike Nínay, goes off unhappily with the aggressive foreign suitor and his sinister father.

Chapter 2

1. The assumption that 1898 marked the end of the Spanish empire is nearly universal and endlessly repeated. It is also wrong. Through much of the twentieth century, Spain clung on to the African colonies of Spanish Guinea and Spanish Sahara as well as ruled a protectorate in Morocco for nearly half a century.

2. Recent efforts at studying Martí and Rizal side by side include John Blanco's essay "Bastards of the Unfinished Revolution" and Koichi Hagimoto's dissertation, "Between the Empires: Martí, Rizal and the Limits of Global Resistance."

3. The verses in "Guantanamera" were taken from different stanzas in Martí's *Versos sencillos* (*Simple Verses*) and, after his death, put to melody. Seeger pays homage to Martí in his *Greatest Hits* album of 1967.

4. See Rafael for details on the geographies involved in the writing, publication, and circulation of the *Fili* (39–40).

5. Rizal himself visited the Americas only once, a brief journey across the United States in 1888.

6. *Mestizo* is a Spanish word borrowed from the New World colonies that indicates individuals of mixed ancestry. In the Philippines, it could signal *indio*-Chinese parentage as well as *indio-filipino* (creole).

7. The backlash over the Cavite Mutiny also impacted the family of Pedro Paterno directly. According to Resil Mojares, his father Maximo "was one of the victims in the crackdown. He was arrested on February 20, 1872, imprisoned in

Fort Santiago, and sentenced by a military tribunal to imprisonment in the Marianas for eight and six years, respectively, for the double offense of 'conspiracy against the national integrity and conspiracy against the constitution of the State.' The particulars of the charge were vague. . . . We do not have word on how these events affected the young Pedro Paterno. What we know is that he led the life of a gentleman of leisure, haunting Madrid's salon society, taking up such hobbies as fencing, and devoting himself to literary and scholarly pursuits" (*Brains*, 8). Mojares adds that Maximo Paterno was amnestied in 1874 and thereafter left Guam for Hong Kong, but "Like the other deportees, he was initially forbidden to go back to the Philippines by the terms of the amnesty. He eventually returned to Manila around 1882" (*Brains*, 8).

8. Today, the two national languages of the Philippines are Filipino, which is based on Tagalog, and English.

9. See Anderson's *Under Three Flags* for extensive historical contextualization that juxtaposes and interrelates events in the Philippines with those in Cuba before and after Rizal's death. The word *filibusterismo*, effectively meaning "subversion" in Rizal's novel, came into Spanish via Dutch. In the middle of the nineteenth century, it was primarily associated with Cuba and attempts by individuals based in the United States to overthrow Spanish power on that island by military means. See Rodrigo Lazo's "Los Filibusteros" for a discussion (in English) of the Cuban context that immediately preceded Rizal. Cuba was more important economically to the Spanish empire than the Philippines. Luis Mariñas estimates that the exports of the American island were approximately six times as great as those of the Asian archipelago (32).

10. See Anderson's *Under Three Flags* for a detailed account of this entire sequence of events.

11. In *Under Three Flags*, Anderson writes that Spanish was "understood by less than 5 percent of the Philippine population" (5). In his 1998 *The Spectre of Comparisons* (the title is a mistranslation from a phrase in the *Noli*), he suggests that "In the 1890s barely 3 per cent of the population knew 'Castilian'" (227). Whatever the true figure, the general point is the same: almost no *indio* in the Philippines could understand the language in which Rizal chose to write.

12. See Mojares, *Origins and Rise of the Filipino Novel*, for the prevailing account of how nonnovelistic texts in vernacular Filipino languages can be considered as antecedents of the novels in Spanish by Paterno and Rizal.

13. According to Mojares, Rizal in 1891 attempted "writing his third novel in Tagalog" but was "unable to complete the work" (*Origins*, 145). Only fragments of that novel are extant; they were published by Ambeth Ocampo as *Makamisa: The Search for Rizal's Third Novel* in 1992. The *Noli* and the *Fili* thus remain, writes Mojares, despite their creation in Spanish, "to date the most important literary works produced by a Filipino writer, animating Filipino consciousness to this day, setting standards no Filipino writer can ignore" (*Origins*, 140–41).

14. See the previous chapter for a discussion of these passages.

15. Given the economic pressures on individuals in the Philippines and the widespread illiteracy in Spanish, the Rizal Law takes into account the challenge

of compliance by including the following clauses as well: "It shall be obligatory on all schools, colleges and universities to keep in their libraries an adequate number of copies of the original and unexpurgated editions of the *Noli Me Tangere* and *El Filibusterismo,* as well as of Rizal's other works and biography. . . . The Board of National Education shall cause the translation of the *Noli Me Tangere* and *El Filibusterismo,* as well as other writings of Jose Rizal into English, Tagalog, and the principal Philippine dialects; cause them to be printed in cheap, popular editions; and cause them to be distributed, free of charge, to persons desiring to read them."

16. The spelling of "Simoun" even seems vaguely French, more so at least than Spanish or English. Work on the disastrous French effort in Panama was abandoned in 1889, that is, in between the publication of the *Noli* and the *Fili.* Construction of the canal as a "yankee" plan of the United States would not commence until 1904. The opening of the Suez Canal in 1869 had been of major importance to the Philippines, for it greatly quickened the voyage time between Spain and the archipelago. The entire generation of Filipinos who went to Europe in the last third of the nineteenth century traveled through it.

17. Anderson critiques Guerrero's bowdlerization of the *Noli* in the "Hard to Imagine" chapter of *The Spectre of Comparisons.* Although Guerrero's translations in the 1960s of both Rizal novels and his corresponding *The First Filipino: A Biography of José Rizal* dominated the market for nearly half a century, the following more recent translations now compete for space and readership: Ma. [María] Soledad Lacson-Locsin's translations into English of the *Noli* and the *Fili* in 1996 and 1997; Virgilio S. Almario's translations of both novels into Filipino (the national language based on Tagalog) in 1998; and Harold Augenbraum's translation into English of the *Noli* for Penguin Classics in 2006. Lacson-Locsin, whose versions seem to be increasingly disseminated, was born in the Philippines during the U.S. colonial period but into a family that still spoke Spanish as a primary language. Late in her life she was asked to undertake the translations because of her childhood proximity to the Spanish of Rizal's era. Her introduction to the *Fili* reads in part, "The *Fili* is just another story to tell, but in its intensity lie the thoughts and the soul of a people, their hopes and their future, the sweep and shape of their destiny, forming part of the parcel of a national heritage" (no pagination).

18. Nick Joaquín makes the case that Simoun/Simón was not meant to represent a revolution to come so much as resonate with those that had taken place decades earlier in the New World possessions of Spain: "During Rizal's youth, it looked as if what had happened in America would happen in the Philippines" (67). This makes particular sense given the abovementioned suggestions by López Jaena and Blanco that the Philippines was part of Latin America for centuries. Blanco develops Joaquín's argument further in "Bastards" (101).

19. López Jaena issued various wildly enthusiastic discourses on the subject of Columbus, even comparing him to Jesus ("La redención," 108–9). The implication is that 1492 marked the splendid start of the European explorations in the Americas to which the Philippines was gratefully heir.

20. The language overheard is not unequivocally English, as the narrator hastily notes that for the passer-by, "todo idioma hablado en Filipinas por los europeos, que no sea español, tiene que ser inglés" ["every language spoken in the Philippines by Europeans, if it were not Spanish, had to be English" (215). Nonetheless, the suggestion remains that the unnamed "estrangero" (the word translates as both "foreigner" and "stranger") is Leeds and that the idiom at hand is English.

21. The stereotype is itself a mishmash of vague associations. The talking head, for instance, though called a "sphinx" does not bear much resemblance to the mythological creature of that name.

22. There is a Chinese character of minor importance in the *Fili* who is represented in somewhat stereotypical terms, but this does not appear to be so much an orientalizing gesture as a weak, racialized attempt at a realistic depiction of a particular ethnic group in the islands. Perhaps significantly, however, the only chapter named after the Chinese character, entitled "Las tribulaciones de un chino" ("The Tribulations of a Chinese"), is the same in which the Leeds/sphinx episode commences. Rizal himself was partially of Chinese descent, which complicates consideration of this question.

23. Florentino Hornedo, the only scholar known to publish a substantive analysis of *Social Dawn*, classifies the collection as the first Filipino novels in Spanish since the *Fili*. This conclusion, however, requires numerous qualifications and caveats and ultimately perhaps will need to be discarded altogether. See chapter 3 for a discussion of the ambiguous history of Filipino novels in Spanish just before and after *Social Dawn*.

24. The word *vosotras* is the familiar, plural form of a collective "you," as opposed to the more formal *Ustedes*. The difference disappears in English, which does not make such distinctions. Here, "vosotras" underlines that an older person of a certain social prestige is addressing a younger, less socially prestigious readership.

25. Actual sex acts, though, are never described explicitly, as Paterno leaves those to ellipses and allusions and premature repentances. The occasional scene of disrobing does take place.

26. A more typical translation of "el *rapto*" would be "kidnapping" or "abduction," but "elopement" seems to make more sense in the context of the story. The customary implications of unwanted force in the word *rapto*, however, are difficult to ignore.

27. "Maring" does have some noteworthy features, though, such as a hero named Berto who recalls somewhat his homonym in *Nínay*. A Berto-Pilar/Berto-Maring comparison would make for an interesting paper. An extended treatment by Paterno of an industrialized work space (an environment also depicted in the *Social Dawn* story "El alma filipina" ["The Filipino Soul"]), "Maring" takes places in an archetypal "Fábrica" ["Factory"] with an evil Inspector who lusts after the eponymous virgin.

28. The meaning of "Espureas" is unclear.

29. By way of example, Mariñas includes in *Social Dawn* only four *novelas:* "El

alma filipina," "La fidelidad," "Los amores de Antipolo" and "Boda a la moderna" (38). Presumably, "Los amores de Antipolo" is the same text that Mojares notes as both "Los amores en Antipolo" and "Leyendas de Antipolo." Alinea lists five *novelas* in *Social Dawn:* "El alma filipina," "Boda a la moderna," "Amor del obrero filipino," "Los heraldos de la raza," and "Los amores de Antipolo." Sycip suggests there are six: "El Alma Filipina," "El Amor de un Día o El Pansol de Calamba," "Boda a la Moderna," "Amor de Obrero Filipino," "Los Heraldos de Mi Raza," and "Los Amores de Antipolo" (5). Zaragoza de Preysler, who does not mention *Nínay* at all, writes that "En sus últimos días, Paterno había dado una nueva orientación a su actividad literaria, publicando una serie de novelas cortas, bajo el título genérico de 'Aurora Social'" ["In his last days, Paterno had given a new orientation to his literary activity, publishing a series of short novels under the generic title of '<u>Social Dawn</u>'"] (cxci). She says that there are seven known *novelas:* "El alma filipina," "Amor de un día," "Boda a la moderna," "Amor del obrero filipino," "La braveza del bayani," "Los heraldos de la raza," and "Los amores en Antipolo" (cxci). Mojares gives the 1910 output as "Los Amores en Antipolo" (aka "Leyendas de Antipolo"), "En el Pansol de Kalamba. Amor de un Dia," "La Braveza del Bayaní," "El Alma Filipina," "La Dalaga Virtuosa y El Puente del Diablo," "Maring, Amor de Obrero filipino," and "Boda a la moderna," but indicates only the last four as part of *Social Dawn* (*Brains*, 534–35). Of the 1911 production, he lists "La Fidelidad," "Los Heraldos de la Raza," and "Los Ultimos Románticos en la Erupcion del Volcan de Taal" (*Brains*, 535). He adds, "It cannot be determined whether some titles announced by Paterno in the bookcovers of his works were actually published. These include: *Genesis Filipino, Haz el Bien y no Mires a Quien, Musica Tagalog: El Kumintang, El Kundiman, el Balitao y La Sampaguita, Gat-Maitan: Heroe de Kainta (Leyenda Filipina), Matando Fanatismos (Novela Filipina), El Codice de Bathala, El Dolor de Amor, S.M. La Usura. Las Espureas, Reglas del Juego de Chongka, El Fruto de dos Educaciones, Amores del Colegio, Matando Precausiones, El Martir de Golgota, El Ultimo Celaje*" (*Brains*, 530). Of these texts, it seems certain that "Haz el bien y no mires a quien" was published because it did receive votes in an *El Ideal* contest. The titles that sound most akin to others in *Social Dawn* are "Gat-Maitan: Heroe de Kainta (Leyenda Filipina)" ("Gat-Maitan: Hero of Kainta (Filipino Legend)") and "Amores del Colegio" ("High School Loves"). Interestingly, Torres's bibliography lists two unpublished novels by Paterno, *Matando fanatismos* (*Killing Fanaticisms*) and *El códice de Bathala* (*The Codex of Bathala*) in the same category of "Novelas" ["Novels"] as *Nínay* but apart from all the *Social Dawn* texts, which he places under the heading "Novelas cortas" ["Short Novels"] (xvi–xvii). The only other mention of these two unpublished novels is in Mojares's list above. Torres gives no dates or further information about either title, though the implication is that they are longer works than those of *Social Dawn*. It is possible that these manuscripts, if they ever did exist, still reside in a Paterno family library or other private collection somewhere in the Philippines or abroad. Such holdings may contain more examples of Filipino literature in Spanish than all the public and university libraries in the country combined. For example, Torres credits Antonio Paterno, nephew of the author, "por habernos permitido usar su biblioteca privada para facilitar nuestra investigación y por habernos proporcionado muchos informes valiosos y familiares sobre nuestro biografiado ["for having permitted us to use his private library to facilitate our investigation and for having provided us many valuable family reports about our biographical subject" (unnumbered acknowledgments page). Torres may have seen the unpublished novels as well as "Haz el bien y no mires a quien," which he also lists, in that private family collection. The Torres bibliography mentions also an extensive list of theatrical pieces written by Paterno, including the drama "El último celaje" (noted by Mojares above), six operas (three of them unpublished), eighteen comedies in one or two acts (mostly in Tagalog), five *zarzuelas* and one *sainete* (xviii–xix). Elderly descendants of Paterno still can be located in greater Manila and may possess some of the missing texts.

30. This is the only book on the subject. Though an indispensable reference, it actually does not mention any novel in Spanish other than *Nínay*, the *Noli*, and the *Fili*, which leaves out *Social Dawn* and later novels by other writers. The absence of any twentieth-century literature in Spanish in *Origins* may be due partly to the absence of translations into Tagalog or English of any Filipino novel in Spanish other than the first three and the much later novel *La loba negra (The Black Wolf)*, a forgery attributed to the nineteenth-century priest Jose Burgos. See Schumacher, *The Making of a Nation*, for information about *La loba negra*.

31. Why "The Virtuous Maiden" in particular keeps getting chosen for republication is puzzling. One possibility is that the text happened to be picked by the first one or two anthologizers and that created enough of a canonization to snowball. Another potential explanation is that its anthologizers find its folkloric qualities to be safely and usefully picturesque.

32. The following is a snapshot of the plots of all the known *novelas* uncommented directly in this chapter: (1) "El alma filipina" is dedicated to Filipina workers and features a young virgin who works in a Factory. The director of the factory seduces her and they live together and have a son. He leaves her to marry someone else, whereupon she kills him in the church on his wedding day. (2) "En el PANSOL de Kalamba: Amor de un día," features Miling and Maneng, a girl and boy who meet each other on the train to the Pansol waterfall and thermal springs. En route, she tells an old Filipino legend that explains the origins of the waterfall, which used to be a virgin in love with the light of the planet Jupiter. Miling and Maneng move in together but ultimately he leaves her for another woman. She eventually dies while being comforted by Noneng, a humble childhood friend from their old village who always had loved her. (3) "La braveza del bayani," set long ago by the Pasig River, focuses on an old, wealthy warrior who goes off to fight against Muslims. In his absence, his virginal daughter falls for a young serenader. When the warrior returns, he challenges the youth to a duel. The story ends with the impressed warrior giving the

hand of his daughter to the serenader. The young couple pledges in turn to bear him a son with "el espíritu libre é indomable de su abuelo" ["the free and indomitable spirit of his grandfather"] (23). (4) "Los heraldos de la raza" is a patriotic allegory of two boys from the provinces who rise to become political and social leaders of the country. Luis studies in the United States and this jumpstarts his political career, but Ramón, who stayed in the Philippines, ultimately rises even higher and becomes president. His final act in the *novela* is to tell Luis to kiss the national flag. (5) "La fidelidad" tells of the love between Paco, a humble fisherman, and Tríning, daughter of a fisherman. One day, Tríning is lost at sea in a tempest. Paco loses his sanity and wanders the beach, not knowing that Tríning has been rescued by a rich and passing ship pilot named Daniel. She lives with Daniel in luxury, unaware that Paco is now in an asylum. One day she returns to Manila and spots Paco on the asylum grounds. He is drawn toward her but does not know why. Eventually, she play-acts her earlier fisherwoman self in front of him and Paco recovers his sanity. They live together happily ever after.

33. The tourist's national identity is not mentioned but he is called a "tourista" rather than a "turista" (which would be the Spanish spelling), an orthographic anglicization. Also, he speaks with the girl "como si no fuera campesina, ni tagala" ["as if she were not a peasant or Tagalog"], which suggests that he is not a Tagalog himself (29). If he were a foreign national—and the alternative of his being a non-Tagalog Filipino seems low—the only serious possibility of that in 1910 would be as a U.S. citizen working with the occupation.

34. In 1910, Paterno published an ostensibly factual account of his experiences entitled *El pacto de Biyak-na-Bato* (*The Pact of Biyak-na-Bato*). Though appearing the same year as many of the *Social Dawn* texts, it follows more regimented organizing principles and is never included as part of the collection of *novelas*. This is not to say, however, that Paterno did not allow himself considerable creative leeway. Ambeth Ocampo, writing in the capacity of chairman of the National Historical Institute, prefaced a 2004 volume that contains an English translation of both *The Pact of Biyak-na-Bato* and *Nínay* by noting, "At one point we toyed with the idea of calling this book 'two works of fiction by Pedro Paterno' but decided to let perceptive readers decide from their own conclusions'" (foreword, vi).

35. Paterno, as usual, apparently thought very highly of his own work. For his Biyak-na-Bato efforts, according to Luis Eugenio Togores Sánchez, "pidió al Gobierno español la concesión de un ducado con grandeza de España, un millón de dólares y el nombramiento de representante de Filipinas en las Cortes. Nada de esto obtuvo" ["he asked the Spanish Government to give him the title of Grand Duke of Spain, a million dollars, and the appointment as representative of the Philippines in Parliament. He obtained none of this"] (726).

36. The massive eruption took place on January 20, 1911, but Paterno dates it as January 30 (title page). The reason for the discrepancy is unknown. Possibly, the second date is that on which he wrote the *novela*, but this seems unlikely.

Chapter 3

1. The Book of Acquisitions does not give the purchase date of any book on the page on which *Social Justice* is listed. Nearby pages list purchase dates of 1950 and late 1949.

2. MacArthur selected the Philippines as a battle site not out of military advisability but in order to satisfy a personal desire to fulfill his famous "I shall return" pledge. He had commanded U.S. forces in the Philippines until Japanese advances led to his relocation to Australia.

3. León María Guerrero is discussed in the *Fili* section of chapter 2 of this book. He is not to be confused with his grandfather of the same name. Paterno used a sketch by the painter Lorenzo Guerrero, the biographer's great-uncle and brother of the first León María Guerrero, as the cover for a printing of "La braveza del bayani." Evangelina Zacarías, the daughter of Fernando María Guerrero, won the 1935 Zóbel Prize (awarded for the best Filipino literature in Spanish) for a book of poetry. Her sister, Nilda Guerrero Barranco, won the 1964 Zóbel for a collection of prose. For a synopsis of the achievements of these and other Guerreros, see Anderson's *The Spectre of Comparisons* (247–49).

4. Alinea suggests that "El 'Periodo de Oro' empieza algunos años después de la muerte de Apolinario Mabini ocurrida el 13 de mayo de 1903 en Nagtahan y se extiende hasta el mes de enero de 1942, inmediatamente después de la ruptura de hostilidades entre los Estados Unidos de América y el Japón" ["The 'Golden Age' begins some years after the death of Apolinario Mabini on May 13, 1903, in Nagtahan and extends up to the month of January in 1942, immediately after the eruption of hostilities between the United States of America and Japan"] (125). Mariñas cites Alinea's position but adds, "Tal vez la última de dichas fechas hubiese que adelantarla, era evidente a partir de 1930, que no surgían ya nuevas figuras entre los escritores filipinos en castellano, eran éstos personalidades nacidas, en general, entre 1870 y 1900, es decir, al final de la era española cuando comenzaban a dar sus frutos las reformas educativas de 1863" ["Perhaps the last of these dates needs to be moved up. It was evident beginning in 1930 that new figures among the Filipino writers in Castilian were no longer appearing. These writers were people born, in general, between 1870 and 1900, that is to say, at the end of the Spanish era when the education reforms of 1863 began to yield fruit"] (51). Sycip prefers 1898–1942, which corresponds exactly to the occupation of the United States in between those of Spain and Japan (1). Tiamson Mendoza writes, "We can speak of a golden chapter of Philippine Poetry in Spanish that began with the works of Rizal and reached its peak in the 1930s" (112). Romanillos refers to the Golden Age as 1880 to 1940, which implies a starting date not of Rizal but of Paterno and his publication of *Sampaguitas* (43). Reyes Soriano chooses a Golden Age that starts with the death of Mabini in 1903 and ends in 1942, but she wrote a year after Alinea and likely based her timeline on his. Alinea's *Historia analítica,* an entrant in the 1964 Zóbel contest, is probably the most influential of all twentieth-century scholarship on Filipino literature in Spanish.

5. Florentino Rodao has suggested that, contrary to conventional belief in a gradual decline of Spanish in the archipelago after 1898, the language would not have been doomed had it not been for the devastations of World War II (personal communication, December 2008). For more of Rodao's insights on the historical interrelations of Spain and Asia, see http://www.florentinorodao.com/. Statistics that seem to support his argument appear in Mojares's *Origins,* where a table of Filipino periodicals in circulation in 1930, 1937, and 1940 actually shows a significant increase in hispanophone media in that decade: sixty Filipino periodicals in Spanish with a circulation of 182,318 jumps ten years later to eighty publications with 447,620 readers (374). No one seems to have combed through these newspapers and magazines for whatever fiction, poetry, and theater they might contain. Sporadic efforts in the second half of the twentieth century to publish periodicals in Spanish never achieved the heights of the prewar decades. Still today among the very elderly and the very elite there are native Spanish speakers in the Philippines, but there is no hispanophone community with a geographic center and material evidence (stores, newspapers, public spaces for entertainment, etc.) as before the war.

6. "Siglo de oro" has fallen out of use in recent decades in North American academic circles. Scholars now tend to prefer a broader and less hyperbolic term such as "Early modern Spain."

7. Additional information on texts submitted for the Zóbel Prize in the 1960s can be found in the various brief reports by Edgar C. Knowlton Jr., a U.S. scholar who saw a number of unpublished manuscripts in his trips to Manila and described them in the journal *Books Abroad.*

8. The library is the Filipinas Heritage Library in Malate, a subsection of greater Manila. It is open to the public for a small fee.

9. Regarding minor errors, for example, Brillantes writes of Buenaventura L. Varona (known by the pseudoynm of "Takio"), an honorable mention awardee of 1933 (no first prize was given that year), that "Very little data exist about [his] novel *El Nieto de Cabesang Tales,* and because it was unpublished, we can only theorize that it possibly was reminiscent of the agrarian rebel in Rizal's novel [the *Fili*]" (112). Several copies of Takio's fiction, however, survive in different Manila libraries. In addition, Brillantes refers twice to *Negros* by 1938 winner Francisco Varona as a "novel" and notes, "Unfortunately, not one copy of *Negros* exists" (138–39). Yet a microfilm of the text does survive, as does a complete translation of it into English that was serialized in the newspaper *Western Visayas Chronicle.* Moreover, both the microfilm and the translation reveal that *Negros* was a historical work rather than a novel. Such occasional inaccuracies should not diminish in any way the importance of *81 Years of Premio Zóbel* as a springboard to further research. Without Brillantes's bibliographic efforts, searches for many of the texts that she lists could not be undertaken because often no one would know they existed.

10. The publication date of *Bankruptcy of Souls* is always given as 1910. The last page of the novel, however, indicates that it was written, or at least concluded, in September and October of 1908 (360).

11. Balmori's third and final novel, *Los pájaros de fuego* (*The Birds of Fire*) was written during the Japanese occupation, three decades after *The Flower Was Stripped*. It was not published at the time. The manuscript survived the war only because Balmori buried the pages as he wrote them in crystal bottles under the garden of his house, which was repeatedly searched by Japanese troops.

12. Alinea's *Historia analítica de la literatura filipinohispana* (*Analytical History of Filipino-Hispanic Literature*), a nominee for the 1964 Zóbel award, has provided the names of numerous authors and titles for various later scholars. This has led to the repetition of his many invaluable contributions to the field but also his omissions. Apart from the well-known trio of early novelists (Paterno, Rizal, and Balmori), Alinea mentions all the same individuals as Hornedo sixteen years later: himself, the two Ripolls, Centenera, Abad, Teodoro, and Mercader, plus one whom Hornedo does not, Francisco Villanueva Jr. (94, 141). Alinea notes that Centenera, Rafael Ripoll, and he himself all serialized their novels in the Manila periodical *La vanguardia* (*The Vanguard*), an important clue for a future researcher interested in locating examples of postwar Filipino novels in Spanish (95). Rafael Ripoll won the 1939 Zóbel for a book of essays, not fiction. In *Historia analítica*, Alinea adds that two short novels by Villanueva are entitled *Las doce uvas de Navidad* (*The Twelve Grapes of Christmas*) and *El lago de los cisnes* (*Swan Lake*) (141); and that Teodoro and Mercader wrote the respective novels *Oleada o realidad* (*Wave or Reality*) and *El Super-economista* (*The Super-Economist*). All these middle to late twentieth-century texts remain unlocated to date. As for Alinea's own works, he wrote *Amor provinciano* (*Provincial Love*) in 1938. In 1941, he submitted to the Zóbel competition *La venganza de la sangre* (*The Vengeance of Blood*); and in 1961, he entered *Bajo las alas de mi bandera* (*Under the Wings of My Flag*) and *Libélulas del trópico* (*Dragonflies of the Tropics*). Some or all of these titles may have been novels. None of their texts is known.

13. Beyond the prize-winning novelists mentioned by Brillantes in her Zóbel retrospective, Tiamson Mendoza adds titles such as *El calvario de una artista* (*The Calvary of an Artist*) by Luis F. Nolasco in 1922, *Nitang* by A. R. (presumably the Anastacio mentioned above) Teodoro in 1935, *Cuando los troncos han caído* (*When the Trunks Have Fallen*) by Centenera in 1938; and various novels by Jose Flaviano Sanchez, a resident of Pampanga rather than greater Manila, including such titles as *Un caballero socarrón, Abrojos, Gay Caballero, El príncipe de Visayas,* and *Rosa de Manila* (*A Crafty Gentleman, Sufferings, Gay Gentleman, The Prince of the Visayan Islands,* and *Rose of Manila*) (117). Tiamson Mendoza makes special note of Centenera's novel *Tomor-Cheg* as perhaps "the last Filipino novel in Spanish, serialized in *El Debate* in 1969"; and of Jose E. Marco's *La loba negra* (*The Black Wolf*) of 1938, which the author "tried to pass off . . . as a novel purportedly written by Fr. Jose A. Burgos in 1869" and which has been translated into English and Tagalog (119). See Schumacher, *The Making of a Nation*, for a detailed analysis of the authenticity issues of *La loba negra*.

14. The other novel by Abad is *El último romántico* (*The Last Romantic*), which received a Zóbel honorable mention in 1928.

15. The judges were Epifanio de los Santos, Jaime C. de Veyra, and Trinidad H. Pardo de Tavera.

16. "Cuando se empeñan ellas" cannot be translated with precision until the text itself surfaces, as "se empeñan" can have multiple meanings. The "They" of the title, corresponding to "ellas," indicates female subjects but whether girls or women also will remain unclear until the *novela* is found.

17. Brillantes gives the author of *Ya hablo en español* as José Sadano rather than José Sedano, but this seems likely to be a typographical mistake (148). Alinea entered the Zóbel that year as well with *La venganza de la sangre* (*The Vengeance of Blood*), whose genre is unknown.

18. Two phrases here are unclear: "se les dará la absoluta" seems to have the sense that those soldiers who choose to stay in the Philippines will be given unconditional freedom from, or forgiveness of, any obligation to the departing Spanish regime; and "estoy yo, tan fresco" seems to imply that, after his decision to stay, Sedano feels vibrantly alive or as good as new.

19. Both men, like many *indio* elites, also had Chinese ancestry.

20. Cebuano is also known as Visayan, although technically this term refers to a family of languages in the central Philippines. Depending on context, "Visayans" may be synonymous with "Cebuanos" or indicate people(s) from the central Philippines in general.

21. This statement is the fifth and final section of Article II, "Declaration of Principles" (1).

22. Each story in *Social Justice* is independently numbered, so this citation is from the first page of "The Tragedy of a Peasant" rather than that of the whole manuscript.

23. The rocky waters prevented a landing proper, so eleven men stayed behind to safeguard the boats (87).

24. Pigafetta guessed over 1,050 (87). A Genoese who also survived the battle reckoned 3,000 to 4,000 (Pigafetta, 163).

25. It is possible that these javelins were actually cutlasses (Pigafetta, 163).

26. Mojares adds that "It is possible that other issues came out after 1912. . . . A large collection of 1904–1912 issues is with the New York Public Library" (*Cebuano*, 57).

27. According to Mojares, *Wala'y Igsoon* by Juan I. Villagonzalo was published earlier the same year (*Origins*, 170).

28. Alburo adds, "the novel is little more than an exemplum. As a narrative, it relies more on telling than showing. The setting has no clear function" (166). This criticism seems less applicable to *Social Justice,* but that collection was composed nearly thirty years later and Alviola might have developed his skills at writing fiction in the meanwhile.

29. This "Period of Emergence," as a chronological division of Philippine literary history, corresponds with no Golden Age time span for Filipino literature in Spanish (a taxonomy and tradition that Racho does not consider) proposed by other scholars nor with major historical events such as the Japanese invasion in World War II or Philippine independence in 1946.

30. Personal communication, summer 2008.

31. The table of contents of *Social Justice* lists the story instead as "Delante de la bandera," but that also translates to "Before the Flag."

32. It is conceivable that he might have written fiction in English and Tagalog too.

33. The "official website of Santander," defunct as of 2010, said unequivocally as late as November 2008 that "Santander was created in 1898" (http://www.santander.gov.ph/). The website *Cebu Daily* affirmed as late as July 2010 that "The town was created in 1898," but the source of its information is not known and may in fact be the vanished official city site (http://www.cebu daily.com/townsandcities/santander/). In any case, the general region of Santander evidently had been inhabited for centuries and possibly millennia. A new church seems to have been built in 1898 in correspondence to the creation of a local parish, and it may be that this development was and is considered by residents to mark the effective beginning of Santander as a municipal entity.

34. Interestingly, the decision by Gerardo to translate "No Vacancy" into Spanish implies that he anticipated a readership literate in the old imperial language but unable to understand such a relatively simple English phrase despite four decades already of the U.S. occupation.

35. The only previous implication of Ismael as a national subject rather than provincial or local is when he begins living in Kamiland and feels some nostalgia for "la tierra que meció su cuna . . . Filipinas" ["the land that rocked his cradle . . . Philippines"] (6). This phrasing is odd, though, because clearly his birthplace and childhood were defined by the village of Santander and not a larger concept of the nation. In any case, again here it is Kamiland that cues his Filipino identity into existence.

36. Mactan is separated from the much larger Cebu island by fewer than three thousand feet. Today, bridges connect the two. The international airport of Cebu is located in Lapu-Lapu City on Mactan.

37. The Spanish *extranjero* could also be translated as "foreigner," which if so rendered here would lessen the resonance with Exodus that Gerardo might have intended.

Chapter 4

1. This episode involved the king Humabon of Cebu; see the introduction to this book for a discussion of his actions vis-à-vis Magellan and his men.

2. In a spring 2011 article in *Foreign Policy*, Ken Silverstein describes current Equatoguinean reality in complementary terms: "Over the past 15 years, Exxon-Mobil, Hess Corp., and other American firms have collectively invested several billion dollars in Equatorial Guinea, which exports more of its crude to the U.S. market than any other country. Energy revenues have flowed into the pockets of the country's elite, but virtually none has trickled down to the poor majority. . . . Nearly four-fifths of its people live in abject poverty; child mortality has increased to the point that today some 15 percent of Equatorial Guinea's children

die before reaching age 5, making it one of the deadliest places on the planet to be young." He adds, "Equatorial Guinea's economy depends almost entirely on oil, which generated revenues last year of well over $4 billion, giving it a per capital annual income of **$37,900, on par with Belgium.** 'The oil has been for us like the **manna that the Jews ate** in the desert,' Obiang has said. It certainly has been for him. Obiang placed eighth on a 2006 list by Forbes of the **world's richest leaders,** with a personal fortune estimated at $600 million. His population hasn't fared so well. Human Rights Watch reports that one in three of Obiang's impoverished subjects dies before age 40."

3. The alleged absence of Filipino novelists in Spanish between Rizal and Balmori is complex and questionable and, pending further research, likely to be discarded eventually as an erroneous understanding of that era of literary production. For the moment, however, there is virtual unanimity among scholars regarding the gap between the two writers. See chapter 3 of this book for a fuller discussion of these matters.

4. Juan Tomás Ávila Laurel, a writer based mostly in Equatorial Guinea, is the most probable candidate to match Paterno in terms of copiousness of output. A case also could be made for Donato Ndongo-Bidyogo owing to his varied work as a scholar and novelist, produced largely in exile in Spain.

5. There is widespread disagreement over the translation of "calabó." It may refer to a type of tree found in Africa or in the tropics elsewhere.

6. Evita's *When the Combes Fought* is set on the Guinean mainland.

7. Ngom writes in another source that Daniel Jones Mathama is the nephew, rather than the son, of Maximiliano Jones ("African Literature," 589).

8. Since those references are invariably fleeting and almost always paraphrased, inaccuracies tend to appear that then multiply as they in turn are paraphrased by yet other scholars in other hasty sketches. One example of textual creep, for example, commences when Antonio M. Carrasco González describes Jones Mathama's background as that of "un fernandino—es decir, nacido en Fernando Poo de padres originarios de otros lugares de África—que ha estudiado y trabajado en España y tiene una educación que supera el ámbito de la colonia" ["a Fernandino—that is to say, born on Fernando Poo to parents originally from other places in Africa—who has studied and worked in Spain and has an education that exceeds the scope of the colony"] (248). Parsed closely, these phrases say nothing specific about Jones Mathama but are vaguely misleading. He is identified as a Fernandino, but the description of the ethnic group is questionable because it allows only for originators coming from Africa. Moreover, transitive logic suggests that Jones Mathama's own parents are of foreign birth, yet there is no hard proof of that in any known published documentation. His father may have been born elsewhere, but that remains a question, and there does not seem to be a single phrase anywhere that gives any information about his mother. The possible erroneousness of these two implications is exaggerated by Marvin A. Lewis, author of the only booklength overview in English of Guinean literature, when he writes, "Carrasco González notes further that Daniel Jones Mathama was born in Equatorial Guinea of foreign parents, educated at Oxford

University, and spent most of his life in Barcelona" (112). The first clause about birthplace is based on taking as factual Carrasco González's inaccurate generality about Fernandinos. Even if Jones Mathama's parents were indeed foreign born, not all Fernandinos' parents were. Indeed, by the twentieth century it was possible to have third- or even fourth-generation Fernandinos on Fernando Poo. Meanwhile, Carrasco González says nothing about Oxford or Barcelona, notwithstanding Lewis's attribution. Those details are surely taken from Ndongo-Bidyogo. On another note, Carrasco González adds that Maximiliano Jones was "de gran importancia en los últimos años españoles de Guinea" ["of great importance during the last Spanish years in Guinea"] but this timing is misplaced (248). Jones played a major role on Fernando Poo in the first third of the twentieth century but surely was dead by the time Spanish rule in the colony ended in 1968, given that by 1887 he was working as a "carpentry professor" (Liniger Goumaz, 22). The only published birth and death dates for Jones seem to be those by Ibrahim Sundiata, who gives his lifespan as 1870 to 1944 (*Equatorial Guinea*, 37). While there is no particular reason to disbelieve this information, Sundiata does not indicate his source for it and no corroborating documentation is otherwise available.

9. It seems likely that he knew Bubi as well, given that he was raised on Fernando Poo. And if his father was Nigerian, he also probably was conversant in one or more Nigerian languages.

10. Adding to these tensions is the discrepancy between the year of the contest and that of publication. *A Spear for the Boabí* appeared in print in 1962, not 1960. If the manuscript were submitted in 1960, then it must have been written in the late 1950s, probably over a long period given its sheer extension. That likelihood would place the writing of *A Spear for the Boabí* rather closer in time to Evita's *When the Combes Fought* of 1953.

11. Ngom published very similar versions of this assessment in 1995 ("Algunos aspectos," 93), 2000 ("Introducción," 20), 2001 ("The Missing Link," approx. 6), and 2003 ("African Literature," 589).

12. See Dunzo, "Hispanic Africa"; Lifshey, "And So the Worm Turns"; and Ugarte, *Africans in Europe*.

13. Alfonso XIII was the king of Spain until 1931, when he fled the country and was replaced by the democratic Second Spanish Republic. That was the same year in which Jones Mathama went to Barcelona from Oxford according to Ndongo-Bidyogo, although Castillo Barril says he arrived two years earlier. The Republic later fell to the fascist forces of Franco.

14. The use of English here and occasionally elsewhere in *A Spear for the Boabí* is a case of code-switching that deserves sustained analysis in a different study. Its origins may lie in the anglophone elements of the Fernandino creole and in the professional anglophone background of Jones Mathama. The inverted and nonliteral self-translation he inserts here, in which he first writes a sentence in English and then parenthetically offers it in Spanish to a presumedly monolingual reader, is a particularly interesting gesture. Its pedantry notwithstanding, the self-translation carries again the political charge of implicitly asserting a

knowledge base that is superior to that of a Spanish reader who knows neither English nor anything about Spanish Guinea.

15. Carlos González Echegaray, the Spaniard who edited and prologued Evita's *When the Combes Fought* in 1953, wrote in 1989 that he had found partial proof of a third lengthy text from the colony: "En 1967 un escritor fang, Marcelo Asistencia Ndongo Mba, que solía usar el seudónimo 'Mandongo', publica un folletón en el semanario de Bata 'Potopoto' titulado *La tumba,* cuya conclusión no he podido constatar por hallarse incompleta la colección de aquel periódico en la Hemeroteca Nacional; sólo llega al capítulo XX" ["In 1967 a Fang writer, Marcelo Asistencia Ndongo Mba, who usually used the pseudonym 'Mandongo,' published a long pamphlet in the weekly newspaper *Potopoto* of Bata entitled *The Tomb,* whose conclusion I have not been able to confirm because I found that the collection of that newspaper in the National Periodical Library is incomplete; it extends only to chapter 20"] ("Etapas," 44). González Echegaray adds that the text revolves around "la vida de un hechicero fang" ["the life of a Fang witch doctor"] and that the author followed it a year later with a shorter but more complete text with a different title and a similar theme (44). González Echegaray seems to imply that these texts are fictional but does not say so outright. It is not clear whether the first text was ever finished by its author or how long it is. The quantity of chapters, however short they might be, would seem to point to at least a novella rather than a short story. *The Tomb* does not seem to be mentioned anywhere else in existing scholarship. Donato Ndongo-Bidyogo does write in his 1984 anthology of Guinean literature that Ndongo Mba was "el escritor más leído de Guinea antes de su independencia" ["the most read Guinean writer before independence"] (96). Ndongo-Bidyogo reproduces in that anthology a short rhyming fable and a brief poem about death by Ndongo Mba, which is all that he believes to remain of a prolific oeuvre. Unaware that the prose that González Echegaray would find still survived in the National Periodical Library in Spain, Ndongo-Bidyogo laments that the dictatorial regime of Macías deliberately destroyed everything else by Ndongo Mba, including his contributions to "*Poto-Poto*" (95). In the larger and only other collection of Guinean literature, published in 2000 and edited by Ndongo-Bidyogo and Ngom, two more narratives attributed to Ndongo Mba appear. His name, however, is followed by a question mark, as if his authorship of those texts is in doubt (93). The longer of the pieces does include the word *tumba* in its title, "Mientras la tumba brama en su selvática canción" ("While the Tomb Roars in Its Sylvan Song") and contains six very short chapters, but it was published originally in the periodical *La Guinea Española* (*Spanish Guinea*) in 1968 and does not seem to be the more extensive narrative partially located by González Echegaray (100). In a biographical blurb, Ndongo-Bidyogo writes that Ndongo Mba was an "integrante de la primera generación de escritores guineanos en lengua española . . . Durante la dictadura de Francisco Macías, fue víctima moral psicológica y física de la irracionalidad del nguemismo [la política del régimen]. Toda su obra literaria fue quemada por ser «subversiva»" ["member of the first generation of Guinean writers in the Spanish language

. . . . During the dictatorship of Francisco Macías, he was a moral, psychological and physical victim of the irrationality of Nguemism (the policies of the regime). All his literary work was burned for being 'subversive' "] (458).

Chapter 5

1. The prize reopened in 1974 but with the eligibility rules changed so that awardees no longer had to be authors but only individuals who had promoted Spanish culture in some way in the Philippines. Recipients thus came to include language teachers and members of the national elite quite removed from the production of literature in Spanish in the archipelago.

2. According to Mbare Ngom, the "folleto titulado *Nueva narrativa guineana,* que fue publicado en Madrid probablemente en los años 70, es el único texto de ficción de ese período" ["short work entitled *New Guinean Narrative,* which was published in Madrid probably in the 1970s, is the only fictional text of that period"] ("Afro-fascismo, 391). Sabrina Brancato writes that "The only works in prose to be published in this period were four short stories collected in a small volume entitled *Nueva narrativa guineana* [New Guinean Fiction] in 1977, among which we find two of the most beautiful tales of exile: Francisco Zamora Loboch's 'Bea' and Donato Ndongo's 'El sueño' [The dream]" (11). An accompanying footnote indicates that the narratives were published in Madrid by "U.R.G.E." (11). Ignacio Tofiño-Quesada, however, says that a short story published in Madrid by "URGE" in 1977 entitled "La última carta del padre Fulgencio Abad, CMF" ("The Last Letter of Father Fulgencio Abad, CMF") was written by an Equatoguinean named Maplal Loboch who, for a first-person narrator, "chooses the voice of a white Spaniard, but he appropriates it and uses it to criticize the Spanish administration" (145). The Spanish character is a Claretian missionary who casts doubt on the efficacy of the evangelizing project. It is unclear whether this text, which like the story "Bea" mentioned by Brancato was authored by someone with the surname "Loboch," was part of the *Nueva narrativa guineana* collection or not. Regarding texts published inside Equatorial Guinea during the Macías years, Ngom adds that "no text came off the Guinean presses, except, of course, pamphlets in praise and favor of the regime" ("African Literature," 590). The rubric "Years of Silence" was used by Donato Ndongo-Bidyogo in an interview with Ngom in August 1992, who in turn increased its currency in his sundry publications (Ngom, "Introducción," 21). Ndongo-Bidyogo utilized the same construction earlier as the title of the lengthy last section of his nonfiction study *Historia y tragedia de Guinea Ecuatorial* (*History and Tragedy of Equatorial Guinea*) of 1977. Ndongo-Bidyogo and Ngom have dominated individually and collectively the early scholarship on Guinean literature to such a great extent that their literary histories and interpretations have become canons in their own right, establishing frameworks and verdicts that only in the first decade of the twenty-first century, though still quite influential, began to be questioned. The sheer repetition of Ngom's studies—he regularly republishes verbatim or near-verbatim passages of his own

work in different forums—has no doubt amplified their impact. This holds true even with inaccurate and dubious statements, such as when he wrote in 1995 of María Nsue Angüe's novel *Ekomo* that "lo interesante en esta novela es el enfoque narrativo desde la perspectiva de Ekomo, el personaje masculino y protagonista del relato. Eso le confiere cierta legitimidad al discurso femenino de María Nsue" ["The interesting thing in this novel is the narrative focus from the perspective of Ekomo, the male character and protagonist of the story. That confers a certain legitimacy upon the feminine discourse of María Nsue"] ("Algunos aspectos," 97). This pronouncement is repeated word for word in his introduction five years later to a major anthology of Guinean literature coedited with Ndongo-Bidyogo, with the only change being typographical: the word "legitimidad" has quotation marks around it (Introducción, 26). The statement is counterfactual in that the novel is not from the perspective of Ekomo but from that of Nnanga, his wife; and that it is Nnanga, not Ekomo, who is the protagonist. An additional problem is the suggestion that the author's "feminine discourse" only acquires legitimacy if authorized by a male character, a depiction that in any case, if true, would paradoxically negate the possibility of "feminine discourse." The work of Ndongo-Bidyogo and Ngom from the 1970s through the turn of the century is foundational and remains very important, opening as it did spaces for nearly all other literary scholarship on Guinea, but even the most meritorious critiques should not be fetishized.

3. There probably were some Filipino novels in Spanish written after 1960 that were never published or that were serialized in newspapers or magazines, but this remains unproven unless such texts surface.

4. In the 2010 novel *The Cobra,* Forsyth returned to the theme of fictionalized political violence in a small West African state, based again in part on his own experiences. This time the setting is the Portuguese-speaking country of Guinea-Bissau.

5. The other novel is *Dark Inheritance,* a potboiler from 2001 by W. Michael Gear and Kathleen O'Neal Gear. It is notably worse than *Chromosome 6.*

6. There is no consensus among scholars as to how to refer to the names of Equatoguinean authors. For example, those critics who are personal friends with the writers, which is very frequently the case, tend to follow even in published essays the Guinean custom of using the first two names, e.g., "María Nsue." Whatever the cultural justification for this approach, it is likely to appear to most readers as surprisingly informal and undistanced, as well as not in keeping with standard procedure in other fields of literary criticism.

7. Ilombé's surname is sometimes spelled Ilonbé.

8. Pope John Paul II also believed that the Obiang regime promised better days. In a 1982 visit to Malabo, according to the *Washington Post,* he affirmed, "I am sure the moral reserves of the Guinean people will bring about a climate of proper morality, both public and private, and lead to a real spiritual and material progress.' He was greeted by President Theodore Obiang Nguema" ("Pope in Equatorial Guinea," A27). The analysis by the pope proved inaccurate.

9. Leoncio Evita's *When the Combes Fought* of 1953 was republished in 1996 and Donato Ndongo-Bidyogo's *Shadows of Your Black Memory* of 1987 was republished in 2000 and 2011.

10. There are no well-known female authors among the earliest Filipino writers in Spanish, though from the second quarter of the twentieth century onward a number of women did win the Zóbel Prize. Research into hispanophone periodicals in the first quarter of the century, however, may reveal published fiction and poetry by a number of Filipinas.

11. See, for example, "Los territorios de la identidad" by Lola Aponte-Ramos, "'Materia reservada' No More" by Nicole Price, and "Entre la espada y la pared" by Dorothy Odartey-Wellington.

12. The author of the thesis, Anna Mester, emphasizes that the novel develops beyond the ethnic and national categorizations to which it is typically consigned. She offers transatlantic readings of certain passages and argues that Nsue Angüe as a writer and *Ekomo* as a novel should be contextualized as Spanish rather than exclusively (as is almost always the case) as Guinean and African. Another of the rare attempts at situating *Ekomo* beyond its conventional national or ethnic frameworks is a shorter, also recent study by Alain Lawo-Sukam that compares it to *The Trial* by Franz Kafka and *Chronicle of a Death Foretold* by Gabriel García Márquez. "El mundo kafkiano y el de macondo," suggests Lawo-Sukam, "no eran tan extraños a la realidad africana llena de fantasías y de magias" ["The worlds of Kafka and of Macondo were not so foreign to the African reality full of fantasies and magic"] (69).

13. The first novelist to write of the remaining major ethnic group, the Annobonese, would be Juan Tomás Ávila Laurel in *Áwala cu sangui* (*Áwala with Blood*) of 2000. The novel, notwithstanding its title, is written in Spanish.

14. Lumumba and his death in 1961 were once broadly familiar to many Africans and some Europeans, but probably not so to an isolated Spanish population then stagnating under Franco or to the potential readership for *Ekomo* in Spain a generation later. It seems likely that the Lumumba reference might only be caught en masse by some readers of the later French translation, who possibly would have greater familiarity with twentieth-century African history because of the more extensive French involvement in the continent.

15. As with *A Spear for the Boabí*, the title character of the novel is often mistaken in scholarship as the protagonist. Marvin Lewis, for instance, author of the only book in English on Guinean literature, affirms inaccurately that "Ekomo is the focus of most of the novel" (131).

16. Carlos González Echegaray, who prologued Leoncio Evita's *When the Combes Fought* in 1953 with a similar Castilian disapproval of Guinean Spanish, commented nearly half a century later on *Ekomo* that Nsue Angüe "trata de eliminar los guineísmos, resultando un castellano correcto" ["tries to eliminate Guineaisms, resulting in a correct Castilian"] ("La novela," 45). He and Granados do not find problematic their roles as linguistic ethnic cleansers. Similarly, Manuel Castillo Barril says of Daniel Jones Mathama's *A Spear for the Boabí*, "en

ocasiones se le escapa alguna que otra vulgaridad, con giros y expresiones que se me dan por llamar 'guineos'" ["on occasion he lets loose one or another vulgarity with turns of phrases and expressions that I call 'Guineaisms'"] (62).

17. The preface by Granados was not included in either the French translation of the novel or its second edition in Spanish, doubtless because of its paternalistic (at best) overtones. It should have been retained, however, because excising the original remarks of a neocolonialist, unfortunate as they may be, is an act of censorship as much as an attempt to edit out indigenous voices. The powers that Granados wielded over the novel, the way he frames it, and the implicit macrocontext of his presence all condition the production, content, and reception of *Ekomo*. At an absolute minimum, readers of later editions should be told explicitly that the original preface existed and offered justifications for its absence.

18. The title of the introduction, "El marco" ("The Framework"), proved to be self-fulfilling in a larger sense, as it set the frame for both the anthology and the entire first generation of criticism on Guinean literature.

19. The name of the narrator/protagonist may confuse many readers because she is not identified as Nnanga until fairly late in the novel, while her grandmother is referred to earlier by the same name. The 2007 reedition of the novel attempts to clarify that there are two Nnangas by amending an early line from the original edition that reads "la voz de Nnanga me viene a la mente" ["the voice of Nnanga comes to my mind"] (26). The same passage in the second edition is rendered "la voz de Nnanga, mi vieja abuela, me viene a la mente" ["the voice of Nnanga, my old grandmother, comes to my mind"] (31). This revision may help the reader follow the plot better but it also lessens any implied symbolic correspondence between the two women. Nnanga the narrator/protagonist accrues additional monikers in the course of *Ekomo,* such as "Paloma de Fuego" ["Dove of Fire"] when she becomes a dancer, and Sara, her Christian name.

20. The death of the "great chief" augured by the ceiba also may resonate for some readers with the murder of Lumumba. That historical event, however, is not tied into the plot of the novel in any organic way, for Lumumba is not mentioned again after the early and ephemeral reference to him.

21. Soon after the lament of "mother Africa," Nfumbaha emerges from the forest metamorphosed into an old man. He tells the villagers that he had shot a deer in the woods who turned out to be the son of his (biological and therefore continental) mother and consequently his own brother; added to his trespasses thereby is fratricide. After relaying this story, "el viejo-joven cayó al suelo muerto, cubriéndose rápidamente de escarcha" ["the old man-youth fell dead to the ground, covering himself up rapidly with frost"] (88). Having violated still more ancestral prohibitions, he is consumed by a white coldness that symbolically recollects his Europeanization.

22. Establishing the birth date of a living author and the publication date of a recent novel should not be challenging, yet so it is in the case of Nsue Angüe. In the 1993 article that brought Guinean literature to the attention of many scholars, Ngom gives her birth year as 1950 and the year of publication of

Ekomo as 1985 ("La literatura africana," 416). In a 1995 article, however, he amends the publication date to 1984 ("Relato," 81). In the 2000 anthology of Guinean literature that Ngom edited with Ndongo-Bidyogo, Nsue Angüe's birth year is given as 1945 (*Literatura de Guinea Ecuatorial,* 459). In a 2003 translation to English of the 1995 article, Ngom shifts her birth year from 1950 to 1948 ("Narrative," 303). Also in 2003, Jorge Salvo writes that *Ekomo* has a printer's note dated 1986 (3). The 2007 reedition of *Ekomo* in Spanish lists the birth year as 1948 but returns the publication year to 1985 (front cover flap). These discrepancies are of very minor importance and would not seem to affect interpretations of *Ekomo* in a substantive way, yet the differences raise important issues about the potential unreliability of any claims about the author and text that are rather more subjective and complex. Determining the extent to which Nsue Angüe spent her formative years in Spain, for example, would be relevant to an assessment of her biographical biculturalism, but here too facts are hard to come by. Nsue Angüe says that she moved to Spain when she was eight years old ("María Nsué Angüe," 117). Salvo writes that she emigrated when she was fourteen years old (3). The 2007 edition of *Ekomo* in Spanish says she moved to Spain when she was ten years old and lived there "hasta el año 1972 en que vuelve a Guinea a pasar sus vacaciones" ["till the year 1972, when she returned to Guinea for her vacation"] (inside cover flap). This itself is a quietly bizarre statement, with Equatorial Guinea in 1972 in the midst of such Macías horrors as the event a year earlier when Alfred Erdos's cook was skinned alive in front of him by goons of the regime. In the early 1970s, with much of the country careening toward death or exile, the concept of heading to Equatorial Guinea for "vacation" needs, at the very least, to be problematized.

23. Personal communication, August 2009. There are several unnamed "locos" who appear in the medicine man chapter. The one most likely to be Nfumbaha is described as "un joven de unos veinte años, a quien trajo su padre explicando que el muchacho había llevado varios años de estudios en Europa. Su hijo sacaba siempre las mejores notas, hasta que le dio por irse con malos amigos que le enseñaron a drogarse, entonces le retiraron la beca y había sido enviado a su país" ["a young man of some twenty years who was brought by his father, who explained that the boy had spent various years studying in Europe. His son always got the best grades until he let himself hang out with bad friends who taught him to take drugs. Then they took away his scholarship and he had been sent back to his country"] (127). This character tells the medicine man that he doubts that he is crazy, notwithstanding the beliefs of everyone else.

24. Personal communication, August 2009.

25. Viewed as a matter of realpolitik, the appearance of a French version could be judged as part of the French efforts over the decades to replace relatively weak Spain as the dominant European country in Equatorial Guinea. With Río Muni bordered by the francophone nations of Cameroon to the north and Gabon to the south and east, the policies of France toward Equatorial Guinea in general reflect an assumption that Equatorial Guinea rightfully belongs within its sphere of interest and influence in Africa.

26. To support her argument, Odartey-Wellington judiciously uses an ellipsis to juxtapose two passages from the last page of *Ekomo* in a way that emphasizes a seeming causality between them, so that the first passage, which does explicitly foreground the suffering of collectivities of women, leads directly to the second that cites the novel's concluding line, "How tremendously alone am I!" (174). In the excised sentences replaced by the ellipsis, however, Nnanga turns her tormented thoughts inward and addresses exclusively herself as an ineffably isolated tragic figure hovering on "La frontera entre la vida y la muerte" ["The border between life and death"] (Nsue Angüe, 194). The novel ends with her just as isolated from the collectivities of women—she is "tremendously alone," after all—as she is from Ekomo and all the other forces that careen in and out of the novel. If anything, the unviability of every phenomenon in the narrative, including sorority, ultimately has freed the strong and rebellious Nnanga from identification with traditional gender roles rather than solidified her metonymic relationship to the same.

27. Nnanga carries this larger social import in her surname. According to Nicole Price, "her last name Abaha is the same word that is used to describe the common building in which the community goes to settle problems or discuss the business of the community" (20).

28. Such is the limited circulation of Guinean literature that the emergence of new novels in the mid-1980s was not necessarily evident even at the time. As late as 1986, Annette Dunzo wrote that "The extreme paucity of creative writing in Spanish during the colonial period, and its total absence since independence, do not augur well for the future of literature in a European language in that unfortunate part of the Black continent" (329).

29. See "Imagined Temporalities" by Adam Lifshey for a contrast of *The Reencounter* with a Senegalese novel *Ex-père de la nation* (*Ex-father of the Nation*) by Aminata Sow Fall.

30. It is apparently due to Balboa Boneke's poetry and nonfiction, rather than his novel, that Igor Cusak suggests that he maintains a "posición prominente en la aparición de una literatura nacional guineoecuatoriana" ["prominent position in the appearance of a national Equatoguinean literature"] (172).

31. Marvin Lewis writes that Balboa Boneke "initially worked with the power structure [of the Obiang regime] when he returned to Equatorial Guinea, hoping to build a better nation. However, for many Equatorial Guinean writers who returned home, the gap between expectation and realization was profound" (38–39).

32. See chapter 4 for a fuller consideration of Fernandinos.

Chapter 6

1. Although Ndongo-Bidyogo is probably considered in general to be the most important Equatoguinean intellectual and the leading voice among exiles against the Obiang government, his historical relationship with that regime is complicated by his repeated willingness to serve it. According to Liniger-

Goumaz, in 1985 Ndongo-Bidyogo was "adviser to the minister of information, culture, and art. . . . In 1986 he became president of the Guinextebank. During the same year, he was arrested and accused of complicity in the attempted coup d'etat by Mba Oña. . . . Obiang Nguema granted him pardon in 1987. In 1993, Ndongo Bidyogo was counsellor to the president for economic affairs . . . [in 1994] he was again forced to seek asylum abroad. . . . In early 1996, he exposed the electoral maneuvering of the 'eternal candidate' Obiang Nguema" (295–96).

2. A *bubisher* is a type of bird that lives in the Western Saharan desert (Alvarado, 10).

3. Jacinto López Gorgé writes in a preface to the 1985 anthology that "La lengua literaria española une en esta ocasión, como en otras precedentes—recordemos, por poner un ejemplo, las revistas hispanoárabes *Al-Motamid y Ketama,* que algunos han olvidado" ["The Spanish literary language unites on this occasion, as in preceding ones—let us remember, to give an example, the Hispano-Arab magazines *Al-Motamid* and *Ketama,* which some have forgotten"] (17–18). Two of the short stories in the anthology, he notes, had appeared previously in *Ketama,* a literary supplement of the periodical *Tamuda,* published in Tetouan (19–20). Fourteen issues of *Ketama* came out between 1953 to 1959 (20). López Gorgé was its director (20). He adds that *Al-Motamid* "era fundamentalmente revista de poesía" ["was fundamentally a poetry magazine"] (18). Its full name, however, was *Al-Motamid (Verso y Prosa) (Al-Motamid (Poetry and Prose))* and it ran from 1947 to 1956, first in Larache and then in Tetouan, for a total of thirty-three issues (20).

4. Statistics on the Guinean residents of Gabon are imprecise and not always reliable. The best information on refugees in general from the Macías regime is from Max Liniger Goumaz, who writes that in 1979 they "numbered as many as 120,000—including 65,000 in Gabon (official estimate); 35,000 in Cameroon; 5,000 in Nigeria; and 9,000 in Europe (of which 8,500 went to Spain)" (409). By 1992, according to Liniger Goumaz, there appeared to be 80,000 refugees living in Europe, while "Gabon confirmed that there were 60,000 Equato-Guinean refugees with political or economic grounds. . . . In 1996, the number of Equato-Guineans who had chosen to seek asylum abroad was still estimated to be 110,000, which represents nearly a quarter of the total population" (410–11).

5. Rich has confirmed the apparent absence of published Equato-Gabonese literature ("Re: Nous, les equatos").

6. Rich notes in passing that Guinean immigrants also live in Nigeria ("Nous," 127). Their oral narratives too merit listening and attempts at analysis.

7. J. M. [Juan Manuel] Davies, a Guinean writer based in New Jersey, seems to be the only published Guinean creative writer who lives permanently in the United States. Coincidentally, he also happens to be a descendant of Maximiliano C. Jones, the father of the novelist Daniel Jones Mathama.

8. Whinnom suggested that Zamboangueño "has fared best, perhaps" of the different dialects of Chabacano but he concluded nonetheless that "This language also, therefore, is doomed to extinction, and that adprobably [sic] in the space of another generation" (14, 15).

9. The last word of the Chabacano postcard refers to Paterno's pretensions to royal lineage. According to Resil Mojares, "Claiming descent from Tagalog nobility, he affected the title of *Maguinoo* ("lord")" (*Brains*, 11). The word *capatid*, which is of vernacular rather than Spanish etymology, can be translated as "brotherhood" or "fraternity" and likely refers to the cohort of Filipino intellectuals in Spain who knew each other and produced such texts as the *Solidarity* newspaper. The repeated use of "di" to indicate future tense is a marker of the Caviteño dialect of Chabacano, that is, the version from the community of Cavite that is relatively near Manila (not to be confused with the now extinct Ermitaño, which was spoken even closer to the capital) (Quilis and Casado-Fresnillo, 458). Zamboangueño, the most spoken dialect of Chabacano that is centered on a peninsula extremely far away from Manila, uses "ay" instead of "di" to construct the future tense (Quilis and Casado-Fresnillo, 458).

10. The categorization of Balmori as the third Filipino novelist in Spanish needs qualifications and perhaps elimination altogether. See chapter 3 for a discussion of this issue.

11. Whinnom reprints the entire story with abundant lexical glosses (23–49). The narrative is also available without Whinnom's addenda as part of the twelfth volume online of *Revista filipina* (*Filipino Magazine*) in spring 2008 at http://revista.carayanpress.com/arena.html. This journal is not the early twentieth-century periodical of the same name.

12. Romanillos reprints the poems and adds English translations (198–200).

13. Other sources of Chabacano literature include *La lengua española en Filipinas* (*The Spanish Language in the Philippines*) by Antonio Quilis and Celia Casado-Fresnillo of 2008. This tome offers more than fifty pages of Chabacano texts, each followed by a translation into Spanish and many accompanied by a phonetic transcription. Compact discs included with new copies of the book offer oral recordings of a number of the texts. Earlier collections of Chabacano literature are Teresita La. Perez-Semorlan's self-published *Mga Leyendang Chavacano* of 1984, which contains sixty-seven legends in Chabacano that can be more or less understood by Spanish speakers even if they cannot read the accompanying translations and commentary in Tagalog; *Zamboanga Chabacano Folk Literature,* a compilation gathered from 1988 to 1990 mostly from elderly oral informants plus "old written records, diaries, magazines, yearbooks and periodicals found in archives of private and public libraries" (vii); and Sonia S. Sicat's *Chavacano Folk Music-Literary Pieces: A Spanish Progeny* of 2003. Sicat, who collaborated with the *Zamboanga Chabacano Folk Literature* project more than a decade earlier, writes that her text is the first of its kind on Chabacano literature because it goes beyond "compendiums of folktales, poems, proverbs, riddles, songs, myths and legends. No study to date has looked into the textual meaning and the rhythmic pattern and meter of the lines much less to capture and transcribe these into musical compositions and pieces" (vi). A thorough account of all the prose and photo collections in Chabacano held by local libraries, parishes, private collectors, and government offices as of June 1991 is in Josefina B. Malindog's graduate thesis "Chabacano Literature in Zamboanga

City: An Annotated Index." Only a few of the hundreds of texts that she found, however, are literary in the traditional sense: a one-act play in Chabacano, five poems, and a short story (163–64). Combing the multitude of linguistic studies of the language might prove the best way of finding further examples of creative texts. For instance, Michael Lawrence Forman's 1972 dissertation "Zamboangueño Texts with Grammatical Analysis: A Study of Philippine Creole Spanish" contains a variety of manifestly literary narratives with such titles as "A folktale: Monkey and Turtle," "An origin story: Pulumbato," and "Tale of the dragon and the three brothers," all in Chabacano and accompanied by English translations (30–52). Another resource is YouTube, where videos of Zamboanga culture are beginning to abound. Apparently, the only books to concentrate on the Cavite variant of Chabacano are *Chabacano Studies: Essays on Cavite's Chabacano Language and Literature* by Romanillos, which is an anthology of his scholarly papers, and *Chabacano . . . for Everyone: A Guide to the Chabacano Language* by Enrique [Ike] R. Escalante, which includes some poetry and short prose in Caviteño at the end. There is also at least one graduate student thesis, "An Analysis of the Basic Structures of Cavite Chavacano" by Librada C. Llamado.

14. Even seemingly unimpeachable projects of the recovery of Filipino texts in Spanish can carry neoimperial or nostagically imperial overtones. It is not a coincidence that the first major book publications of fiction in Spanish in the Philippines in half a century, outside of Rizal reprints, is originating not among Filipinos but from the Cervantes Institute, a cultural arm of the Spanish government. The erstwhile empire can afford to lose money in printing fine editions of old texts. Its series *Clásicos Hispanofilipinos* (*Filipino Hispanic Classics*), launched in 2010, is supposed to put out two books a year as noncommercial archival products. These texts are not intended for retail in the Philippines.

Works Cited

Agoncillo, Teodoro A. *History of the Filipino People*. 8th ed. Quezon City: Garotech, 1990. Print.

Alburo, Erlinda K. "A Sociological Study of the Pre-War Cebuano Novel." Thesis. Silliman U, 1987. Print. Available at the Cebuano Studies Center of the U of San Carlos in Cebu City, Philippines.

Alinea, Estanislao B. *Historia analítica de la literatura filipinohispana (desde 1566 hasta mediados de 1964)*. Manila/Ciudad de Quezon [Quezon City]: Imprenta Los Filipinos, 1964. Print.

Alvarado, María Jesús. Prólogo. *Bubisher: Poesía saharaui contemporánea*. Ed. María Jesús Alvarado. Las Palmas de Gran Canaria: Puentepalo, 2003. 9–11. Print.

Anderson, Benedict. *Imagined Communities: Reflections on the Origins and Spread of Nationalism*. Rev. ed. London: Verso, 1991. Print.

Anderson, Benedict. *The Spectre of Comparisons: Nationalism, Southeast Asia and the World*. London: Verso, 1998. Print.

Anderson, Benedict. *Under Three Flags: Anarchism and the Anti-Colonial Imagination*. London: Verso, 2005. Print.

Añoranza: Imágenes del pueblo saharaui. Ed. La Associació d'Amics I Amigues del Poble Sahrauí de les Illes Balears. 2002. Print.

Antología de la literatura guineana. Ed. Donato Ndongo-Bidyogo. Madrid: Nacional, 1984. Print.

Antología de relatos marroquíes en lengua española. Ed. Mohammed Chakor y Jacinto López Gorgé. Granada: A. Ubago, 1985. Print.

Aponte-Ramos, Lola. "Los territorios de la identidad: Transgénero y trasnacionalidad en *Ekomo* de María Nsué Angüe." *La recuperación de la memoria: creación cultural e identidad nacional en la literatura hispano-negroafricana*. Ed. M'bare N'gom. Universidad de Alcalá, 2004. 101–13. Print.

Aspillera, Paraluman. *Basic Tagalog for Foreigners and Non-Tagalogs*. 2nd ed. Revised by Yolanda C. Hernandez. Singapore: Tuttle, 2007. Print.

Bakhtin, M. M. "Epic and Novel." *The Dialogic Imagination: Four Essays*. Ed. Michael Holquist. Trans. Caryl Emerson and Michael Holquist. Austin: U of Texas P, 1981. 3–40. Print.

Balboa Boneke, Juan. *El reencuentro: el retorno del exiliado.* Madrid: Ediciones Guinea, 1985.

Balmori, Jesús. *Bancarrota de almas.* Manila: Imprenta y Litografía de Juan Fajardo, 1910. Print.

Barnet, Miguel. *Biografía de un cimarrón.* Barcelona: Ariel, 1968. Print.

Blanco, Jody [John D.]. "Patterns of Reform, Repetition, and Return in the First Centennial of the Filipino Revolution, 1896–1996." *Positively No Filipinos Allowed: Building Communities and Discourse.* Ed. Antonio T. Tiongson, Jr. et al. Philadelphia: Temple UP, 2006. 17–25. Print.

Blanco, John D. "Bastards of the Unfinished Revolution: Bolívar's Ismael and Rizal's Martí at the Turn of the Twentieth Century." *Radical History Review* 89 (Spring 2004): 92–114. Print.

Blanco, John D. *Frontier Constitutions: Christianity and Colonial Empire in the Nineteenth-Century Philippines.* Berkeley: U of California P, 2009. Print.

Bolekia Boleká, Justo. *Aproximación a la historia de Guinea Ecuatorial.* Salamanca: Amarú, 2003. Print.

Bouissef Rekab, Mohammed. "Después del advenimiento de la independencia de Marruecos." In "Literatura marroquí de expresión española." *Instituto Cervantes.* July 1, 2010. Web. http://cvc.cervantes.es/lengua/anuario/an uario_05/bouissef/.

Bouissef Rekab, Mohammed. "Hispanistas que cierran el siglo XX y abren el nuevo milenio." In "Literatura marroquí de expresión española." *Instituto Cervantes.* July 1, 2010. Web. http://cvc.cervantes.es/lengua/anuario/an uario_05/bouissef/.

Brancato, Sabrina. "Voices Lost in a Non-Place—African Writing in Spain." *Transcultural Modernities: Narrating Africa in Europe.* Ed. Elisabeth Bekers et al. Amsterdam: Rodopi, 2009. 3–17. Print. Also available in *Matatu: Journal for African Culture and Society* 36 (2008): 3–17. Print.

Brillantes, Lourdes [Castrillo] [de]. *80 años del Premio Zóbel.* Instituto Cervantes y Fundación Santiago: 2000. Print.

Brillantes, Lourdes [Castrillo] [de]. *81 Years of Premio Zóbel: A Legacy of Philippine Literature in Spanish.* Makati City: Georgina Padilla y Zóbel Filipinas Heritage Library, 2006. Print.

Bubisher: Poesía saharaui contemporánea. Ed. María Jesús Alvarado. Las Palmas de Gran Canaria: Puentepalo, 2003. Print.

Cabuag, VG. "RP Sailors Unsung Heroes of Industry." *Business Mirror Online Space* June 21, 2010. Web. June 22, 2010. http://businessmirror.com.ph/in dex.php?option=com_content&view=article&id=26777:rp-sailors-unsung-heroes-of-industry&catid=23:topnews&Itemid=58.

Cailles Unson, Ben. "La literatura hispanofilipina." *Archivum: revista de la Facultad de Filología, Universidad de Oviedo* 19 (1969): 275–91. Print.

Carrasco González, Antonio M. *La novela colonial hispanoafricana: las colonias africanas de España a través de la historia de la novela.* Madrid: SIAL, 2000. Print.

Castillo Barril, Manuel. "La influencia de las lenguas nativas en el español de La Guinea Ecuatorial." *Archivos del Instituto de Estudios Africanos* 20:79 (April 1966): 45–71. Print.

del Castillo y Tuazon, Teofilo, and Buenaventura S. Medina, Jr. *Philippine Literature from Ancient Times to the Present.* Quezon City: Philippine Graphic Arts, 1966. Print.

Castrillo Brillantes, Lourdes. See Brillantes, Lourdes [Castrillo][de].

"El certamen: Concurso de novelas: Laudo del jurado." *Cultura Filipina* 3:1 (October 1912): 1–3. Print.

Chavacano Reader. Rommel M. Miravite et al. Ed. R. David Zorc. Hyattsville, MD: Dunwoody P, 2009. Print.

"Constitution of the Philippines." Adopted by the Philippines Constitutional Convention at the City of Manila, Philippine Islands on the 8th Day of February 1935. U.S. Government Printing Office. Washington, DC, 1935. Print.

Cook, Robin. *Chromosome 6.* New York: Berkley Books, 1997. Print.

"Creación de la AEMLE." Asociación de Escritores Marroquíes en Lengua Española. Web. July 1, 2010. http://usuarios.multimania.es/aemle/_private/creacion_aemle.htm.

Cusack, Igor. "'¡Qué en mis pupilas se perpetúe el fulgor de las estrellas!': Literatura e identidad nacional en Guinea Ecuatorial." *La recuperación de la memoria: creación cultural e identidad nacional en la literatura hispano-negroafricana.* Ed. M'bare N'gom. Universidad de Alcalá, 2004. 156–81. Print.

Daughters of the Diaspora: Afra-Hispanic Writers. Ed. Miriam DeCosta-Willis. Kingston, Jamaica: Ian Randle, 2003. Print.

DeCosta-Willis, Miriam. "María Nsue Angüe Equatorial Guinea/Spain." *Daughters of the Diaspora: Afra-Hispanic Writers.* Ed. Miriam DeCosta-Willis. Kingston, Jamaica: Ian Randle, 2003. 286–87. Print.

Dizon, Alma Jill. "Rizal's Novels: A Divergence from Melodrama." *Philippine Studies* 44:3 (1996): 412–26. Print.

Dunzo, Annette I. "Hispanic Africa." *European-Language Writing in Sub-Saharan Africa.* Ed. Albert S. Gérard. Vol. 1. Budapest: Akadémiai Kiadó, 1986. 321–29. Print.

"Editors' Choice: The Best Books of 1990." *New York Times Book Review.* December 2, 1990. Web. August 1, 2010. http://www.nytimes.com/1990/12/02/books/editors-choice-the-best-books-of-1990.html?ref=bookreviews&pagewanted=1.

Erdos, Chris. "Heart of Darkness." *Foreign Service Journal* (April 2008): 43–48. Print. Web. May 9, 2011. http://uniset.ca/misc/heartOf.pdf .

Escalante, Enrique R. *Chabacano . . . for Everyone: A Guide to the Chabacano Language.* Malate, Manila: Baby Dragon Printing P, 2005. Print.

"Estatuto de la Asociación de Escritores Marroquíes en Lengua Española." Asociación de Escritores Marroquíes en Lengua Española. Web. July 1, 2010. http://usuarios.multimania.es/aemle/_private/estatuto_de_la_aemle.htm.

Evita, Leoncio. *Cuando los Combes luchaban.* Madrid: Consejo Superior de Investigaciones Científicas, 1953. Print.

Farolan, Edmundo. *Literatura filipino-hispana: una breve antología editada y compilada.* Manila: Versman, 1980. Print.

Forman, Michael Lawrence. "Zamboangueño Texts with Grammatical Analysis: A Study of Philippine Creole Spanish." Diss. Cornell U, 1972. Print.

Forsyth, Frederick. *The Cobra.* New York: G.P. Putnam's Sons, 2010. Print.

Forsyth, Frederick. *The Dogs of War.* New York: Viking, 1974. Print.

Fryer, T. Bruce. "Aspectos políticos de Guinea Ecuatorial: Raíces hispánicas en África." *Afro-Hispanic Review* 9:1 (Spring 2000): 3–10. Print.

García Castellón, Manuel. *Estampas y cuentos de la Filipinas Hispánica.* Madrid: Clan, 2001. Print.

García Castellón, Manuel. "Miguel Zaragoza, el primer poeta hispano-filipino." *Revista filipina* 12:2 (Spring 2008). Web. August 8, 2010. http://www.re vista.carayanpress.com/mzaragoza.html.

García Márquez, Gabriel. *One Hundred Years of Solitude.* Trans. Gregory Rabassa. New York: Perennial Classics, 1998. Print.

García Márquez, Gabriel. "La soledad de América Latina." *Nobelprize.org.* Web. July 28, 2010. http://nobelprize.org/nobel_prizes/literature/laureates/1982/marquez-lecture-sp.html.

Gedda, George, "'Heart of Darkness' or a Challenge?" Associated Press. Reprinted in the *Los Angeles Times,* October 1993: A39, col. 1. Print.

Gerardo, Félix. *Justicia social y otros cuentos.* Cebu?: 1941? Available at the National Lib. of the Philippines, Manila. Print.

Golay, Frank Hindman. *Face of Empire: United States—Philippine Relations, 1898–1946.* Madison: U of Wisconsin–Madison Center for Southeast Asian Studies, 1998. Print.

Gómez-Rivera, Guillermo. *Texto para español 4-N: La literatura filipina y su relacion al nacionalismo filipino (Revisado): Un Análisis de la Evolución de la Nacionalidad Filipina a Traves de su Literatura. Con los Comentarios, Vocabularios, Ejercicios Gramaticales y Cuestionarios Adecuados.* Manila: n.p., 1972. Print. Available at the library of the Cervantes Institute of Manila.

González Echegaray, Carlos. "[untitled prologue]." *Cuando los Combes luchaban.* By Leoncio Evita. Madrid: Consejo Superior de Investigaciones Científicas, 1953. 5–6. Print.

González Echegaray, Carlos. "La novela en lengua española sobre Guinea Ecuatorial: Etapas de una producción literaria." *Africa 2000* 9 (1989): 41–45. Print. [N.b.: the surname of the author is misspelled in the byline as "Echagaray."]

Granados, Vicente. "Ekomo, de María Nsue Angüe." Preface. *Ekomo.* By María Nsue Angüe. Madrid: Universidad Nacional de Educación a Distancia, 1985. 9–13. Print.

Guerrero, León Ma [María]. *The First Filipino: A Biography of José Rizal.* Manila: Guerrero, 1998. Print.

Guerrero, León Ma [María]. Trans. *El filibusterismo.* By José Rizal. Manila: Guerrero, 1996. Print.

De Guinea Ecuatorial a las literaturas hispanoafricanas. Ed. Landry-Wilfrid Miampika and Patricia Arroyo. Madrid: Verbum, 2010. Print.

Hagimoto, Koichi. "Between the Empires: Martí, Rizal and the Limits of Global Resistance." Diss. U of Pittsburgh, 2010. Print.

Hau, Caroline S. *Necessary Fictions: Philippine Literature and the Nation, 1946–1980.* Manila: Ateneo de Manila UP, 2000. Print.

Hazelton, Hugh. *Latinocanadá: a Critical Study of Ten Latin American Writers of Canada.* Montreal: McGill-Queen's UP, 2007. Print.

Hendel, Mischa G. "Conversación con Juan Balboa Boneke." *Afro-Hispanic Review* 28:2 (Fall 2009): 431–38. Print. Also available on *Subvaloradas, sin ser vistas: Voces literarias de Guinea Ecuatorial.* Dir. Mischa G. Hendel (2009). Film.

Hernandez Chung, Lilia. *Facts in Fiction: A Study of Peninsular Prose Fiction: 1859–1897.* Manila: De La Salle UP, 1998. Print.

Hornedo, Florentino H. "Notes on the Filipino Novel in Spanish." *Saint Louis University Research Journal* (Baguio City) 11:3 (September 1980): 383–422. Print.

Joaquín, Nick. *A Question of Heroes: Essays in Criticism on Ten Key Figures of Philippine History.* Pasig City: Anvil, 2005. Print.

Jones Mathama, Daniel. *Una lanza por el Boabí.* Barcelona, 1962. Print.

"Juan Balboa Boneke." *Diálogos con Guinea: panorama de la literatura guineoecuatoriana de expresión castellana a través de sus protagonistas.* Ed. Mbare Faye Ngom. Madrid: Labrys 54, 1996. 91–100. Print.

Klitgaard, Robert. *Tropical Gangsters: One Man's Experience with Development and Decadence in Deepest Africa.* New York: Basic Books, 1990. Print.

Knowlton, Edgar C., Jr. "Philippine and Other Exotic Loan Words in Paterno's *Nínay.*" *Proceedings of the Ninth Pacific Science Congress of the Pacific Science Association Held at Chulalongkorn University, Bangkok, November 18th to December 9th, 1957.* Vol. 3. 99–102. Print.

Lacson-Locsin, Ma. [María] Soledad. Trans. *El filibusterismo.* By José Rizal. Makati City, Philippines: Bookmark, 1997. Print.

Lawo-Sukam, Alain. "*El proceso* de Kafka, *Crónica de una muerte anunciada* de Gabriel García Márquez y *Ekomo* de Nsue Angue: la problemática de la cuestión existencial." *Neophilologus* 94 (2010): 67–80. Print.

Lazo, Rodrigo J. "Los Filibusteros: Cuban Writers in the United States and Deterritorialized Print Culture." *American Literary History* 15:1 (Spring 2003): 87–106. Print.

Lewis, Marvin A. *An Introduction to the Literature of Equatorial Guinea: Between Colonialism and Dictatorship.* Columbia: U of Missouri P, 2007. Print.

Licsi Espino, F. [Federico]. "Pedro A. Paterno: the Neglected Poet." *Archipelago* 4.A-39 (or 4–7) (July 1977): 13–15. Print.

Lifshey, Adam. "Imagined Temporalities: The Temporalizing of Neocolonialism and Nation-Narrations in Aminata Sow Fall's *Ex-père de la nation* and Juan Balboa Boneke's *El reencuentro: el retorno del exiliado.*" *Lucero* 14 (2003): 100–108. Print.

Lifshey, Adam. "And So the Worm Turns: The Impossibility of Imperial Imitation in *Una lanza por el Boabí* by Daniel Jones Mathama." *Chasqui* 36:1 (May 2007): 108–20. Print.

Lifshey, Adam. *Specters of Conquest: Indigenous Absence in Transatlantic Literatures.* New York: Fordham UP, 2010. Print.

Liniger-Goumaz, Max. *Historical Dictionary of Equatorial Guinea.* 3rd ed. Lanham, MD: Scarecrow P, 2000. Print.

Literatura de Guinea Ecuatorial (Antología). Ed. Donato Ndongo-Bidyogo y Mbaré Ngom. Madrid: Casa de África, 2000. Print.

Literatura hispano-filipina (Selecciones). Vol. 4. Ed. Rosario C. Estanislao et al. [Quezon City]: Universidad de Filipinas, 1976. Print.

López Gorgé, Jacinto. "Justificación de este libro." *Antología de relatos marroquíes en lengua española.* Ed. Mohammed Chakor y Jacinto López Gorgé. Granada: A. Ubago, 1985. 17–20. Print.

López Jaena, Graciano. "Homenaje a la memoria de Colón." *Discursos y artículos varios.* Manila: Bureau of Printing, 1951. 22–26. Print.

López Jaena, Graciano. "La redención social." *Discursos y artículos varios.* Manila: Bureau of Printing, 1951. 107–9. Print.

Madrigal y Centenera, Vida Ma. [María] and Arlene de León y del Rosario. *Filipinas es mi patria: Español 4-N; Selecciones de literatura filipina en español.* N.p.: De Paul Printing P, 1981. Print.

Magallon, Epifania L., comp. *List of Cebuano Pseudonyms.* February 1977. Cebuano Studies Center of the U of San Carlos, Cebu City, Philippines. Print.

Malindog, Josefina B. "Chabacano Literature in Zamboanga City: An Annotated Index." MS thesis. U of San Carlos, 1993. Print. Available at the National Lib. of the Philippines, Manila.

"María Nsué Angüe." *Diálogos con Guinea: panorama de la literatura guineoecuatoriana de expresión castellana a través de sus protagonistas.* Ed. Mbare Faye Ngom. Madrid: Labrys 54, 1996. 113–18. Print.

Mariñas, Luis. *La literatura filipina en castellano.* Madrid: Nacional, 1974. Print.

Martín-Márquez, Susan. *Disorientations: Spanish Colonialism in Africa and the Performance of Identity.* New Haven: Yale UP, 2008. Print.

Matibag, Eugenio. "The Spirit of Nínay: Pedro Paterno and the First Philippine Novel." *Humanities Diliman* 7:2 (2010): 34–59. Print.

Melville, Herman. *Moby-Dick.* Ed. Harrison Hayford and Hershel Parker. New York: W. W. Norton, 1967. Print.

Mester, Anna. "Repensar Ekomo de María Nsué Angüe: Un desafío ecuatoguineano a la hispanidad." BA thesis. Mount Holyoke College, 2009. Print.

Miampika, Landry-Wilfrid. "Plaidoirie équato-guinéenne: chronique d'une littérature émergente." *Notre Librairie: Revue des littératures du Sud* 138–39 (September 1999–March 2000): 14–17. Print.

Minsongui Dieudonné, Mendogo. "Mujer y creación literaria en Guinea Ecuatorial." *EPOS* 13 (1997): 209–18. Print.

Mojares, Resil B. *Brains of the Nation: Pedro Paterno, T.H. Pardo de Tavera, Isabelo de los Reyes and the Production of Modern Knowledge.* Manila: Ateneo de Manila UP, 2006. Print.

Mojares, Resil B. "Catechisms of the Body." *Waiting for Mariang Makiling: Essays in Philippine Cultural History.* Manila: Ateneo de Manila UP, 2002. 171–97. Print.

Mojares, Resil B. *Cebuano Literature: A Survey and Bio-bibliography with Finding List.* Cebu: U of San Carlos, 1975. Print.

Mojares, Resil B. *Origins and Rise of the Filipino Novel: A Generic Study of the Novel until 1940.* 1998 ed. Quezon City: U of the Philippines P, 1983. Print.

Ndongo-Bidyogo, Donato. *Historia y tragedia de Guinea Ecuatorial.* Madrid: Cambio 16, 1977. Print.

Ndongo-Bidyogo, Donato. "La literatura moderna hispanófona en Guinea Ecuatorial." *Afro-Hispanic Review* 9:1 (Spring 2000): 39–44. Print.

Ndongo-Bidyogo, Donato. "El marco." Foreword. *Antología de la literatura guineana.* Ed. Donato Ndongo-Bidyogo. Madrid: Nacional, 1984. 99–102. Print.

Ndongo-Bidyogo, Donato. "María Nsue Angüe." *Antología de la literatura guineana.* Ed. Donato Ndongo-Bidyogo. Madrid: Nacional, 1984. 99–102. Print.

Ndongo-Bidyogo, Donato. *Las tinieblas de tu memoria negra.* Madrid: Fundamentos, 1987. Print.

"The Need for EG Justice." *EG Justice.* Web. August 4, 2010. http://www.egjustice.org/?q=need-eg-justice.

N'gom, M'bare. "African Literature in Spanish." *The Cambridge History of African and Caribbean Literature.* New York: Cambridge UP, 2003. 584–602. Print.

Ngom, Mbaré. "Afro-fascismo y creación cultural en Guinea Ecuatorial: 1969–1979." *Revista Canadiense de Estudios Hispánicos* 21:2 (Invierno 1997): 385–95. Print.

Ngom, Mbaré. "Algunos aspectos de la literatura hispano-negroafricana: la creación cultural en Guinea Ecuatorial." *Cuadernos para investigación de la literatura hispánica* 20 (1995): 89–99. Print.

Ngom, Mbaré. Introducción. *Literatura de Guinea Ecuatorial (Antología).* Ed. Donato Ndongo-Bidyogo y Mbaré Ngom. Madrid: Casa de África, 2000. 11–29. Print.

Ngom, Mbaré. "La literatura africana de expresión castellana: la creación literaria en Guinea Ecuatorial." *Hispania* 76 (September 1993): 410–18. Print.

Ngom, Mbaré. "La literatura hispano-negroafricana e identidad cultural en la posindependencia." *Letras peninsulares* 13:2.3 (Fall 2000): 545–59. Print.

Ngom, Mbaré. "Memoria y exilio en la obra Juan Balboa Boneke." *La recuperación de la memoria: creación cultural e identidad nacional en la literatura hispano-negroafricana.* Comp. M'bare N'gom. [Madrid?]: Universidad de Alcalá, 2004. 45–61. Print.

N'gom, M'baré. "The Missing Link: African Hispanism at the Dawn of the Millennium." *Arachne@Rutgers: Journal of Iberian and Latin American Literary and Cultural Studies* 1:1 (2001): 1–19. *Arachne.rutgers.edu*. Web. http://arachne.rut gers.edu/vol1_1ngom.htm. May 9, 2011.

N'gom, M'baré. "Narrative of a Woman's Life and Writing: María Nsue Angüe's *Ekomo*." Trans. Antonio Olliz Boyd. *Daughters of the Diaspora: Afra-Hispanic Writers*. Ed. Miriam De-Costa-Willis. Kingston, Jamaica: Ian Randle, 2003. 300–309. Print.

N'gom, M'baré. "Novelística y espacio femenino: entrevista a María Nsue Angüe." *Afro-Hispanic Review* 19:1 (Spring 2000): 102–3. Print.

Ngom, Mbaré. "Relato de una vida y escritura femenina: *Ekomo*, de María Nsue Angüe." *Journal of Afro-Latin American Studies & Literature* 3:1 (Fall 1995): 77–92. Print.

Ngugi, wa Thiong'o. "The Language of African Literature." *Colonial Discourse and Post-colonial Theory*. Ed. Patrick Williams and Laura Chrisman. New York: Columbia UP, 1994. 435–55. Print.

Nistal, Gloria. Prólogo para la nueva edición de *Ekomo*. *Ekomo*. By María Nsue Angüe. 2nd ed. Madrid: Casa de África, 2007. 7–14. Print.

Nkogo, Eugenio. "Despedida." Message to Adam Lifshey. December 23, 2009. E-mail.

Nsue, Angüe, María. *Ekomo*. Madrid: Casa de África, 2007. Print.

Nsue, Angüe, María. *Ekomo*. Madrid: Universidad Nacional de Educación a Distancia, 1985. Print.

Nsue, Angüe, María. *Ekomo: Au cœur de la forêt guinéenne*. Trans. Françoise Harraca. Paris: L'Harmattan, 1995. Print.

Ocampo, Ambeth. Foreword. *The Pact of Biyak-na-Bato and Ninay by Pedro A. Paterno*. Manila: National Historical Institute, 2004. v–vi. Print.

Ocampo, Ambeth. *Makamisa: The Search for Rizal's Third Novel*. Manila: Anvil, 1992. Print.

Ocampo, Ambeth. "Rizal Law Not Being Followed." *Philippine Daily Inquirer*. February 21, 2008. Web. March 5, 2008. http://opinion.inquirer.net/ inquireropinion/columns/view/20080221–120379/Rizal-Law-not-being-followed.

Odartey-Wellington, Dorothy. "Entre la espada y la pared: la voz de la mediadora en Ekomo, una novela afrohispana." *Revista canadiense de estudios hispánicos* 32:1 (Autumn 2007): 165–75. Print.

Odartey-Wellington, Dorothy. "La necrosis poscolonial: patologías e identidades en la novela afrohispana, *Ekomo*." *El cuerpo enfermo: representación e imágenes de la enfermedad*. Ed. R. [Ricardo] de la Fuente Ballesteros y J. Pérez Magallón. Valladolid: Universitas Castellae, 2006. 147–55. Print.

Ortiz Armengol, Pedro. *Letras en Filipinas*. Madrid: Dirección General de Relaciones Culturales y Científicas, 1999. Print.

Osubita, Juan Bautista. "La muerte de Ekomo en Ekomo." *Africa 2000* 16 (1992): 48–50. Print.

Oubali, Ahmed. "La literatura marroquí de expresión española." Web. July 1, 2010. http://usuarios.multimania.es/aemle/_private/activ_aemle_presenta cion_literatura_marroqui_oubali.htm.

Oyono, Ferdinand. *Une vie de boy.* Paris: René Julliard, 1956. Print.

Palés Matos, Luis. *Tuntún de pasa y grifería: poemas afroantillanos.* San Juan: Familia de Luis Palés Matos, 1974. Print.

Paterno, Pedro A. *El alma filipina.* Manila: La República, 1910. Print.

Paterno, Pedro A. *Boda a la moderna.* Manila: La República, 1910. Print.

Paterno, Pedro A. *La braveza del bayani.* Manila: La República, 1911. Print. [Possibly also printed at some point in the periodical *El ideal* after having received votes in one of its contests.]

Paterno, Pedro A. *La dalaga virtuosa y el puente del diablo.* Manila: La República, 1910. Print.

Paterno, Pedro A. *La fidelidad.* Manila: La República, 1911. Print. [Possibly also printed at some point in the periodical *El ideal* after having received votes in one of its contests dated December 30, 1910.]

Paterno, Pedro A. *Los heraldos de la raza.* Manila: La República, 1911. Print.

Paterno, [Pedro] Alejandro. *Leyendas de Antipolo.* Manila: La República, 1910. Print.

Paterno, Pedro A. *Maring, amor de obrero filipino.* Manila: La República, 1910. Print.

Paterno, [Pedro] Alejandro. *Ninay.* In *The Pact of Biyak-na-Bato and Nínay.* Manila: National Historical Institute, 2004. Print. Reprint of *Ninay (Philippine Customs).* Trans. E. F. du Fresne. Manila: La República, 1907. [N.b.: the surname of the translator on the title page of this reprint is given as "Frensne" but everywhere else, including all bibliographic references, credit him as "Fresne."]

Paterno, Pedro A. *Nínay (Costumbres filipinas).* Madrid: Fortanet, 1885. Print.

Paterno, Pedro A. *Ninay (Ugali nang Catagalugan).* Trans. Roman G. Reyes. Maynila: De La Salle UP, 2002. Print.

Paterno, Pedro A. *Ninay (Ugali nang Catagalugan).* Trans. R. Reyes. Maynila: La República, 1908. Print.

Paterno, Pedro A. *En el PANSOL de Kalamba: Amor de un día.* Manila: La República, 1910. Print.

Paterno, Pedro A. *Sampaguitas.* Madrid: F. Cao y D. De Val, 1881. Print.

Paterno, Pedro A. *Los últimos románticos.* Manila: La República, 1911. Print.

Peralta-Imson, Ma. Elinora. "Philippine Literature: Spanish Evolving a National Literature." *Linguae et Litterae* 2:1–19. Published by the Department of European Languages, University of the Philippines Diliman. Print.

Pérez, Remigia et al. *Español 4-N: La literatura filipina y su relacion al nacionalismo filipino.* [Manila?]: n.p., 1978? Print. Available at the library of the Cervantes Institute of Manila.

Perez-Semorlan, Teresita La. *Mga Leyendang Chavacano.* Iligan City, Philippines: n.p., 1984. Print.

Pié Jahn, Guillermo. "Aproximación a la poesía hispanocamerunesa." *La situación actual del español en África: Actas del II Congreso Internacional de Hispanistas en África*. Ed. Gloria Nistal Rosique and Guillermo Pié Jahn. Madrid: Casa de África/SIAL Ediciones, 2007. 203–45. Print.

Pons García, Araceli. "Filipino Writers in Spanish and Their Works: Historico-Bibliographic Study." Thesis. Manila: U of Santo Tomás, 1950. Print.

"Pope in Equatorial Guinea." *Washington Post*. February 19, 1982, final ed., 1st sec., World News: A27. Print.

"Presentación." *Generación de la amistad saharaui*. Web. June 29, 2009. http://www.generacionamistadsaharaui.com/quienes_somos.htm.

Price, Nicole Denise. "'Materia reservada' No More: The Post-Colonial in the Equato-Guinean Narrative." Diss. U of Missouri–Columbia, 2005. Print.

Pynchon, Thomas. *Mason & Dixon*. New York: Henry Holt, 1997. Print.

Quilis, Antonio, and Celia Casado-Fresnillo. *La lengua española en Filipinas: Historia. Situación actual. El chabacano. Antología de textos*. Madrid: Consejo Superior de Investigaciones Científicas, 2008. Print.

Racho, Evelyn S. "The Historical Growth of the Cebuano Short Story: 1901–1971." MA thesis. U of San Carlos, 1975. Print.

Rafael, Vicente L. *The Promise of the Foreign: Nationalism and the Technics of Translation in the Spanish Philippines*. Durham: Duke UP, 2005. Print.

Rebollos, Grace Jimeno and Fr. Angel Calvo, C.M.F. *The Lady of the Forest/El Señora del fuerte*. Zamboanga City: UP Western Mindanao State U, 2002. Print.

Republic Act No. 1425. 3rd Congress of the Philippines. *Filipiniana.net*. Manila: 1956. Web. March 5, 2008. http://www.filipiniana.net/ArtifactView.do?artifactID=L00000000010&query=rizal%20law.

Revista filipina. Web. July 29, 2010. http://www.revista.carayanpress.com/.

Reyes, Portia L. "A 'Treasonous' History of Filipino Historiography: The Life and Times of Pedro Paterno, 1858–1911." *South East Asia Research* 14:1 (March 2006): 87–121. Print.

Reyes Soriano, Rosa. *Cultura Hispano-Filipina: Breve historia de la literatura hispana filipina*. 2nd ed. Manila: Nueva Era, 1965. Print.

Rich, Jeremy. "*Nous, les équatos:* Equatorial Guinean Immigrants in Contemporary Gabon." *Afro-Hispanic Review* 28:2 (Fall 2009): 113–30. Print.

Rich, Jeremy. "re: Nous, les equatos." Message to Adam Lifshey. June 21, 2010. E-mail.

Rizal, José. *El filibusterismo*. Madrid: Cultura Hispánica, 1997. Print.

Rizal, José. *Noli me tangere*. Caracas: Biblioteca Ayacucho, Galaxia Gutenberg, Círculo de Lectores, 1982. Print.

Romanillos, Emmanuel Luis A. *Chabacano Studies: Essays on Cavite's Chabacano Language and Literature*. N.p.: Cavite Historical Society, 2006. Print.

Salazar, Danica. "Elementos Costumbristas en 'Nínay'." *Linguae et Litterae* 6:109–15. Published by the Department of European Languages, Univesity of the Philippines Diliman. Print.

Salvo, Jorge A. "La formación de la identidad en la novela hispano africana 1950–1990." Diss. Florida State U, 2003. Print. *Biblioteca virtual Miguel de Cervantes.* Web. July 29, 2010. http://www.cervantesvirtual.com/Ficha Obra.html?ref=13525&portal=0.

Sampedro, Benita Vizcaya. "African Poetry in Spanish Exile: Seeking Refuge in the Metropolis." *Bulletin of Hispanic Studies* 81:2 (April 2004): 201–14. Print.

Sampedro, Benita Vizcaya. "Theorizing Equatorial Guinea." *Afro-Hispanic Review* 28:2 (Fall 2009): 15–19. Print.

de San Agustín, Delfina. "La literatura castellana en Filipinas." Thesis. U of Santo Tomás, 1935. Print.

de Sánchez, Mercedes C. [Conchú]. "El desarrollo de la literatura hispano-filipina." Thesis. U of Santo Tomás, 1958. Print.

de Sánchez, Mercedes C. [Conchú]. *Literatura filipino-española.* Madrid: U Central de Madrid: 1961. Print. [Abridged version of above thesis.]

Sayahi, Lotfi. "El español en el norte de Marruecos: historia y análisis." *Hispanic Research Journal* 6:3 (October 2005): 195–207. Print.

Schumacher, John N. "The Literature of Protest: Pelaez to the Propagandists." *Brown Heritage: Essays on Philippine Cultural Tradition and Literature.* Ed. Antonio G. Manuud. Quezon City: Ateneo de Manila UP, 1967. 483–507. Print.

Schumacher, John N. *The Making of a Nation: Essays on Nineteenth-Century Filipino Nationalism.* Manila: Ateneo de Manila UP, 1991. Print.

Schumacher, John N. *The Propaganda Movement 1880–1895.* Rev. ed. Manila: Ateneo de Manila UP, 1997. Print.

Sedano y Calonge, José. *La madrastra: novela histórico-contemporánea.* 2nd ed. Manila: Juan Fajardo, 1910. Print.

Sedano [y] Calonge, José. "Mi mala sombra." *Soy de tu raza, Castila: Recopilación de novelas relámpago.* Manila: n.p., 1936. 12–20. Print.

Sedano [y] Calonge, José. *Soy de tu raza, Castila: Recopilación de novelas relámpago.* Manila: n.p., 1936. Print.

Seeger, Pete. *Greatest Hits.* Columbia, 1967. LP.

Shurtleff, Len. "A Foreign Service Murder." *Foreign Service Journal* (October 2007): 51–55. Print. Web. May 9, 2011. http://www.uniset.ca/misc/fsj_erdos.pdf.

Sicat, Sonia S. *Chavacano Folk Music-Literary Pieces: A Spanish Progeny.* Zamboanga City: Western Mindanao State U, 2003. Print.

Silverstein, Ken. "Teodorin's World." *Foreign Policy* (March–April 2011). Web. March 6, 2011. http://www.foreignpolicy.com/articles/2011/02/22/teodorins_world.

Sommer, Doris. *Foundational Fictions: The National Romances of Latin America.* Berkeley: U of California P, 1991. Print.

Sumsky, Victor V. "The Prophet of Two Revolutions." *Philippine Studies* 49:2 (2001): 236–54. Print.

Sundiata, Ibrahim K. *Equatorial Guinea: Colonialism, State Terror, and the Search for Stability.* Boulder, CO: Westview, 1990. Print.

Sundiata, Ibrahim K. "The Fernandinos: Labor and Community in Santa Isabel de Fernando Poo, 1827–1931." Diss. Northwestern U. 1972. Print.

Sycip, Victoria. "The Golden Age of Philippine Literature in Spanish." Thesis. Department of English and Comparative Literature at U of ?, 1972. Print.

Tadiar, Neferti X. M. *Things Fall Away: Philippine Historical Experience and the Makings of Globalization.* Durham: Duke UP, 2009. Print.

Tiamson Mendoza, Edgardo. "A Re-appreciation of Philippine Literature in Spanish." Diss. U of the Philippines, 1993. Instituto Cervantes Lib., Manila. Print. [N.b.: this text consists of two volumes with irregular pagination in that some page numbers appear twice but indicate different pages.]

Tiongson, Jr., Antonio T. "On Filipinos, Filipino Americans, and U.S. Imperialism: Interview with Oscar V. Campomanes." *Positively No Filipinos Allowed: Building Communities and Discourse.* Ed. Antonio T. Tiongsono Jr. et al. [Philadelphia?]: Temple UP, 2008. 26–42.

Tofiño-Quesada, Ignacio. "Spanish Orientalism: Uses of the Past in Spain's Colonization in Africa." *Comparative Studies of South Asia, Africa and the Middle East* 23:1–2 (2003): 141–48. Print.

Togores Sánchez, Luis Eugenio [identified as "LTS" in byline]. "Paterno, Pedro Alejandro." *Diccionario histórico, geográfico y cultural de Filipinas y el Pacífico.* Ed. Leoncio Cabrero Fernández et al. Vol. 2. Madrid: Agencia Española de Cooperación Internacional, 2008. 726–27. Print.

Torres, Máyolo G. "Estudio de las influencias de los novelistas costumbristas españoles en la primera novela hispanofilipina—Nínay." Diss. Colegio de San Juan de Letrán Graduate School (Manila), 1967. Print.

Ugarte, Michael. *Africans in Europe: The Culture of Exile and Emigration from Equatorial Guinea to Spain.* Urbana: U of Illinois P, 2010. Print.

Whinnom, Keith. *Spanish Contact Vernaculars in the Philippines.* London: Hong Kong UP, 1956. Print.

Zamboanga Chabacano Folk Literature. Project leader Orlando B. Cuartocruz. Tokyo: Toyota Foundation, 1990. Print.

Zaragoza Viuda de Preysler, Margarita. "Temática de la poesía filipina en su siglo de oro—(1870–1930)." Thesis. U of Santo Tomás, 1955. Print.

Zielina Limonta, María. "*Ekomo:* representación del pensamiento mítico, la magia y la psicología de un pueblo 'Fang.'" *Afro-Hispanic Review* 19:1 (Spring 2000): 93–101. Print.

Index